Marketing Communication

Principles and practice

Richard J. Varey

LONDON & NEW YORK

First published 2002
by Routledge
11 New Fetter Lane, London EC4P 4EE

Simultaneously published in the USA and Canada
by Routledge
29 West 35th Street, New York, NY 10001

Routledge is an imprint of the Taylor & Francis Group

Typeset in Plantin and Rockwell by Keystroke, Jacaranda Lodge, Wolverhampton
Printed and bound in Great Britain by TJ International Ltd, Padstow, Cornwall

British Library Cataloguing in Publication Data
A catalogue record for this book is available from the British Library

Library of Congress Cataloging in Publication Data
Varey, Richard J., 1955–
    Marketing communication : principles and practice /
    Richard J. Varey
        p. cm.
    Includes bibliographical references and index.
    1. Communication in marketing. I Title.

HF5415.123 .V37 2001
658.8′02—dc21   2001019948

ISBN 0–415–23039–X (hbk)
ISBN 0–415–23040–3 (pbk)

Contents

Figures

Case studies

Boxes

Tables

Structure of the book

The discussion is predicated, in chapter one, on the need to adopt a particular conception of the role of communication in marketing, and to understand marketing communication as the mode of managing exchange.

In chapter two we reflect on the conception of communication that pervades our daily discourses outside of our awareness, to recover marketing as a social process in which people come first, and products follow. Marketing communication is imagined as managed conversations and this approach is compared and contrasted with the notion of designed messages.

Theory is applied, in chapter three, in examining consumer behaviour in order to appreciate the problem of engaging people in value exchanges within the context of market relationships. The nature and role of products in fulfilling social needs in consumption communities are considered.

Next, in chapter four, the intentions of marketers in attempting communication with consumers and buyers and other people are examined. Marketing communication programme design decisions are related to assumptions about communication styles, and it is shown that it is necessary to adopt a broader view of the role of marketing communication than is found in many textbooks.

This shows, in chapter five, that we need to take a broadened view of the role of marketing communication in contemporary management by considering the whole system of relationships that provides the context for exchange and communicative behaviour for marketing purposes.

We rightly identify contemporary marketing as an essentially intercultural communication system, and go on to recognize aspects of culture that are major intermediaries of meaning-making in contemporary society, and their significance in marketing communication management. Thus, in chapter six, we come to appreciate the manner in which words, pictures, and products have social value – their meaning is particular to the culture in which they are apprehended.

Next we consider some important aspects of managing marketing communication to realize the various facets of a product offering that are attended to by managers, and by buyers and consumers. This requires that we re-examine the marketing mix in a more holistic manner that identifies marketing's social functions. Readers of chapter seven are thus encouraged to shift their thinking of marketing communication as mass communication to a more relationship-oriented style.

In chapter eight we examine the nature and role of product brand management to appreciate further the communicative nature of a brand. We connect brand design with marketing communication objectives. Finally, we suggest the value of thinking of a brand as akin to a product-provider reputation.

The next step in constructing our management perspective on marketing communication is to understand the range of media available, and to examine ways of comparing media suitability. In chapter nine we take account of major changes in media options, without losing sight of central marketing communication objectives.

We move on to identify the relevance of the concepts of corporate identity, corporate image, and corporate reputation to the management of marketing communication. In chapter ten we distinguish and relate the concepts of identity, image, and reputation, and distinguish and relate the respective roles of marketing and public relations.

The organization of a business impacts on the ability of marketing management to contribute to competitive performance through customer satisfaction, so it is necessary to explore the concept of internal marketing. In chapter eleven we consider internal marketing as a responsible, responsive approach to managing communication for the management of marketing communication, and connect communication and marketing through the concept of exchange.

In chapter twelve we ask why relationship marketing has become of major importance in marketing management. We connect the concept of relationship to the concept of communication, and realize some implications for marketing planners. We highlight the importance of planning for communicating before, during, and after a value exchange.

Managers need to appreciate fully the development of the integrated marketing communication approach and managerial approach to marketing communication. In chapter thirteen we consider the added-value for provider and consumer/buyer of an integrated marketing communication (IMC) strategy, and identify some obstacles to practical IMC operation.

As advertising is the most prevalent practice in marketing communication, we examine this in order to appreciate its contemporary use in its many forms. In chapter fourteen we critically examine advertising as a corporate, supposedly credible and creative phenomenon that pervades our lives in attempting to link products with satisfactions. We do this in order to understand better how and why advertising form and use are changing.

Now we begin to construct a management framework, by recognizing the role of strategy-making and communication objective-setting. We distinguish, in chapter fifteen, marketing objectives, marketing communication objectives, and communication objectives. It is necessary, it is argued, to broaden our thinking as managers beyond promotional intentions, to consider objectives for total communication systems.

In chapter sixteen we conceptualize marketing communication planning in terms of the appreciative system introduced earlier, to consider planning in relation to the overall marketing communication system and communication programme requirements for marketing performance. This helps to structure our thinking about planning around a simple, coherent planning framework that is based on evaluation and control as essential management functions.

Having established the nature of the task of communicating for marketing purposes, we then anticipate the nature of the job of the marketing communication manager in terms of role and responsibilities within the management system as communication catalyst, interpreter, mediator, and communicator. We consider, in chapter seventeen, the need for, and obligations of, the responsible and responsive communicator (i.e. the ethics of communicating).

Finally, we look at how the marketing communication environment is changing in order to appreciate how marketing communication practices are developing. In chapter eighteen we locate marketing communication strategically within the corporate communication managing system.

Case studies and provocative comments and queries are provided throughout the text to focus thinking on contemporary practices and the underlying 'working' theories that support or divert (even subvert) the management of marketing communication as a social process.

Preface

For many people who have not studied marketing as a specialism, marketing is promotion or 'marketing communications': advertising, mailed brochures, sales promotions, exhibitions, and people selling. Expectations concerning marketers are often of people with something to sell – expressers of what is great, good, and irresistible about a product. People with job and role titles of 'marketer' are often engaged in firing 'messages' at 'targets' with the intention of hitting them in order to persuade and induce purchase. We will take a necessarily broader, more powerful perspective – that all marketing activity is intercultural social communication. Communication is social action among people who differ in their values, beliefs, and motivations.

It would be naïve to imagine that marketing is merely a tool of business. Marketing communication is a cultural enterprise that has a cultural impact. But do marketing managers ask questions about the cultural impact of their system of marketing communications? We examine this problem further in chapter two as the basis for the approach taken in this book. Unlike most marketing and marketing communication textbooks, this book does not assume that it is possible to separate the social (culture) and economic (business) aspects of markets. Thus, the scope of this book is broader than most in this field, since it does not restrict itself to the management of marketing communication from a business perspective. Chapter two provides the detailed rationale for this approach.

This is an introductory textbook for advanced undergraduate, masters, doctoral, and professional students. It has been designed to build on the traditional body of knowledge for marketing communication by connecting principles that are applicable in contemporary society with academic rigour and practice applications. This not an orthodox (conservative) textbook nor a radical rewriting of marketing communication principles. Rather, it is a necessary 'third way' critical reflection on the received wisdom of management courses. Readers will find the content complementary to the contemporary syllabus, as it raises the possibility of constructive change in management as a social and political ideology and set of practices. Thus, this book represents a reflective introduction to the field of managed marketing communication for those engaged in a serious and advanced study of management.

A comprehensive holistic framework is presented for the management of integrated marketing communication programmes. Key features are:

- important concepts and theories of human communication, culture, democratic process, and marketing
- a broader view of the social process of managed communication for marketing purposes than is to be found in other textbooks in this field
- a perspective that takes marketing communication as a relational process and not merely tools and artefacts of business
- links to strategic management and marketing planning, and a stakeholder perspective in managing relationships with customers and other people in the context of 'new media'
- current concise and diverse case studies of contemporary management practices, situation vignettes, and study prompts

The text aims to provide a framework for the management of marketing communication processes focused on a planned, integrated marketing communication programme. I develop an approach that examines the nature, role, and contribution to corporate performance and marketing objectives. This requires a perspective that forwards communication as a social process between 'cultures', the critical mode of management, and the fundamental basis for organized purposive work. This requires a connection to corporate communication as a system of managing.

The reader of the text will be able to:

- appreciate the management of promotional and other necessary purposive communicative activities in the context of markets operating in wider social groupings
- apply some judgement and skills to this
- take a broad view of managed communication for marketing purposes
- apply a framework for developing marketing communication strategies
- identify links to strategic management and marketing planning with a stakeholder perspective

The text takes a contemporary view in considering the advent of electronic media as part of the communication context. Thus 'new media' are not considered as merely an update or supplement to a more traditional marketing communication framework. Second, rather than distinguishing promotion management from marketing communication as has been the tradition (especially in US textbooks), a holistic communication management approach is constructed. Care is taken to present marketing as a social process and not merely a management technology. Rather than treating marketing communication at an international level as a special case, all marketing communication is treated as intercultural. This integrates consumption, communication, culture, marketing, and management.

Thus, a contemporary approach to managing communication for marketing purposes is presented that deals with the management of legitimate commercial and social communicative acts of corporate and private actors, and does not presume intentions and effects centred on consumption that can be unsustainable or unethical. This critical view of marketing locates this particular communication system as organized dialogical communication acts in a dynamic network of stakeholder relationships.

This textbook is the first written by a UK scholar that transcends the constraining dogma of orthodox marketing discipline to integrate a democratic managerial perspective with contemporary communication theory and marketing theory. Academic rigour has been applied in setting out key principles, and these are connected to relevant practices covering issues of significance to SMEs (Small and medium enterprises), the public sector, service providers, and MNEs (Multi-national enterprises) – i.e. the total intercultural marketing system.

The book forwards the entire marketing mix as communicative – and marketing as a particular set of communication behaviours operated in a particular context for a particular purpose. Communication theory is provided as a firm basis for a managerial framework, and this is contemporary, incorporating an exchange relationship perspective to avoid the simplistic 'informing' notion of communicating.

Marketing communication is related to other communication behaviours required in business enterprise. Marketing is seen as an algorithm (or way of working) for exploiting opportunities to further the productive adoption and diffusion of ideas in society.

I wish to acknowledge the encouragement of Michelle Gallagher (Routledge), Dr Jim Blythe, and an anonymous second reviewer, in my pursuit of a (somewhat intentionally) radical review of the orthodoxy. Thank you for allowing me a voice in pushing forward the boundary.

Dr Richard Varey
University of Salford, UK
January 2001

chapter

one

AN INTRODUCTION TO MARKETING COMMUNICATION

LEARNING POINTS

Careful study of this chapter will help you to:

- adopt a particular conception of the role of communication in marketing

- understand marketing communication as the mode of managing exchange

- critically engage with the questions of what and why, before limiting your thinking by asking how

> The sign brings customers
>
> (The Fortune-Tellers, Fable 15)

INTRODUCTION

As far back as 1954, Peter Drucker said that any business has two basic requirements: marketing and innovation. Marketing assumes the task of guaranteeing the conditions of communication and information that allow demand for need fulfilment to be met through production of goods and services. Managers have long realized that it is as important to organize the demand as it is to organize the supply. Thus, straight away we can see the significance of managed communication – exchange relationships are needed and ideas must be generated and deployed. Ultimately, it is customers (buyers and users) who determine the nature of the businesses that can operate.

Integrated marketing actions, when applied to meeting the needs of consumers and buyers, can generate profits and other corporate results through customer satisfaction. This matching of corporate and customer interests requires the parties to communicate. This communication can be spontaneous and ad hoc, but experience shows that careful management of marketing communication can add value for all involved.

Since the rise of consumer marketing in the USA in the 1950s, there has been a shift from personal relationships with customers to mediated actions directed towards consumers. Recent developments in information and communication technologies, and market conditions, have spurred a further shift, back to dealing with relationships again. With the emergence of new forms of mass communication and information, it is time to bring the marketing communication knowledge-base up to date.

We must beware of a contradiction in traditional discussions. Do we view consumers as sovereign, or as easily manipulated, seduced, and outwitted? This is an important question, for it locates our stance on communication as either a transportation tool or a participatory human experience.

The advent of electronic media produces situations that cannot be adequately explained by conventional marketing theory. Some of the answer lies in adopting up-to-date communication theory, something that has not happened yet in even the most recent textbooks on marketing communications.

We can benefit from systematic study of marketing communication, as this helps guide judgement and decision-making. The logic begins with the needs of providers and consumers, to guide marketing interventions. In turn, communication needs can then be established, and these will indicate suitable communication objectives (Figure 1.1).

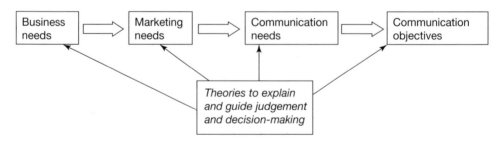

Figure 1.1 **What to study for marketing communication management**

THE MARKETING TASK

The term 'marketing' is not a modern invention, it has been in use in the English language for some considerable time. *Webster's Dictionary* of 1880 gave a meaning as 'the act of purchasing in a market'. Interestingly, this is consistent with the idea that both producer and consumer can be a marketer!

Profit is made from people, not products

(Anon)

The idea of 'marketing' first appeared in the economics literature at the end of the nineteenth century and was developed as 'merchandising and selling' in the scientific management of Frederick Winslow Taylor (Taylor, 1929). The concept became widely applied in the middle of the twentieth century. Promotional communication gained emphasis with the emergence, initially in the USA, of national product brands with widespread distribution.

In 1931 the American Association of Marketing and Advertising Professors issued an official definition:

> *all* the business activities implicated in the flow of goods and service from producer to consumer, with the sole exception of activities that imply a change of form.
>
> (Mattelart, 1996: 292, emphasis added)

This offers a historical insight that can be of great help to us in better understanding the communicative role of marketing. Marketing – as a managerial discipline for organizing demand and supply – was preceded by advertising by at least 100 years (see chapter thirteen for a brief historical account).

The management practice of marketing has emerged as a coordinating function (discipline) that acts as a bridge between the needs of the provider (to stay in business and to prosper), and the needs of buyers and consumers (for access to desirable value-for-money products), and other stakeholders in a society that has normative, expressive, cognitive, as well as instrumental institutions (see Figure 1.2).

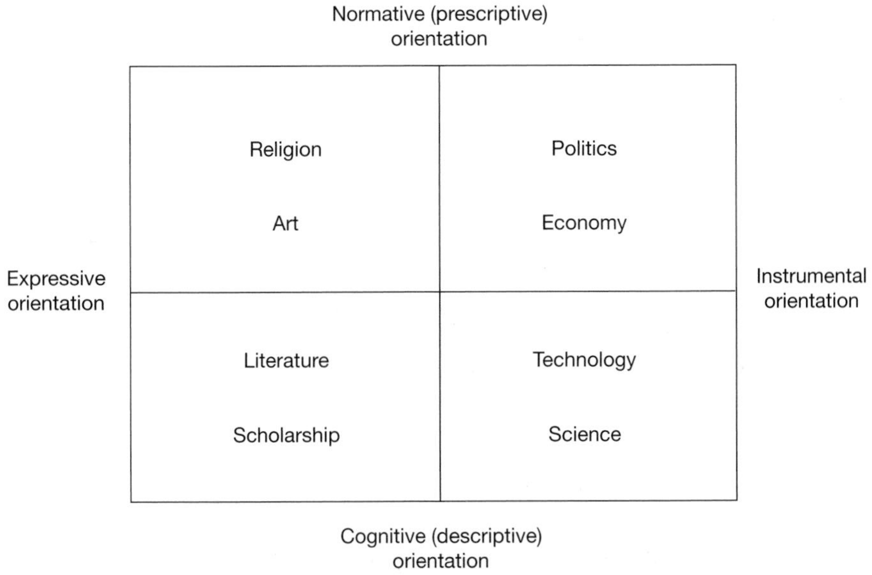

Figure 1.2 **The place of marketing in societal culture: the cultural value system**
Source: Rosengren, 1999, Figure 3.1

Thus, while management and the management of marketing have an instrumental character, they cannot be properly understood as standing divorced from other ways of living.

MARKETING, CONSUMPTION, AND COMMUNICATION

Consumerism is the production, distribution, desiring, obtaining, owning, and using of **symbolic** products. Consumption does not only satisfy material longing for food and wealth. Symbols are manipulated for a host of reasons. For the person, consuming constructs identity, the self, and relationships with others (see Box 1.1). For society, consumption sustains the continuing existence of institutions, groups, and other such structures.

BOX 1.1   A WORKING DEFINITION OF MARKETING

Marketing is concerned with creating and sustaining mutually satisfying exchanges of value between producer/servers and their customers. It has both a managerial orientation and an organizational/social function.

Certain conditions are necessary for an exchange to take place. Each party must:

- have something valued by the other
- be capable of communicating about the offering
- be capable of making the offering available
- believe that it is appropriate or desirable to trade with the other party
- value the offered benefits sufficiently to offset the efforts and risks involved in the exchange.

Marketing communication is like a coin – it has two sides:

1 **The offer** (expression): One part of marketing communication is concerned with effectively and efficiently providing information about the business and the products to chosen customer groups. But in isolation, what to say and to whom can be nothing more than a risky second-guessing about the interests and allegiances of other people. The answer, to paraphrase Stephen Covey (1989), is first to seek to understand before seeking to be understood.
2 **The inquiry** (impression): This part of the marketing communication task is concerned with learning from others about their interests and values, and relating this to the interests of the people working in the business. This action should logically precede the promotion of a point of view on product desirability and related consumer satisfaction.

Creating	Marketing helps to direct production to the creation of products that serve a purpose for buyers and consumers
Sustaining	Marketing is a bridge between those people who have a need to be fulfilled though interaction
Mutual	Neither party is exploiter of the other
Satisfying	The outcome of the interaction is desirable
Exchange	Products of value are traded
Value	Parties are free to determine the worth, desirability, utility, and associated qualities
Producer/server	The manufacturer who coordinates and delivers the product
Customer	The person who makes the purchase
Managerial orientation	Clearly understood relating of clearly purposeful actions and decisions in the coordination of resource use
Organizational function	The bringing about of a state or condition of being organized

Figure 1.3 **The essential aspects of marketing as exchange**

The overall outcome of this effort is intended to be the positioning of the provider as an efficient preferred source of solutions to problems experienced by people as buyers and consumers. This is the managerial aim in managing marketing communication. The challenge is to ensure that *expressive communicative activity* is clear, consistent and coherent, while also enabling and facilitating *impressive communicative activity* that aids judgement and decision-making. Marketing communication is widening in scope to embrace the idea that healthy relationships between customers and suppliers are the basis for the prosperity of each. Expectations are growing for authentic communication as part of a stakeholder relationship based on trust and commitment (see Box 1.2).

BOX 1.2 COMMENT: BRANSON'S PERSPECTIVE ON THE FUTURE OF BUSINESSES

Richard Branson does not believe that the Internet will be the driver of business. Corporations must focus on what their customers want and not on what they own.

Successful businesses will be organised virtually – they will contract with third parties to provide services to their customers. They will concentrate on personal relationships with their customers. Assets will be those resources that provide value to customers. They will be owned, according to Branson, by those who are best able to give personal service. Customers will get cheaper and better quality of service. Mobile phones and transport are examples.

(Shares, 8 January 2000)

MARKETING AS A MANAGEMENT TECHNOLOGY: MICRO-MARKETING

The origins of macro-marketing (Fisk, 1986; Sheth *et al.*, 1988) in social imperatives have been somehow nudged aside as the micro-economic (managerial) foundations have taken a firm grip on most managers' thinking in the past 30 years or so.

A major review of marketing literature by Sheth *et al.* (1988) produced a classification of marketing theory that reveals a range of foci. An overview is now given to highlight some alternative paradigms. Table 1.1 summarizes the focus of each of the various schools of thought, with particular comment on those ways of imagining marketing that have direct interest to business enterprise management. Note that the most prevalent 'micro-marketing' perspective differs from that of consumer behaviour, and is but one way of seeing marketing.

Sheth *et al.* (1988) additionally classified these twelve schools of marketing theory into four dimensions:

1 **The economic dimension** recognizes that actions may be driven by economic values, is normative in nature, and is derived from economic theory.
2 **The non-economic dimension** considers the social and psychological factors influencing the respective behaviours of the buyer and seller, is descriptive, and is derived from an anthropological perspective.
3 **The interactive dimension** examines the balance of power between buyers and sellers in interdependent exchange relationships, considers relations and effects, recognizes that either party may conduct marketing functions, and adopts an interactionism perspective in recognizing that neither party acts in isolation.
4 **The non-interactive dimension** considers the buyer to be passive and to have their behaviour acted upon by the active producer through persuasion and buying and selling.

Table 1.1 **The total field of marketing theory**

'School' of marketing thought	Focus of theory	Comments
Commodity	The objects of market transactions – i.e. distribution	
Functional	The marketing functions performed in market transactions	
Regional	Spatial separations between buyers and sellers	
Institutional	Intermediaries and channels of distribution	
Functionalist	The function of marketing systems	
Managerial (micro-marketing)	Marketing practice	Urges marketers to analyse consumer/customer needs. Emphasizes the marketing concept. Too simplistic, constraining and artificial in emphasizing the 'marketing mix'. Assumes economic values dominant
Buyer behaviour	Marketing from the buyer's perspective	Concentrates on purchase and brand choice behaviour – but from consumer, packaged goods field
Activist	Ad hoc issues of consumer interests	
Macro-marketing	The relationship between marketing and society	Useful if the organization's stakeholders are the 'society'
Organizational dynamics	Psychological aspects of behaviour of marketing channel members	
Systems	All functions and institutions of marketing and marketing as an institution in society	
Social exchange	The market as the focal point of exchanges	Exchange is seen as the fundamental foundation of marketing

Source: Adapted from Sheth *et al.*, 1988

In considering these dimensions, two particular dichotomies are of interest:

- **interactive/non-interactive**: examines the role of marketing and its objectives
- **economic/non-economic**: examines approaches to achieving the objectives of marketing

Much of the weakness in prevailing marketing communication accounts stems from a failure to address both of these concerns together. It considers only how marketing objectives can be achieved, thus often allowing assumptions about the appropriateness of marketing objectives and the nature and role of marketing to remain unrecognized and unchallenged.

The twelve schools of marketing theory have been classified by Sheth *et al.* (1988) to highlight their perspective on the role and nature of marketing. This is summarized in Table 1.2 to highlight the differing bases of marketing thinking, and to identify schools of thought which might contribute to a broader conception of marketing communication.

Rosengren (1999) uses his 'Great Wheel of Culture in Society' model to explain all societal structures. Two pairs of value orientations are the basis for society: truth and righteousness, and beauty and usefulness. These can also be termed cognitive/descriptive and normative/prescriptive, and expressive and instrumental, respectively. As early as the Greek philosophers, these were discussed as logos and ethos, and pathos and praxis, respectively. These basic value orientations are recognized by contemporary students of advertising and public relations.

Table 1.2 **Schools of marketing theory**

Approaches to the study of marketing	Economic	Non-economic	Interactive	Non-interactive
Commodity	✓			✓
Functional	✓			✓
Regional	✓			✓
Buyer behaviour		✓		✓
Activist		✓		✓
Macro-marketing		✓		✓
Institutional	✓		✓	
Functional	✓		✓	
Managerial	✓		✓	
Organization dynamics		✓	✓	
Systems		✓	✓	
Social exchange		✓	✓	

Ideas, actions, and artefacts in society are linked by culture as communicative and coordinating. Thus, religion and politics, politics and science, science and technology, technology and religion, religion and scholarship, and so on are continually mutually interacting. All of these relationships have to be established through action – the special type of action in which we are interested – namely communication. A never-ending process of differentiation proceeds through the face-to-face and mediated interactions of people. Yet, the institutions remain interdependent.

MARKETING AS A SOCIAL PROCESS: MACRO-MARKETING

Professor Theodore Levitt was clear that marketing is not a means of doing business, but the mode of sustainable business enterprise. 'Marketing is not the devious art of separating the unwary from his [*sic*] loose change . . . It is a consolidating view of the entire business process' (Levitt 1969: vii). This orientation shifts attention from what is done, to **why** it is done. Instead of operating against standards (cost, efficiency, productivity, etc.), it operates against competitors to earn patronage from consumers who become customers who constantly change the terms on which they will choose one product and/or supplier over another.

Kline (1993) shows that products in contemporary markets either are cultural products (e.g. films, TV programmes, art, books, games, sports, toys, music) or have social value (e.g. prestige, power, style, personal identity, ceremonial display) related to their ownership and use as both objects and social symbols.

WEAKNESSES IN TRADITIONAL TEXTBOOK EXPLANATIONS OF MARKETING

The institution of the market now ensures that all products are valued primarily through their exchange. All products are cultural artefacts – selling them is mostly a matter of communication. As Raymond Williams, scholar of culture and communication, has noted: 'marketing communication is a form of social narrative with the primary task of conveying those fictional social relations that can only be fulfilled in and through product ownership and use' (Williams, 1980).

Most marketing textbooks, and even marketing communication textbooks, however, include a discussion of 'communication' as merely a promotional tool. They seem to miss the point that marketing **is** communication designed to contrive the overlapping of fields of experience.

As Usunier (1993) pointed out also, these textbooks have downplayed or ignored the need to consider the impact on various cultures (and even on our conception of culture) of the global marketplace. Marketers need to understand people as consumers and customers, but also as citizens in their own lived context.

Usunier's solution is to recognize that global marketing can be more usefully understood as intercultural marketing. This properly recognizes the interaction between people, products, and symbols, as buyers and sellers who have different national cultural backgrounds.

In another review of marketing thinking, Gummesson (1993) identifies six further weaknesses in the way marketing is presented in traditional textbooks (summarized in Table 1.3). He simply does not believe that most textbooks in this field meet the claim that they cover every important marketing topic in detail. Ironically, some advertising of marketing textbooks has been misleading and unethical!

Marketing enterprise depends on, and perpetuates, the notion that consumer choice is rational (O'Shaughnessy, 1987). The intellectual task for marketers is to find order and reason in what might appear emotional or unreasonable. Consumer behaviour towards brands and as consumers has been described as schizophrenic. The marketing task is to plot the predictability of the unpredictability, and to provide rules for what may seem random.

Marketing itself, as we now know it, is a cultural borrowing, with its origins in the industrialization of the USA (Usunier, 1993). In many countries it is merely the word marketing that has been imported – the US-originated concept and social practices have been merely superimposed on to and merged into local selling practices, rather than replacing them (Allen, 1978).

WEAKNESS IN TRADITIONAL TEXTBOOK EXPLANATIONS OF MARKETING COMMUNICATION

In writing this book as a contemporary introduction to marketing communication, the author has attempted to respond to the past shortcomings by examining marketing communication as a cultural enterprise and products as social symbols. This makes the management of marketing communication an essentially intercultural problem of enabling and facilitating commerce in a complex intertwining of market-based exchange and social relationships.

Orthodox economists emphasized 'goods' with utility value. We consider products to include goods (manufactures) and services.

Marketing communication is almost always presented in textbooks as promotion of producer and product to a predetermined audience to elicit a desired response. If only it were actually that simple! The communication needs of marketing are much broader – even including the possibility that consumers may wish to consider the purchase of your product, and thereby become your customers! Marketing efforts, even when pre-planned, emerge through the interactions (negotiations or encounters) of interested actors.

Market research is clearly communication between producer and consumer – but is mostly not promotional – although even distinction is difficult, since in asking people to consider aspects of your provisional offering (product characteristics, pricing policy, distribution arrangements, and so on) you create an impression. All of the design, production, promotion, and delivery

Table 1.3 **Objections to established textbook versions of marketing**

Version of marketing	Objection
Textbook presentations of marketing are based on limited real-world data	Most of the theory presented is drawn from US packaged consumer goods activity and cannot be generalized to the broader cultural domain of instrumentally oriented economy
Services are treated as a special case, when goods are a minor part of total marketing attention	Services account for the majority of GNP, employment, and new companies. Well-managed service operations are a condition for goods to be sought and utilized. Many textbooks do not cover the actual composition of the economy satisfactorily
Industrial and business marketing are treated as a special case – consumer marketing dominates	Consumer marketing does not actually dominate the economy, despite being portrayed as doing so. Much marketing and purchasing takes place between corporate bodies and is invisible to most people, while consumer marketing and purchasing is a personal experience. Most textbooks do not reflect this
The knowledge is a patchwork, with little integration of new knowledge with established knowledge	New developments in thinking and practice are treated in separate chapters as add-on detail, when synthesis is necessary. Many 'new' ideas are obsolete by the time they reach the textbooks. Researchers devote too much attention to testing established theories
Pedagogical form overrides substance – design is better than content	Aesthetic values of presentation have, in many cases, overtaken the attention necessary to content. What is discussed is incomplete and lacks integration, but is attractively packaged
European thinking is subverted by the domination of US thinking	US textbook authors and gurus have been successfully colonizing our thinking for decades. Arguably, they are less critical in their thinking when they are successful in terms of book sales. European academics and practitioners default to mere bystanders, and fail to recognize the particular market environment from which much of the textbook content emanates

Source: Gummesson, 1993

is communicative when it comes into the awareness of a person operating as a consumer.

The marketing concept is centred on the concept of exchange. We need a communication theory basis for marketing communication that is also based on exchange, and should also be able to account for the co-production of identity, meaning, and knowledge (Deetz, 1992).

Compare:

1. **The orthodox 'marketing' perspective**: Communication is 'a transactional process between two or more parties whereby meaning is exchanged through the intentional use of symbols' (Engel *et al.*, 1994, quoted in Blythe, 2000: 1).
2. **The communication theorist perspective**: Communication is 'interaction (i.e. mutual influence), which is intersubjective (i.e. mutually conscious), intentional and purposive, and is carried out by means of a system of signs, mostly building on a system of verbal symbols, characterized by double articulation, and in turn building on fully developed systems of phonology, syntax, semantics and pragmatics' (Rosengren, 1999: 38). Rosengren summarizes this as 'intersubjective, purposive interaction by means of doubly articulated human language based on symbols'.

An alternative conception of communication and a further elaboration of the need for this can be found in chapter two.

In this book, communicating is taken to be the mode for marketing. We need a definition that acknowledges the central notion that marketing is communication for particular reasons, rather than allows the misleading view that communication is simply the promotion part of the whole.

Grönroos (2000) very helpfully uses the term *market communication*. This is, in a sense, a clearer concept than marketing communication. It implies that buyers and sellers form a market together and that they have to communicate in order to buy and sell, respectively. Thus, the management responsibility is to provide and operate effective and efficient systems to enable the making and keeping of promises – this of course is essentially relational. As Professor Grönroos points out: 'everything communicates something about a firm and its good and services – regardless of whether the marketer accepts this and acts upon it or not' (Grönroos, 2000: 264). Let us add that both buyer and seller may initiate marketing activity, and communication may be unplanned.

This perspective is complex, but necessarily comprehensive. Marketing is a social process consisting of individual and collective communicative activities performed by people as producers, intermediaries, and/or purchasers that facilitate and expedite participation in voluntary chosen satisfying tangible and intangible exchanges in social relationships by creating, maintaining or altering attitudes and/or behaviours in a dynamic environment through the joint and interactive creation, distribution, promotion, and pricing of valued goods and services, and the promotion of ideas, causes, places, and people.

Clearly, it is not intended that you memorize, word-for-word, this verbose statement. There are plenty of relevant definitions elsewhere. This carefully crafted description is dissected in chapter two so as to allow a full appreciation of the significance of a communication process perspective on marketing and marketing communication.

THE CONTRIVED EVOLUTION OF HUMAN COMMUNICATION TECHNOLOGIES

Although the real task of the student of marketing communication is to look forward to better possibilities, there is considerable benefit in taking a historical review to help us to understand the contemporary place of marketing in society. We cannot separate developments in marketing from the environment, which of course provided technologies for communicating. Each new development enables further possibilities.

Rosengren (1999), for example, shows that in 'the great wheel of culture in society', economy and technology are adjacent basic societal institutions that share an instrumental value orientation. By 'instrumental' we mean focused on use or purpose.

The expansion of media systems has increasingly enabled merchants to become marketers in speaking to consumers of the availability and desirability of their goods and services (Kline, 1993). In the second half of the nineteenth century, advertising became a valued instrument of merchandising, and became seen as a valuable diversion of capital from production and product improvement. Promotion became an investment. Table 1.4 is intended summarily to suggest that the application of a marketing concept and related social practices has been an aspect of social conditions. It is not implied that technologies were the drivers, though it is true that the availability of certain technologies provided marketers with an enhanced capacity to communicate.

Communication tools have become what their users wanted, only limited by availability of technology and science. Largely, in Western capitalist societies, developments in the tools for communicating have been driven by marketing ambitions (Fang, 1997). Indeed, many of the social systems have developed into industries in their own right, e.g. newspapers, radio, TV, cinema, the Internet. Mass communication made possible mass advertising to generate the necessary 'hungers' that led to mass consumption. This, in turn, gave purpose to mass production.

Table 1.4 **The evolution of the context for marketing developments**

Era	Business orientation	New technologies for communicating
Pre-1850	Craft manufacturing and local merchanting	Newspapers, pamphlets (notices and announcements)
1850–1920	Mass production – consumer demand for manufactured goods outstripped production capacity	Telegraph, telephone, phonograph, roll film, linotype and monotype printing, wireless, magazines, catalogues
1920–50	Selling – demand subsided, so products had to be advertised and personal selling was considered most important	Cinema, radio
1950–70	Marketing – efficient production and extensive promotion were not sufficient to ensure purchase of products. Meeting of needs now emphasized, therefore customer orientation was pre-eminent	Television, computers
1970–95	Post-industrial society characterized by a service economy in which encounter or communicating is central to the relationship between consumer and producer – no longer mediated by machines	Telex, facsimile machine, VCR
Post-1995	Consumers are increasingly active, differentiated searchers who use interactive multimedia to gather information. Mass customization of products is promoted and delivered via new media formed from newly merged media and marketing systems	Internet, WWW, mobile telephone, digital TV, e-mail, CD-ROM, low-cost PC, EDI (electronic data interchange), home shopping

CASE STUDY 1   THE ELOQUENCE OF HERMES, THE BOUNDARY SPANNER

In Hellenic (Greek) mythology, Hermes Mercurius, son of Zeus and Maia, and father of Pan and others, was the messenger of the Olympian gods, as well as the plebeian (common) Arcadian god of science and commerce (exchange, trade), and protector of merchants and traders, and patron to travellers (by road), gamblers, thieves, and cheats (wealth, luck, cunning)! He was god of eloquence (communication), master philosopher, revealer of hidden wisdom and guardian to occult knowledge.

Also associated with fertility and young men, as well as wrestling, sports stadia, and the manual arts (i.e. everything that required skill and dexterity), he is credited with inventing the lyre (presumably on his day off?). To the Romans, Hermes was Mercury and associated with the day Wednesday.

A prankster and inventive genius from birth, Hermes was known for his helpfulness to mankind, but also as a feared foe, often as a thief and trickster. He was known to be a master of boundaries and transitions. He was also responsible for leading souls across the river Styx to the Underworld (Hades). His name has been associated with business ventures such as BT's pension fund, the Lincoln Mercury car, the rock singer Freddie Mercury, an EU telecommunications development project, and Mercury Records, among others.

Hermes can be thought of as the necessary and knowledgeable mediator between consumption and production, being concerned with productivity and well-being. But, given the nature of his character, could he always be trusted?

Today, commerce has come to mean 'the activity embracing all forms of the purchase and sale of goods and services' and 'social relations' (*Collins Dictionary*). If we adopt Usunier's notion of 'rehabilitating' commerce as intercultural marketing, we favour the social interaction of provider and consumer.

WHAT DO YOU THINK?

1   Why is marketing communication almost always relegated to be a sub-element of a 'promotions' mix?

2   How does dialogue differ from monologue? Think of some business activities that are purported to be marketing, and are: (a) obviously expressive and (b) obviously impressive (i.e. the provider learns about and is influenced by the customer's perspective).

3   Describe a situation that you have experienced where the communication was initiated by you rather than by a supplier.

4   Consider the social construction of identity, meaning, and knowledge, and the suggested focus on relationships, networks, and interaction. What are the implications for students and managers who adopt the conventional models of human communication?

5   Can we still use models of the 'free market' of mechanisms created for the exchange of commodity goods to explain the possibility of the contribution of 'informational goods' to social well-being?

6   Professor Stephen Kline argues that 'for many people consumption is definitional to the modern way of life'. What role does marketing communication play in this?

7   Consider the meanings of the terms commerce, custom (customer), merchant, and trading. What do you conclude about marketing ideology and practice today?

8   Distinguish global marketing from intercultural marketing (see chapter six for further discussion).

9   Is Hermes a good role model for marketing communication managers?

10 What is the origin of popular marketing ideology? Do economists, social theorists, communication theorists, anthropologists or other specialists have the best theory of marketing?

RATIONALE FOR THE BOOK

The 'easy' way to sell a textbook is to reproduce the success formula of those that have gone before. If Professor Gummesson is right, this does a disservice to students who are asked to have faith that the so-called experts are telling the whole and true story. At the very least, such cultural products as textbooks should be promoted honestly.

In response to Gummesson's polemical critique of marketing textbooks, and in anticipation of a similar criticism of marketing communication textbooks from Professor Buttle (see chapter two), this book has been designed with the following principles:

- closer to reality by moving beyond simplistic stimulus–response models of communication
- attempt to integrate, not merely compile fragmented knowledge
- avoid taking the 4Ps (product, price, place, promotion) as a general theory of marketing
- avoid equating marketing communication only or mostly with mass communication
- incorporate quality management knowledge
- integrate around concepts of relationships, networks, and interaction
- examine a social constructionist approach as an alternative approach to explaining marketing and consumer behaviour
- consider marketing communication processes to be discursive, not merely expressive
- directly consider a communication mix to fully recognize marketing as a social process, rather than fragment our thinking to a promotion mix within a marketing mix

Marketing communication is thus a management process that enables and facilitates a dialogue among consumers (and in certain cases other stakeholders).

The key points of each chapter are highlighted in the 'What Do You Think?' section with a set of questions that catalyse reflection on the preceding discussion, and build a link into the subsequent chapter. These questions can also be the departure point for further reading and thinking.

'Comment' sections are interspersed with the text to provide links into day-to-day experiences that you may have had yourself, or that can be brought forward from other people's experiences. These illustrate or challenge the point of view presented and can be used as the basis of class discussion.

FURTHER READING

Blythe, J. (2000) *Marketing Communications*, London: Prentice-Hall.

Covey, S. R. (1989) *The Seven Habits of Highly Effective People: Restoring the Character Ethic*, New York: Simon & Schuster.

Engel, J. F., Warshaw, M. R. and Kinnear, T. C. (1994) *Promotional Strategy: Managing the Marketing Communication Process*, 8th edn, Burr Ridge, IL: Irwin.

Fang, I. (1997) *A History of Mass Communication: Six Information Revolutions*, Boston, MA: Focal Press.

Levinson, P. (1997) *The Soft Edge: A Natural History and Future of the Information Revolution*, London: Routledge.

Pine, B. J., Peppers, D. and Rogers, M. (1995) 'Do you want to keep your customers forever?', *Harvard Business Review*, March–April: 103–14.

chapter *two*

A COMMUNICATION CONCEPT FOR COMMUNICATING

LEARNING POINTS

Careful study of this chapter will help you to:

- reflect on the conception of communication that pervades our daily discourses outside of our awareness

- recover marketing as a social process in which people come first, products follow

- imagine marketing communication as managed conversations and to compare and contrast this with the notion of designed messages

- examine our ideas about communicators and their interchanges in markets

In a capitalist market-based society, relationships are coercive and turn people into things

INTRODUCTION

It is the provider's task to establish a meaningful relationship with selected consumers and buyers as a basis for influence and exchange. Today products are similar (often identical) in design, price, and performance – i.e. in terms of core benefits to users and consumers – so must be differentiated through benefit augmentation to attract buyer and consumer attention when promoted. Thus, nowadays marketing communication is much more than notifications of availability. Daily experience and our knowledge of marketing principles show that communication in marketing is much more than informing, since we can observe such actions as sponsorship, product repositioning, consumer targeting, image redefinition, brand renewal, and so on.

Marketing communication is a set of purposive activities, linked and coordinated to some degree. These activities are simply some of the actions that occur in a situation, impart some influence on the situation and are in turn influenced by the context in which they arise. Contexts are not isolated sets of circumstances that are easily identified – rarely do we have full knowledge. A particular situation is the intersection of people, technologies, and processes.

The traditional models of communication – both linear and 'two-way' versions – emphasize individual behaviour and fail to account for the social nature of the human communication process. They treat identity, meaning, and knowledge as if they arise in the mind of the individual in isolation of their environment. But, it is clear that in communicating we are mutually participative in constructing our own identity and those of others we encounter, in generating meanings in our minds that cannot be directly 'shared' with others, and in producing knowledge. We will refer to an appreciative system in which all this happens (explained in chapter three).

The cultural (interactional) approach is considered. This identifies persons as role players in the process of communication. This approach will be seen to be more sensible than the now outmoded conduit metaphor or transmission model, but it also has a weakness. The context within which communicating is pursued as an activity is not accounted for, and so a relational approach is needed.

The transmission model is convenient for a management that is centred on control and authority. Deetz (1992) warns of the limiting effect of such hegemonic managerialistic thinking and practices. The possibility of responsive and responsible management is lost. Response is central to marketing, and we will return to the problem of responsibility in chapter eighteen. Deetz defined managerialism as 'a kind of systemic logic, a set of routine practices, and an ideology'. He goes on to specify that it is

> a way of conceptualising, reasoning through, and discussing events
> . . . [involving] a set of routine practices, a real structure of rewards,
> and a code of representation. It is a way of doing and being in
> corporations that partially structures all groups and conflicts with, and
> at times suppresses, each group's other modes of thinking.
> (Deetz, 1992: 222)

This is a political explanation for the communicative practices of many marketing managers.

THE ORTHODOX VIEW OF MARKETING COMMUNICATION

Our textbooks provide a simple model of human communication when explaining the role of communication in marketing and management. The trouble is, the models used are not just simple, they are also simplistic – and misleading. Consider our everyday terminology as set out in Box 2.1.

BOX 2.1 SIMPLISTIC MODELS OF THE ROLE OF COMMUNICATION

'I received a communication'

'She is our Communications Manager'

'Did they get our message?'

'My perception of the company is that they are successful'

'He perceived a change of emphasis'

Stop and reflect carefully on what is meant by such use of the terms 'communication', 'message', 'perception', and so on. The terminology is confused and our use of it is confusing.

Traditional marketing thinking presupposes that producers produce and communicate, while consumers receive and consume. In the marketing process (i.e. in taking a product into the marketplace) production, communication, and consumption are separate processes. The task of the marketer is seen to be to reach, and stay in, the minds of consumers. In this ideology, it is believed that consumers will buy if persuaded (euphemistically termed 'informed') through messages to understand what is offered to them and how to act on that knowledge. This transmission model is now examined.

The necessary reconception of communication

Buttle's (1995) review of the treatment of marketing communications marketing textbooks showed that very few marketing specialists have attempted to produce comprehensive, integrative theory for marketing communication at both the interpersonal and mediated levels. He found that while all 101 texts surveyed did not try to provide some theoretical basis for the development of managerial strategies, many did so only implicitly and did not explicitly recognize the theoretical grounds of their discussion. Buttle shows that the work of Wilbur Schramm (first published in 1948) has been by far the most widely adopted in promoting a set of communication practices designed to produce cognitive, affective or behavioural outcomes among a specified internal or external target audience.

Schramm's work remains disproportionately influential and is still the main basis of the prevailing orthodoxy in the consideration of the communication aspects of marketing. Although Schramm did update his thinking (in 1971) to spell the demise of the earlier 'bullet theory of communication', he still retained the encoder–message–decoder model, and this has become firmly entrenched in marketing texts. In fairness, Schramm's thinking did shift to communication as 'a relationship, an act of sharing, rather than something which someone does to someone else' (1971: 8). This was a considerable development from the earlier view that communication was a 'magic bullet' (Klapper's [1960] term 'hypodermic effect' also become popular in mass communication studies) that 'transferred ideas or feelings or knowledge or motivations from one mind to another' (1971: 8). At last, communication was seen as the study of people in relationship. Indeed, Schramm claimed that all communication necessarily functions within a broader framework of social relations: the physical/spatial relationship between sender and receiver; the situational context; role expectations; and social norms. Yet, this conclusion and essential orientation has not yet percolated into marketing texts. Another problem is that some texts have taken an interpersonal or mediated communication perspective, thus failing to cope with the diversity of activities that fall within the field of marketing communication.

Buttle (1995) concludes from his meta-analysis that marketing textbooks share, because of the common ancestry for their theories of communication, four themes and assumptions (Table 2.1).

Buttle highlights the problem that the very themes and assumptions upon which marketing and marketing communication textbooks are designed (he terms this 'normal marketing communication theory') have been questioned by contemporary communication theorists. It seems that these fields do not readily communicate! The wider communication literature can better deal with the weaknesses and omissions of popular (textbook version of) marketing communication theory. What resides in most textbooks is outdated, ill-informed, and in need of revision. Perhaps marketing communication texts should be (at least) co-authored by a communication and/or culture scholar (perhaps an anthropologist untainted by managerialistic thinking?).

Ray (1982) treats marketing as strategic communication. DeLozier's (1976) characterization of marketing communication is an example of this outmoded thinking that is still prevalent:

> The process of presenting an integrated set of stimuli to a market with the intent of evoking a desired set of responses within that market set and setting up channels to receive, interpret and act upon messages from the market for the purposes of modifying present company messages and identifying new communication opportunities.
>
> (DeLozier, 1976: 168)

In fairness, DeLozier is one of the few clearly to identify both modes of communication: impression and expression. However, his definition of communication is limiting because:

- it does not recognize that meaning and interpretation of messages are framed in differing environments and widely differing fields of experience
- it says nothing about symbolism at product and producer levels

Table 2.1 **Critique of prevailing themes in marketing communication theory**

Textbook theme	*Critique*
The individual is the appropriate unit of analysis	Marketing has communicative effects at household, family, institutional and cultural levels, yet, in common with other fields of enquiry, there has been bracketing of human experience – the exclusion of some elements while including others – to simplify the complex situation to make it more accessible to explanation. This ignores the systemic character of the social world
The principal concern is the effect of particular messages	Marketing communication has a pervasive, inescapable presence in our day-to-day consciousness. Consumers can find meaning in almost any publicly accessible information about corporations, products, people, etc. All elements of the 'marketing mix' are (at least potentially) communicative.
The intention of the source determines the meaning of a message	Assumes that the audience is passive and that the receiver is relatively powerless in how they respond to the content of a message to which they are exposed. Recent communication theory development has introduced the notion of interpretative community members deriving meaning by interacting with the content
Communication is 'effective' when the receiver's decoding of message content produces the same meaning as intended by the encoder	Assumes that the content of marketing communication is closed, but accessible to a competent receiver. But people contextualize received messages – co-orientation and fidelity are unlikely once the message is released out into others' interpretative frames

Source: Adapted from Buttle, 1995

- it places presentation ahead of attention (apprehension)
- it assumes that desired responses can be evoked
- it is premised on a transmission conception of communication

Perhaps DeLozier can be forgiven for the inadequacy of his thinking, but contemporary slips are unforgivable. Kotler (2000), for example, unashamedly explains the communication process as a linear series of encoding and decoding acts, even though this does not sensibly explain human interaction. Professor Kotler does not appear to acknowledge that the model he adopts is challenged by alternative approaches.

A contemporary perspective on the field of marketing communication

The consequence of recognising the concerns of communication theorists is that a contemporary textbook will be newly selective in the presentation of relevant concepts and principles, and will be particularly critical of certain traditional practices (see Table 2.2).

The more up-to-date concerns of the 'abnormal' marketing communication theory takes contemporary communication theories as the basis for examining marketing communication principles and practices. This textbook will, therefore, not follow the outmoded orthodoxy: models to explain the effects of intentional messages on individuals premised on a 'conduit' conception of human communication. Instead, rather more helpfully, we will

Table 2.2 **Priority topics in the 'old' vs. 'new' marketing communication theory**

'Normal'/traditional marketing communication theory is concerned with:	'Abnormal'/contemporized marketing communication theory is concerned with:
The psychology of interpersonal and mediated communication effects on the individual: a simple stimulus–response model	1 The complex, rule-governed relationships of families and households with advertising media and content 2 The institutional effects of advertising 3 Cognitive and critical perspectives on the cultural effects of advertising: social reality; beliefs, values, moral orders and knowledge claims; enculturation; socialization; hegemony
Effects of single messages or campaigns on identified individuals	The cumulative effect of marketing communication as central to meaning production in our post-industrial consumer society – symbolic interaction
Passive audiences that do not actively interpret messages and are relatively powerless towards the message content to which they are exposed	Interpretative communities: Uses and Gratifications model; the interactive model
Commonness or co-orientation – sharing understandings through information	Interpretative frames – communication as co-productive interaction – conjoint action – meaning not transferred or shared but jointly produced in social 'interaction'

base our exploration of contemporary practices by establishing contemporary principles from contemporary communication theory. This will allow students of marketing communication to understand better the process and effects of marketing communication by examining theories that attempt to describe, explain, and interpret phenomena in a manner that normal marketing communication theory cannot. If you simply wish to bring about short-term cognitive, affective, and behavioural change in a managerialistic fashion, then read one of the other books!

Social approaches to theorizing on communication

Proceeding from Buttle's end-view, we need an abnormal marketing communication theory. A social constructionist perspective, hinted at by Schramm but for some reason not picked up by subsequent marketing textbook authors, offers this improvement.

Social approaches to communication are in opposition to a psychological approach (see Britt, 1978, as an example from the marketing field), and characterized as 'organic' rather than 'mechanistic', concerned with 'ritual' rather than 'transmission', and fundamentally 'interpretive' rather than 'scientific' (Leeds-Hurwitz, 1995, provides a comprehensive collection of essays around this 'new paradigm').

Social approaches to communication describe events occurring between people in the process of interacting. This is in contrast to the reporting of how events are perceived through a single individual's understanding. Thus, communication is thought of as inherently collaborative and cooperative visible behaviour, rather than as merely personal cognition.

A particular definition of what constitutes communication is adopted. This focuses on process as well as product or outcome. For example, Carey (1975: 17) defines communication as 'a symbolic process whereby reality is produced, maintained, repaired, and transformed'. More will be said about this particular conception of communication below.

Social reality and experience

Social reality is not seen as a fact or set of facts existing prior to human activity – it is created in human interaction. Berger and Luckmann (1966) analysed knowledge in society in the context of a theory of society as a dialectical process between objective and subjective reality. They concluded that people interact and produce meaningful behaviour patterns that construct a shared reality. We create our social world through our words and other symbols and through our behaviours. Such an approach requires us to question the validity of traditional 'scientific' experiments. The business of the interpretivist is not to reveal the world to us but to create some part of the world for us. Interaction is forwarded as a creative social accomplishment. Deetz feels very strongly that 'If the study of human communication is not ultimately the study of how we *make* the world in which we have our human existence, then it is as trivial as our dominant "model" of it would seem to say it is' (1995: 130). Further, 'Communication, then, is the process in which we create and maintain the "objective" world, and, in doing so, create and maintain the only human existences we can have' (ibid.: 203). The dominant model will be critiqued below.

Meanings and culture

The central problem attended to is how social meanings are created. The focus is on people not as passive rule followers operating within pre-existing regulations, but as active agents – rule makers within social contexts. Identity is seen as a social construction, and study of social role and cultural identity leads to a study of power and what happens when particular identities are chosen or ascribed by others.

The concept of culture is central and is defined as the knowledge that people must learn to become appropriate members of a given society. Cultural contexts include the community in which particular communicative behaviours arise. Social approaches are mostly holistic – the study of interaction requires the whole picture to understand how the multiple components are related.

Ideas as objects

Reddy (1993) observed that our major metaphor for communication takes ideas as objects that can be put into words, language as their container, thought as the manipulation of these objects, and memory as storage. In this view we send ideas in words through a conduit – a channel of communication – to someone else who then extracts the ideas from the words. A consequence of this metaphor is that we believe that ideas can be extracted and can exist independently of people. We also expect that when communication occurs, someone extracts the same idea from the language that was put in by someone else. Meaning is taken to be a thing. But the conduit metaphor hides all of the effort that is involved in communication, and many people take it as a definition of communication.

Co-construction of meanings

Mantovani (1996) heralds the obsolescence of the old model of communication as the transfer of information from one person to another. No longer should we be satisfied with an outmoded model which conceives of communication as 'the transportation of an inert material – the information that actors exchange with each other – from one point to another along a "pipeline"'. There is no account of the cooperation that stimulates reciprocal responsibility for interaction and the series of subtle adaptations which occur among 'interlocutors'. Nor does the old model consider that communication is possible only to the extent that participants have some common ground for shared beliefs: they recognize reciprocal expectations, and accept rules for interaction which anchor the developing conversation. The old theory of communication treats knowledge as an object (i.e. as a body of information or as independent facts to be processed) existing independently of the participants that can be carried through channels and possessed by a receiver when communication is successful.

The new, alternative conception of communication is of a common construction of meanings. Information is not moved from one place to another but is always a means to an end, produced and used by social actors to attain their goals in daily life. Meaning is a mutual aspect of knowledge – it is a joint production manifested in and through discursive practices. Meaning and message are often assumed to be synonymous. But human communication is not merely information processing.

The politics of communication models

Why do so many of us retain this outmoded way of thinking of communication? The conduit metaphor of communication, shows Deetz (1992), is thoroughly taken for granted in institutional structures and everyday thinking, aligning well with dominant power structures and liberal notions of democracy. It supports the dominant group (i.e. the corporation is the management group) in accomplishing control over those they choose to subordinate. We retain a conception of the communicative process that gives liberal guidance to communicative practice – in the face of corporations as communication systems of control. In this way we misconceive how human perception and expression work. Yet the denial of democracy is an everyday occurrence not necessarily done for the purpose of control. A web of strategic moves of asymmetrical power-based relationships is enacted through discursive practices; managed (corporate) communication is needed to avoid managerialistic (the traditional 'corporate') communication. In systematically distorted communication systems, managers become locked into praising each other, discussing the difficulties of the job, making endless agenda lists, inventing elaborate strategies, and trying to decide what to do, and yet they communicate in ways that inhibit resolution of problems and rarely say what they mean – thus they cannot really manage!

The contemporary everyday conception of interacting with others through effective communication is conceptually flawed as the basis for participatory democracy. Identity is fixed in distorted communication systems, and actors are denied the possibility of regaining (constructive) conflict and self-formation. Counter to the common-sense view, communication is not for self-expression but for 'self-destruction' – a social act to overcome one's fixed subjectivity, one's conceptions, one's strategies. Identity, meaning, and knowledge are opened to the indeterminacy of people and the external environment.

Our everyday work experience includes the self-deception that individuals are engaging in communication action in pursuit of mutual understanding. In fact they are engaged in concealed strategic action (even concealed from themselves), which result from confusing the pursuit of mutual understanding with the pursuit of success. What is missing is a productive rather than a reproductive conception of communication as the fundamental process by which mutual understanding arises in regard to the subject matter rather than in the sharing of opinions. Conversation is the ongoing process of creating mutual understanding through the open formation of experience.

Most of us are still operating in outmoded instrumental-technical modes in pursuit of control. Communication is seen as a conduit for the transmission or transportation of expressions of self-interest (i.e. informational for understanding), but these no longer suffice. Information conceptions of communication only work in situations in which consensus on meaning, identities, construction of knowledge, and basic values can be taken for granted; this is no longer a realistic view of our world! If we control through information systems, we are in danger of non-responsive self-referentiality. Hayek (1990) called this the 'fatal deceit': we don't ask questions because we think we have the answers. Some crucial questions are never asked. Imaginary worlds are misrecognized as real. Management practice distorts, manufactures (artificial) consent, excludes, and suppresses differences – asymmetrical power relations suppress natural conflicts. Social divisions are assumed to be fixed and in need of promotion. Consensus over problems, personal identities, knowledge claims, norms of interaction, and policies for directing joint action are assumed as the basis for interaction, when they need to be negotiated through interaction for creativity and to meet diverse stakeholder interests. When the 'corporation' = the management team, all other stakeholders are externalized as costs to be contained. Then, stakeholders are managed for the managers' benefit.

Most corporate communication systems are systems of corporate control, when participation is required. A Corporate Communication Managing System as a corporate participation system has been proposed (Varey, 1998). The Corporate Communication Research Unit at the University of Salford is one of a number of groups working in this field to bring the benefits (and values) of contemporary communication thinking into management (and marketing) practice.

We must shift from our general belief in liberal quasi-'democracy' and its adversarial expression of self-interest, opinion advocacy and persuasion, to a constitutive real participatory democracy of negotiated co-determination through interaction ('It's good to talk' is a moral stance). We need to move from controlling to stewardship and this requires a mindshift from self-interest to service; from patriarchy to partnership; from consent to coordination; from dependency to empowerment; from involvement to participation.

Conversations

'Communications' are best understood as interaction acts, not as objects and artefacts. We communicate when we interact. Communication is best understood as constitutive – interests should be understood as social products, often produced by decisions and opportunities.

We must often speak when we do not know – not knowing is a reason to talk with others! We can reach consensus if we interact. We need a **conversational model** of corporate life that we can apply in pursuit of dialogue before expression – Stephen Covey (1989) teaches us why we should 'seek to understand before seeking to be understood'. Such organized gossip can lead to serendipity; the repair of faulty mental maps; and productive 'interchanges'.

The conversing corporation is full of natural talk, curiosity, discussion, and questions. Conversing corporations can expect:

- more satisfactory goal accomplishment
- recognition of an important value in a pluralistic society in which a wider range of social values and lifestyle options are emerging
- equality in pay-in (contribution) and pay-out (benefit)
- fair representation of interests
- products and services that fulfil customers' needs and desires, and meet workers' needs for fulfilment and pride
- a self-correcting whole, promising genuine opportunity and progress
- people to have a voice

These benefits are realized when managers take responsibility and account-ability for constructing and driving systems for communication that enable and facilitate questioning, paraphrasing, story-telling, and so on. These systems are capable of overcoming the natural outcome of efforts to communicate – misunderstanding – that is inherent in the nature of language use (see Heyman, 1994). Counter-productive behaviour is exposed in such systems.

An interaction can be thought of as a behaviour that produces a response. Communication is thus a special kind of interaction that produces meanings. We often speak of interactive communication; actually, 'communicative interaction' is what is needed in the workplace.

Much 'communication' and 'interaction' practice is ping-pong in nature, with individuals talking past each other in a dyadic pair of monologues rather than with each other. Two temporally and spatially co-located, but inde-pendent, communication systems are operating in this situation. 'Feedback' is purported to complete the cycle, but often is little more than reaction (in the terms of the speaker). Heyman (1994) clarifies the manner in which each person contributes talk, but there is only limited communication (Figure 2.1).

Note, however, that talking past each other in a monological dyad is not the same as dialogue. Communicating is better seen as interaction that co-constructs meaning by making context differences explicit, leading through common interpretation to a shared understanding. Why does this not naturally occur?

According to Heyman, ethnomethodology (a sociological movement founded by Harold Garfinkel) shows that language use (talk) inherently creates misunderstanding, because language is necessarily **indexical** (i.e. context gives meaning to our talk), and **reflexive** (i.e. context depends on meaning). The context for understanding each other does not automatically

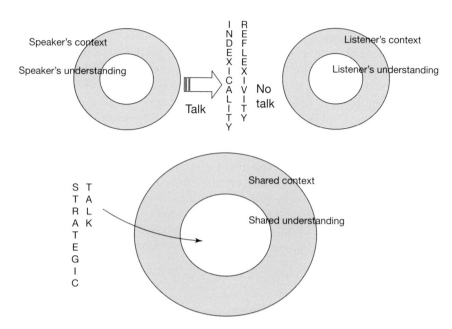

Figure 2.1 **Constructing shared context for understanding**
Source: Based on Heyman, 1994

arise (it is not pre-existent); rather, we are responsible for creating our own context for understanding. The meaning of a situation comes from the combination of person, place, time, and so on. Sociolinguistics provides a way of analysing the manner in which we choose our language use in the situation in which we believe that we find ourselves. Talk is naturally ambiguous – we never know all that the other person knows. All language use is in a context, therefore meaning-making comes through interpretation. It is not the words of language that are the basis of communication, it is previous and current interaction that is at the heart of communicating, to provide understanding. Interaction does the communicating; language use clarifies. Experience may be past and present.

Misunderstanding arises when the communicators create differing contexts for understanding. In this context misunderstanding is differing under-standing. Personal context is a taken-for-granted knowledge. The shared context necessary for shared understanding is created in interaction.

What are the implications of the inherent indexicality and reflexivity of language that are a barrier to shared understanding? First, interactors (communicators) have a responsibility for creating shared context for understanding. Second, we need to understand misunderstanding to create shared understanding founded on shared context through strategic talk. Third, the service encounter has to be a mutual context-creating interaction (we jointly create the world we experience).

Misunderstanding is natural but can be avoided through what Heyman calls 'strategic talk', that is a conscious effort to talk in order to create context and understanding, using techniques of formulations, questions and answers, paraphrasing, examples, and stories.

Without such effort to construct understanding, we 'climb the ladder of inference' (Argyris, 1990), rapidly leaping from observable data about a situation to conclusions and actions based on assumptions and beliefs with scarcely a moment to reflect. Because most of these conclusions are never openly discussed, there is no way to check them and they provide the basis for misunderstanding (Figure 2.2).

This inevitably leads to diverging meanings and understandings (Figure 2.3), unless communicators engage in conscious 'strategic talk'.

When communicating is taken as no more than objective informing, much is lost that is possible in dialogue. In this ultimate level of communication, each party seeks to share, perhaps only hypothetically, the other's appreciation and to open their own to the other's persuasion with a view to enlarging the approaching mutual understanding, if not also shared appreciation.

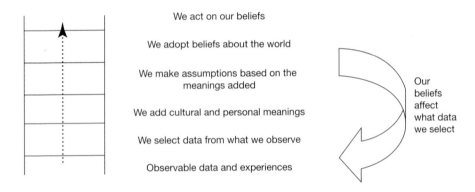

Figure 2.2 **The ladder of inference**

Source: Based on Argyris, 1990

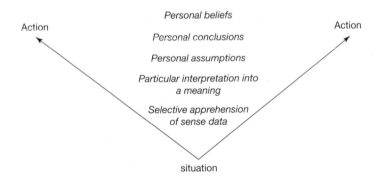

Figure 2.3 **Intersubjective divergence**

Morality of communication practices

The moral question is whether all positions are granted an equal right of co-determination. Morally, psychology pursues reflective autonomy (of the person), sociology pursues legitimate social order (of the collective), and communication pursues equable participation (in the social system). We need a communication theory of managing (this is largely a personal value decision) about why rather than how.

We no longer have cosmos (an ordered, predictable system), instead the (post)modern world is chaos (formless, utter confusion). There is no longer fundamental consensus on what things mean – interaction has become about values and differing meanings. We no longer have a stable, homogeneous society. The problem of 'inadequate communication' is not merely one of divergent understandings but of divergent interests. We need real communication, not 'more' or 'better' communication. Interaction can no longer be the expression and transmission of meaning (an information process). It has become about the construction and negotiation of meaning (a communication process).

Marketing is theorized as participative, i.e. voluntary exchange (a negotiative constitution), but is most practised as strategic or consensual (a dominant constitution supported by systematic distortions). For example, advertising is almost always dominant expression and is selected as the means of communication because it is so. Yet goals cannot be preconceived but are co-determinate.

Figure 2.4 summarizes the alternative conceptions of human communication. Since this book is taking an intercultural approach to defining marketing communication, it is the cultural model that will be assumed to underlie most of the remainder of the discussion in the following chapters.

As we shall see in chapter four, it is the motives and intentions of communicating marketers that are often inconsistent with the concept of marketing (see also Box 2.2).

BOX 2.2 COMMENT: PERCEPTION–CONCEPTION AND THE APPRECIATIVE SYSTEM

When we say that we have a perception of a situation or event, we usually mean that we have a particular meaning or understanding of it. Perhaps our thinking would be straighter if we spoke of a conception rather than a perception.

The appreciative system captures data through perception. This is translated into meaning before being judged in advance of deciding what action to take.

THREE PERSPECTIVES ON MESSAGES

A 'message' can be best be defined as an intended meaning for a written, aural or visual text. But how it will be interpreted depends upon the reception

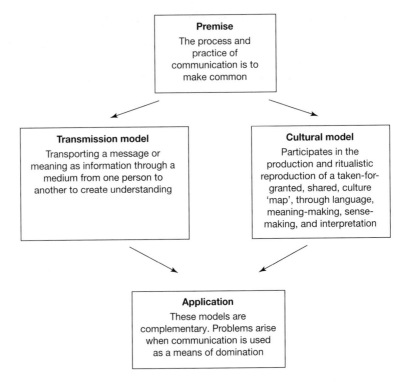

Figure 2.4 **Complementary models of communication**

Source: Based on Grossberg *et al.*, 1998: 15–26

environment: not only the linguistic and ideological codes of the producer and 'viewer', but also alternative information. We can call this environment the culture of the consumer.

O'Keefe (1988) shows that when messages are designed, one of three design logics or conceptions of communication underlies the style, format, content, and medium selected (Figure 2.5).

Expressive logic	Communication is a mode of self-expression of feelings and thoughts, with little regard for the needs or desires of others
Conventional logic	Communication is a game to be played by rules – self-expression guided according to accepted rules and norms, usually polite and appropriate
Rhetorical logic	Communication is a way of changing the rules through negotiation – flexible, insightful, person-centred

Figure 2.5 **Message logics**

COMMUNICATOR CHARACTERISTICS

Several factors can be thought of as intervening between communicators, with resulting effects on outcomes. These are summarized as source credibility, source attractiveness, and anticipated source intention (Figure 2.6).

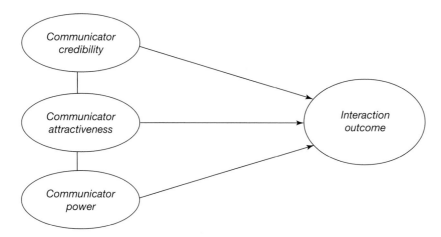

Figure 2.6 **Influences on communication outcome**
Source: Kelman, 1961

'Credibility' is the extent to which a communicator believes that the other communicator is able and willing to give a open opinion based on sufficient relevant expertise. Highly credible people are usually more persuasive than others. Trust is very important – a person's input to a communication system will be taken negatively if they are believed to be biased in their view. 'Selfishness' and 'hidden agendas' are manifestations of this, occurring when one person believes that the other is trying to beat them or exploit them.

'Identification' arises when one person finds another attractive. This can be observed when one person is motivated to seek a relationship with another and so adopts a similar position. Thus we might only maintain an attitude or behaviour as long as it is supported by the attractive other, or as long as they remain attractive to us. Is Gary Glitter still influential as a pop icon? (Ask your mother and father!)

Credibility is sometimes established by encouraging people to identify with a situation in which a product is shown resolving a recognized problem.

When one person believes that the other is able to confer reward or punishment in a situation, they may choose to comply with requests in order to receive a desired reward or benefit or to avoid a undesired punishment or cost. 'Power' is always an attribute of a relationship, since it implies that one person can have an effect on the other's situation.

The derived self

The self is composed of multiple identities with associated loyalty to relationships of ethnic community, religion, locality, and nation or supranation. Dittmar (1992) argues that identity is located at the individual–society interface, linking self and consumption. With some products, we develop a sort of relationship in which they come to be important parts of our identity. Others cannot be so readily accommodated. These, if they are to be absorbed, require an exploration of identity – 'the quest for outer difference becomes a quest for inner meaning' (Gabriel and Lang, 1995: 78). Consumption has become an opportunity to display one's identity – but is this creative opportunity or cultural determinism? Certain objects are vital elements of our identity as if physical extensions of our bodies. McLuhan (1964) saw these extensions of our physical existence as communication media – anything that amplifies or intensifies a bodily organ, sense or function. These also act as filters to organize and interpret our social existence – each affects the whole psychic and social complex. As communicator, the consumer uses products as bridges to relate to other people. As identity-seeker, the consumer searches for a real self in consumed objects (see Gabriel and Lang, 1995).

We derive a sense of self (personal identity) from 'what we are not' – from what surrounds us, i.e. from our experience of the world (Russell, 1982). This externally derived sense of identity, from our interaction with others, may be our only sense of identity, and yet it is as transitory and ephemeral as the experiences from which it is derived. Almost all human activity is towards establishing and defending our identities.

Identification increases susceptibility to influence (Kelman, 1961). It pays us to identify. In developing and maintaining a favourable, self-defining social relationship (often subtle and unrecognized) with a controlling agent, we are able to construct a favourable self-image. This type of conformity facilitates the adoption of collective norms and values – for example, consider the decision to buy and wear clothing that bears a corporate label. Celebrity product endorsement aims to promote the possibility of identification by exploiting the social attractiveness of the person, group, or corporation. We are prompted to ask ourselves 'who am I?', 'who are you?', and 'who may I be(come) if I (am) associate(d) with you?'

Russell (1982) argues that we acquire possessions to show who we are and to confer status upon ourselves – 'many advertisements prey upon the need to reaffirm a sense of self' (Russell 1982: 106) – they solve problems on the level of image. The derived self constantly strives to reaffirm its existence by identifying with something larger, such as a group or belief system. The 'right' association supports the identity. Following a fashion reaffirms 'belongingness'. The intrinsic self (character) has given way to a mouldable extrinsic self (personality), while consumer goods provide instruments for the construction of the self – the 'self as other'.

Kenneth Burke (1950) proposed three sources of identification: material, idealistic, and formal.

- **Material identification** results from goods, possessions, things – I am like you because we own the same model of car or have the same taste in clothes, music, books, etc.

- **Idealistic identification** is based on shared ideas, attitudes, feelings, and values. We attend the same church or are members of the same political party, etc.

- **Formal identification** results from arrangement, form, or organization of an event in which both participate.

Identification is the opposite of division.

Belief systems are a strong source of identity. We may use selective perception, diversion, appeal to authority, misrepresentation, defamation, jargon, etc. to defend our identity. The 'skin-encapsulated ego' (Watts, 1972) is at once driven to individualism (difference and competition) and yet craves social contact (the derived identity needs other people). We use self-deception to distort our relationships and day-to-day lives as our means of psychological self-preservation (Goleman, 1985), yet we derive our sense of identity from those same people, things, places, institutions, and informational structures with which we relate (see Toffler, 1970). Watts, among others, has urged that we learn to balance the nourishment and protection of our individuality and separateness with that of our belonging and unity. Healthy society requires healthy members whose actions are not dominated by the ego and are appropriate to the situation at hand. Satisfaction of self-centred needs cannot accomplish this healthy state. The derived self cannot be allowed to dominate. Is the effect of modern-day 'branding' to create 'mindless xenophobia'? In a society in which consumption has replaced production and creation as the primary seat of self-definition, is tribalism rekindled on consumption decisions through sought relationships (in the marketplace), in place of kinship? 'All of us become at some point, and for however little time, what we buy' (Tomlinson, 1994: 35).

Identity provides the means by which individuals create and survive social change. Tomlinson (1994) sees the debate on consumerism as essentially about stages of cultural transformation – fundamental shifts in values – about confusions over class, regional, generational, and gender identities. Style, for example, is a visible manifestation of power relations and a process of creating commodity images (cf. 'imagination') for people to emulate and believe in. Fromm (1966) argued that one way we reject our sense of impotence and try to restore our capacity to act on the world is to submit to and identify with a person or group having power. By this symbolic participation with another person's life, we have the illusion of acting, when in reality we only submit to and become part of those who act.

ZONES OF MEANING

Realms of understanding are dynamic 'envelopes' of values, attitudes, interpretations, and knowledge that we apply in dealing with the situations in which we find ourselves. They are the product of our appreciative system (see chapter three), operating in advance of our decisions on how to act. Traditional 'communication theory' argues that communication is effective to the degree that these realms of understanding are coincident (overlap).

Communities of action have their own way of looking at things that supports social order within the group, but may cause conflict in interactions with other groups.

People apply interpretative schema or frames to their situations to make sense of (i.e. generate meanings for) the actions, relationships, and expectations that surround them. These meaning are socially constructed realities that are negotiated in interaction within relationships. People enact with others in a social environment using a dominant theme. This theme helps them to explain what goes on around them and how they should respond. People interacting constitute the 'structure' of the market. Within the market system, subcultures operate. These are the segments that are sought in product positioning (see Box 2.3).

BOX 2.3 REFLEXIVE COMMUNICATION

Recognition that each person's worldview is culturally conditioned and individually developed. Reflexive communication is a practical and pragmatic approach to mitigate the problems of stereotyping. It considers effective communication to be more than information transmission, it is mutual understanding. The approach addresses the problem of communicating from different cultural paradigms. Reflexive communication is non-hierarchical, collaborative, and inclusive.

(See Kikoski and Kikoski, 1996)

As we have seen earlier, enactment is the process of people putting things out into their environment that they can perceive and negotiate with others about perceiving. This transpires through communication processes – the act, interact (react), and double-interact (react to the interact).

In the daily discourse of people pursuing 'life projects' there is operating a mutually agreed language within established 'zones of meaning' (Heath, 1994). These zones can only be based on social learning, determined by what the group need to learn in order to maintain relationships. Therefore, relationships should be envisioned as collaborative projects encouraging constant re-evaluation, refinement and modification of 'zones'. Without a successful 'web of social learning', corporations are failed human institutions. Corporate communication provides a synthesized approach to elaborating, maintaining, and progressing zones of shared meaning.

Inconsistency or misalignment of values leads to cognitive dissonance. Heath (1994) has discussed zones of meaning as differing social realities. Some degree of shared meaning is necessary to define work-related situations, interpret and attribute meaning for the behaviour of others, and establish the basis for control, motivation, and the performance of roles. Meaning helps us to understand information and to define relationships and the communication that is appropriate within them. The job of the corporate communication manager is to act as a boundary-spanner who represents constituents in bringing differing zones of meaning into sufficient alignment for cooperative working to achieve corporate and personal goals.

COMMUNICATION NETWORKS

Communicators (persons, groups, corporations, market sectors) become interconnected in patterns of communication to a greater or lesser degree of integration or connectedness. Communication systems are collectivities of interacting (inter-acting) communicators who modify their apprehension, interpretations, judgements (values), and actions in taking account of each other and fellow members of the 'net', 'web', or network.

- **prescribed network**   formalized patterns of communication brought about through intended structures
- **emergent networks**   informal and dynamic patterns of communication that emerge in response to the social and task needs of the participants

This approach to understanding what happens when people act with others as their context or environment is entirely compatible with the notion of relational exchanges that is the basis of contemporary thinking in the field of marketing. The patterns of communication within social networks at least partially reflect the diversity of interests in a social group.

COMMUNICATION AND CULTURE

All products are cultural artefacts, so selling and buying them is mostly a matter of communication. Products may be understood as utilities, symbols of social status, representations of personal characteristics of the owner, and/or reflections of the person's choices of lifestyle. Products have social uses – they have social meaning and value within a particular cultural milieu. Our social values, fashions, and lifestyles are nowadays articulated through our choice of products. At the same time, commercial media are vital agencies of socialization. What greater justification can there be for marketers and their managers and critics to understand that marketing is a cultural enterprise and communication must be understood for the purpose of connecting intercultural life experiences in mutually beneficial exchanges of value?

CASE STUDY 2   WHAT WE WEAR IS WHO WE ARE

In October 1978 Renzo Rosso, a 20-year-old son of a farmer, started Diesel SpA in Molvena, Italy, with other manufacturers (the Genius Group) to produce casual garments for other companies. The name came from the oil crisis of the time. Soon their expertise allowed them independently to produce their own designs and to develop the distinctive sales and product polices that would become the Diesel brand. In 1985 Rosso decided to separate Diesel from the group and to produce clothes that he liked to wear and that represented his lifestyle.

Sales in 1985 totalled 7 billion lira. By 1998 that had been increased to 530 billion lira. The company now sells its products in 81 countries, mainly through department stores and its own retail shops, including several megastores in the USA. According to the company website,

> Beginning as a company focused on making quality clothing, Diesel has become part of youth culture worldwide. It can legitimately claim to be the first brand to believe truly in the global village and to embrace it with open arms.

In 1991 an innovative (and risky) communication strategy was introduced – a single creative execution run in every market to address the 'global village' with one message – this turned Diesel into a world-famous brand name. The brand name Diesel is a proper name, needing no translation and is internationally understood. 'Industrial' is juxtaposed with paradoxical 'anti-fashion' fashion. Today Diesel loudly proclaim 'Diesel – For Successful Living'. This is interpreted ironically in advertisements. In 1998 the corporation was awarded Advertiser of the Year at the 45th Cannes International Advertising Festival for the 'outstanding quality of the company's communications strategy'.

The Diesel brand is focused on a hip, alternative image for wearers of avant-garde jeans and unusual but modish casual and workwear. Advertising uses remarkable imagery as an implied selling proposition. A love of kitsch and global pop culture references are the hallmarks of Diesel advertisements. The Internet has become an integral part of the communication strategy (check out the UK Virtual Store). The company even built The Pelican Hotel on Miami South Beach to embody the wit and style of the company. The differently themed rooms attract European tourists, designers, artists, and youngsters – all of whom 'get it' on different levels.

Diesel competes with Calvin Klein, Armani, and Tommy Hilfiger. According to Rosso,

> We don't sell a product, we sell a style of life. I think we have created a movement . . . the Diesel concept is everything. It's the way we live, it's the way to wear, it's the way to do something.

> (Quoted in *Paper* magazine)

The extensive Diesel denim product range (in common with other fashion designers, called a collection) caters for children to grandparents, although the core market is women aged 15–30. Hugely successful in the USA, the clothes are designed and made in Italy – this is unique in a market dominated by Levi and others who manufacture in Asia and Mexico. Key to the Diesel market position are: quality, fit, fabric, and image – hip, cool, edgy. Careful market segmentation in each country has revealed similar lifestyles and ideas about fashion wear. Analysis of trends in habits and preferences in the most active markets has enabled careful tailoring to local product demand differences.

Advertising appeals to the intellect and teases the senses. Recently, advertisements for jeans have celebrated the bizarre in poking fun at convention and what are taken to be normal situations. For example, in one ad humans are shown serving a roasted girl to pigs sat at a table covered with exotic foods. The autumn/winter 1999 collection was launched under the banner of 'The Luxury of Dirt'. Diesel advertising doesn't preach and avoids the earnest messages of Benetton. Diesel messages are more direct and heavily ironic. Diesel wearers react to the naughtiness with 'whatever!'

Founder, president, and designer Renzo Rosso explained, 'we give them [consumers] a free interpretation of what they want. We are not pushing like everybody did, especially in the eighties.' People want to wear the style and accomplish the associated attitude. Victorian outrage and decadent, Oscar Wilde said it all: 'In matters of great importance it is style not sincerity that counts.'

Professor Philip Kotler in 1996 wrote a case study bearing the title 'We're all different. But aren't we all different in the same way?'. This is surely the positioning slogan of the Diesel brand.

(See www.diesel.com and http://ukstore.diesel.com)

WHAT DO YOU THINK?

1 What is lost in abandoning the traditional linear model or conduit metaphor for human communication?

2 Why has a mass communication basis for marketing communication passed out of currency?

3 Today, technologies for communicating are high on the management agenda. The content of communication media is referred to as 'communications'. Explain how this conception and terminology can be unhelpful.

4 In what circumstances would a transmission model be helpful in supporting marketing management?

5 Review your working situation. Tabulate some examples of activities and actions than can be explained by the transmission model and others that require a cultural model of communication. What implications does your analysis have for management?

6 Diesel advertising is standardized and used in all its country markets. Comment on this policy.

7 Attempt to explain the notion that all marketing communication is intercultural.

8 How do you communicate with product providers? Do they understand your communication needs?

9 Write a short essay on 'marketing communication as a conversation'.

10 The Diesel advertisers have claimed to have abandoned the expectation that they can persuade people to buy their products. Why then spend so much money on advertising?

FURTHER READING

Fill, C. (1999) *Marketing Communications: Contexts, Contents, and Strategies*, 2nd edn, London: Prentice-Hall.

Fromm, E. (1966) *The Heart of Man*, London: Routledge & Kegan Paul.

Heath, R. L. (1994) *Management of Corporate Communication: From Interpersonal Contacts to External Affairs*, Hillsdale, NJ: Lawrence Erlbaum Associates Inc.

Heyman, R. (1994) *Why Didn't You Say That in the First Place?: How to Be Understood at Work*, San Francisco, CA: Jossey-Bass.

Kotler, P. (1996) *Principles of Marketing*, 2nd European edn, London: Prentice-Hall, case study no. 19.

Littlejohn, S. W. (1999) *Theories of Human Communication*, 6th edn, London: International Thompson Business Press.

McLuhan, H. M. (1964) *Understanding Media: The Extensions of Man*, New York: Signet Books.

Toffler, M. (1970) *Future Shock*, London: Bodley Head.

chapter three

CONSUMER BEHAVIOUR AND COMMUNICATION

LEARNING POINTS

Careful study of this chapter will help you to:

- apply some theory to examine consumer behaviour in order to appreciate the problem of engaging people in value exchanges within the context of market relationships

- consider the nature and role of products in fulfilling social needs

- view market segments as consumption communities

Shop 'til you drop, spend 'til you end, buy 'til you die.
(Marketer's war cry – or consumer's anthem?)

Life is a chain of unrequited need: men want women, women want children, and children want hamsters.
(Alice Thomas Ellis)

No man makes greater haste to the market than he who seeks that which is to be bought.
(Anon)

INTRODUCTION

Consumer behaviour is what people do as consumers as they seek to live their lives, including exchanging some things for value products or services that satisfy their needs – this includes processes of browsing (e.g. 'window-shopping', reading magazines, watching television, etc.) and selection, purchase, use, evaluation and influencing others, and disposal. There are two sides to the consumer behaviour coin:

- Consumers decide how to spend their time and money to buy and consume products and services that satisfy their own recognized needs (response to hunger, love, vanity, fear, identity, recognition, insecurity, stimulation, etc.).
- 'Marketers'[1] offer products and services so that consumers will buy from them, thus satisfying consumer needs for money, which, in turn, satisfies their own needs.

The field of consumer behaviour study has developed, originally as part of marketing study and more recently as a distinct discipline, since the 1960s, with contributions from psychology, economics, sociology, organizational behaviour, and anthropology. The economists have explained consumer behaviour as engagement in securing scarce resources in a free market. Thus, according to this view, marketing is an allocation process.

Consumer behaviour has both logical/cognitive and emotional/affective aspects. Psychology helps to explain the processes you enact as an individual in interacting with your world. Thoughts, feelings, and attitudes are emphasized. Sociology emphasizes the effects of social arrangements on consumer behaviour. The act of consumption is rarely a solitary one. Anthropology, on the other hand, focuses on the effects of culture and values on direct and symbolic choices (product selection is discussed at length later in this chapter). We can apply an understanding of corporate structures and culture in understanding the role of corporate actors in exchanges with consumers.

As managers, we are concerned with where and when we can cause representations of ourselves and our products to enter the minds of relevant buyers and consumers. Consumption is communicative and requires human interaction for it to make sense – consumption is derived through communication.

There has been a tendency for writers of marketing textbooks to rely on the burgeoning field of consumer behaviour, while ignoring another important perspective on the behaviour of people in society – cultural studies. An attempt is made here to correct this weakness by locating this discussion of marketing communication within the field of popular culture. This does not take for granted that marketing, advertising, public relations, and news

---

1 Actually, both the consumer and producer are 'marketers' in the sense of coming into a notional 'marketplace' to effect an exchange (interaction for interchange).

reporting are necessarily an industry of culture creation. Culture arises through the needs of people. Commodities can be used as cultural resources for reworking to generate an own culture.

PEOPLE AS CONSUMERS

The acquisition and consumption of products (goods and services) can be thought of as problem-solving behaviour. In this chapter we examine explanations of people's actions to solve problems (unmet needs) and their search for what is needed to solve their problem, and where it is available.

Gabriel and Lang (1995) define a number of possible roles in which people may be selectors, acquirers, and/or consumers (Table 3.1).

Table 3.1 describes largely alternative faces for consumers, that are neither fully compatible nor incompatible. They do, however, provide food for thought in considering the motivations of consumers and the ability of marketers to influence their decisions and attitudes.

We all are consumers, and as such we participate in activities that are motivated by a desire to fulfil a recognized need. We search for a product to meet our need, select one that we believe will meet the need, then use it and dispose of it, or terminate a service, once it has met our need. It can be argued that consumption is, itself, a form of production – the production of meaning.

The central concept of marketing and consumer behaviour is **exchange**. Because we cannot produce all of the things that we want to fulfil our need, we must look to 'the market' for other people who produce what we want. To get what we want, we exchange money with producers to satisfy their needs. Gratification is a basic human pursuit. Money is a generalized exchange medium, since it allows us to make satisfying exchanges without having to provide a specific object.

Exchange is explored more fully in chapter four, when we examine the concept from a communication perspective.

THEORIES OF PURCHASE BEHAVIOUR

Why are we taking the trouble to examine some aspects of consumer behaviour in a textbook on marketing communication? Essentially, we need to consider how people react to marketing communication actions. Although, at this point, we are mostly looking at marketing relationships from the perspective of the provider, we should not forget that both marketers – the provider and the buyer/consumer – may initiate communication situations. At certain points in this book we will reflect on how the provider may react to marketing communication actions.

A critical survey of the consumer behaviour literature will show that a number of theories have become established as the usual frameworks for explaining consumer behaviour. However, as is the case with communication theory in marketing, there are weaknesses and alternatives perspectives that can be of value. Three approaches to consumer action are considered here, and summarized in Table 3.2.

Table 3.1 **Images of consumers**

Consumer concept	Characterization
Explorer	Thirsting after new experiences and meanings to discover, in search of goods, marketplaces, and signs. Insatiable curiosity is manifest in shopping
Chooser	Focuses on the consumer as a decision-maker, with choice as the central feature of consumerism. Choice is good and consumers want more choice – the decision is not whether to consume, but what to consume
Identity-seeker	Consumers try to find a real self in the objects he/she consumes – a life project in exercising freedom in search of satisfactions. Brands are seen as the emblems of the self
Hedonist or artist	Concerned above all with personal pleasure. Consumption liberates the person who has a right and obligation to seek pleasure – to enjoy life
Victim	The consumer hopes for a better future from consumption of commodities – and this can never come to fruition – there is endless dissatisfaction, promoted by the want-creating machinery of mass marketing. Further, the consumer is powerless in the face of the might and sophistication of vast corporations whose resources and techniques they cannot match. Consumers are passive objects of manipulation – seducible and manageable
Rebel	Commodities are used as symbols of rebellion – functioning as icons of disaffection and defiance. Consumers rebel against producers, advertisers, and merchandisers by discovering uses (meanings) distinctly different from those intended – commodities are redefined, reclaimed, and re-appropriated. The ultimate consumer rebel simply consumes less and is unmanageable! Or is rebellion another form of consumption?
Activist	Consumers as morally driven people seeking collectively to improve their positions relative to markets and marketers
Citizen	The consumer acts beyond his or her own interests as a consumer, and takes responsibility for the future
Communicator	Using objects as bridges to relate to fellow humans, the consumer is a communicator of meanings with others and with the self. Consumption defines social status, establishing differences and similarities. Thus material objects are not simply connected with physical and social needs, but are carriers of meaning

Source: Summarized from Gabriel and Lang, 1995

Table 3.2 **Theories of consumer behaviour**

Approach	How is purchase treated?	Weakness	Implication for marketing communication management
Cognitive	Decision-making in problem-solving	Consumers seem to be not very systematic and rational in decision-making	Provide information and persuade
Reinforcement	Consumption is seen as learned behaviour in response to aspects of the consumer's situation	Complex behaviour cannot be traced to multitudinous past experiences	Change the consumer's situation
Habit	A pre-established pattern of behaviour is elicited routinely in particular contexts	?	Use specific stimuli associated with desired behaviour

Textbooks from US authors tend to favour and emphasize the cognitive approach (see Engel *et al.*, 1995, as a classic example), while British authors mostly favour the reinforcement approach. A smaller number of critical authors have challenged both of these approaches as being unsupported by empirical data, and have forwarded the habit approach as being a more realistic explanation of actual consumer behaviour (see the work of Andrew Ehrenberg, for example).

The cognitive approach

In the decision-making paradigm, consumer behaviour is seen as a problem-solving and decision-making sequence, in which the cognitive consumer processes information, conducts comparative evaluation, and makes a rational selection. Much management strategy and marketing thinking is underpinned by this belief. But reflect for a moment how in many purchase situations no decision is made. Much consumer behaviour is not buying behaviour – window-shopping is a pleasant pastime for some people!

Behaviour may be based on past experience and cues that come from the consumer's situation. Decision-making may be pre-empted. Consumer theorists seem to agree that some behaviour results from the situation and other behaviour is deliberate and preceded by planning. The cognitive and reinforcement theories may be complementary rather than competing views. But insufficient attention has been given to habitual behaviour (East, 1997). Scholars such as Engel *et al.* (1995) have tried to provide an all-encompassing model of consumer behaviour with a decision process continuum, which includes habitual decision-making. But, points out East, this is contradictory. If behaviour is habitual, then there is no conscious cognitive processing before action (i.e. there is no 'decision' as such). Engel *et al.* have offered their rational model as a normative tool that indicates to managers what they need to find out about consumers. However, it is not universally accepted as a true representation of how consumers behave.

Habits seem, from observation, to account for much of consumption behaviour, but habit is much more than simply the absence of thought. Simon (1957) explained the typical decision-making based on limited information as the adoption of a 'good enough' solution to a problem – what he called 'satisficing behaviour'. Typically, we assess a situation and identify a possible option or action. Then we evaluate the option to decide if it will give a satisfactory outcome. Only if it fails will we seek a further option. Mostly, we do not compare old and new options, or generate a set of options and make comparisons among them. If consumers rarely extend much thought to purchase and consumption decisions, and satisfice to keep their consumption efficient, then the extended-problem-solving model of Engel *et al.*, favoured by almost all other textbooks, is of little real value in trying to influence consumer behaviour.

The reinforcement approach

Purchase may be thought of as learned behaviour. A satisfactory purchase outcome may increase the likelihood of a further selection in the future, whereas an unsatisfactory outcome may be avoided next time.

Learning theory systematically describes and explains the connection between experience and subsequent behaviour.

Classical conditioning (Watson and Raynor, 1920) can be used to explain how colours, aromas, music, brand names, and the context of purchase and consumption become associated with the buying of particular products. Some advertising is intended to create such associations between brands and stimuli. The conditioned stimulus is supposed to support identification and increase purchasing tendency.

Another explanation is found in **reinforcement learning** (Skinner, 1938). Reinforcers are rewards or cost reductions – experiences that raise the frequency of responses associated. East (1997) gives the example of Air Miles sales promotion awards for the use of particular products, used to reinforce purchase or use. Skinner introduced the idea of behaviour shaping, whereby behaviour is altered from one form to a desired other form by selectively reinforcing the behaviours that show movement in the preferred direction. The evolution of product forms and features in recent years may indicate shaping. Heavily used reinforcers may lose their power to elicit a response when the consumer becomes satiated. Advertisement wear-out may be explained by this. Stimulus satiation can also produce desensitization, when people get used to unsatisfactory or unpleasant conditions without desire for change. Learning can be reinforced each time a response is reproduced (continuously) or may be intermittent. Learning is faster in continuous reinforcement. However, greater reinforcement is obtained from intermittent reinforcement.

Foxall (1992) argues that learning theory should be applied more systematically to define and control consumption environments for profit enhancement. He distinguishes pleasure and information reinforcers. For example, flights offer free drinks as an extra to the basic service, as well as in-flight information on TV screens. Foxall wants us to consider more carefully the aspects of a consumer's situation that affect behaviour. Managers can then more carefully alter cues and reinforcers.

Habitual approach

We can see that learning theory is relevant here too. The cognitive and reinforcement approaches emphasize the modification of consumer behaviour and thus help to explain the changes that occur in purchasing. But there is much stability in markets too. Brands and stores are patronized over long periods. There is clearly a major habitual aspect to consumption.

When similar situations (context) prompt the same behaviour, we can say that people display habits. These habits simplify our responses to our surroundings by removing the need to make decisions. This absence of problem-solving or planning before action does not imply irrationality or a lack of reflection. Often, people think about their actions after the event. Repeated brand purchase, for example, would not arise if an experience were unsatisfactory.

HOW CAN WE EXPLAIN BUYER BEHAVIOUR?

There have been many attempts to explain and predict the behaviour of people in the roles of buyer and consumer. The field of consumer behaviour has grown extensively over the past 30 years. Classic generic models of a supposed purchase decision process are to be found in all marketing textbooks. Are they really very helpful? Perhaps only immersion in the actual world of the consumer/buyer can yield a proper understanding and reveal what motivates particular purchases. Ritson (2000), for example, has suggested that asking customers to tell their 'story' – how they started by knowing nothing about a brand and later came to buy it – might give a better understanding from the buyer/consumer's point of view. In each market segment, the purchase process may differ in detail.

Simple models of consumer response to marketing activity assumed that attracting a consumer's attention would automatically lead to desire for the product and the action of purchase. For example, the AIDA (proposed around 1900 by E. St Elmo Lewis – see Strong, 1925) model describes a process of consumer thinking (or communication effect) shifting logically from grabbing attention, to creating interest, that leads to desire, that drives action (i.e. purchase and consumption). Later, it was realized that, more realistically, attention and interest are more likely to arise from recognition of a need. Today, few still cling to the idea that consumers are passive recipients of promotional messages. Even when messages are transmitted, there is interaction between the apprehender and the message – it is interpreted in a particular context, attitudes and beliefs. The conduit metaphor for communication does not explain this adequately, and yet it is still used as an explanation! The traditional notion of a seller always taking the marketing initiative in making an offer (promise) to which a buyer responds is being challenged. Today buyers are more realistically seen as often active searchers for suppliers and their products to fulfil their needs. This phenomenon is termed 'reverse marketing', 'proactive procurement', and 'buyer initiative'.

A rather more sophisticated (and complex) model that relates an information-processing sequence to a purchase decision-making process, and which has gained considerable respect, is the Howard–Sheth model of consumer behaviour. This shows inputs processed by and into perceptions, interpretations, judgements, learning, and so on. Figure 3.1 shows informing connections (solid lines) and feedback effects (broken lines).

We will examine some key elements of the Howard–Sheth model. Significance factors can be addressed in pictures and words during the information search phase when you are actively attending to marketing communication materials and activities. Symbolic factors are concerned with identity and image relative to other people and our self-esteem, and arise mostly before the active information search, often outside our awareness. Social factors are power, wealth, prestige, and so on, relating consumption and purchase and use of products to culture. According to the theory of symbolic interactionism, our behaviour towards an object or event depends on the symbolic meaning ascribed by referent others in society. As consumers, we behave towards goods and services, according to this theory, according

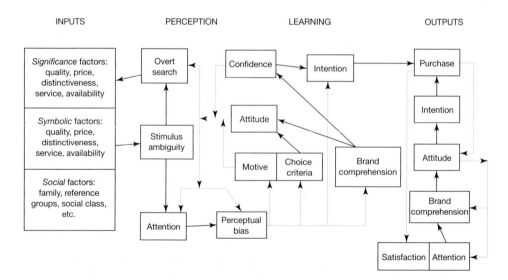

Figure 3.1 **A simplified version of the Howard–Sheth model of consumer behaviour**

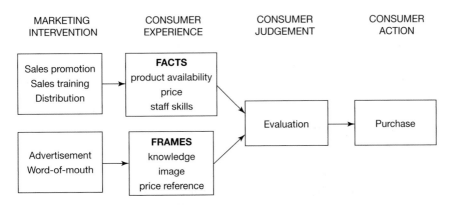

Figure 3.2 **Some effects of marketing interventions on consumers**
Source: East, 1997: 23

to the symbols attached to them by other social entities (reference groups, persons, societies, etc.).

The two components of a judgement are **facts** and **frames** (see Figure 3.2). Basic facts often come from the environment, whereas frames are personal cognitive maps. People differ in their judgements because their frames differ. Some influences can affect our knowledge but not the frames we use to judge facts, while other influences have more effect on our frame of reference. As we shall see in chapter fourteen, advertising may be designed to make relatively durable modifications to the frames used to evaluate products.

Several underlying factors can be identified to explain the actions of consumers. Wells and Prensky (1996) suggest a set of consumer background characteristics and a set of behavioural processes. These are each introduced here and then each is explored in greater detail.

Consumer background characteristics

These are the stable aspects of a person's life, describing individual attributes and the place of the person in their social structure and environment. Some are never changed (race or gender?), some require major reorientation if they are to be changed (lifestyle, reference group, geographical location of residence), while others evolve gradually as the person matures (age, life cycle stage):

- culture and values
- personality, lifestyle, and psychographics
- demographics
- reference groups

Much of the information we take into our decision process is not controlled directly by marketers, despite their best efforts to influence us. Our friends and family give us highly credible views about products, suppliers, places, and people. Often such role models are featured in advertisements to demonstrate desirability of purchase and use. Often there is an implication that if we adopt a specific product, we will be able to join a better group (aspiration). Another form of role model is the authority figure who may be employed to endorse the product (men in white coats were seen as scientists and expert in the early selling of soap powders). Thus role models show us how to behave.

Behavioural processes

These are situationally specific 'tools' used by people in recognizing their feelings, gathering and utilizing information, and formulating thoughts and opinions in order to interact with the world. Marketers are particularly interested in these because they appear to offer opportunities to exert influence over buying and consumption behaviour.

Motivation

Motivation can be thought of as the recognition of a need that is followed by action-taking to satisfy it.

A need is a drive to realize an ideal state (goal) by shifting from a non-ideal state. The term **innate need** refers to biological conditions for staying alive, while the term **acquired need** refers to social and psychological needs. A person does not recognize a need for which there is no attainable goal, while a goal does not motivate action unless a need to achieve it is seen. A product can satisfy a need (i.e. it has value) when it offers a benefit or outcome from its use. A core benefit is basic to a particular product or class of products and is expected by every buyer. These are not motivators, but their absence demotivates. Motivators are specific to a person (see Figure 3.3) and are attended to by marketers in segmenting and targeting groups of buyers and consumers (see chapter fourteen).

The driving force in recognizing needs and electing goals to satisfy them is motivation. We prioritize the effort we make towards satisfying out needs, generally giving more time and effort to those needs that have higher costs and benefits and that are more important, interesting, and relevant to us.

Our level of involvement reflects the benefits and costs we expect to receive from buying a product to satisfy a need in a situation. Factors that affect our level of involvement are those background characteristics that we saw in Figure 3.3, as well as characteristics of the product (such as attributes and benefits, costs, and perceived risks of purchase, ownership, and use), and situational effects (such as purchase and use occasion, and competing needs).

We judge things in terms of importance and relevance to us in a given situation or context. Involvement is a judgement relating to a feeling of risk of negative outcome, social sanction, and ego. For example, will buying that jacket be a mistake (poor value for money, say), will it make me look out of

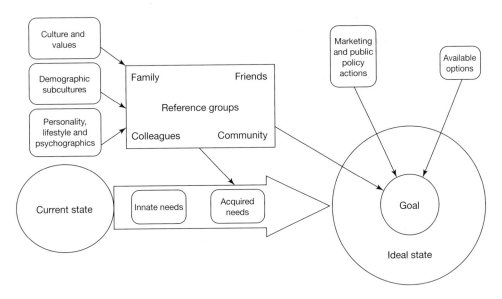

Figure 3.3 **Need, motivation, and goal**
Source: Adapted from Wells and Prensky, 1996: 227

place in my social group, and does it seem right for my own sense of my image (self-image)? Involvement is an important concept for marketing communication because it relates to the likelihood that a person will pay attention to a communication activity.

Involvement explains the different levels of cognitive activity created by advertising and purchase situations. East (1997) argues that low involvement is habitual whereas high involvement requires planning, since purchase risk raises potential costs.

Purchase and possessions have an indicative function (Veblen, 1963). Veblen coined the term 'conspicuous consumption' to describe expenditure that shows others what kind of person the consumer is. People manage the impression that others have of them through their choice of action, words, and dress (Goffman, 1959). In a sense, we are what others think we are. The consumption of valuable goods, including entertainment, is a sign of social prestige and status. This 'means of reputability' is a lifestyle, a behaviour to be imitated (Veblen, 1963). More recently (Mason, 1998), the support of consuming for personal identity and style in pursuit of status has become the defining purpose of manufacturers, retailers, and advertising agencies.

Consider the differing sense of involvement from two potential purchase scenarios:

1 **a house**: high cost, long-term commitment, contract, many uncertain factors, infrequent decision needed
2 **a chocolate bar**: low cost, little risk of loss, frequent purchase

Perception

Perception is the process by which a person generates data from the environment, through the sense organs of the body, for incorporation into cognitive processes of meaning and knowledge construction through generation and synthesis. There is so much going on around us that we select for attention from present experience only that which is most immediate or interesting, rejecting that which is evaluated as not relevant or in conflict with our adopted ideas (see the discussion on mindfulness later in this chapter). Thus, we never have a full 'mental map' of the total possible world, and our thinking is bound within our own 'sub-world' of live perception, previous experience, and analogies drawn from other situations. Our mental map is influenced by a number of factors (Table 3.3).

Table 3.3 **Influences on our personal mental map**

Influencing factor	Reaction on mental map
Expectations	New data are interpreted in a particular way
Previous experience	Sights, sounds and smells trigger 'automatic' particular responses
Selectivity	Some data are ignored or subverted
Subjectivity	A personal world-view is unique
Categorization	Data are related to knowledge and may be prejudged

Learning

How do we turn our apprehension of what is going on around us into a basis for judgement and action? We learn from what we observe as outcomes from our past behaviour and may use this learning to modify our subsequent actions. Several models of the cognitive process by which we translate data about our environment into knowledge have been proposed. One such model that is helpful to us is McGuire's (1978) information-processing sequence (Figure 3.4).

If a purchase is accompanied by undesirable outcomes, it may be rejected in future action. On the other hand, satisfaction with product may increase the likelihood that it will be selected the next time a similar need is felt. Learning theory tries systematically to relate experience and subsequent action.

Messages in marketing communication are bundles of data constructed by the producer as communicator that can be selectively attended to by other people as corresponding communicators. These data can provide the basis for the information sought in the purchase decision-making process.

Apprehend	Exposure/Presentation	Cognitive (thought)
Attend	Attention	
Interpret	Comprehension	
Judge/Value	Yielding/Acceptance	Affective (emotion)
	Retention	
Act	Behaviour/Action	Conative (desire)

Figure 3.4 **The cognitive process of a person as problem-solver**

Knowledge

What we know of a product, a purchase situation, product usage, and so on, is a framework within which further purchase decisions are made. Attitudes are formed to help organize and simplify knowledge of what goes on around us into simple evaluations that can be used to facilitate the decision-making process.

Figure 3.5 shows a set of elements of a man's knowledge that he considers when thinking about a possible car purchase. Each element invokes characteristics that prompt choice. Try following through the sequence of choices represented in the diagram. The Mazda sports car is selected because it has all of the desired characteristics.

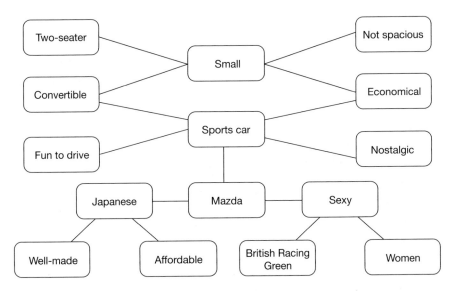

Figure 3.5 **A consumer's knowledge structure for a car**
Source: Shimp, 1997: 126

Attitude

Attitude is what we feel about a concept (brand, category, person, ideology, and so on); i.e. an attitude is an evaluation. Important for marketers are attitudes about forms of action, such as buying, using, eating, etc. Thus an attitude is a learned tendency to respond to something in a consistently positive or negative manner. Attitudes can be inferred from behaviour, or measurement can be attempted using a scale (for example: 'How would you rate playing the Lottery on a scale from a waste of money (−3) to a good investment (+3)?').

When we are motivated to seek a satisfier for a need by processing information, we form attitudes when exposed to data about a concept (product or supplier, for example). As we interrogate the environment in the search for a satisfier, we form salient beliefs about products, upon which we can make a judgement about appropriate action (reject, buy, recommend, etc.).

Attitude change can be accomplished when the balance or consistency of cognition, affect, and conation is altered by adding a new salient belief, changing the strength of influence of a salient belief, or changing the evaluation of a held belief. Beyond a certain threshold of inconsistency, a mental readjustment is brought about to restore stability in the belief. Three mechanisms have been identified:

1 new information is rejected so as to maintain the status quo of the cognitive element of the attitude
2 the information is accepted as true but countered with the view that the person's own situation is exceptional
3 the attitude is changed to accommodate the new information

Rosenberg (1960) showed that a change in one element of an attitude usually causes a change in the others. New data causing a change in cognition will change feelings about a product, usually leading to an alteration in intention towards the product. For example, a mailed leaflet informs me that a software product has been upgraded and reduced in price. This seems to be better value for money and will perform some functions that are useful to me. I decide that the product is appropriate and decide to write an order.

Cognitive change and affective change are modelled in the Elaboration Likelihood Model (ELM) at various levels of involvement. The extent to which you need to develop and refine information in order to make a decision is termed 'elaboration'. Elaboration is high when your ability to process information is high and you are highly motivated to do so. The model is shown in Figure 3.6.

The central route to attitude change involves appeals to rational, cognitive thinking by active, involved decision-makers. When considering a car purchase, for example, they would be willing to read informative brochures and to act upon their judgement of the arguments used to position the product as suitable for them. When the ability to process information and likelihood

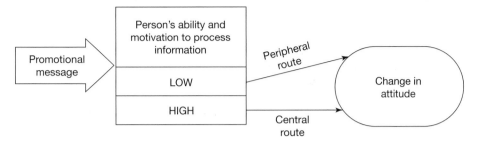

Figure 3.6 **The Elaboration Likelihood Model**

Source: Based on Petty and Cacioppo, 1983

of engaging in cognitive processing are seen as low, the peripheral route is taken, offering cues that are essentially incidental to the content of the promotional message. In celebrity endorsement of a product, feelings towards the star become attached to the product – there is little reasoned evaluation.

The halo effect arises when the attitudes of a salient belief influence attitudes about another. One is said to 'rub off' on another. From the marketer's point of view, the halo effect can be highly advantageous – when, for example, the advertising of one brand helps to sell another. On the other hand, this can be damaging when a dislike for a competitor's product leads to rejection of one's own. When a halo effect is positive, spending on product advertising can be very efficient.

When a person's beliefs do not fit together, they become aroused, leading to a change of thought, feeling, or action so as to improve the 'fit'. This condition of cognitive dissonance (Festinger, 1964) is felt when we commit ourselves to a course of action that is inconsistent with our other behaviour or beliefs, or which later turns out to have undesirable consequences that we might have foreseen. Thus, after a purchase decision is made, we might feel tense about our decision, perhaps because the product fails to meet our expectations or because we become aware of a superior alternative. Ever felt like you had missed out on the best deal after buying a PC and then seeing an advertisement for an even better equipped model at a lower price? When such discomfort occurs, we may change one or other of the views held or introduce a third view that accounts for the discrepancy. Of course, the cheaper, better-equipped PC can't possibly be as reliable as the one we are now lumbered with!

Dissonance has important implications for managing marketing communication systems. The arousal of dissonance is associated with involvement, and generally leads to some further action beyond purchase. The buyer may complain to the provider, or to friends, relatives, and colleagues, or to a trade or consumer protection body.

Communication strategy should take account of the level of cognitive processing that consumers and buyers are expected to engage in and the route taken to effect attitude change. When motivation and involvement are low, for example, the peripheral route should be dominant with a focus on emotions.

THE PURCHASE DECISION-MAKING PROCESS

An understanding of how we make decisions and what influences our decision-making is important to managing communicative actions by both buyers and suppliers. This should be the basis for planning marketing communication systems and activities.

A general decision-making process model is shown in Figure 3.7. Of course, we may not actually proceed through the steps in strict sequence in every case.

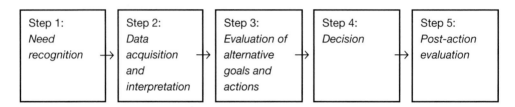

| Step 1: Need recognition | Step 2: Data acquisition and interpretation | Step 3: Evaluation of alternative goals and actions | Step 4: Decision | Step 5: Post-action evaluation |

Figure 3.7 **Steps to ordered decision-making**

An example of this (simplified) cognitive, affective, and conative process in given in Figure 3.8.

Need recognition

We each have different needs at different times and recognize them in different ways. To a hungry walker, a country orchard is a place for nourishing food, while the artist sees an opportunity for a magnificent landscape painting. The next person may see the possibility of a job during the harvesting season. Needs may be simple and physical (for example, hunger), or complex and socially produced (recognized success, for example). As consumers, we may readily recognize our needs, while other people may act to spur us to recognize other needs. Healthy people know when they are hungry, but it may take an advertisement or comments from friends to provoke a desire to try a new restaurant.

Consider joining the fitness gym (Figure 3.8). What need may motivate this? Do you want to look good in your shorts? When you played tennis at the weekend, did you tire easily? Has you doctor advised you to lose weight for health reasons? Are some of your friends regular users, so you can meet up there? Are you preparing for a fundraising run? Does vigorous exercise help you to relax after a day at work? We seek to fulfil different needs.

Search

What are the general ways available to you to meet your recognized need? Consumer habit renders an answer from memory of what has satisfied us in the past. We might ask friends or relatives how they have satisfied their similar need. We might scan through a magazine or check entries in *Yellow Pages*. Some advertisements are designed to alert us to a new alternative.

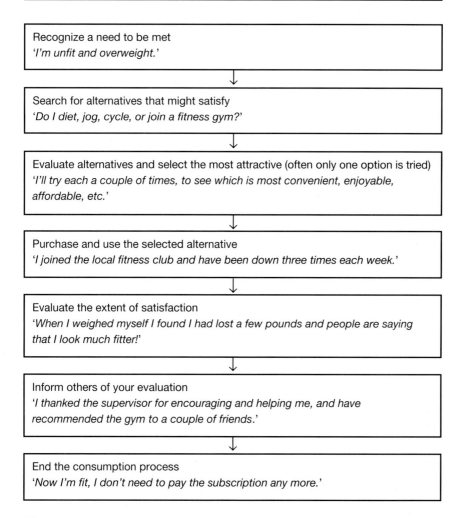

Recognize a need to be met
'I'm unfit and overweight.'

Search for alternatives that might satisfy
'Do I diet, jog, cycle, or join a fitness gym?'

Evaluate alternatives and select the most attractive (often only one option is tried)
'I'll try each a couple of times, to see which is most convenient, enjoyable, affordable, etc.'

Purchase and use the selected alternative
'I joined the local fitness club and have been down three times each week.'

Evaluate the extent of satisfaction
'When I weighed myself I found I had lost a few pounds and people are saying that I look much fitter!'

Inform others of your evaluation
'I thanked the supervisor for encouraging and helping me, and have recommended the gym to a couple of friends.'

End the consumption process
'Now I'm fit, I don't need to pay the subscription any more.'

Figure 3.8 **Purchase and consumption activities**

Once a particular way of satisfying the need is identified, we can seek more specific options. Have we driven past a gym locally? Where do your friends go? Who is listed in the telephone directory under the heading 'Fitness & Health'?

Selection

Which of the various alternatives is best for me? Before we can evaluate alternatives, we need criteria or standards to guide our choice: price, brand name, capabilities, convenience, proximity. If several criteria are important, how do you prioritize them?

Purchase

Once an alternative is selected, the purchase can take place. This is at the heart of consumer behaviour, since it is the exchange that interests both the acquirer/consumer and the producer/supplier.

Who sells the product or service, and where can you get it from? What are the payment options?

Evaluation of the consumption experience

During or after consumption we can make a judgement about the extent to which the purchase experience and consumption experience are satisfactory. This evaluation is significant because it is remembered when it is necessary to search for alternatives to meet the same need again in the future. How do you judge your experiences? Were your expectations met? This is an important question, since advertisements can influence our expectations of the product or service prior to purchase.

Feedback

Complaints and compliments to suppliers are important. A partial refund may be requested because the gym was closed at the weekend for maintenance. You might ask the supervisor to close later, so as to get more value from your attendance.

We tell our friends about what we like and don't like, and we may try to discourage them from buying the latter. We might even write a letter to the editor of the local newspaper, if we feel strongly about something.

Termination

We may simply stop using a product and dispose of its packaging. Growing concern about our environment has made product disposal an important aspect of consumer behaviour for marketing managers.

BOX 3.1 COMMENT: RATIONAL CONSUMPTION

Consumer choice is assumed to be undertaken on rational grounds by many textbooks. Indeed, the entire marketing enterprise depends on and perpetuates this notion. Yet consumer behaviour is complex and not readily understood. See Gabriel and Lang (1995) and Barnes (1995) for implications of this for marketing management.

Intangible products require more formal steps to end the consumption process. Membership of the fitness gym may require that notice is given. Some consumers may continue to use products and services through inertia – they don't get around to stopping!

SOME FURTHER KEY CONCEPTS

We could write a whole book on consumer behaviour (actually it's been done before!). That is not the aim here. Rather, we need a comprehensive basis for critically considering essential aspects of the challenge in managing communication systems for marketing purposes. There is a considerable toolkit available for this purpose (see Table 3.4 for some guidelines on further reading and the bodies of knowledge that are examined in classes on consumer behaviour, marketing management, and corporate communication management).

Table 3.4 **Understanding consumer actions**

Action	Approach
Important vs. trivial choice	A *cognitive approach* to understanding decision-making is relevant
New vs. repeated actions	A *learning approach* is helpful to understanding habit and desensitization
Free vs. constrained	*Attribution theory* helps to explain why some of us do not try to change our behaviour
Individual vs. group-based	Social influence can be understood by examining behaviour with *exchange theory*

Source: East, 1997

Freedom of choice

The decision-making emphasis seems to exaggerate the degree of freedom that consumers have to choose. As East (1997) points out, to be free requires that we know that we can choose from more than one option without coercion, and that we can reject all options if they are unsatisfactory. But the cognitive approach sets the consumer up as resisting the commercial persuader by their own purposeful and goal-oriented actions. Consumers may have much autonomy, with only partial influence from providers, but they are not really fully in control. With little time to invest in consumption choices, we find ourselves putting petrol in our cars and selecting from almost identical brands in the supermarket. Alternative products may not be available, and we can become dependent (in a psychological sense) on cigarettes, alcohol, and pharmaceuticals.

Frustration arises when no options are available. Some minor frustrations lead to thoughtful problem-solving behaviour, while some modes of consumption are rational responses to frustrations. There is a lesson here for product designers – seek designs that avoid common frustrations. Service breakdown usually results in an aggressive response. Other related concepts are consumer satisfaction and dissatisfaction, and consumer complaining behaviour, discussed later in this chapter.

Attribution

When things don't go the way we want them to, we can blame ourselves (internal attribution) or the situation (external attribution). We tend to see our social situation as predictable and controllable and to make the same kinds of predictions about social phenomena as about physical phenomena. The conditions for events to occur may be situational or impersonal, or regarded as internal to yourself or others, such as ability or personality (Heider, 1958). There are two components in any judgement – the basic nature of the situation, and the frame we use to interpret that situation. People use different frames, and advertising is intended to change interpretative frames (see Figure 3.9).

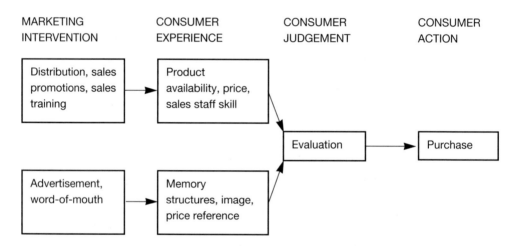

Figure 3.9 **The effects of marketing interventions on consumers**
Source: East, 1997: 23

Social influences

The theory of planned behaviour (Ajzen, 1988) sees the determinants of a person's intention to perform a voluntary action as:

- the perceived gains and losses
- the beliefs about what other important people think about the action
- the 'perceived' conditions that make the action more, or less, easy to perform

From the cognitive perspective, people act out roles as sets of mutually related expectations about how they should act in relation to others and vice versa.

For example, as a customer, we take into account what we think other customers and sales staff expect from us, and we expect them to behave in certain ways. Years ago, as a student, I witnessed a friend approach a salesperson in a well-known discount electrical retailer, with the greeting 'go on then, sell me something'. The situation was unusual! From a learning theory perspective, these roles must be learned when the actions of others are reinforcers or punishers. The habitual perspective sees roles as established patterns of behaviours elicited by familiar situations and the behaviour of others.

Exchange theory

Exchanges are interactions between people that are maintained through reinforcement, according to this view. Continuing exchanges are those that are expected to bring more benefit than expected from alternative activities. People learn to expect certain behaviours from others in response to their own actions (Homans, 1961). In exchange, affection and respect are extended to those who act in the ways that are valued. This reinforces that behaviour. Thus, the exchange of goods and services for money is only a part of a much wider (and deeper) process of social exchange.

Regular habits of interaction become established – notions of fair exchange develop. Exchange theory can help to explain the service encounter (see chapter ten).

Consumer satisfaction and dissatisfaction

We evaluate our experience with a product by considering the extent to which our needs were satisfied and how the experience compared with our pre-purchase expectations about how the product would perform.

Alternative products are evaluated on their attributes that represent the benefits that satisfy our needs. When we evaluate performance, we compare this to what we expected. Three outcomes are possible:

- **positive disconfirmation**: the products perform better than we expected
- **confirmation**: we got what we expected
- **negative disconfirmation**: our expectations were not met

Here is a lesson for designers and quality managers: good performance may not be enough, we can still be disappointed when our expectation is not met.

Consumer complaining behaviour

If we feel satisfied with a product purchase and/or use experience, we may be more inclined to remain committed to that supplier and/or product when next we have a need that can be similarly satisfied. When dissatisfied, points out Singh (1988), we may:

- **voice our dissatisfaction to the supplier** by complaining of poor performance and suggesting ways for improvement; often we want a response, perhaps in the form of a refund, discount, or additional service to compensate and/or increase performance
- **voice our dissatisfaction privately** to people in our reference groups in word-of-mouth communication
- **seek the support of a third party** by writing letters of complaint to newspaper, magazine, and TV consumer advocates, or to trade and government bodies, or we may seek legal recourse
- **decide to not repeat our purchase** of this product, perhaps choosing one from another supplier

There are implications here too for the design of marketing communication systems and activities, as well as performance criteria for both marketing and communication management.

MINDFULNESS

The personal perspective on people communicating for marketing and consumption purposes can be thought of as the pursuit of healthy communicator interactions that lead to mutual need satisfaction through the exchange of valued products, etc.

Psychologist Edith Langer's concept of 'mindfulness' (Langer, 1989) suggests that dysfunctional behaviour is based on unnecessarily limiting thought processes. Mindful thinking requires that the communicator:

- creates new categories for new information about the perceived world, rather than trying to force it to fit existing categories
- is open to the new information which is added to his/her expanding, and increasingly differentiated, information base
- is aware that there is usually more than one perspective on a situation, i.e. is sensitive to context
- pays attention to the process before its outcomes

Langer has a view on rationality and the connection between cognition and perception:

> In dealing with the world rationally, we hold it constant, by means of categories formed in the past. Through intuition, on the other hand, we grasp the world as a whole, in flux.

> (Langer, 1989: 123)

This has interesting implications for marketing as a communication system, as we saw in chapter two. Marketing simply cannot be merely a one-way informing technology – unless we want to be responsible for an unhealthy society. We deal with ethical issues in chapter seventeen.

BOX 3.2   INITIATORS, APPREHENDERS, AND APPRECIATION

We must abandon the notion of senders and receivers because, as we will see throughout this book, the transmission or transportation model of human communication is outmoded.

The initiator begins the process of communicating with an intention, while the apprehender is drawn into a joint system of communication when they try to interpret the other person's intention.

THE APPRECIATIVE SYSTEM

How can we understand the healthy communication system from a social perspective? One way is to understand communication as 'appreciation'.

Every act of a person is interpreted by other people and so becomes communication only when meaning is attributed to it by the other(s), i.e. when it is perceived and appreciated. Sir Geoffrey Vickers (1984) could find no accepted word to describe the attaching of meaning to perceived signals to create communication. He thus referred to this mental activity as 'appreciation', the code it uses as its 'appreciative system', and the state of the code as the 'appreciative setting'. Note the similarity of this model to that of McGuire's information-processing sequence, but also that Vickers did not limit his explanation to 'information', rather than choosing the larger and distinctly different concept of 'communication'. We will discuss this further as a valuable insight can be brought into thinking about managing.

Vickers has clarified the nature of the problem. Culture and communication cannot be separated. For us to communicate and cooperate, we must share some common assumptions about the world we live in, and some common standards by which to judge our own and other people's actions. These shared epistemological assumptions must correspond sufficiently with reality to make common action effective. The shared ethical assumptions must meet the minimal mutual needs that the members of our society have of each other. 'Culture' is the shared basis of appreciation and action which communication develops within any political system (a corporation is a subsystem of wider society).

Acceptance arises from the apprehender's choices, not the initiator's intentions. Participants to a communicative event take part in a process of creating shared meaning. First we interpret the situation, then act, influencing one another.

We all have concerns, in response to each of which we construct an inner representation of the situation that is relevant to that concern. The appreciative system (Vickers, 1984) is a pattern of concerns and their simulated relevant situations, constantly revised and confirmed by the need for it to correspond with reality sufficiently to guide action, to be sufficiently shared among people to mediate communication, and to be sufficiently acceptable for a 'good' life. The appreciative system is thus a mental construct, partly subjective, largely intersubjective (i.e. based on a shared subjective judgement), constantly challenged or confirmed by experience.

Only if the appreciative mind classifies the situation as changeable or in need of preservation, does the person devise possible responses and evaluates them with criteria determined by their other concerns. Thus 'problems' are discerned and 'solutions' sought. Action may or may not follow.

This perspective provides a simple and yet profound way of understanding what has to happen for a communication system to function. It has rarely been applied in the management of marketing communication. Are you willing to develop your thinking in this way?

DIFFUSION OF INNOVATIONS

When the compact disc was introduced in 1983 in Europe, how did so many people become committed to buying and using it? We had no prior experience of this product. Very few of us woke up screaming one night, in search of a life-enhancing 12 cm shiny flat plastic disc with a hole in the middle. But today, almost every household has a player and numerous discs. Many have a Walkman version and another in their car. Almost all PC software is now supplied on a disk, so many of us see a CD-ROM drive as essential equipment. How did this come about? Through the best efforts of certain professional marketers! But how exactly?

Innovation in a market may be through behaviour change or technology change. Products may be modified (through varying degrees of technological change), or novel introductions made (requiring new purchase and usage behaviours). The CD was a technology change. Soon they may become obsolete as we can download MP3 and other format music files directly from the Internet. We will then be able to choose whether to visit the downtown record shop in the rain so as to thumb through disorganized CDs before joining a queue of coughing people to pay too much for them!

Once again, in trying to explain the process by which a new product spreads through a market through purchase by adopters, we have a choice of models. Figure 3.10 summarizes four such models.

The process has a number of stages identified, each with certain factors that are of importance to planning marketing communication. Note how similar these process models are to the decision-making process model(s) discussed earlier in this chapter. As we move through these stages, we tend to use different media as means of finding data and for taking action. Rogers (1981(with Kincaid), 1983, 1986) gives a sound account of this process in terms of communication.

Over time the process of aggregate adoption is termed 'diffusion'. Rogers explains diffusion as the process by which an innovation is communicated over a period of time among members of a social system. In terms of segmentation, five categories of adopter have been defined:

1 **innovators**: like new ideas, have discretionary money to spend, and take risks

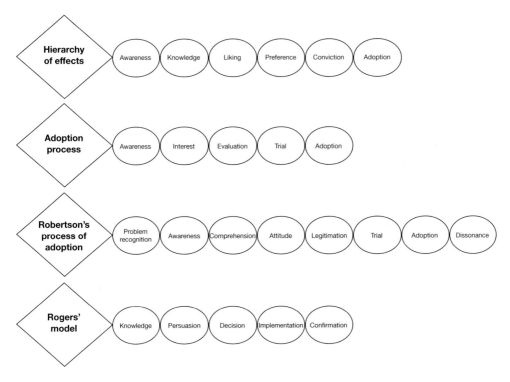

Figure 3.10 **Models of the adoption/diffusion process**

Source: Based on Wells and Prensky, 1996: 493

2 **early adopters**: well-educated opinion leaders who are open to new ideas
3 **early majority**: opinion followers who rely on informal sources of data
4 **late majority**: sceptical about new ideas, only adopting new products for social and economic reasons
5 **laggards**: suspicious of new ideas and very fixed in their thinking, with little disposable income

People whose behaviour mostly falls into one of these categories for a given product will have distinct communication behaviours, such as media use, and so on.

PERSONAL INFLUENCE AND OPINION LEADERS

We should keep in mind that 'organizations', companies, firms, and so on are not living things and cannot communicate. It is people who communicate with one another, either in their own right or on behalf of a legally recognized entity (a company or firm or partnership).

It is a gross oversimplification to imagine that an organization directs information like an arrow or bullet at a target audience. Not only do people communicate with people, but also communication is not merely information transfer, as we saw in chapter two. As David Bernstein (1984) wrote, we don't communicate with targets, we hit them! In addition, both technologies and people often mediate communication. Here we are interested in the influence that people may have in the marketing communication system.

Some people apprehend a message directly, while others may interact with them but will not have heard or read the message directly (Figure 3.11).

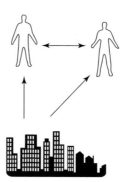

Figure 3.11 **Direct and indirect interaction**

Mediators may reinforce or undermine through reinterpretation of the message in their interactions. Presenters in TV travel shows are opinion formers in that they can experience a place or event 'on our behalf' and give us an opinion for something that we have not ourselves experienced directly. Reviews and tests have the same impact. Credibility of the mediator is crucial to the outcome.

Word-of-mouth communication is significant because our customers and those consumers with whom we might wish to forge a trading relationship may interact with highly influential people. The recommendations of highly credible people are sought, especially during the evaluation phase of the purchase decision process.

Some people are active in receiving data, interpreting it, and communicating about their judgements with others (Katz & Lazarsfeld, 1955). These **opinion leaders** are more persuasive in exerting interpersonal influence than those who interact directly through mass media. Opinion leadership can be simulated in product testimonial advertising. These people are very important to managed product diffusion, but are very difficult to identify through conventional market research methods.

Opinion formers are able to exert personal influence because they have authority or status. Others seek information and advice from them because they are recognized as expert. They are gatekeepers, relatively easy to identify, and are often 'lobbied' in an effort to persuade them to pursue opinions and policies that are favourable to the lobbier.

People act within a network of other people. The challenge for marketers is to identify those customers and prospective customers who are significant because they are influential to others and those who are not amenable to mediation and will apprehend messages directly. As we saw earlier, dissatisfied buyers and users will voice negative criticisms. Word-of-mouth remains a much under-exploited marketing communication system. This is a challenge in planning and operating the marketing communication system.

CORPORATE BUYING BEHAVIOUR

'Consumer' behaviour also occurs in business settings where people act as purchasing agents guided by corporate procedures to acquire products and services for use by themselves and others in their won value-creating processes.

Business-to-business marketing includes industrial and public sector buying and the selling of materials, components, consumables, and services. Although there are far fewer corporate buyers, less frequent purchases are made through formal orders of higher value. It is usual for contractual arrangements to be made for continuing supply over an extended period of time, often through a process of competitive bidding and negotiation.

There is considerable similarity between consumer purchasing and business-to-business purchasing, although there are differences between communication activities that are important to note (see Table 3.5 below). Primarily, purchases are made as contributions to corporate goals and objectives, yet it is important to realize also that the needs of buyers may be personal (promotion, financial reward, job satisfaction, and so on). Buyers are mostly professionally trained in a range of skills, and rely on information and formal decision-making.

Decision-making units (DMUs) have members from various parts of the organization, each of whom has some interest in the outcome of purchasing efforts. Users initiate the process of acquiring products, and evaluate their performance. Influencers participate in setting technical specifications for products as well as assessing options during the search stage. Deciders, usually authorized managers, make the purchase decision. Buyers or purchasing managers may select which product to buy and from whom. Alternatively, this decision is made by the manager, and the buyer may influence and then administer the placing of orders and so on. Gatekeepers (technicians and engineers, secretaries, receptionists, etc.) control the information that is available to the members of the DMU. The number of people involved in purchasing will depend upon the complexity of the need, the value of the purchase, and the degree of risk believed to be attached to the decision. The role occupants alter with each new purchase situation.

It is vital that suppliers identify members of the DMU and recognize their particular needs so that communication efforts can be tailored in each case. The marketing communication manager must be able to treat each member of the DMU as an active problem-solver (perhaps more so than consumers, because defined goals are involved).

The requirement for particular marketing communication effort depends on the nature of the buying situation. In consumer purchase situations, we

Table 3.5 **Characteristics of purchase situations**

Buying situation	Familiarity	Information need	Option search
First-time buy	Decision-makers have not faced this problem before	Lots of information	All options are new
Rebuy	The problem has been faced before	Little or none	Alternative solutions are not needed
Modified rebuy	The problem significantly differs from past experience	Past experience is supplemented with new information	New solutions are sought

can think of limited, extended, and routine purchases. Here these are called first-time buy (novel), rebuy, and modified rebuy situations (Table 3.5).

Influences on corporate buying behaviour come from the organization itself, from stakeholders, and from the interpersonal relationships of the DMU members.

The cost of switching from one supplier to another can be considerable. When the cost is considerable, the motivation to switch is low, but this leads to relative inflexibility for the user. Cost of switching can work to the benefit of the supplier, but in the long run can be a point of contention in a buyer–seller relationship. Other major influences come from corporate business strategy, culture and values, resources (cash flow, for example), and purchasing policies and procedures.

A network of relationships develops between the various stakeholders of a business enterprise (employees, customers, shareholders, regulators, community, etc.). (Stakeholder relationships are examined in chapter five). The climate of the exchange relationship and the communication style both affect buying decisions. Cooperative and productive relationships are based on trust and mutual support, with a long-term perspective. (The relational approach to marketing is examined in chapter twelve). Short-term thinking borne out in 'arm's-length' behaviour may lack commitment and may be driven more by self-interest, convenience, and instrumentality.

Each member of the DMU will have some view on the consequences of their contribution to buying decisions. Participation and influence are greater when members believe that blame or praise will stem from good and bad decisions. A further communication problem in DMUs, as in other work groups, is the relative power of each member to control resource deployment and information inputs (i.e. data gathering and interpretation).

The effective DMU is really another example of an appreciative system. The group captures data from the environment about needs and options for satisfying them. The members interpret the data into meaning and make judgements about the situation, and then decide how to act. Like the consumer buying process, a number of phases can be described that apply

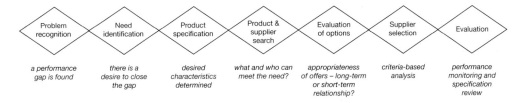

Figure 3.12 **Phases of the corporate buying decision process**

mostly to the first-time buy, with certain phases omitted for repeat purchases because they are not necessary (Figure 3.12).

Marketing communication for consumer markets differs from that of business-to-business markets. These are summarized in Table 3.6.

Table 3.6 **Consumer vs. business-to-business marketing communication**

Factor	Consumer	Business-to-business
Communication context	Informal, for self	Formal, on behalf of others
Size of DMU	One or few	Many
Promotional methods	Mostly advertising and sales promotions	Primarily personal selling
Orientation	Emotions and imagery	Rational, logical informing
Decision period	Short	Lengthy
Word-of-mouth impact	Close social network	Wider network in organization and beyond
Targeting and research	Sophicated methods widlely used	Limited but increasing use
Budget	Mostly for brand management	Mostly for sales management
Evaluation and measurement	Range of techniques	A limited number of techniques

Source: Adapted from Fill, 1999: 113

IMPLICATIONS FOR MANAGERS

The marketing manager must be able to analyse buyer and consumer behaviour, as follows (adapted from Wells and Prensky, 1996: 59–60):

1. Identify the activities of consumers when they are purchasing and consuming.

2. Distinguish the activities of diverse consumer market segments during the purchase and use of a particular product, and recognize the factors that contribute to the different patterns of activities.
3. Determine which of the background characteristics explain which segments carry out the purchase activities in different ways.
4. Understand how consumers enact behavioural processes when they buy and use a product.

CASE STUDY 3   THE MEANINGS OF DINNER

Patterns of habit, preference, and behaviour may be thought of as a lifestyle, chosen and pursued. This may bear a characteristic consumption style that may identify the person with a particular social group or consumption community. Consider the now largely passed era of ceremonial dining, and compare it with today's social gathering at the barbecue.

The structured meal patterns that emerged in Victorian Britain ceased to be concerned only with mere nourishment. Dining became centred on the mechanics of social interaction, social rank, and the need for conspicuous display. Both content and timing became crucially significant. The hour at which a meal was served might show the rank or aspirations of the host. The form, including garnishes, table decoration, and rules for serving guests, also communicated much. At the heart was an obsession with correctness that helped to define the Victoria era.

A complex formal etiquette governed the use of space, time, objects, cuisine, and labour to define those who dined in their appropriate social circles. Dining *à la Russe* overtly divided those who knew how to dine from the others. Also important for maintaining social distance was that servants mediated between hosts and guests. Since almost all activity was delegated to the servants, interaction between diners was considerably reduced, and was regulated by formal rules.

In the early years of the twentieth century, the imperial train of the Russian Tsar and his family had one car devoted entirely to dining. The car was equipped with a kitchen, a dining room with a table for 20 people, and an ante-room in which zakouski (an assortment of *hors d'œuvres* served with chilled vodka) was served before every meal. The Russian custom of self-service from a table was strictly observed. At dinner, Nicolas always sat at the middle of the long table with his daughters sat beside him, while the court functionaries sat opposite. The Empress ate alone on the train. At Tsarskoe Selo, near St Petersburg, dinner at midday was the ceremonial meal. The meal began, according to Russian custom, with a priest's blessing. Teas were always the same, year after year. Small, white-draped tables were set with the same glasses in silver holders, the same plates of hot bread, the same English biscuits. There was a rigid routine for tea. Every day, at the same time, the Emperor would enter the room and sit at the tea table. He would butter a piece of bread and sip his tea – always two glasses of tea – and read his telegrams and newspapers.

Why do we eat as we do? Dining has long been an almost universal medium of relationships – the means of creating community. Consider the many meanings of the ritual of a formal dinner, a family dinner, or a summer Saturday barbecue. In the emerging browsing or snack culture of the present, what has become of the social ritual that was dining?

(Sources: Massie, 1969; Visser, 1991; Wilson, 1994)

WHAT DO YOU THINK?

1 To what extent are purchase decisions really made by people as discrete decision-makers?

2 In what circumstances are you an innovator or a laggard? What implications has this categorizing scheme for planning communication activities?

3 People have a limited capacity to 'process' information. What implications has this for the design of marketing communication systems and activities?

4 Find an example of a recent innovation in applying consumer behaviour theory to the management of marketing communication.

5 What considerations must a communication manager make in supporting new product development?

6 Explain how the rational treatment of consumer behaviour will fail when choice is not free.

7 How might the growth in use of the Internet affect consumer response to traditional marketing communication activities?

8 What communication 'tools' are used close to the buyer decision point?

9 Explain how buyers incrementally learn as they progressively solve their problems.

10 It is reported that corporations can save large sums of money by enabling people to use the Internet more. Suggest ways in which this might work, and identify implications for communication managers (how do buyer and consumer interventions affect marketers?).

FURTHER READING

Arnott, D. and Fitzgerald, M. (eds) (2000) *Marketing Communications Classics: An International Collection of Classic and Contemporary Papers*, London: Thomson Learning/Business Press.

Barnes, B. (1995) *The Elements of Social Theory*, London: University College London Press.

Blythe, J. (2000) *Marketing Communications*, London: Financial Times/Prentice-Hall.

East, R. (1997) *Consumer Behaviour: Advances and Applications in Marketing*, London: Prentice-Hall.

Foxall, G. R. (1992) 'The behavioral perspective model of purchase and consumption: from consumer theory to marketing practice', *Journal of the Academy of Marketing Science* 20 (2): 189–98.

Gabriel, Y. and Lang, T. (1995) *The Unmanageable Consumer: Contemporary Consumption and Its Fragmentation*, London: Sage.

Stiff, J. B. (1994) *Persuasive Communication*, New York: Guilford Press.

Wells, W. D. and Prensky, D. (1996) *Consumer Behavior*, New York: John Wiley & Sons.

chapter
four

**MARKETING
COMMUNICATION
IDEOLOGY**

LEARNING POINTS

Careful study of this chapter will help you to:

- examine the intentions of marketers in attempting communication with consumers and buyers and other people

- relate marketing communication programme design decisions to assumptions about communication styles

- take a necessarily broader view of the role of marketing communication than is found in many textbooks

> The basic principle of marketing is supply and demand
> (Ian Beale, 'entrepreneur', *EastEnders*, BBC TV)

INTRODUCTION

Was Ian Beal forwarding a theory of marketing based on exchange? Probably not, since his comment was a retort to accusations of unnecessary competition. So why is so much marketing practice essentially aggressive and therefore pathological in its focus on competing when the marketing concept is widely accepted intellectually as healthily providing a focus on exchange and thus requires assertive behaviour? In this chapter we explain why a broader application of communication styles is necessary than is often the case in business enterprise. The concept of 'communication' is understood in the light of what we intend of its purpose (Kline, 1993: chapter 2).

COMMUNICATION IS RELATIONAL

We each construct our self-identity in terms of what we are and are not – we are who we are because we are different or similar to others. We are what we are in relation to others. Thus, a relational theory of communication would seem to be more sensitive to our needs as social beings. This sense of identity is expressed in many ways in society, especially in how we treat one another. In each dichotomous behaviour system, one behaviour is considered positive (good) and the other negative (bad): Box 4.1.

BOX 4.1   DICHOTOMOUS BEHAVIOUR SYSTEMS

aggressive–submissive

dominant–deferent

attacking–defending

dissenting–obedient

superior–inferior

controlling–controlled

active–passive

proactive–reactive

selfish–selfless

authoritarian–permissive

conservative–radical

This reveals types of behaviour that we can term egocentric (centred on me), sociocentric (concerned with us, i.e. the middle way), and 'other-centric' (elevating you above me). These social orientations are independent, interdependent, and dependent, respectively. Such behaviour tendencies are learned, manifesting our beliefs about the locus of control (either intrinsic or extrinsic). When we locate social actions as truly social, i.e. between independence and dependence, then joint social action is recognized (see chapter two). Figure 4.1 summarizes the communication theories that may thus be operative in our business enterprise.

Exploitation act	Transactional process
One-way influence	Each person expects to give and take
Somebody else's propaganda is conveyed	equally
• One party does something to the other	• A bargain is involved
• The 'communicator' takes the initiative	• Not all exchanges are exactly equitable
• The effect is exclusively on the audience	• Inequities can favour either person
	• People select what they attend to
[Morally asymmetrical, alienated]	• People evaluate credibility

Figure 4.1 **Alternative underlying theories of communicating**
Source: Based on Grossberg *et al.*, 1998

Traditionally, only one party has been thought of, by managers, as the 'communicator'. In the marketer-dominated communication system, the consumer and buyer are seen as information receivers in a process initiated and controlled by the provider. In the consumer/buyer-dominated communication system, the consumer or buyer is seen as an information seeker who uses interpersonal sources, many of which are complementary rather than competing, that are not under the control of the provider. The news and entertainment media, for example, are influences among other contributory agents. An alternative dialogic view has both provider and consumer/buyer in communication together within a complex web of influence in which knowledge transactions occur to meet the needs of both parties as marketers (i.e. in seeking out satisfying transactions).

The communication style adopted by managers is determined by their assumptions about:

1. *what motivates other people to act – the problem to be solved is seen to be how to cause them to behave in a manner advantageous to me*
2. *the effects of communicative behaviours: how available communication activities work – the problem to be solved is how to get desirable behaviour to come about through communicating*

Figure 4.2 summarizes several possible behaviours that we may have towards other people in our work.

The list shown in Figure 4.2, from a highly influential analysis of management roles, says little about learning and invention.

The prevailing style in (competitive) capitalist society is domination/ control. The transmission model of human communication is convenient for this, since the 'communicator' is dominant. Yet, marketing communication as merely promotional action is but one part of a four-part process. Promotional communication (i.e. communicating to promote) offers products and their providers as need satisfiers. Clearly, marketing is concerned with much more than this. Marketing is much more than selling

Tells	The manager makes a decision and informs others
Sells	The manager makes the decision and explains it to others to get their cooperation
Tests	The manager presents ideas and invites questions
Suggests	The manager presents a tentative decision, subject to change
Consults	The manager presents a problem, listens to suggestions, then makes a decision
Shares	The manager defines limits and asks others to make the decision, with the leader as an equal member
Delegates	The manager allows others to operate within defined limits

Figure 4.2 **Management styles**

Source: Based on Tannenbaum and Schmidt, [1958] 1973

(if it were mostly selling, it would be called 'selling'). The overall task is to create and retain customers by defining, producing, and delivering value. This is a social (joint) task, since people in the consumer role will adopt the customer role with a particular supplier only so long as they believe that there is real benefit from the instrumental relationship. As consumers, we do not take kindly to impositions of what is right and good for us – we assume the right to define what is good value in satisfying our needs.

We should, perhaps, be surprised that marketing thinking and practice has not more generally adopted the participatory conception of communication set out in chapter two. Marketing has long been seen as conceptually founded on exchange, while assertive behaviour is premised on the possibility and desirability of joint action to satisfy the needs and wants of both parties. We will now examine the implications of these various orientations and their associated attitudes.

Vickers (1984) distinguished seven overlapping and coexisting ascending levels of trust and shared appreciation (Figure 4.3).

Arguably, much marketing practice is superficial, even trivial. Although military metaphors and analogies still prevail in some quarters, behaviours are neither truly aggressive nor truly cooperative. Vickers would place much marketing communication at the information and persuasion levels in Figure 4.3. It would appear that the marketing concept is not really the central focus of much marketing behaviour. Is that behaviour then legitimate as marketing?

COMMUNICATION AS A MODE OF EXCHANGE

In a sense, marketing communication is no different to other forms of human communication and arises between people who communicate in their own

Violence	Erodes trust and evokes a response to contain it and to abate it, but has no specific communicative purpose
Threat	The conditional 'do it or else' – involves trust only to the extent that the threatened party needs to believe both that the threatener can and will carry out a threat unless the condition is fulfilled and that to fulfil the condition will avert the threat
Bargain	Involves a greater shared assumption – each party has to be confident that the other regards the situation as a bargain – the attempt to negotiate an exchange on terms acceptable to all the parties – each must believe that the other parties can and will carry out their undertakings if agreement is reached – each is free to make not merely an acceptable bargain but the best they can, or to withdraw from the negotiation
Information	The receiver must not only trust the giver's competence and reliability, they must also be assured that the giver's appreciative system corresponds sufficiently with their own to ensure that what is received fits the receiver's needs. Even if it does, it will, to some extent, alter the setting of their appreciative system
Persuasion	The giver actively seeks to change the way in which the other perceives some situation and thus to change the setting of their appreciative system more radically
Argument	When the process is mutual, each party strives to alter the other's view while maintaining his/her own
Dialogue	Each party seeks to share, perhaps only hypothetically, the other's appreciation and to open his/her own to the other's persuasion with a view to enlarging the approaching mutual understanding, if not shared appreciation

Figure 4.3 **Levels at which human communication may arise (Vickers, 1984)**

right and on behalf of an employer. Decisions about how to communicate are driven by assumptions about what motivates people to behave in certain ways and how to satisfy their own needs and those of the corporation.

How do we get what we want? Locus of control refers to beliefs about our own ability to determine what happens to us. An external locus of control places the origin of events and situations outside our own control – they just happen to us. An internal locus of control places the responsibility for control with us.

A competitive basis for accomplishment and benefit acquisition leads to a belief that winning is necessary, and that this may be justifiably at the expense of others. Such behaviour may be termed aggressive. In behaving this way, we stand up for our own rights in such a way that we violate the rights of other people. We ignore or dismiss the needs, wants, opinions, feelings, and beliefs of other people. We express our own honest or dishonest needs, wants, and opinions in inappropriate ways.

The other side of the competition-based stance on accomplishment and benefits is submissive behaviour. This stance avoids conflict by taking the needs and wants of others as more important than your own and assuming that they have rights while you do not. Needs, wants, opinions, and feelings are not expressed in an honest way, but in apologetic, diffident, and self-effacing ways.

The alternative assertive behaviours aim to satisfy the needs and wants of both parties to a situation, based on beliefs that each has needs to be satisfied and is able to contribute. Rights are pursued without violation of those of other people, while needs, wants, opinions, feelings, and beliefs are expressed in direct, honest, and appropriate ways (Box 4.2).

BOX 4.2   PRESENTATION, CONVERSATION, ELICITATION

'I get what I want by helping you to get what you want' – interdependence

'I get what I want, with no regard for other(s)' – independence

'I get what you want by deferring to your authority' – dependence

---

The intended outcome of a communicative interaction is the driver for the selection of a particular communication style (method). Communication styles may conflict (Figure 4.4).

Marketing, we have suggested, is more constructive if premised on an exchange concept. In a market exchange, it can be predicted that the loser in a competitive situation will not wish to repeat the outcome and will withdraw. Customers often defect to alternative suppliers in the hope of fairer or more responsive treatment because they feel that they are losing out on expected benefits while the supplier may be winning. Of course, it also works the other way around. The shrewd marketing manager would not wish to continue trading with a customer in a relationship that does not generate benefits for the business (profit, profile, new knowledge, etc.). Of course, if one party is willing to be the loser, a submissive–aggressive system is established in which one party is prepared to be controlled and the other is thus encouraged to reciprocate with control.

When both customer and supplier feel that they are losing, then it is highly unlikely that further interaction will occur. When both feel that they are benefiting from the relationship, then interaction is likely to increase in quantity and frequency – the virtuous circle of escalating benefits. It is clear that win-win outcomes result from exchange – the question is the extent

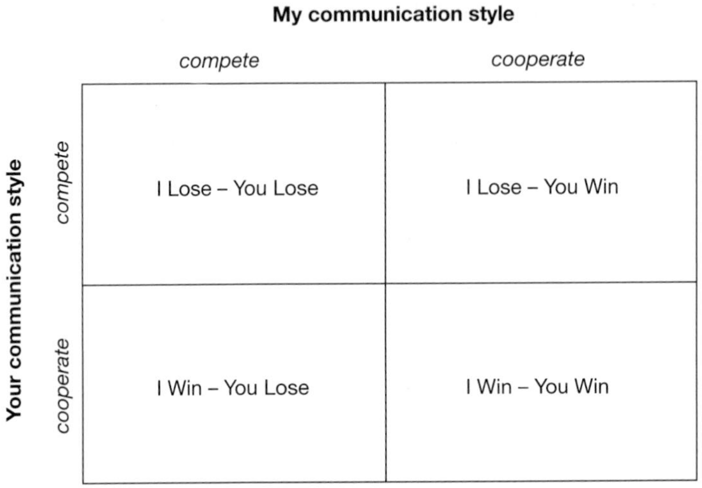

My communication style

Figure 4.4 **Outcomes of possible communication style combinations**

to which participants benefit. Cooperation can increase the benefits gained (Box 4.3).

BOX 4.3   MARKETER STANCES

Give them what profits them – we have no long-term business – we feel exploited

Give them what profits me – there is no long-term business – they feel exploited

Give them what profits us – a healthy prospect is brought about through negotiated exchange.

Thayer (1968) pointed out the lack of a satisfactory way of saying what is necessary to human communication – that each communicator takes something other than themselves into account in their thinking and expressing of ideas. 'When we have learned how to express what others will comprehend, and to comprehend what others will express, we will have learned how to communicate, and, in communication, we know' (Thayer, 1997: 7).

In order to be a proficient communicator, a person must have the ability and the susceptibility to take some things into account. Wherever and whenever human communication occurs there must be at least one person taking something into account. Susceptibility simply means openness, sensitivity, or impressionability. Appreciation (Vickers, 1984) is a good term for this 'taking-into-account'. Langer used the term mindful (as we saw in chapter three). Later, Thayer (1997) used the term 'minding' to suggest that communication is the process in which we create and maintain the 'objective' world.

> Our assumption, given the nature of the biases of our Western *mentalité*, is that one first has a mind, and merely learns how to 'express' it in words, or in communication; or that one has feelings, and then merely learns how to 'express' them to others, or to comprehend others' expression of 'them'; or that one first somehow 'knows' something, and then merely learns how to 'communicate' that knowledge to others. This is not so. Minds and feelings and attitudes and thoughts are literally communicated into existence; and then they have only that existence that their communicability permits – enables or constrains. It is not that we communicate the way we do because we are the way we are; it is that we are the way we are because we communicate (or not) the way we do.
>
> (Thayer, 1997: 203)

Our communication attitude is largely determined by our assumptions about human motivation and individual capabilities. We choose to include or exclude other people in order to fulfil our own needs, seeking others as either allies or enemies. The exchange basis for marketing should logically place each customer (and other important stakeholders) within our social circle rather than without. The commonly observed behaviours may be explained in terms of a communication model in use (Table 4.1, note the similarity with Tannenbaum and Schmidt's managerial styles – see Figure 4.2 in this volume, p. 75).

MARKETING COMMUNICATION IN THE VALUE-CREATING SYSTEM

The corporation can be thought of as a knowledge-conversion system that creates value for a range of knowledge network members. For some members, value is created directly through products that can be used to meet needs. We refer to these members as 'customers'. Other members acquire benefit from their membership indirectly. For example, shareholders gain financially when the system is profitable in producing and supplying value to customers. Employees similarly receive benefits such as job security, bonuses, and job satisfaction, when customers' needs are satisfied.

Wikström and Normann (1994) model the corporation as part of a value creation network that organizes processes of generation, production, and representation and creates value by transforming knowledge. This approach differs from the traditional supply chain management view that is linear, monological, and fragmented, emphasizing persuasion and 'informing'. Instead, a holistic, dialogical, integrated, synchronous, and reciprocal system of knowledge exploitation is envisaged in which productivity is taken to be value creation. Within this, corporate conversations take place to generate knowledge, make offerings, and exchange valued goods and services (tangible

Table 4.1 **Possible communication behaviours**

Communication model in use	Intention in communicating	Underlying ideology	Comment
Press agentry (TELL)	Instruct – promotion of the corporation and its products through publicity	Non-interactive (one-way) communication activities help to control the publics that affect the corporation	The complete truth is not always told, so that a favourable impression may be made
Public information (TELL)	Inform – disseminate truthful and accurate information	We know what facts are for public consumption	'Journalists-in-residence' try to represent the interests of both sides
Two-way, asymmetric (SELL)	Consult/involve – use feedback to manipulate public attitudes into agreeing with the corporation's point of view	We're in control, but we need to know what will motivate you to cooperate with us in our way of thinking to accomplish our goal	Market research may ask questions of customers and consumers, but the interest is only to the extent that this will help us to get what we want from you
Two-way, symmetric (NEGOTIATE)	Collaborate – attempt to reach a state of affairs that is acceptable to all by developing mutual understanding	Conceives of both parties as participating in and engaged in an exchange	Conflict resolution comes through co-produced identities, meanings, and knowledge, in social action

Source: Based on Grunig, 1992

and intangible). There is temporal integration between the three basic processes (Figures 4.5, 4.6, and 4.7).

Generative processes construct knowledge in activities aimed at solving problems by attending to both the internal and external domains of the operating environment (the corporation is not other than the environment, it is part of it). We saw the need for this when we examined mindfulness and appreciation in chapter three.

Productive processes then use the knowledge to provide products as part of the offerings to be made to customers. Goods and services are manifest knowledge that has use value. All businesses sell knowledge in some form or other.

Representative processes relate manifest knowledge to customers in a manner in which they can incorporate this knowledge into their own value-

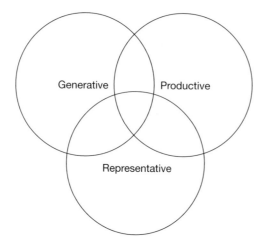

Figure 4.5 **The knowledge system processes**

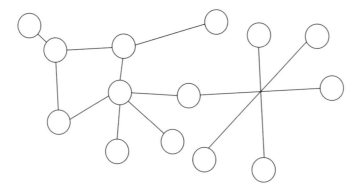

Figure 4.6 **A value star network**

creating processes. (Fan belts are added to car engines, whereas cream cakes are added to my stomach!)

The corporation is a contributing and benefiting part of a social network of value-creators and value-users who are linked by commonalities in their needs and competences for satisfying them.

COOPERATION, COLLABORATION, COMPETITION

Marketing may be operated managerially or managerialistically. In examining the politics of corporate life, Deetz observed that managerialism is a kind of logic, a set of routine practices, and an ideology. This managerialistic way of dealing with situations and people is 'a way of conceptualising, reasoning, through, and discussing events' (a 'discursive genre') but, it also involves 'a set of routine practices, a real structure of rewards, and a code of

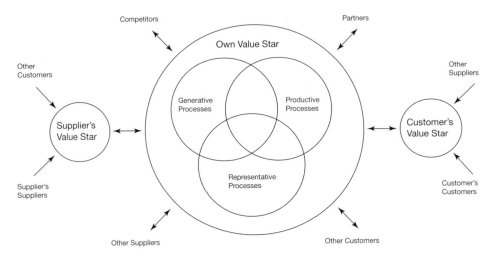

Figure 4.7 **The network as a knowledge-creating value star**
Source: Based on Wikström and Normann, 1994

representation. It is a way of doing and being in corporations that partially structures small groups and conflicts with, and at times suppresses, each group's other modes of thinking' (Deetz, 1992: 222).

In much of marketing management, as well as management, and life in general, competition is taken to be the basis for relating, rather than co-operation. Tasks are considered central. Yet, interactions arise within relationships. A market interaction is transactional, is entered into independently of previous or subsequent exchanges, is short-term in outlook, and is primarily motivated by self-interest. A relational interaction, on the other hand, is a development of a long-term supportive relationship (see Table 4.2).

The implication of the analysis of relationship characteristics (Table 4.2) is that managers should, beneficially, attend more to relationships than to transactions. We examine this further in chapters eleven and twelve when we review current thinking on internal marketing and relationship marketing.

A collaborative communication strategy focuses on making a relationship that works for all participants and contributors. An autonomous communication strategy assumes benefit will arise from depersonalizing interactions (see also chapter fourteen on strategy formation and implementation).

MARKETING COMMUNICATION OBJECTIVES

What should the marketing manager pay attention to when facing the communicative needs of the business? Most textbooks on marketing communication treat the field as if only promotional message broadcasting and related activities are communicative or necessary and relevant.

Take, for example, the hierarchy of effects (outlined in chapter three). This and similar models can usefully be applied to explain how advertising may work. Thus a potential customer may, through marketing activities, be

Table 4.2 **Impact of relationship characteristics on interactions**

Nature of relationship	Nature of interaction			
	Relative frequency	*Mode*	*Subject*	*Form*
Form				
Market	Lower	Monologue	Behaviour	Formal
Relational	Higher	Dialogue	Beliefs and attitudes	Informal
Climate				
Supportive	Higher	Dialogue	Beliefs and attitudes	Informal
Unsupportive	Lower	Monologue	Behaviour	Informal
Relative power				
Asymmetrical	Lower	Monologue	Beliefs and attitudes	Informal
Symmetrical	Higher	Dialogue	Beliefs and attitudes	Informal

Source: Based on Mohr and Nevin, 1990

encouraged to mentally pass through a series of steps from ignorance to purchase, as each stage is fulfilled before passing on to the next. It is not helpful, however, to apply such thinking to try to explain or predict how a person will behave in response to communication activity in other situations. How, for example, can such a model explain communication behaviour that is initiated by the consumer? We need to look at consumption behaviour from the consumer's point of view.

A scale of degree of connectedness between two or more people is shown in Figure 4.8. Of course, this applies both ways in a relationship. Perhaps,

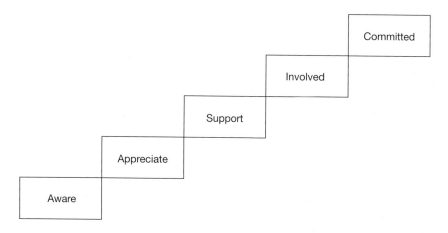

Figure 4.8 **Levels of a relationship**

it is the recognition that two people can each be a marketer seeking his or her progression from the other that advances a social (communication) orientation to the management of marketing communication.

Fill (1999) provides an interesting and comprehensive account of the role and nature of marketing communication. But even this well-written and attractive 656-page textbook provides an incomplete picture of the marketing communication task. Fill offers a simple acronym (DRIP) for remembering the uses of marketing communication:

- **differentiating**: trying to exclude competing products from consumer decision-making by making your own more attractive and a closer match to their needs
- **reminding**: trying to ensure that when options for consumption are being assessed, your product is included
- **informing**: providing data into the consumer's mindful and appreciative thought processes to ensure that your product is considered as an attractive option in consumption
- **persuading**: effort to induce desired favourable behaviour from the consumer.

This is, however, only the expressive part of the task. To accomplish efficient and effective generation, the corporation must also ensure that at least some of its members attend to the problem of impression. Decision-making on what to do and how in the productive processes of the business enterprise must receive inputs that take into account the marketing environment: customers' recognized needs, competitors' offerings, technologies, social values, and so on.

The emphasis should be balanced between asking and telling, but will depend on the attitude of managers and workers towards people and task achievement. Possible orientations are:

- **commanding**: giving orders in exercising authority over people to control them for the purpose of domination
- **persuading**: inducing belief or action through reason
- **influencing**: manipulating beliefs and actions of others from a superior stance
- **collaborating**: pursuing jointly held goals for mutual benefit

Commanding, persuading, and influencing are authoritarian methods for egocentric pursuit of goals, whereas collaborating is a participatory process of joint social action motivated by sociocentric interests. We are arguing here that a conversation model of marketing communication comes much closer to the contemporary need for responsible business responsiveness than does the traditional and now outmoded expressive model (Box 4.4).

BOX 4.4   CONVERSATION IN THE CONTEXT OF MARKETING OBJECTIVES

Conversation is:

Consensual – both parties willingly come together to engage in communicating for a purpose

Control-less – neither party is in control or intends to assume control over the other

Change – recognized as possible (and necessary?) for both parties (why else communicate?)

> (*Source*: Based on a presentation by Don Peppers,
> Royal Mail Conference on One-to-One Marketing, 1995)

If marketing communication is strategic corporate gossip, perhaps a more sophisticated acronym is that represented by Figure 4.9, and compare Figure 4.10.

> **C**onnect
> **R**elate
> **I**nform
> **P**ersuade
> **C**onstruct
> **L**earn
> **I**nvent
> **E**xchange

Figure 4.9 **An acronym for marketing communication**

Thus marketing is enabled and facilitated when we take into account (appreciate) before we seek to be taken into account (to be appreciated). This assertive behaviour was identified by Covey, who advocated seeing to understand before seeking to be understood. There is a good lesson in this for marketing practice.

Of course, another way of saying this is Vickers' appreciative system:

> **A**pprehend the environment
> **I**nterpret meaning
> **V**alue and judge
> **A**ct accordingly

Figure 4.10 **Vickers' appreciative system (as an acronym)**
Source: Based on Vickers, 1984

MESSAGES

In pretty well every account of advertising and marketing communications, a central concept is the 'message', i.e. the content of the 'communication' package or event. So, what is a 'message'? We can make some sense of this rather abstract idea by thinking of the message as an intended meaning for a written, aural or visual text. But how can another person possibly 'know' what was intended? Only through interpretation can a meaning be given to a communicative act, and of course this requires that the message was apprehended in the first place.

The interpretation given to a message, and the act which provides it, will depend on the reception environment of the apprehender. This is a complex of linguistic and ideological codes of the producer and 'viewer', as well as alternative information from other sources (including beliefs, memory, various third parties, etc.).

Hall (1961) identifies three components of a message. A set is a distinguishable combination of parts. For example, words can be combined into a set (a sentence), and products offered for sale are a set (a product range). The sets that are perceived in a given situation will depend upon the person's interests, expectations, and cultural background. Brazilians rank coffee highly, whereas an Englishman may rank coffee low and tea high. Cultures rank products as sets differently. Comparable sets in different cultures may have different parts. Consider, for example, the set we call the midday meal. In some places this comprises wine and bread. Elsewhere, this may be the main meal of the day and have several courses and lots of social interaction. Somewhere else, there may be no meal at this time of day, and the main cooked meal will be at 7 p.m. (which is dinner in your culture?). The isolate is a component part of the set. The sounds that make up the words in a phrase are isolates. So are the package, parts, and other attributes of a product. The pattern is the third message component. Sets are arranged through implicit cultural rules so as to take on meaning. Grammar is such a formalized pattern. A sales method is a pattern that arranges a group of sets in a meaningful fashion. Of course, through marketing research the marketing manager seeks to understand how patterns, sets, and isolates focus sense perceptions into responses to products and promotional appeals. Viewing a selected group of people in terms of culturally prescribed patterns may help in designing marketing communication programmes of objectives and activities. Patterns, sets, and isolates must direct appeals to the set of ideas, attitudes, and habits of the buyers (Zaltman, 1965).

Another way of examining the concept of a message is to identify properties. Content is the ideas, questions, and so on that are intended to inform, interest, persuade, and motivate. Structure is the sequence in which items of content are presented. Format is the physical presentation (personal, aural, written, still or moving pictures, etc.). The source may be overt, implied, or assumed and may be the product provider or an expert or celebrity endorser. More will be said when we examine advertising design in chapter fourteen.

MARKET EDUCATION

Marketing intervention seeks to influence (i.e. make change to) buyer and consumer behaviour. Marketing activity is educational when it provides a public service in identifying and discussing the existence and nature of a problem. On the other hand, when the intention is to induce purchase by suggesting a specific solution that favours both parties, marketing activity is promotional. We are, of course, clear that any other activity that seeks to favour the supplier over the buyer or consumer is not really marketing, but merely a sales pitch.

Examples are to be found in health and medicine. For instance, people can be familiarized with significant findings from research studies on the effects of cigarette-smoking or wearing seat belts in cars, etc. However, we should note that public service is not the same as marketing that is of service to publics.

The consumer learning curve of a market, from the situation in which no one is using a product to the desired situation of fully saturated adoption, can be likened to the familiar product 'life cycle'. The latter is a managerial construction for the management (driven or contrived) of the evolution of the demand and use of products. The diffusion of innovations that transforms ignorance into awareness and then into adoption is a gradual learning process in which people come to accept the legitimacy of a product, and then to appreciate its utility and to recognize its value. For major innovations to take off, people have to unlearn old value systems and learn to accept and value a new value system. Once we had no cars, telephones, televisions, personal computers, CDs, and so on. Now they are ubiquitous in daily life.

Market education is an attempt to initiate the early introduction of a product, to accelerate growth in demand for it, or to postpone maturity and decline in demand. Often, this attempt to extend the life of a product–market relationship is the purpose of product and brand repositioning (see chapter fourteen). Particular strategies are related to the stage in the product life cycle. Product purchase and consumption are provoked by communicative interventions in consumer behaviour.

Learning here may be thought of as changing the cognitive links among concepts attended to by a person. Some advertising research has shown that these links can be strengthened by repeated claims, creative presentation of features, and more concrete presentation. Alternatively, new linkages can be established by reporting previously unknown benefits – often how pharmaceuticals, for example, are promoted based on clinical trials. Much learning has, in years gone by, been little more than acculturation – the process of taking on the values, the experiences, and the biases of those who preceded us. Today, many technological developments are so substantially novel and rapid in appearance that acculturation is not sufficient. We have to deal with an overload of novel possibilities, many of which fundamentally challenge what we take for granted as the basis of our society and our own lives within it.

Consumers and buyers may come to hear about your product through various means, but will also hear about others too. The principle of 'market education' is that people are more likely to respond to your selling message when they understand what is being sold. Market education, or pre-selling, can have the following effect on advertising:

- it will help to make it more readily acceptable and to produce more response
- it can save considerable sums of money since the public relations activity will cost much less than a commensurate level of advertising
- the advertising run will be more cost-effective

As well a helping the customer to learn, marketing communication systems can (and should) help the corporation to learn. Thus, market research and customer complaints are mechanisms by which customers educate the marketer.

RESPONSE TO MARKETING ACTION

What seems to be forgotten in much discussion of marketing, is that sometimes it is the consumers and buyers, not the providers, who initiate marketing actions. Traditional marketing focuses on attention-getting and persuasion to attract consumers to become customers. Interactive marketing has a different, more strategic, agenda – to maintain a healthy customer–supplier relationship with each consumer or buyer.

Expressive communication actions – from the marketer to the consumer – are intended to affect consumer and buyer behaviour in a way that is advantageous to the supplier, through promotional messages. Impressive communication actions can, on the other hand, affect the marketer's behaviour as well. These are intended to be advantageous to both. Thus, elicitation should come as an early input to the value-creation process (at the generative phase). Table 4.3 attempts to provide the manager's learning framework.

Figure 4.11 and Box 4.5 consider some of the classic questions posed by marketing.

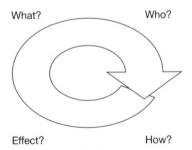

Figure 4.11 **The classic marketing questions**

Table 4.3 **Who does what in the marketing encounter?**

Marketer's question	Marketer's action	Consumer's action
What should we offer?	Market research, analysis of complaints, analysis of enquiries, review of competitive offers, audit of competences, and so on	Enquiries, complaints, choice-making, selection, criticism, word-of-mouth celebration, etc.
Who should we make the offer to?	Market segmentation, advertising, selling	Purchase and use
Who is using our product and in what way does this satisfy their needs?	Observation, trials, customer surveys, EPOS data analysis, mystery shopper, etc.	
What do our customers think of our product?	Quality improvement, new product development, refined advertising design, and so on	Consumption, word-of-mouth evaluation

---

BOX 4.5   BUY MORE STUFF!

Ask the non-specialist 'what is the essence of marketing?' and he/she will almost invariably equate this to mean persuasive advertising that aims to get people to buy more of a certain product brand. Yet, research shows, persuasive communication is more likely to reinforce existing opinions than to change them. People generally read and listen to what interests them, therefore they have considerable information and fixed opinions. Those most likely to attend to a message are those most difficult to change. Those who can be converted do not look or listen.

CASE STUDY 4   THE BENETTON NETWORK

The Benetton Group is a long-established Italian international retailer of knitted fashion clothing, established in the 1960s, whose brand name and logo is prominently displayed around the world along with associated images that allow premium pricing. Typical customers are other-directed consumers – aware of what meaning other people will give to their consumption of the Benetton product. Customers see themselves as members of an exclusive club. This is borne out further, as we shall see, by a central theme in the brand advertising.

Formed as part of the INVEP Group by Luciano, one of three brothers and a sister, Benetton opened their first shop in Belluno in northern Italy, and by 1982 had sold 27 million units through 1,900 shops, nearly half of which was exported. By the late 1980s, Benetton employed

2,000 people in eight factories in northern Italy. Additionally, the firm used about 220 contractors or groupers and their many subcontractors that employed a further 10,000 people. We could view the size of the firm as 2,000, or as 12,000 because the firm controls the contractors, many of which are owned or part-owned by Benetton employees. In 1989 some 185,000 people were working in 4,600 franchised shops, of which 1,300 were sited in Italy. Other factories were located in France and Scotland.

The prize in Europe for inventiveness, creativity and business aptitude certainly goes to the Italians. Their remarkable qualities for adaptation, as well as their art for compromise, have even given them the reputation of being chameleons. Enthusiasm, creativity and dynamism are elements of their character. The Italians appreciate people who have ideas, who innovate, because they themselves are without any particular prejudices and are open to everything new. They are naturally curious and inventive and have a very sophisticated business sense. This entrepreneurship, Italian style, has been exported and is the hallmark of Italian success abroad, the Benetton phenomenon (in the top-six Italian retailers) being an example. This gift of Italian entrepreneurs has created a style, and added to that gift is their unmatched artistic sense for aesthetics, refinement, design and fashion. European teenagers seek the latest trends in fashion through the stores, which are popular in many city retail quarters and airport shopping malls. About 80% of customers are aged 18–34, while almost 90% buy on quality and style/fashion. Some 83% of customers surveyed said that they would pay more for a Benetton product even if an equivalent was available elsewhere at a lower price. Only 13% felt that another retailer had a colour range that matched or was better than that available from their local Benetton shop (Schmidt *et al.*, 1994). Stores are bright with almost all stock on the shelves, creating ambience and vibrancy – the garments are brightly coloured – especially effective in attracting in 'window-shoppers' aged 19–25. In Italy, the Benetton brand is subdivided into '012 Benetton' (children's wear), 'Mt Market' (higher-fashion content), 'Sisley' (sophisticated menswear), 'Mercerie' (sophisticated womenswear), and 'Tomato' (trousers and knitwear for the urban youth market).

The opportunistic strategy is popular for competing in the garments industry. For example, Benetton's global network of suppliers, agents, and retailers is managed by using a global information system. Benetton's designers create new apparel offerings from the corporate headquarters in northern Italy. The information system transmits orders and designs to producers. Benetton makes extensive use of independent suppliers, drawing on the depth of experience in dyed knitwear production in the regional community. The company enters new geographical markets and develops new apparel designs as consumer preferences change and market opportunities are identified.

To gain control over their channels of distribution, spoken agreements based on trust were made with 'agents' across Europe. Each of these people set out to recruit small investors and store operators with the 'Benetton mentality' with whom individual partnerships were established at the single store level. By 1982 there were 70 such agents. It seems that the term 'franchise' is in this case something of a misnomer. Although stores do not pay a fee or royalty, they must stock only Benetton products, use their fixtures, adhere to strict price mark-ups and payments schedules, follow basic merchandising concepts, and develop 'an understanding of Benetton's way of doing business'.

Sales promotion is firmly founded on carefully selected store location and bright, inviting store appearance, often with sparing window displays and a clear view of open shelves of colourful merchandise.

Ask for what is Benetton known, and most people will recall the infamous attention-getting and controversial imagery employed in their advertising. A social controversy theme can be easily identified throughout their advertising run over two decades. The controversial and at times shocking (and even offensive) images often cause controversy in themselves. This is reported as news, further raising awareness of the Benetton brand beyond customers. On several occasions they have gone too far for some people. Advertisements featuring death in various forms were described as shock tactics and bad taste. They have pursued an international format, thus avoiding the cultural or linguistic inadequacies of presenting a single nationality. This approach has been presented under the banner 'United Colours of Benetton'. In highlighting colour as being more than black and white, they have challenged many racial tensions head on.

Do Benetton advertisements reflect social issues? Their series of wild, attention-getting images has been rationalized, after the event, as expressing the corporation's concerns. However, we might ask whether their creative ideas might not have led to a much better positioning strategy statement than was originally conceived. This is 'after-the-fact positioning strategy'. Benetton claim that the pictures they present should not be viewed as advertisements but as statements – images of social issues to raise public awareness and debate. They claim that nothing could be further from their minds than simply selling jumpers.

The core values of a nation define acceptable market relationships. Advertisers must understand their own and others' so that they do not violate them. Consider, for example, most Americans never see their more provocative advertisements because they are banned as too provocative and offensive. Minority groups have complained, for example, of racism when a black man was shown handcuffed to a white man. This implied, they claimed, that the former was a criminal. They may have lost many sales and even previously loyal customers in sticking to their strongly held core values. Yet, perhaps, rather than being a weakness in management, this demonstrates a willingness to decide with whom to trade. This is product-market targeting in action.

Does Benetton advertising cause unnecessary offence and even damage in society? The Advertising Standards Authority (ASA) in the UK has ruled several times against Benetton and its advertising agency for failing to show respect, their 'apparent willingness to provoke distress', and their 'disregard for the sensitivities of the public'.

Benetton marketers have been able to use high-impact, relatively low-cost media: magazines (emphasizing colour and the Benetton 'lifestyle', billboards, and posters (with TV spots in Europe emphasizing 'sport' and 'youth'). They sought public sites, and billboards generally do not need prior approval from advertising regulators, and can be changed relatively quickly in response to feedback. This has paid off several times in the face of public outrage and consequent backlash. In the UK, the new-born baby campaign caused over 800 complaints to the ASA, as well as to Trading Standards Offices (and even to the police). Other brand awareness campaigns have tackled civil rights, birth control, and world peace.

In 1993, the $25 million global campaign replaced images of a dying AIDS victim and oil-drenched seagulls with that of a naked Chairman Luciano Benetton with the strap line 'I want my clothes back'. This avoided adverse media criticism and presented a softer, more caring identity. In combining brand promotion with a social concern, the advertisements appealed for consumers to return their old unwanted clothes for recycling. In association with the International Red Cross, clothes gathered were sent to many problem areas.

Benetton remain unapologetic about their campaigns, claiming that all they ever wanted to do was help people to understand their point of view, recognizing that there will always be a cynical point of view and that they have never expected everyone to be with them on all issues.

Colours have a strong impact on peoples' feelings, moods, and thought processes. The corporation sponsors a range of sports that represent their values and interests of dynamism, loyalty, and competition. In 1991 a magazine entitled *Colours* was launched. The Benetton corporate brand personality is based on colours. The 'World of Colours' theme has rocketed Benetton to an international retail brand based on beliefs and values centred on equality and social responsibility. Members seek to influence those who dislike racial inequality and unfairness in the world. This 'cause marketing', which stresses harmony among the races, has been the basis for the long-term corporation–customer relationship.

It is the corporation that is seen as the presenter of a strong and extremely heterogeneous main message of pure emotion, for an existential generic positioning in the minds of consumers, that, nonetheless, is highly persuasive. Personal peer-group influence has augmented the frequent advertising. This social diffusion of the advertising message has been mostly by word of mouth, but also visually when customers are seen wearing the distinction label by others in their reference group. This promotional approach has been financially very successful worldwide, except in the USA. In the early 1990s profits world-wide grew by 24% but fell to nearly break-even in the USA, where many felt they overstepped the mark of decency.

The corporation saw rapid international development in the 1970s and 1980s, built on an elaborate network of suppliers, agents, and independent retail outlets, with a retail franchise based on a core marketing strategy with a clearly defined brand proposition. The network is a highly responsive supply chain distributing 50 million items of clothing each year, linked and supported by an international electronic data interchange system. The information system, managed by a subcontracted specialist facilities management company, has become the bedrock of their continued success by allowing continuous monitoring of global daily sales. This information is processed every day and analysis is translated into reprogramming of production. The lag between events in the shops and corporate response is kept to a minimum. Wikström and Normann (1994) point out that such a system is close to the idea of mass customization of products, and is leading to a blurring of the traditional functional distinctions between producer, marketer, purchaser, customer, wholesaler, retailer, media, supplier, and so on. Benetton operations are organized as a unique partner system between the central corporation and a very large number of subcontractors and around 6,500 franchised shops in 100 countries.

Founder Luciano Benetton and 200 staff tour the stores to exercise leadership and to gather personal impressions of trading conditions. Gummesson (1999) explains that this is both a close and distant relationship. There is lots of personal contact, state-of-the-art IT, and streamlined logistics in the network.

Marketing management decisions are based on fast learning about current customer response to products in-store, rather than on abstract ritualized 'market research'. Seemingly, it pays to be the expert and knowledgeable marketing operation for a complex network of small producers rather than trying to control the whole value chain in a fixed hierarchy. Supply chain management, both supply side and demand side, has been a source of defensible competitive advantage.

More recently, the photographer whose collection of photographs has been the basis of the long-running advertising approach has resigned from employment with Benetton. Now what will happen?

Do all stakeholders benefit from the particular managerial approach adopted in the Benetton network? Is the manner in which marketing communication is managed beneficial to all?

WHAT DO YOU THINK?

1 The verb 'appreciate' is defined in dictionaries as 'recognize', 'understand', 'be sensitive to'. How might this concept be applied in setting communication objectives?

2 Marketing thinking has long assumed that the supplier is dominant over consumers and customers. Increasingly, such hierarchical asymmetrical relationships are being replaced by symmetrical relating in which consumers are active problem-solvers. Why is this happening? Identify some market situations where customers are dominant.

3 Who needs to be the learner? How can marketing communication management provide learning mechanisms for the truly exchange-oriented business enterprise?

4 Much marketing activity would seem to be fairly superficial, even trivial. In what ways may the broader view of communicating be integrated into marketing management practices?

5 The broader range of marketing communication objectives suggested in this chapter includes connection, informing, persuading, learning, and inventing. All are aspects of cooperative interaction or interchange. Can you suggest others that might apply in particular situations?

6 Why is so much that is passed off as marketing actually rather cynical behaviour? How could this be avoided?

7 What are Benetton managers trying to achieve with their controversial approach?

8 Think of a market relationship that you have currently in which the intentions of the provider are more sophisticated than mere persuasion. What do they gain from this? Ask them if you cannot answer this question yourself.

9 What constitutes effective and efficient marketing communication?

10 Is (typically) mass communication theory appropriate in explaining and guiding all marketing activity?

FURTHER READING

Back, K. and Back. K. (1982) *Assertiveness at Work: A Practical Guide to Handling Awkward Situations*, London: McGraw-Hill Book Co. (UK).

Fromm, E. (1942) *The Sane Society*, New York: Rinehart & Co.

Fromm, E. (1978) *To Have or to Be?*, London: Abacus Books.

Gummesson E. (1999) *Total Relationship Marketing: Rethinking Marketing Management – From 4Ps to 30Rs*, Oxford: Butterworth-Heinemann.

Hall, E. T. (1961) *The Silent Language*, New York: Anchor Books.

Kline, S. (1993) 'Communication analysis for the age of marketing', chapter 2 in *Out of the Garden: Toys and Children's Culture in the Age of TV Advertising*, London: Verso, pp. 22–43.

Thayer, L. (1997) *Pieces: Toward a Revisioning of Communication/Life*, London: Ablex Publishing Corporation.

Varey, R. J. and Lewis, B. R. (eds) (2000) *Internal Marketing: Directions for Management*, London: Routledge.

Varey, R. J. (2000) *Corporate Communication Management: A Relationship Perspective*, unpublished book manuscript.

Vickers, G. (1984) *Human Systems Are Different*, London: Harper & Row.

Wikström, S. and Normann, R. (eds) (1994) *Knowledge and Value: A New Perspective on Corporate Transformation*, London: Routledge.

chapter
five

MANAGING WITH STAKEHOLDERS IN MIND

LEARNING POINTS

Careful study of this chapter will help you to:

- take a broadened view of the role of marketing communication in contemporary management

- consider the whole system of relationships that provides the context for exchange and communicative behaviour for marketing purposes

- examine the stakes that can be affected by marketing actions

> Surplus wealth is a sacred trust which its possessor is bound to administer in his lifetime for the good of the community.
> (Andrew Carnegie, 1889)

INTRODUCTION

Some critics of marketing practice have argued that marketing in modern society is no more than the seduction of people into dependence on marginal product benefits in markets concocted by corporations for profit. Products are offered through communication that is merely persuasive – the planned communication simply transmits the corporation's preferred messages.

Other social commentators have suggested that marketing communication can be dialogical interaction to find a distinct and 'visible' value-creating 'voice' among stakeholders. Values are offered in a participative process of co-constructing meaning, identity, and knowledge.

The societal marketing movement has sought to satisfy consumers and generate profits while also encompassing the interests of society. This requires marketing managers to widen their view of roles and responsibilities beyond their engagement with the particular group of customers that they serve.

THE MARKETING ENVIRONMENT

The marketing environment is a complex set of interacting people, processes, situations, and technologies, including the marketing corporation, that can significantly impact upon the nature and performance of the business enterprise. Typically, this system is examined in political, economic, social, and technical terms when managing marketing.

We can think of the total environment as a system comprising four sub-systems of ascending levels of complexity and distance or abstraction from the marketer. Rather like a set of Russian dolls, the corporation operates within markets, which are themselves within a stakeholder network, which is within the social network (Figure 5.1).

The micro-environment is the corporation and its close markets, whereas we may term the wider environment within which marketers operate as the macro-environment. Arguably, the micro-environment is controllable in managing marketing, but the macro-environment has a greater influence on the ability of the corporate members to fulfil their ambitions than they can exert on the more distant (in a number of terms) elements of the environment.

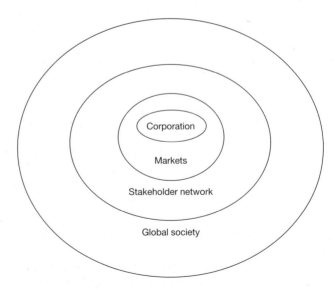

Figure 5.1 **Nested subsystems of society**

A business enterprise operates within the context of a network of people who have differing interests and stakes, often with conflicting motivations and values. The value star is a development of the value chain concept (modelling the organization of value production as a series of specialist transformations) that recognizes that a network of interdependent people have some stake in what the marketer does and why.

Nowadays, the stakeholder system should be thought of as a negotiated environment in which relationships have to be carefully managed. The corporation is only one of a set of publics that must maintain contact. The management task in the twenty-first century is to ensure mutually productive relating. This is highly significant for marketing, since the climate of these relationships – with customers, suppliers, regulators, shareholders, communities, professional groups, and so on – can strongly affect the performance of the enterprise in aspects such as brand image, product acceptance, customer service, competitor behaviour, employee relations, and corporate reputation.

AUDIENCES, MARKETS, AND PUBLICS

Many unsatisfactory situations arise (we tend to refer to many of these as 'communication problems') because the definitions given by one party of the other party are incompatible. For example, traditional 'corporate communications' treats the employee group as an audience, when the employed individual sees him/herself as part of a public.

An audience has a focus on and loyalty to the content or medium, and its members are consumers of the information, music, etc. This communication system operates on the basis of personality (of the 'performer'), its genre, and an author as source. The relationship is transient, based on some normative attachment through identification and involvement. A fan club is an example, as is a newspaper. The response sought from communication effort is primarily attention.

A market is an aggregate of individuals engaged in consumption behaviour that is calculative and concerned primarily with self-interest. A market is defined by the producer of a good or service through offer to consumers or users. Gratification is the primary motive for communicating. Product endorsement is an attempt by producers to shift the relationship into the audience mode.

A public forms normative ties (in a sharing mode) with a sense of identity and purpose, and is defined by its members. Communication is necessarily seen as arising through interaction. The primary motivation is conflict resolution.

These modes of relationship may be located within the internal environment of the corporation or span the boundary with the 'external' environment.

Our intended mode of relationship with another communicator (person, group, corporation) may be mismatched and dysfunctional. Figure 5.2 identifies some consequences.

Communicator one's intended mode of relationship

	Attention	Gratification	Sharing
Attention	*Each shouting across the chasm*		
Gratification		*Both ask them selves 'what's in it for me?'*	
Sharing			*Coming together to construct a mutually satisfying outcome*

Communicator two's intended mode of relationship

Figure 5.2 **Communication strategies: functional and dysfunctional interfaces**

We know from experience that as a party to intentional communication we do not always get what we set out to get or believe that we need from the interaction. Intentions are not always compatible. Do we then compromise, exploit, or negotiate? The field of social psychology deals with such questions.

When two parties come together to attempt communication, the internal structure of their communication system governs the outcome. We can consider the degree of social differentiation, the extent of social interaction, and existence of processes of normative control within the communicating system. These should form the basis for selecting a particular relationship mode and associated communication strategy. Far too often, however, the judgement is made with an introspective bias that considers only preferences or past experience.

STAKEHOLDING

A corporate stakeholder is a person who can affect or is affected by the accomplishment of corporate purpose (Freeman, 1984). When someone suffers a loss or receives a benefit from some action, they are a stakeholder. Carroll's (1993) stakeholder view of the firm requires that managers see stakeholder groups and their subgroups, at least until the legitimacy of claims and respective power have been examined, as both:

1. those who the management group thinks have some stake (an interest, right, or ownership) in the enterprise
2. those who themselves think they have some stake in the enterprise

It is then necessary to examine the nature of each relationship (in terms of duration, intensity, and function), as well as recognizing that some stakeholder groups also have relationships with each other.

According to Leaver (1995), 'capital' is the stock and flow of resources needed to produce outputs from inputs. In this sense, an 'investor' is someone who contributes in order to gain a return, and a corporate member is a steward of the resources and transformation processes employed to create value for the stakeholders. Thus, stakeholders are those who invest something in the enterprise (Table 5.1 and see Table 5.2).

Table 5.1 **Total stakeholder commonwealth**

Source of capital	Stakeholder ('investor')	What steward is accountable for	Stakeholder's pay-back ('bottom-line')
Human and intellectual capital	Workers	Know-how, brain use, effort, soul	Core competence
Social capital	Citizens	Talent, energy, and goodwill of citizens and their communities	Well-being of the community
Natural capital	Nature	Abundance of raw materials	Sustenance
Consumer capital	Customer	Buying power	Strength of truthful franchise in the market
Financial capital	Shareholder	Money	Profit

Source: Based on Leaver, 1995

Table 5.2 **Primary influence of stakeholders**

Stake	Shareholders, Directors	Employers, Owners	Dissident shareholders
Equity share	Preferred debtors	Suppliers Customers Employees Competitors	Local government Consumer lobby Trade unions
Exchange relationship	External directors Licensors	Regulators	Trade associations Environmental groups
Other influence	Formal control	Market forces	Legislation and regulation

Source: Based on Freeman, 1984

Freeman (1984) shows that it is important to identify those people who have a stake because they can be or are influenced by the policies and strategies of the corporation. He proposes that a stakeholder analysis be part of strategic management work, to identify who influences aims, objectives, and strategies. Table 5.2 shows an example of an analysis that identifies the dominant role and related influence of each stakeholder.

DO WE HAVE A STAKEHOLDER SOCIETY IN THE UK?

In the run-up to the 1997 general election in the UK, our major political parties each talked of their preferred society, based on capitalist economics, for the future. Each offered a vision of a relationship between corporate governance and national policy.

The Liberal Democrat manifesto spoke of the need to deal with a divided society, run-down public services, a fractured sense of community, and an underperforming economy. The Lib-Dem vision was for a more prosperous, fair and open society with the market economy delivering prosperity and distributing economic benefits. But market mechanisms on their own would not be able to ensure good services for everyone, or promote employment opportunities, or tackle economic inequality, or protect the environment. What they offered was a society in which every citizen shares rights and responsibilities to the wider community, with power and opportunity widely spread to avoid conformity and authoritarian centralized government. This 'citizen's society' would require active government which invests in people, promotes long-term prosperity and welfare, safeguards their security, and is answerable to them for its actions. Citizenship means political inclusion – writer Michael Ignatieff calls this the 'civic' model – a community of equal, rights-bearing citizens, united in a patriotic attachment to a shared set of political practices and values.

The Conservative plan was more about 'a people's share' of wealth created in an enterprise economy. To give greater public (vs. private) ownership of capital to the people, share ownership was to have been widened, with free shares for employees, more portable pensions, and the establishment of personal pension schemes for small firms.

Whereas the right's vision is for a 'shareholder' society, (New) Labour's 'stakeholder society' has at heart the interests of the many instead of the few – one nation, with shared values and purpose. Merit overrides privilege, and 'a government will govern in the interest of the many, the broad majority of people who work hard, play by the rules, pay their dues and feel let down by a political system that gives the breaks to the few, to an elite at the top increasingly out of touch with the rest of us' (from the 1997 Labour Party manifesto document). The vision promotes equal worth for all, with fairness and justice within strong communities. Ambition and compassion are to be partners not opposites. Public service is valued as well as material wealth. Many aims are held in common and people work together to achieve them instead of pursuing their own individual aims. The Labour government contract with the people is to work as partners with all people of the nation to rebuild a bond of trust so that democracy can flourish.

The stakeholder society pivots on the concept of inclusion – the individual is a member, a citizen, and a potential partner in a relationship with reciprocal obligations as well as rights. A stakeholder economy goes hand in hand with a stakeholder polity. Political reform is necessary. The (new) centre-left seek a partnership between government and corporations, at a time when power is shifting to big business. Perhaps that is the only way to have a hand in the power of the future? Some have argued that a stakeholder society is merely a reconciliation of the discipline of the free market with 'supply-side' socialism. Government then, through the law, protects the interests of those stakeholders who cannot do it themselves. Government is less intrusive, but civil order is retained. Perhaps we should consider the prospects for more of a culture of a corporate governance which recognizes that employees and customers, as well as shareholders, have a stake in an enterprise. Then we would not so willingly allow owners to leverage financial gain by treating people and their work as commodities to be traded for profit?

Will Hutton sees stakeholding as a different political economy of capitalism, with different assumptions based on a different value system – social inclusion, membership, trust, cooperation, long-termism, equality of opportunity, participation, active citizenship, rights and obligations. This is in sharp contrast to the political right's notions of opting-out, privatization, the primacy of individual choice, maximization of shareholder value, and the 'burden' of welfare and social costs. Large industrial organizations were bureaucracies who arbitrated between rival claims – a necessary function in any industrial economy, whether market capitalist or market socialist. Adoption of a stakeholder value system requires us to rethink the idea of a company as a network of reciprocal claims between customers, shareholders, employees, bankers, suppliers, and managers.

Critics claim that we have yet to see a clear definition of the 'stakeholder society' – they expect that it exists out there to be captured – merely the rebirth of post-flower-power corporatism. Perhaps they might wish to help to create a corporate community which truly distinguishes the negativity of selfishness from the constructivity of individualism through the promotion of a democracy which creates as well as presupposes shared values, giving everybody a sense of shared rights and responsibilities. The consequences of a quasi-democratic form of corporate governance could be staggering. Resolution of the business–society conflict could create a more productive form of free enterprise, better serving economic **and** social needs.

Surely, we must see that this question is fundamentally one concerning the nature of relationships in our society. Some critics have labelled Labour's vision as a return to a 'communitarianism'. If this means cooperation and communication, leading to accord, fellowship, and reciprocity, to supersede conflict, theft, and insecurity, then count me in.

One final question remains. As the global village becomes a reality through computer–telecommunications convergence, where does the corporate community reside? National borders are easily transcended by electronically mediated communication. If the citizen lives in one state, where does the corporation live? Nationalism based on kinship has been eroded by corporatism based on ownership. Where will this take us in the long run? Do we care?

THE THIRD- AND FOURTH-WAVE SOCIETY OF THE NEW MILLENNIUM

The nature of business and that of the society within which it is nested are changing. The world-views which characterize the outmoded (but still operational) industrial age (the second wave) and the emerging post-industrial age (the third wave) are characterized by Maynard and Mehrtens (1996) and discussed at length by Professor Bill Halal (1996) of George Washington University. Maynard and Mehrtens urge to think ahead into the twenty-first century when the fourth wave will emerge. These world-views are summarized below because their values, principles, and assumptions will have profound implications for the creation and management of systems of communication.

The second wave: 1750–1970 (approx.)

Mankind assumed supremacy over the environment and nature through exploitation. Values stressed separation, individualism, and competition, based on a drive for self-preservation. Success meant material gain – consumption required production. Business is the way to make a living. 'Consumeritis' resulted from winning by beating competitors – consumers were of secondary importance, so corporate imperialism resulted. Hierarchies of control and authority ensured that those who had power could retain it. Yet, all suffered from the denial of reality which sprang from co-dependence, in the pursuit of profit, efficiency, bigness, and growth.

The third wave: 1970 to early twenty-first century

In the third wave, values are shifting towards conservation, cooperation, balance, and sustainability. Team processes are emerging as ways to create value in projects to serve stakeholders – the new way to accomplish within limits to growth. Workplace democracy, collective learning, diversity, and self-management characterize the working environment, in which communication is open and direct, resulting in trust and collaboration for a shared purpose.

The fourth wave: from around 2030–50 onwards?

Corporations take on responsibility for a wider contribution to well-being – the business of business is no longer only business. Corporations strive to serve their stakeholders, with integrated business principles, environmental concern, personal integrity, and spiritual values. This stewardship takes effect within a democratic community which values participation and contribution in ethical decision-making and life is lived more intentionally. The collapse of 'privatism' is brought about by a quest for wholeness – interconnection and caring for all, based on honesty, truth, conviction, self-worth, and a concern for the quality of relationships and personal fulfilment. Business becomes the means to promote economic and social justice

Communication assumptions and styles will shift from dominance or passivity, to an assertive leadership in community.

THE INCLUSIVE COMPANY

Debate continues about that part of the overall management task having to do with the management of important relationships, and with communication with groups in these relationships. This 'sub-task' may be argued over by marketing, customer relations, and human resource management or public relations specialists. Its importance has been emphasized in recent years by the extensive study of the Royal Society for the Encouragement of the Arts, Manufactures and Commerce on the sustainable success of the company of the future (RSA, 1995).

The study report was the result of an enquiry lasting more than two years and involving some of the UK's most prominent companies. It aimed to stimulate competitiveness, offering a broad view of the possible sources of sustainable business success. The study concluded that an inclusive approach to business leadership, investment needs, people and society is needed for world-class business success. The approach requires companies to:

- clearly define purpose and values and communicate these consistently to all those people and groups who are important to success
- develop their own success models, drawing on stated purposes and values
- value reciprocal relationships, working actively to build these
- expect relationships to contribute to maintenance of a strong 'license to operate'

The RSA study concluded that the successful company of the future will be inclusive, that is, it will recognize and respond to the interests of those with a stake in a company's success, and will 'include' all such groups.

The part of management concerned with the management of relationships is public relations, which may also be described as: 'public affairs'; 'corporate communications'; and 'corporate affairs'. These terms do have different meanings: public relations is the practice of managing important relationships, and public affairs deals with relationships involved in public policy development (with government, political parties, pressure groups and the media, as they contribute to public policy debate), and with issues management. 'Corporate communications' recognizes the importance of managed communication in relationships and includes forms of communication used for corporate[1] purposes.

---

1 The term 'corporate' here is taken to mean the total social collectivity, as distinct from the minority dominant coalition or shareholder groups. Thus this is premised on a total system model of organizing.

The RSA study advocates inclusion, and values the interest of stakeholder groups. Where important internal stakeholder groups are involved, other studies have shown that they are more willing to come forward with ideas, feel able to express ideas, and trust the corporation to use rather than criticize the ideas that are put forward. Drawing in, and including stakeholders, means identifying them, and then using communication to establish a dialogue with them which allows for:

- the expression of interests
- clarification of interests
- conciliation of what may be conflicting interests

Communication is central to the approach of the RSA's study, and communication between people is the core of business activity.

Interdependence is not the same as unity

Communication enhances group effectiveness, partly by limiting the destructive effects of social dilemmas – situations in which members are faced with a conflict between maximizing personal interests and maximizing collective interests. Communication enhances cooperation. Increasing diversity and uncertainty increases the likelihood that people will concentrate on serving their own interests. Intelligent communication can offset this tendency for the benefit of all contributors. Carter (1999) is clear that management in the 'renaissance organisation' will be concerned to accomplish the 'alignment and co-ordination of individuals in such a way to enable them to make a high-value energy contribution to an organisation, both to sustain that organisation and to meet their own needs' (Carter 1999: 211).

The pursuit of economies of scale, which may lower prices but cost us in terms of remoteness and lost understanding, is being abandoned in favour of intimacy and understanding. Smaller units can be more symmetrical and exhibit reciprocity, embodying emotional range beyond mere abstract rules. The profusion of smaller units demands greater connectivity and thus more communication between as well as within groups. Paradoxically, as more connexity (interconnectedness) arises, people want membership of small cells (Mulgan, 1997). Thus society and its corporations are becoming cellular structures held together by communication.

MANAGING WITH STAKEHOLDERS IN MIND

Professor Bill Halal's 1996 study shows us that we are already moving past the idea that stakeholders are to be managed. Rather, what is now becoming the basis for management practice in many corporations is a recognition that, as we make the transition into an information age, stakeholders can be working partners in the creation of value.

All healthy social systems depend on reciprocity and are thus vulnerable to the abuse of reciprocal behaviour. All relationships entail some 'give and

---

BOX 5.1   ORGANIZATION DEVELOPMENT INTERVENTIONS

Likening the leadership role to that of the aircraft pilot, Labovitz and Rosansky identify four key aspects of the 'cockpit instrumentation' that must be attended to in avoiding serious pathologies of misalignment. Alignment arises when, simultaneously, a balance is achieved between strategy and people, and between processes and customers. Strategy must be developed and deployed, but must link with the needs and abilities of the people who work in the open system we call the corporation. This must be achieved while integrating customer needs with processes for continuous improvement in value creation and service delivery. Many tensions have to be overcome, and the design and operation of systems of communication is central to corporate performance. For example, increasing knowledge and task specialization drives differentiation, yet people relate to those who are most like themselves. We are building barriers to necessary cooperation into the corporate system ourselves!

The overall message is clear. True leadership creates consistency among corporate vision, goals, management systems, and incentive mechanisms. Alignment through communicative behaviour is the key.

Labovitz and Rosansky, 1997

---

take'. Mechanisms are needed to ensure that reward is taken in line with contribution. The manager as steward will have a greater significance. Mulgan (1997) has termed this requirement 'adult politics'. Maynard and Mehrtens (1996) consider biopolitics to be the adoption of environmental and biological awareness in order to be able to govern evolution.

CORPORATE COMMUNITY

One particularly central facet of the emerging context for management is the notion of co-evolution. This sees business operating in society under a holistic paradigm of people fully open to and supportive of each other, all forms of diversity embraced, a seamless connection between work and personal lives, and an integration of life and fulfilment of purpose to achieve preservation (Maynard and Mehrtens, 1996) and see Box 5.2.

This community provides a way of living and of doing business that supports the individual in the context of being with others. Community brings people together in place and time, and also removes the defensive barriers

---

BOX 5.2   DEFINITIONS OF COMMUNITY

A group of individuals who have learned how to communicate honestly with each other, whose relationships go deeper than their masks of composure, and who have developed some significant commitment to . . . make others' condition their own.

A group of people and a way of being.

M. Scott Peck, 1987

---

that stop people from opening up to each other. Bonding arises through a sense of mutual trust and reliance.

Corporate community is the new form of organization governance that shifts emphasis from profit to democracy by unifying the goals of all parties – by focusing on the needs of the corporation's constituents. The old profit-centred model of business is too limited because it ignores the reality that business is both an economic and a social institution. Corporate governance can evolve towards collaboration among all stakeholders. The shift from profit to democracy requires the creation of a coalition of investors, employees, customers, business partners, and the public. Such a corporate community can serve all interests better.

The onset of a knowledge economy has made cooperation efficient and thus there is no longer a need to consider business as a zero-sum game in which one party gains at the loss of another. The capitalist theory that profit is the driving force of economic progress is at last being challenged. The question is no longer whether to focus on making money or on serving society.

The old model required a focus on serving the interest of shareholders. The interests of employees, customers, and other stakeholders were not really goals of the company, but simply a means to meet the interests of shareholders – to make money. If the goal of enterprise is to make money, then the interest of business is opposed to the interests of society.

Even the concept of 'corporate social responsibility' has not remedied the problem. It has proved useful in educating people in business about their social obligations, but in focusing on social service, the economic realities of productivity, revenues, and profits have been ignored.

In recent years, however, major changes in corporate governance have been underway. Collaboration with stakeholders is now occurring as they gain power and because managers need their support. Institutional investors have become more involved in the management of large corporations, including 'ethical investors'. Employee participation, often in the form of shareholding, has grown significantly, especially in the USA. Feminist moves are becoming more influential in business, thereby bringing cooperative, community-oriented values into management practice. Other social constituencies have gained influence in recent years: relationship marketing to build trust and commitment with customers in long-term relationships; partnership agreements with suppliers and government; voluntary moves to protect the environment; and so on.

Halal proposes a stakeholder model of the corporation (1996: 64), which views the corporation as a socio-economic system composed of various equally important constituencies: employees, customers, suppliers, the public and its government representatives, and investors. Each stakeholder has obligations to the corporation as well as rights. This view is gaining wide acceptance because managers realize that they need the support of these groups. Halal's return-on-resources model shows that all stakeholders invest financial and social resources, they incur costs, and expect gains – these resources are their stake in the organization (see also Heath, 1994, chapter

6, for a discussion of negotiated enactment of stakeholder interests). Halal's analysis leads to a theory of the nature of the firm:

> Corporate managers are dependent on stakeholders because the economic role of the firm is to combine as effectively as possible the unique resources each stakeholder contributes: the risk capital of investors; the talents, training, and efforts of employees; the continued patronage of customers; the capabilities of business partners; and the economic infrastructure provided by government.
>
> (1996: 67)

In this view, managers act as stewards engaged in a 'social contract' to draw together this mix of resources and transform it into financial and social wealth, which they can distribute among stakeholders to reward their contributions. The closer the integration into a cohesive community, the greater the wealth. Stakeholders have different interests according to their unique roles in the corporate community. These interests can be reconciled if they are organized to create a more successful enterprise. The goal of business, therefore, should be to serve the public welfare of all stakeholders.

There are some problems to be resolved in putting this into practice, but there are compelling reasons why the transition will occur:

- the liberating power of information
- the benefits of cooperation
- the rising aspirations of people
- democratic ideals being extended into everyday life
- the new business model offers increasing productivity and social benefits, without clashing with the profit-centred model of business – it is a logical extension which helps to resolve the 'cultural contradictions of capitalism'.

(Bell, 1974)

The industrial age was characterized by analysis that rationally broke down complex problems into constituent parts, which then required hierarchical structures to coordinate these diverse parts – the age of specialism and division. The information age has the opposite need: the synthesis of disparate nations, social diversity, and other fragmented subsystems into a balanced, integral, functioning whole (Halal, 1996).

What is needed is a balance between internal markets and corporate community:

> the marketplace fosters competition, a focus on profit, individualism, diversity, and constantly shifting relations – while community encourages co-operation, social welfare, unity, equity, and commitment.
>
> (Halal, 1996: 88)

Rather than seeing all others as sources of conflict and competition, in which desired resources must be won, many managers are seeing their other stakeholders as providing a 'licence to operate'. Halal (1996) demonstrates that business is a socio-economic institution in which democracy and enterprise can operate harmoniously if there is cooperation between the various stakeholders who balance their various interests and responsibilities. This requires cooperation. When business is about dividing the finite 'pie', it is competitive; when it is concerned with creating the 'pie', then business is cooperative.

Halal (1996) provides considerable evidence of a fundamental shift from rigid bureaucratic forms of business organization towards organization around changing clusters of entrepreneurial units working together to form 'internal markets' which are integrated into a 'corporate community' that unites the interests of investors, workers, clients, business partners, and the public. Managers create the organizational structure, communication channels and activities, and financial systems that support the internal enterprises and stakeholders, connect them together, and coordinate their functions (Halal, 1996: 91). Moore (1996) has spoken of 'total system leadership' in place of outmoded competition.

CONCEPTS OF COMMUNICATION AND COMMUNICATION PURPOSE

When hierarchy and control were the only sensible way to run a business enterprise, we accepted the frustrations of delayed and distorted communication, and islands of local coherence set in a wider sea of poor cooperation, as the inevitable character of big 'organizations'. We envisioned our workplace as a huge machine with ourselves as small cogs. The new engineering and science of electricity and computers gave us a pipeline notion of 'communications' messages that could cascade down reporting lines. Things, we can readily observe, are changing.

Mulgan sums up the rally call for the new management of the connected future world:

> In a democratic culture . . . people expect some engagement in the causes they give their life to, even if their engagement comes through the contract of work. They expect their emotions and motivations to be engaged. If the work is creative, or uncertain, or if it demands that they respond quickly to the needs of customers in ways that cannot be clearly specified, then it is essential that something beyond narrowly defined function should bind them into the organisation [sic]. If communication is richer and more ubiquitous, then it is natural that it does more than pass down commands or pass up results, but rather communicates emotions and desires too.
>
> (Mulgan, 1997: 243)

If some of us can achieve this vision, then we will have become good managers and good at being managed. Such should be the desire of the designers and managers of our corporate communication system of managing human relationships.

Communication will be easier in the fourth wave, because the point of view of each person will be honoured, allowing the individual to discover what similar values, standards, and expectations he/she shares. We will progressively abandon communication as a tool for acting upon people. Communication will become conceived of as a process for active participation in the construction of identity, meaning, and knowledge.

MARKETING CHANNELS AND NETWORKS

In recent years, managers and scholars in the field of marketing communication have come to view the channels through which products are accessed by consumers and buyers as networks of coordinated distribution activity. As we have seen from our stakeholder perspective, these networks (often referred to as markets) are also intimately part of the wider stakeholder system. The crucial point to grasp about this perspective is that the actions of each member of the network more or less impact on many other members, and not only those to whom they are directed. The network is a web of interdependent and reciprocal relationships (Achrol, 1997). This view fits well with the recent notion of relationship marketing that we will examine in chapter twelve. A distribution channel is thus a performance network coupled with a support network, whose members assist in satisfying customer needs in order to accomplish their own purpose.

This network perspective is important because it recognizes that the position of a marketer is determined by his/her couplings to others and the identity of those with whom he/she relates. Communication must be managed if these necessary relationships are to be maintained and enhanced. The value star (see Figure 4.6, p. 81) is a contemporary model for the network of collaborating partners who work together to provide end-customer satisfaction. Of course, some of the people in the network will have conflicting interests and motivators. Within the value star, the marketer will try to add value by managing the performance of the generative, productive, and representative systems of the corporation. The stakeholder system is a negotiated trading environment. Marketing action will be required and will be effective to the extent that relationships are mutually productive. The state of the relationships can exert a powerful effect upon brand image, product acceptability, service quality, reputation, and so on.

CASE STUDY 5   LISTENING AND RESPONDING

In 1996 Shell International began extensively auditing the views of stakeholders: customers, employees, other companies, governments, non-government groups, and all those affected by their operations and products. Managers as decision-makers have a role to play in helping to ensure that the legitimate aspirations of all the stakeholders involved – government, communities, business and others – are recognized and addressed in a balanced, fair manner for the long-term benefit of all.

In 1999 – a corporate communication campaign was launched to start up a dialogue with their stakeholders about the critical economic (commercial), ethical (social responsibility), and environmental (sustainable development) issues of the business. This dialogue had become necessary because of changing expectations. In the past, Shell companies had met society's expectations and had an excellent reputation. But greater scepticism and questioning were now raising concerns about Shell's work and values, and how managers were discharging their responsibility to society – in return for a societal 'licence to operate'. Greater engagement through dialogue was necessary to deal responsibly with the knowledge gap that had developed between their values and those that their various stakeholders believed they held and managed by.

The approach to engagement through dialogue was designed to operate on the basis of direct and personal contact (relationship), reaching out among stakeholders to seek and value others' views, transparency and openness through performance reporting, and verification by independent experts and other ways to ensure independent assurance.

Active communicating about the issues and the corporation's point of view has been progressive over the past two years. The stakeholder forums have produced intensive discussion and debate between staff and stakeholder representatives. The corporate website was redesigned and relaunched in late 1998 to include publications, statements, news, and e-mail. The 'Profits & Principles' global television advertising campaign began in the spring of 1999 to stimulate debate and comment.

Up to the time of writing in early 2001, the programme has revealed a positive shift in stakeholder views, and the corporation have demonstrated that they are committed to be better at communicating by listening and responding.

(See www.shell.com)

WHAT DO YOU THINK?

1 Who are the main stakeholders for your place of study? Try to rank them in order of importance. What criteria did you use?

2 Do you believe that Benetton's unique advertising approach (see chapter four) adds value to its brand image and sales performance?

3 To what extent has the network management approach helped Benetton to prosper in difficult trading conditions in Europe? What have been the gains for stakeholders?

4 How can marketers ensure that their decisions and actions do not adversely impact upon stakeholders?

5 Societal marketing was the first step to relationship-oriented marketing, according to Ken Peattie (1992). Do you accept this point of view, or was relationship marketing the precursor to societal marketing?

6 The essential nature of marketing is the organized response to consumer and buyer needs and wants. How must marketing communication management practices change in a stakeholder perspective?

7 The entire marketing system (i.e. the organized deployment of the marketing concept in the overall business process) involves various forms of communication among a number of people. Apply a stakeholder framework to review the marketing system of a company with which you are familiar, from a communication perspective. List implications for managers.

8 To what extent are corporations focusing their objectives and decisions on social added value? What evidence can you find?

9 Why should marketing managers consider stakeholders?

10 How does stakeholder management relate to relationship marketing and integrated marketing communication?

FURTHER READING

Andersson, P. (1992) 'Analysing distribution channel dynamics: loose and tight coupling in distribution networks', *European Journal of Marketing* 26 (2): 47–68.

Button, J. (1988) *A Dictionary of Green Ideas: Vocabulary for a Sane and Sustainable Future*, London: Routledge.

Halal, W. E. (1996) *The New Management: Democracy and Enterprise Are Transforming Organizations*, San Francisco, CA: Berrett-Koehler.

Moore, J. F. (1996) *The Death of Competition: Leadership and Strategy in the Age of Business Ecosystems*, New York: John Wiley & Sons.

Peattie, K. (1992) *Green Marketing*, London: Pitman/M&E Handbooks.

RSA (1995) *Tomorrow's Company*, report of the inquiry of the Royal Society for the Encouragement of the Arts, Manufactures and Commerce, London.

Wheeler, D. and Sillanpää, M. (1997) *The Stakeholder Corporation: A Blueprint for Maximizing Stakeholder Value*, London: Pitman Publishing.

chapter six

INTERCULTURAL COMMUNICATION

LEARNING POINTS

Careful study of this chapter will help you to:

- identify contemporary marketing as an essentially intercultural communication system

- recognize aspects of culture that are major intermediaries of meaning-making in contemporary society, and their significance in marketing communication management

- appreciate the manner in which words, pictures, and products have social value – their meaning is particular to the culture in which they are apprehended

A lot of trouble is caused by combining a narrow mind with a wide mouth

Anon

Look beyond your own culture

Julian Cope

INTRODUCTION

Deregulation, including the abolition of trade barriers, together with accelerating changes in communication and computer technology have reinforced the movement towards the globalization of business in an integrated market. Increasingly, producers compete in an international market, while markets themselves are becoming transnational. Germany and Japan have overtaken France and the UK as economic leaders, while the European Union matches the USA as an economic power. Latin America is putting forward vibrant economies. The four tiger economies of Singapore, Taiwan, Hong Kong, and South Korea, along with China, India, and Indonesia are accelerating. The world's focal point of economic weight and performance is shifting. There is no longer an East separated from the West.

Technological advances have rendered national boundaries more open. While states retain sovereignty, governmental authority is eroding. The corporation is colonizing more of our lives, although not everyone lives in the world of media communication. In 1992, for example, annual sales of General Motors and Exxon each exceeded the gross national products of Saudi Arabia, Indonesia, Norway, Pakistan, Nigeria, and Egypt. Travel to almost any city and you will be able to find a McDonald's outlet and pervasive Coca-Cola advertising. Foreign cultures and lifestyles are exposed through transnational media. Money and information now flow around the globe. Corporations are buying, selling, and investing in the growth regions – without having to relocate people. Consumer buying patterns are changing, so that Nike wearers have more in common with each other than with their parents or cultural background. Global marketing is heading towards homogeneous buying patterns. Thinking globally requires understanding markets in terms of sources of demand, sources of supply, and methods of management and marketing.

Corporations may operate at one or more of several levels of cross-cultural business. The following categorizations are based on the work of Bartlett and Ghoshal (1991):

- **domestic marketing**: customers and competitors are located within the corporation's own culture and geographic/national boundaries
- **export marketing**: some products and services are sold to customers in other national and cultural territories
- **international marketing**: as above, the focus is domestic customers, while 'foreign' customers are offered the standard marketing 'mix'
- **multinational marketing**: overseas business is a portfolio of independent contributors with their own marketing mixes
- **global marketing**: overseas activities are seen as paths to a unified market with a single marketing mix
- **transnational marketing**: overseas activities are regarded as operating in a complex network of coordinated cooperative management, flexibly deploying global resources to best serve local markets

Communication in an international arena is now almost impossible to avoid, and indeed is highly desirable both economically and culturally to expand contact between satisfiers (providers) and needers (consumers and buyers). Of course, this all started a long time ago (around the thirteenth century in Western Europe, for example).

Similarity of people greatly facilitates friendly relationship – this is why intercultural marketing is a special challenge. When people see others as dissimilar, competition tends to arise in place of cooperation.

CULTURE AND MARKETING

Trading is a universal way of living a life. We should not be surprised, therefore, that marketing has apparently been readily adopted in almost all countries. But we should be aware that the marketing concept arose in the USA and has been borrowed and adapted when integrated into different cultures (Usunier, 1993).

Marketing is social – an exchange process based on communication. Thus, we need to understand how cultural background influences communication and exchange. Indeed, the very notion of communicating differs among cultures. Consider the nature of relationships, communication, and other social phenomena in Anglo-Saxon and Asian cultures. It is important when importing marketing as a word and as a slogan of developing economy, that the cultural roots and precise meaning of the concept are not forgotten. Ironically, perhaps, marketers operating in intercultural environments are often unaware of the cultural origins of their craft. Not everyone sees marketing as rational and logical. For some, including customers, the value is in the irrational art.

As Professor Usunier points out (1993), intercultural marketing implies commerce. The reintroduction of the term commerce into management talk emphasizes the social interaction between provider and consumer/buyer (see also Barabba and Zaltman (1991) and Prus (1989) for further discussion of this interactionist relationship-oriented style of marketing) rather than the ritual of strategy.

CULTURE AS COMMUNICATION

There is little doubt that culture significantly affects communication:

> it determines the time and timing of interpersonal events, the places where it is appropriate to discuss particular topics, the physical distance separating one speaker from another, the tone of voice that is appropriate to the subject-matter . . . Culture includes the **relationship of what is said to what is meant**.
>
> (Hall and Whyte, 1960: 6, authors' emphasis)

Based on the work of Edward T. Hall (1961), we can identify ten ways in which culture is expressed in human behaviour. These provide ten 'languages' that may be used when communicating with potential customers.

According to Hall, culture is not constituted as a simple whole. There are ten areas of human activities that combine to produce culture (Figure 6.1). These he calls 'primary message systems'. They are closely connected to each other. We can not only investigate each separately, but also examine how they work together to form a culture as a whole system.

Interaction	Temporality
Association	Learning
Subsistence	Play
Bisexuality	Defence
Territoriality	Exploitation

Figure 6.1 **Hall's primary message systems**

All things that people do involve interaction with something or somebody else. One of the most elaborated forms of interaction is speech. Association refers to conventions that govern the groupings of people and the roles that people play, rank and hierarchy, class and formal organization, and so on. Subsistence means the processes by which a society satisfies the basic physical needs of daily life and the attitudes towards such matters as food, drink and work. Bisexuality is concerned with both the way the sexes are distinguished and the relationships which are permitted between them. Territoriality refers to conventions which govern the division of space between people and its allocation for different purposes. Temporality is concerned with conventions which govern the way that time is constructed and used. These conventions govern when to do things, in what order to do them, and how much time is allowed for doing each of them. Learning refers to the conventions that govern being taught and teaching. Play is concerned with whatever a society regards as entertaining, for example painting, music, literature, sports, games, etc. Defence refers to protective activities or techniques which the individual and the community need, not only against potentially hostile forces in nature, but also against such forces within human society. Exploitation is concerned with how to develop and make use of resources.

Hall suggests that each of these message systems communicates at formal, informal, and technical levels. Formal behaviour patterns are mostly learned in childhood through rules and warning. Informal behaviour patterns are learned through imitation, usually out of the awareness of both learner and model. These are usually subconscious rules of behaviour until broken. Technical learning occurs at a high level of consciousness.

Hall proposed a general theory of change: change moves from formal to informal to technical levels, and then, perhaps, to a new formal level (i.e. the change is circular rather than linear). For example, consider the message system of exploitation. A change in the concept of comfort (formal) may cause a change in resource use (informal) which may require a change of technology (technical). But what if the technology is not changed? Over a period of time, a change in the concept of comfort may arise.

The marketing management task is to identify which informal adaptations are most successful in daily operations and to bring these to the technical level of awareness. This requires a change agent – perhaps a salesperson or members of a reference group (see Box 6.1).

BOX 6.1   CULTURE, LANGUAGE, AND COMMUNICATION

Cultural background, language, and ways of communicating differ among people. This problem is complex because language influences culture and culture influences language. Language creates categories in our thinking, which influence what we judge to be similar and what should be differentiated. Our way of observing, describing, interacting with and constructing reality are thus determined. Also, vocabulary has its own capacities and limits.

CROSS-CULTURAL CONSUMER BEHAVIOUR

Consumers buy meanings and marketers (consumers and providers) communicate meanings through various forms of communication media, including products and advertisements. These meanings are co-produced in social groups.

Culture provides a set of rules for how people will interact in exchange relationships – what constraints and ways in behaviour and decisions are acceptable.

Consumption decisions are largely determined by the culture of the marketing environment. Consequently, marketing management objectives and strategies are affected by cultural values and norms.

At least four cross-cultural factors should influence marketing strategies (Figure 6.2).

There is cross-cultural variation that cannot be ignored, even though in general terms consumer behaviour has strong universal elements. In fact, even the models, theories, and so on, of marketing vary between cultures. However, let us simply identify several points at which the cultural influence of consumer behaviour impacts on marketing management considerations.

Dominant values may determine which needs are to be attended to as priorities and in what manner their satisfaction may be sought. Consumers may not be autonomous in making purchase and consumption decisions. Consumers may not be free to act individualistically. Institutionalized cultural conventions structure daily life and determine consumption behaviour. We have examined eating in chapter three, for example. Loyalty to brands and providers is not a universal given. Not all consumers enjoy stability or change. The involvement of consumers in product purchase or consumption differs

Customs and values	Differences in attitude to time, place in society, age, materialism, achievement, and so on, will result in differences in product preferences and product use
Language	Language is the means of communicating the customs and beliefs of a culture. Subtleties of vocabulary and dialect are often not easily translated
Symbols	Cultures are particularly sensitive to meanings associated with particular colours and the accepted social meaning of symbols
The economic environment	Standard of living, economic infrastructure, and economic policies influence consumer behaviour

Figure 6.2 **Cross-cultural factors to be accounted for in marketing management**

among cultures. Perceived risk differs among cultures, as does cognitive style, i.e. how consumers reach decisions and are influenced by their environment.

Basic cultural assumptions have been identified in a number of studies:

- what constitutes personal and what does not
- patterns of time
- attitude to action, and the significance of information
- self-concept and concept of others
- individuality and collectivity
- basis of reality

Multiculturalism is not only a global characteristic. Within many countries (for example, Japan), there is considerable homogeneity, while in others multicultural markets (North America, for example) are found. Thus, even corporations operating locally, regionally, or nationally will have to deal with differences in at least kinship and family patterns, religion, education systems, time-related organization patterns, valuation of the individual and the group, friendship patterns, criteria of aesthetic appreciation, and work and leisure expectations and habits.

The cross-cultural analysis of consumer behaviour is essential to a growing number of marketing managers, especially as they are increasingly required to operate within global business strategies. Engel *et al.* (1993) suggest six specific tasks in seeking to understand differences and similarities in the behavioural aspects of cultures, from the point of view of what consumers think in the particular consumer/buyer group (Figure 6.3).

A qualified understanding of consumption behaviour, marketing, and management at a global level is far more important than knowledge of selling

Relevant motivations in the culture	What needs do buyers/consumers see as fulfilled by this product? How are these met? Do they readily recognize these needs?
Characteristic behaviour patterns	How is the family structured? How are roles determined? Frequency of purchase? Pack sizes usually purchased? Does the product performance conflict with usual behaviours?
Broad cultural values relevant to the product	Are there relevant strong values around work, morality, religion, family relations, etc. Does the product suggest conflicting values? Can the product be identified with positive value?
Characteristic forms of decision-making	How do people reach decisions? How are innovations received? What information sources are important? How are alternatives evaluated?
Appropriate communication methods	What is the role of advertising? What words, ideas, and images are taboo? Who would be acceptable as a salesperson? What language problems might arise in translation?
Appropriate institutions for the product, in the mind of consumers	What types of outlets are available? What services are expected and are they available? Should changes in the distribution structure be made, and will they be accepted?

Figure 6.3 **The analysis of cultural differences and similarities in consumer behaviour**

or sourcing in several particular countries. The limited thinking of your own local markets can be termed ethnocentric (i.e. clannish and exclusionary) and leads to business failures when necessary standardizations and adaptations are missed. What works at home almost certainly will not work elsewhere in every case. Recently, Coca-Cola has fallen foul of local preferences for traditionally brewed beverages in Russia. Yet, even the culturally particular (i.e. very British) Fawlty Towers comedy show (starring John Cleese and Andrew Sachs) has been hugely popular in other countries (Manuel, the waiter, was converted to an Italian for the Spanish market).

INTERNATIONAL STRATEGIES

Standardization of advertising and other communication activities is attractive, particularly in terms of cost, and when TV airtime is considered. This is less so for press advertising, where, unlike TV, production costs do not almost equal broadcast fees. Table 6.1 briefly summarizes the four general situations in which decisions about product and communicating about it have

Table 6.1 **International communication strategies: standardize or adapt?**

	Same product	Different products
Same communication	Product and use is the same	Product formulation differs
Different communication	Product need differs, but use is the same	Different needs and product use

to be faced (interested readers are referred to fuller discussions of this issue elsewhere). The term 'communication' refers here to style, format, content, objectives, etc.

Most brands do not travel well between cultures (you can think of some exceptions to this). There continues to be a debate about when to standardize (extend) and when to adapt to local culture.

Cultural and media differences need to be taken into account when planning a marketing communication programme. Failure in this key management task will produce unpredictable and possibly damaging results, and at least will waste scarce budget and resources.

Differences in language, symbolic meaning, and the aesthetics of products and promotional activities and associated materials can have an immediate and direct effect on the outcome of any effort to communicate.

Family, work, politics, religion, and communication technologies provide reference points to people, and differences in them can alter the meaning of messages.

Values are perhaps the most understood of the factors to consider, with major insights derived from a large-scale study by Hofstede (1981, 1991). Although care is needed because the interviews and surveys were conducted twenty years ago (much has changed), only among IBM employees, and its generalizations could lead to stereotyping, this study showed that cultures differ in the degree to which individual versus group interests are emphasized. Languages differ in context. A high-context use of language provides information through the speaker's identity and behaviour, leaving many things unsaid because they are generally understood (Asia). A low-context use of language relies much more on the choice of words spoken (Western Europe) (see Figure 6.4). Power–distance is a measure of the degree of authority. Authority figures play a leading role in decision-making in some cultures, whereas information is sought in others for reasoned decisions. High uncertainty-avoidance cultures rely on formal rules and expert advice.

Studies of culture and advertising industry conditions in a range of countries (Zandpour & Harich, 1996) showed that countries differ in their receptiveness to advertising messages. Some respond to logical, rational, information-based appeals, whereas others are more receptive to emotional and dramatic appeals. Advertising in Western cultures emphasizes individualism, comparison and competition, whereas Eastern cultures emphasize status, emotions, indirect expression, and the avoidance of comparisons.

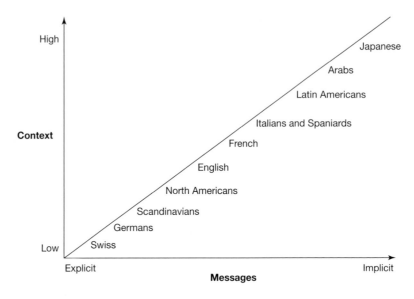

Figure 6.4 **Messages and context in various cultures**

Communication media are not uniformly available to consumers and buyers. Major restructuring of the media industries is being driven by technological development and deregulation. International networks of media companies are evolving and the concentration of ownership is increasing. The result is much cross-ownership of a range of media, allowing one-stop-shopping for media buyers on an international basis.

BOX 6.2   ACCOMMODATION THEORY

In part, the question of whether or not to adapt advertising and other communication activities to local cultures can be addressed from the point of view of accommodation. What might be the consequences of adapting or not adapting our choice of language, vocabulary, imagery, and other aspects of our communication patterns? Simply put, accommodation in our communication behaviour is the conscious adaptation by one or more persons of their style, content, and means of communication to that expected and referred to by the other(s).

When people believe that another person is like themselves, they are more inclined to like them. Thus, accommodation theory suggests that constructive communication is most likely to occur between people who present themselves as similar in the way they behave and treat the other. This is an especially important problem when communicating with members of minority groups (who, by definition, are dissimilar to the majority).

This way of thinking suggests that marketing messages should not be translated between languages but should be designed specifically with each culture in mind, to harness the differences rather than to try to minimize them. Standardization within an international market segmented by actual cultural differences is a sensible option.

Setting a strategy

Standardize when:

- buyers have similar characteristics, so that brand images and propositions have universal meaning
- local programmes of communication activity lack resources, experience and expertise, and cooperation can provide competitive advantage
- widening media and travel experiences allow a strong brand image to develop
- the central management group requires control of creative input, planning and implementation, freeing local managers to run the programme
- economies of scale can be accomplished in media buying, packaging, and so on
- message consistency and integration can improve cost-effectiveness.

Adapt when:

- consumer and buyer needs differ, and experiences generate different meanings
- the infrastructure needed to support the necessary communication objectives and actions varies with location
- educational levels (literacy, etc.) vary
- local regulations reflect differing economic, social, and political concerns
- a lack of the sense of ownership by local managers may jeopardize the programme – local managers may be more motivated to support locally developed plans

INTERNATIONAL ADVERTISING

While advertising experts generally agree that the advertising task is the same in most markets – to provide information and persuasive appeals – specific messages and media strategy may vary from country to country. The words, symbols, illustrations, and so on may have to be selected to match the market. People and their motives may be very similar, but the ways in which we satisfy our needs are not. Demand for particular products, and the appeals that promote sales and use, are determined largely by specific cultural and socio-economic characteristics. The overall message conveyed, the product image, and media characteristics may vary between countries.

Advertising is dependent on the cultural and linguistic attitudes of the local people, but is also a privileged method of cultural borrowing, mirroring changes in social behaviour. Not everyone sees the value of advertising – some believe that it is wasteful (see Davidson, 1992, for example). As we shall see in chapter fourteen, comparative advertising is frowned upon in some cultures, and may even have been made illegal. Cultures also differ in the primary role attributed to advertising: persuasive, informative, or dream-oriented (the latter is favoured in French and Italian advertising, for example, where escape from reality is emphasized).

Advertising designed specifically for a culture will usually be superior to that imported from another. Good campaigns are expensive to produce, however. Therefore it seems to make sense to test an advertisement in another country before beginning from scratch. Local people who have an intimate knowledge of the market should, of course, handle final copy and media selection decisions. For marketing communications managers, the critical questions are when and when not to make adjustments to a standard campaign.

CASE STUDY 6 FROM SNICKERS ABOUT KNICKERS TO WORLDWIDE SNICKERS: THE MARATHON IMPACT OF A NAME CHANGE

Have you ever wondered why the Snickers malt, peanut and caramel bar is called Snickers?

In the 1980s, Managers at Mars Inc. in the UK changed the name of their well-known Marathon Bar (one of Mars' three mega-brands) to Snickers to fit within a global brand name communication strategy. First manufactured in 1930, Snickers became the number-one selling candy bar in the USA.

For years there had been no advertising – Mars managers had let the product 'sell itself'. In 1989, the world-wide rights to use the Chuck Berry song 'Satisfaction' (made famous by the Rolling Stones cover version) were purchased for $2m. During the 1994 football World Cup, some 34 billion viewers saw the Snickers name as major sponsor – made possible only by the globalization of the brand. During the Euro 1996 football championship, Mars sponsored the tournament and ran promotional advertising in several countries in Europe. The viability of a number of ideas was assessed by brand managers in each country, and it was decided to run the following strap line only in the UK because language translation would cause problems in meanings: 'Snickers – tackles your hunger in a big way' (described in Smith, 1998). Mars have for many years made efforts to link candy and health: 'A Snickers really satisfies'. In the 1980s, advertisements featured athletes eating Snickers bars. Mars paid $5m to make M&Ms 'the official snack food of the 1984 Olympic Games'. Before the advent of satellite TV, jet travel, and the Internet, people didn't see advertisements when run in other countries. Once Mars chose to sponsor the 1984 Olympics, they needed to harmonize their brand presentation on wrappers, and in their advertising and sales promotions. The name change became inevitable – prior to that decision there was no brand that could be advertised at the Olympic events (for the benefit of TV coverage) that could be recognized in every nation. Snickers continued the programme by later becoming world-wide games sponsor in 1988 and 1992, with vast expense on Olympics-related brand and product promotion.

Earlier, the Snickers bar had been known by many different names, e.g. Marathon in the UK. Many years earlier, Forrest Mars Senior had changed the name because it rhymed with knickers (a 'rude joke' word in the UK) – he didn't want consumers to make the association – but he did want to conquer the world with snacks! In the 1990s, all the major Mars brands were relaunched with one name and the same advertising message in all countries. The smaller selling brands are still marketed on a local level, giving Mars the flexibility needed to respond to national tastes while allowing capitalization on economies of scale when marketing the big selling 'flagship' brands.

By continuing to pursue the business objective of brand leadership through very efficient high-volume production (avoidance of niche markets) and strong advertising, Mars has built Snickers into a sponsorship (stand-alone) brand. By adopting a single brand identity, economies of scale are possible in sharing the promotion investment world-wide and in intensive product distribution. Mars do not seek corporate growth through innovation, but rather through global expansion. On Thanksgiving Day 1990, during the Gulf War, for example, frozen Snickers bars were to be found on every US soldier's plate, along with the turkey and reconstituted potato.

In Russia, on the other hand, things didn't go so well for a while. The brand name became the butt of comedians' routines after a series of poorly dubbed US advertisements were heavily scheduled on TV. At the time, people in Russia simply were not comfortable with TV advertising, and the poor quality of the presentation caused more irritation than amusement. Today, Snickers is the number-one selling candy bar in Russia. In Peru, also, Snickers is very popular.

A study by Lavenka (1991) showed that the name Snickers has considerable brand equity. When given six different unwrapped, unlabelled chocolate bars to taste, the Snickers bar was by far the preferred product on the basis of flavour. When the brand names were revealed, the rating increased considerably. When the bar was revealed in its point-of-sale wrapping its rating increased again, although only marginally. The (Cadbury's) Bounty bar was actually downrated when its name and wrapper were revealed.

So, does a global brand communication programme work for Mars? According to David Badger (Mars), 'There is no question in my mind [now] that our major brands, Mars, Snickers, Twix, M&Ms, know no boundaries. The consumer demand for sweets is universal' (quoted in Brenner, 1999: 286).

One thing is clear. Snickers is a successful product. With annual sales of $400m, Snickers is big! The brand is still the best-selling candy bar in the USA, despite consistently losing market share since 1994. A witty new advertising campaign was launched by BBDO in autumn 1996. Sales increased as the brand advertising was made more entertaining, less didactic, creating more emotional connection with consumers.

(See www.snickers.com and www.mars.com and Brenner (1999))

WHAT DO YOU THINK?

1 Which brands **are** apparently consistent across intercultural divides? Why is this so?
2 Communication can be thought of as a form of industrial production. Explain this point of view.
3 There is no such thing as international marketing, only local marketing around the world. Do you agree, and why?
4 Take the example of a product which is familiar to you and which has been 'imported' from another culture. What adaptations, if any, have been made and how successful have they been?
5 Can you find an example where international marketing efforts went

wrong? In what ways did they say the wrong thing and did they fail to understand the culture they were trying to connect with?

6 Discuss some practical issues around the notion of consistency and flexibility at global and regional levels of marketing communication.

7 Coca-Cola, Unilever, Toyota, and others, are successful around the world. How do they manage this?

8 From a communication perspective, distinguish 'international' from 'global'.

9 Communication may be explained as 'informational' and 'transformational'. Consider the issues raised when these conceptions of communication are applied in intercultural marketing communication.

10 Since marketing is simply a purposeful system of communication, why do textbooks on marketing rarely deal with intercultural social interaction?

FURTHER READING

Anholt, S. (2000) *Another One Bites the Grass: Creating International Ad Campaigns That Make Sense*, London: John Wiley & Sons.

Barabba, V. P. and Zaltman, G. (1991) *Hearing the Voice of the Market*, Cambridge, MA: Harvard Business School Press.

Bartlett, C. and Ghoshal, S. (1991) *Managing Across Borders: The Transnational Solution*, Cambridge, MA: Harvard Business School Press.

Davidson, M. (1992) *The Consumerist Manifesto: Advertising in Postmodern Times*, London: Routledge.

Hall, E. T. (1961) *The Silent Language*, New York: Anchor Books.

Hofstede, G. (1991) *Cultures and Organizations: Software of the Mind – Intercultural Cooperation and Its Importance for Survival*, New York: McGraw-Hill.

Levitt, T. (1983) 'The globalization of markets', *Harvard Business Review* 61 (3): 69–81.

Naisbitt, J. (1994) *Global Paradox*, London: Nicholas Brealey Publishing.

Prus, R. (1989) *Making Sales and Pursuing Customers*, Newbury Park, CA: Sage Publications.

Robock, S. H. and Simmonds, K. (1989) *International Business and Multinational Enterprises*, 4th edn, Homewood, IL: Irwin.

Usunier, J.-C. (1993) *International Marketing: A Cultural Approach*, New York: Prentice-Hall.

Varey, R. J. (1999) 'What the world needs now is . . . better intercultural communication', *Professional Manager* 8 (8): 16–19, London: Institute of Management (reprinted by the Open University as part of a reader for the MESOL programme for healthcare and social services managers).

chapter seven

THE MARKETING MIX AS SOCIAL COMMUNICATOR

LEARNING POINTS

Careful study of this chapter will help you to:

- consider some important aspects of managing marketing communication
- learn about the various facets of a product offering that are attended to by managers, and by buyers and consumers
- re-examine the marketing mix in a more holistic manner that identifies marketing's social functions
- encourage a shift in thinking of marketing communication as mass communication to a more relationship-oriented style

Communication is the most important form of marketing
Akio Morita, co-founder of SONY

INTRODUCTION

The widely accepted 4P classification of 'marketing mix' tools offers managers a simple framework for organizing marketing decision subjects around possible actions, and judgements on the objectives, interactions, and restrictions of a range of available tools for accomplishing marketing and business goals. Instead of limiting our thinking about marketing communication to a set of promotional activities, as is usually the case, we can think of the entire marketing mix as communicative in pursuing exchanges of value that match needs with capabilities to provide.

Marketing communication is an invention for the purpose of bringing about exchanges of value that are beneficial to people. The framework provides a range of logically connected activities for the generation and expression of knowledge in a variety of forms. Marketing communication is ultimately about the purposeful trading of ideas.

The aim is to bring two of what Vickers would explain as appreciative systems (see chapter three) together to interact in striving to accomplish the satisfaction of their respective needs. Thus two parties will apprehend aspects of their environment, interpret the data into information that has meaning for them, make a judgement, and decide how to act. The – what is usually termed – 'market research' is, to some degree, a systematic effort to learn about a situation in terms of needs as motivators, alternative ways of satisfying those needs, and relationships as the context for need-satisfying action. Persuasion then is intended to influence beneficially the consumption and purchase activity.

We recognize that marketing communication can be observed from two perspectives. From the provider's point-of-view, they can deploy various tools in an effort to intervene in the consumption and purchase behaviour of those with whom an exchange relationship is, or various reasons, desirable. From the consumer/purchaser's perspective, marketing communication is a way of expressing their motivation to fulfil their needs, as well as one of a number of sources of data to be selectively interpreted, judged, and acted upon.

Each party takes into account his/her own needs and the likely motives and actions of the other, to some degree, in **appreciating** their situation.

We have an intimate interest in the success of marketing communication effort. We are all consumers, and most of us are employees of enterprises that have to sell at a profit to stay in business. The social value of marketing is the meaning of what product providers do.

Because marketing communication, especially advertising, is such a public form of communication, we have to be clear that we pursue objectives and organize activities that are consistent with a socially responsible purpose (Figure 7.1).

With so much public communication activity, we can sometimes lose sight of what happens when people spend so much time reading, listening to, and hearing various types of mass media content. Perhaps it would be more responsible of managers to pay more attention to the use that people make of the 'mass' media that carries so much of their effort. Just when does advertising and publicity become propaganda (see Figure 7.2 and Box 7.1)?

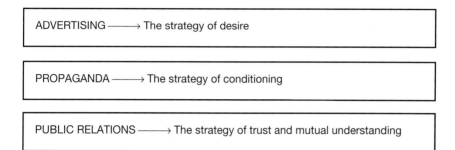

ADVERTISING ⟶ The strategy of desire

PROPAGANDA ⟶ The strategy of conditioning

PUBLIC RELATIONS ⟶ The strategy of trust and mutual understanding

Figure 7.1 **Marketing communication motives**

News	Factual reporting of 'real' phenomena that break the normal flow of events
Advertising and publicity	True accounts that often present a more advantageous version than actual reality in order to elicit consumption, biased to the interests of the initiator
Commercial propaganda	Along with indoctrination, socialization to a particular point of view, biased to the interests of the initiato

Figure 7.2 **Modes of marketing communication**

BOX 7.1   COMMENT: INFOMERCIALS AND ADVERTORIALS

Infomercials and advertorials have blurred the distinctions between what is reported news, what is advertising, and what is merely commercial propaganda. Today, the editorial process may be less an expression of the journalist's views or an account of 'fact' than the painting of a company or product in favourable light.

THE ELEMENTS OF THE MODERN MARKETING MIX

Traditionally, the marketing mix is seen as a collection of tools to be used to elicit desired responses from target markets in pursuit of business objectives. But, until fairly recently, almost all marketing communication textbooks discussed only the 'promotion' element, and most did not even equate this with the wider concept of communicating. Mostly, promotion has meant persuasion to buy, rather than provocation to exchange. Recently, a more holistic conception of marketing communication has been brought forward with the advent of the integrated marketing communication approach (that begins to recognize a convergence of marketing and public relations into a more strategic management framework).

The 4P system is the traditional classification of the marketing mix. It reminds managers of some basic principles and is easy to remember. It is also lacking in clarity. The 'promotion' (the Latin root 'promo' means to bring forward) element really has two dimensions: communication and persuasion (and not all communication has the purpose of persuading or selling). Are the 'mix' elements activities or objects (i.e. tools or instruments)? How are the properties or characteristics by which elements are classified actually specified? Does not sales promotion overlap with advertising and personal selling and with the product, price, and place categories? Should product really cover products so as to reveal cost, sales, and competition interdependencies among a range of products? Does the marketing mix coincide with marketing functions and the associated marketing objectives?

Grönroos (2000) explains the limits of the marketing mix way of thinking about the marketing needs of a business. Efforts have been made to elaborate usefully the 4P framework to better deal with the managerial problems of service business (see, for example, the 7P model of Booms and Bitner).

Mostly, even today, marketing communication is taken to be only promotional and persuasive message-making and broadcast. We take a much broader approach in this book (Box 7.2).

BOX 7.2   AN ALTERNATIVE DEFINITION OF MARKETING COMMUNICATION

The managerial system that ensures timely and comprehensive input to the corporate information and decision-making (generative) process, and the consequent production and expression of credible, persuasive representations of beneficial exchange opportunities with actual and prospective customers and other stakeholders. Marketing is thus the interface element of the corporate appreciative system.

The buyer/consumer's point of view on an exchange

Our excursion into buyer and consumer behaviour in chapter three introduced some ideas on linking communication, thinking, and action in an attempt to identify things that can be managed in a marketing process. Here we take another look at the, often implicit, questions asked by a person as they move towards a purchase activity. How do they arrive at recognition of the possibility and desirability of a particular exchange?

- What is my need?
- What/who will satisfy this for me?
- Who is offering something appropriate?

- How will it satisfy my need?
- Which option offers the best value with an acceptable level of risk?
- When?
- Where?
- How much will it cost me?

The provider's point of view on an exchange

In trying to understand consumer and buyer behaviour, the manager is trying to anticipate such questions and to influence the answers in order to create an exchange. The traditional notion of the marketing mix is a detailed definition of the decisions to be made on a range of facets of an offering (sometimes referred to as the value package). The manager has to ask:

- Who do we wish to trade with?
- Why?
- What is their need?
- How can we satisfy it better than competitors?
- How best can we make an offer to them?

Marketing functions and management decisions

Remember that we have defined the business enterprise system as a knowledge transformation system that creates and provides value. In essence, the manager has to ensure that activities and decisions logically include the definition of a need satisfier, the translation of the consumer's or buyer's need into the language of the production system in order to invent a technical means of producing and delivering the promised and agreed value. Throughout this generative and productive process, representation of particular knowledge is necessary in purposeful interaction.

van Waterschoot and Van den Bulte (1992) identify four generic marketing functions for engaging in actions that can consummate exchanges (see Table 7.1). Marketing functions are intermediate outputs of the marketing system that lead to outcomes, while activities or tools are inputs. The manager should pay attention to the function of each marketing and communication tool. Any classification should be based on how mix elements are used, rather than on any inherent characteristic (that might determine how to use them). The various tools may or may not be promotional, depending on how they are used. It seems that managers most often assume that they are promotional and thus use them for that purpose. But what other purposes or functions might the various tools serve?

Each tool has a primary (basic) role in the consummation of an exchange, as well as a complementary role. Some tools have a fixed contribution over a long period, while others are applied for a short period as additional (situational) incentives to move the exchange forward.

Promotional communication is intended to create awareness, construct knowledge, and motivate purchase. Persuasive communication effort is

Table 7.1 Generic marketing functions [primary concern shown in brackets]

Function	Tools used or activities performed
Configuration of something valued by the prospective 'exchanger' [product design and production]	Market research, design, trial and testing, modification, etc.
Valuation of the compensation and sacrifices the prospective exchanger must make in exchange for the offering [financial aspects]	Cost–benefit analysis, trial and comparison, etc.
Facilitation of the exchange by placing the offering as accessible to the prospective exchanger [provision]	Retailing, delivery, installation, mail order, online ordering, telesales, markets, etc.
Symbolization of the offering to bring it to the attention of the prospective exchanger and to influence feelings and preferences about the offer [promotion]	Advertising, personal selling, demonstration, samples, models, etc.

Figure 7.3 **Sales promotion bridges the communicative marketing mix elements**

undertaken to overcome a lack of awareness, a lack of credibility, or to change the preference structure of a 'chooser'.

We see in Figure 7.3 that sales promotion is not a separate aspect of the promotion category of tools, but rather an underpinning bridge. What are often termed sales promotion tools are tactical situational adaptations that support the strategic aspect of the offering – usually the product itself. For example, the buyer's need is mainly fulfilled by the product features as benefits, but in certain cases a high price can satisfy the status needs of a consumer, as can the use of an exclusive distribution network or advertising the brand through a highly regarded medium. Sales promotion acts to overcome barriers to purchase action. Buyers experience a sense of risk about acting in certain ways, in terms of psychosocial, well-being, financial, and time costs. Sales promotion tools trigger action by providing situationally

Table 7.2 **The basic marketing mix (above the line)**

The offering	Description	Examples
Total product	Tools to satisfy the needs of the prospective exchanger	Product feature options, brand name, packaging, guarantee
Total price	Tools that fix the size and way of payment exchanged for the product	Price list, payment terms, discounts
Total distribution	Tools that determine how the products are available to the exchanger	Merchandising, advice, profit margins
Impersonal communication	Announcement of the offer and maintenance of favourable feelings and removal of barriers to purchase, including third-party endorsement	Themed advertising, sponsorship, permanent exhibition, press releases and conferences, journalist visits
Personal communication	Announcement of the offer and maintenance of favourable feelings and removal of barriers to purchase, including third-party endorsement	Selling efforts, rewards

Source: Based on van Waterschoot and Van den Bulte, 1992

Table 7.3 **The supplementary and complementary promotion mix (below the line)**

Promotion	Description	Examples
Product	Inducement to immediate action by strengthening the basic product offering for a short period	Special offer multi-packs, temporary extra features
Price	Inducement to immediate action by strengthening the basic price offering for a short period	Sales, temporary discounts, coupons
Distribution	Inducement to immediate action by strengthening the basic distribution offering for a short period	Sales contests, additional POS (point-of-sale) materials

Table 7.3 (*continued*)

Promotion	Description	Examples
Impersonal communication	Inducement to immediate action by strengthening the mass communication of the basic offering for a short period	Advertising, competitions, samples, exhibitions, all efforts to generate favourable media coverage
Personal communication	Inducement to immediate action by strengthening the personal communication of the basic offering for a short period	Salesforce contests, temporary demonstrations

Source: Based on van Waterschoot and Van den Bulte (1992)

specific direct inducement to purchase. They do not alone bring about an exchange.

Tables 7.2 and 7.3 are adapted from van Waterschoot and Van den Bulte's (1992) enhanced classification of the marketing mix. They are keen to stress that 'promotion' is a set of inducements and is not a sub-mix of the traditional promotional mix which is here termed overt communication. It must be noted, very importantly, that in this revised marketing mix system all of the four categories of tools are communicative: product, price, and distribution are covert communicators about the offering. Components of the marketing mix serve various functions:

- **generative marketing communication** activities include: market research, product design, new product development, research and development, product planning, market testing
- **representative marketing communication** activities include: advertising, pricing, branding, various sales promotion inducements
- **productive marketing communication** activities include: manufacturing, servicing, distributing, delivering, tailoring, configuring

It seems that, often, the interaction of mix elements is a problem, producing undesirable effects:

> Too often a company will imply one thing about its product in its mass-media ads and contradict it at point of sale, deny it with its direct-selling tactics, and muddle it with its product service policy . . . In short, the communications job which advertising and good product design so laboriously and expensively undertook is scuttled by the customer's actual experience with the many other communications the company send out. The overall message that will finally have got through to the customer will be self-contradictory and confusing instead of self-reinforcing and reassuring.
>
> (Levitt, 1962)

When unintended meanings arise in the minds of consumers and purchasers, apparent contradictions will undermine the credibility (and thus believability) of marketing communication activities. Levitt called this tendency for business activities to shift away from the intended as centrifugal marketing. When specific objectives are accomplished with specific customers, centripetal marketing is practised. This requires coordination of intended and unintended communication to ensure consistency and coherence in positioning and actions.

The primary job of the marketing manager is to manage the attraction, satisfaction, and retention of those customers whose exchanges contribute to the profits of the business. This requires attention to management practices, marketing activities and associated means, and the key relationships within which communication is the **mode** of management and marketing. Thus we can think of the marketing mix elements as communicators. Table 7.4 outlines the communicative effect from the consumer/buyer perspective and highlights the manager's intention. By thinking of the marketing mix as a system of communication, we emphasize the interlocking nature of the various aspects of tangibles and intangibles that 'say something' to consumers/buyers. So, each marketing mix decision should be considered to be a problem of communicating with consumers so that a satisfying exchange will arise.

As Table 7.5 suggests, the successful marketing communication management programme will enable and facilitate the economical and convenient meeting of customer and provider needs.

One important problem that faces the marketing manager is that of matching the marketing mix to the position of the provider and customer – all marketing management decisions must consider the provider–customer relationship and not either the provider position or the customer position in isolation. Maile and Kizilbash (1977) examined the ability of marketing communication activities to persuade consumers. Persuasive communicative acts are attempts to influence buyer actions. These marketing communication interventions feature some degree of discrepancy or attitude gap. A provider of goods and services expresses a position on an issue with rational or emotional argumentation. Their credibility as a provider stems from how believable their messages are in terms of the expected veracity. Newly established unknown providers have low credibility, while prominent, long-established providers have high credibility. An attitude gap exists when there is a discrepancy between the consumer's initial attitude and that advocated by the provider. The buyer's self-esteem is their sense of their own value and worth.

Research has shown that low-credibility providers can maximize their profit by trading with low-esteem buyers, while high-credibility providers should trade with high-self-esteem buyers. Persuasiveness increases with credibility. The marketing manager wishes to know which buyers to make offers to and how much to deviate from traditional forms of product, distribution, price, and promotion.

The degree of deviation of the offer from the expectation of the buyer will affect the degree of persuasiveness. Low-esteem buyers should be offered

Table 7.4 **Communicative aspects of the marketing situation that can be decided by the marketing manager**

The offering[a]	What this can communicate	Example
Product mix		
Variety	Personality	Choice of colours
Quality	Integrity	Fine detail and finish
Design	Taste	Aesthetic appearance
Features	Flexibility	Dual purpose
Brand name	Assurance	Meaningful name
Packaging	Protection and care	Carrying case
Sizes	Consideration	Range of options
Services	Support	Installation and demonstration
Warranties	Peace of mind	Telephone hotline
Returns	Confidence	Pre-paid mailing label
Price mix		
Cost of product	Expectations of quality	Premium price relative to others
Discounts and allowances	Value for money	Special offer voucher
Payment period	Affordability	Instalment plan
Credit terms	Cost	Interest-free period payment
Place mix		
Channels	Convenience and status	Respected outlets
Coverage	Availability	Stocked by prominent stores
Assortments	Choice	Range of colours, etc.
Locations	Convenience and status	High-street stockist
Inventory	Availability	Always in stock
Transport	Availability	Prompt home delivery
People		
Service staff	Competence	Confident, attentive checkout
Physical environment		
Ambience	Comfort	Tasteful decor

Process

| Transaction | Impression | Prompt attention |

Making the offer

Advertising	Identity	Clearly stated valuation
Publicity	Expertise	Comment on social issue
Sales promotion	Value	Buy 2, get 1 free offer
Direct marketing	Personalized offer	Follow-up offer
Personal selling	Attention and concern	Problem resolved

Note: [a] This list of mix elements is based on Kotler, 2000; and Dibb *et al.*, 1999

Table 7.5 **The marketing mix as a communication system**

	Marketer's intention	*How consumers might 'read' this*
Product	Positioning on benefits that creates attractiveness and preferences	A solution to a problem or way of satisfying a need
Price	Enhance intention to buy by creating attractive value for customers	The cost of acquiring the solution or satisfaction
Place	Adequate availability and service to facilitate purchase	Convenience
Promotion	Create awareness of product and its benefits	Connection

conventional products, outlets, media, and price levels by low-credibility providers. High-esteem buyers can be attracted with highly innovative offerings by high-credibility providers.

The limits of the marketing mix approach

Arising from mass-market consumer goods marketing management, the 4P marketing mix approach was suitable for managing in growing markets and exchange did not require considerable interaction between consumer and producer. Transaction marketing was productive, and still is – in some situations. However, as markets have matured, as competition has increased, and as both have moved to a global environment, the attraction of exchangers (customers) has ceased to be adequate.

The relatively recent shift in attention to recognizing the interactions between provider and buyer (discussed more in chapter thirteen), has identified customers as relationship partners. The marketing mix framework does not tell the whole story of management decisions and Grönroos (2000) has pioneered the notion of interactive marketing. This requires attention to matters that are not best explained by the 4Ps. The shift in thinking is from exchange to relationship, or sequences of (perhaps connected) exchanges within a relationship. The focus is on the value-creating process rather than merely on outcome. Promises are made and given – and fulfilled – mutually. Thus, many facets of the required decision-making for the management of the relationship fall outside of the marketing mix framework.

THE TRADITIONAL COMMUNICATION TOOLS

The role of each traditional communication 'tool' was to sell – by attracting attention, promoting and persuading, prior to making the sale. We here argue that this is only part of the whole story, which has two aspects:

- **Asking**: eliciting views from consumers and buyers (i.e. understanding the consumer/buyer need for a product).
- **Telling**: informing and reminding to raise awareness of the product for inclusion in the decision set, to persuade for acceptance, and to prompt purchase action (i.e. selling the product to increase the level of business and to accelerate the diffusion process).

This is on an ongoing dialogue between provider interests and consumer/buyer interests, which is represented by Figure 7.4.

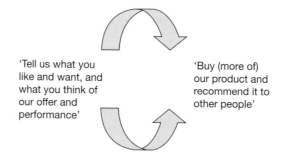

'Tell us what you like and want, and what you think of our offer and performance'

'Buy (more of) our product and recommend it to other people'

Figure 7.4 **Desired responses to marketing communication**

The degree of organization of such communicative events varies considerably in different situations, depending on the nature of the competitive environment, consumption pattern, and product attributes and benefits (Table 7.6).

Today, the fact that there are so many options available for impersonal communication means that this has become in many ways the defining style of communication. It seems that interpersonal communication, for many, is for special occasions only!

Table 7.6 **Some examples of the range of marketing communication styles**

	Personal	Impersonal
Informal	Consumer-dominated: face-to-face conversation	Internet 'chat room'
Formal	Market research focus group	Marketer-dominated: advertising

BUYER STATE

If we imagine, from the provider's point of view, that each consumer or buyer is mentally located along a continuum of purchasing readiness from total ignorance at one extreme to brand ambassador at the other, we can attempt to select communication means that are suitable for the communication objective set (Table 7.7).

The general roles of the main means of promotional communication are suggested in Figure 7.5.

Advertising	Immediate effect on awareness, with delayed effect on sales due to learning curve of customers
Publicity	Continuous background effect of making other communication efforts credible
Personal selling	Immediate effect on sales
Sales promotion	Immediate effect in stimulating impulse purchases

Figure 7.5 **Contributions of main means of marketing communication**

COMMUNICATING IN MARKETING CHANNELS

Communication in marketing channels can enable people to persuade, inform, foster participative decision-making, coordinate programmes, exercise power, and encourage commitment and loyalty. When things go wrong and there is no appropriate communication strategy, manufacturers and resellers can suffer exclusion from decision-making that affects them, misunderstandings, inappropriate actions, and dysfunctional feelings of frustration.

Communication moderates distribution channel conditions (which may be structural and behavioural, such as the pattern of exchange relationships, power, climate, etc., for example in contracted trading) and channel

Table 7.7 **Aligning communication objectives and means with mental preparedness**

Buyer state	Behaviour	Communication objective(s)	Main tools
Naïve	Problems and solutions not recognized	Educate to create awareness	Information and demonstration
Ignorant	Your brand not included in their decision set	Attract attention	Promotion, sample, and advocacy
Hobo	Drifts from one problem/solution to another	Attract attention	Special offer discounts, free trial
Promiscuous	Shops around	Build preference	Special offer discounts, free trial, bulk purchase bonus
Pathological	The purchase event itself is the objective	Attract attention and motivate to action	Sale events, prominent retail location, easy ordering service
Committed	Loyal	Assure	Show other satisfied purchasers/users
Advocate	Loyal and influential	Assure and motivate to action	Reward for word-of-mouth recommendation, discounts for linked purchases
Professional	Expert purchasing on behalf of others	Remind and motivate to action	Regular personal selling meetings, online (automated) reordering, online catalogue

management outcomes (such as member coordination, satisfaction, level of commitment, performance, and so on, as represented by Figure 7.6 and Table 7.8).

Research has shown that channel outcomes are enhanced when:

1. a collaborative communication strategy is pursued in relational, supportive, symmetrical channel conditions
2. an autonomous communication strategy is pursued in transactional, unsupportive, asymmetrical channel conditions

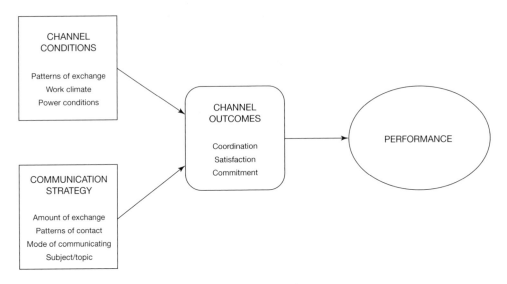

Figure 7.6 **Influences on distribution channel performance**
Source: Based on Mohr and Nevin, 1990

Table 7.8 **Communication strategies in differing channel conditions**

Collaborative communication strategy	*Autonomous communication strategy*
Interaction is frequent and prolonged with bi-directional flows of data through informal media, and direct efforts to change behaviour through requests, recommendations, promises, and appeals to legal obligations The structure is relational (joint planning, long-term perspective on high interdependence) with a supportive climate and a symmetrical balance of power.	Interaction is infrequent and mostly uni-directional and formal, concentrating on indirect efforts to change the beliefs and attitudes about the desirability of intended behaviour with no specific request for action (e.g. discussion of general business issues and operating procedures) The structure is centred on discrete exchanges on an ad hoc basis with a short-term orientation and low interdependence

Source: Based on Mohr and Nevin, 1990

Thus, managers can make decisions about how to manage communication with other members of the distribution channels upon which they depend for access to buyers and consumers. We will examine relationship marketing and compare it with transactional marketing in chapter twelve. Figure 7.7 shows how marketing communication bridges the gap between producing and offering and exchanging.

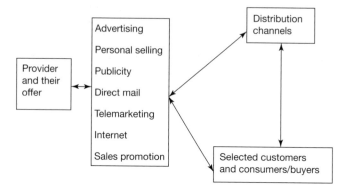

Figure 7.7 **Interaction of exchange parties is a dialogue**

All of the decisions and activities of the marketing system require the application of Covey's golden rule for social competence:

seek to understand before seeking to be understood.

INVESTING IN WORD-OF-MOUTH PROMOTION

The one-step flow model of the role of opinion leaders, opinion formers, and opinion influencers (Figure 7.8) is, of course, an oversimplification and views consumers as passive receivers of information. It is, however, useful in highlighting the mediating role of media and the way in which communication between the provider and the consumer/buyer is often indirect and again mediated by third parties. This helps to explain the value of publicity and public relations, as we have seen in chapter five in looking at the marketing environment as a web of stakeholders. We will revisit this issue of the interdependence of marketing and public relations (both communication management disciplines) in chapter ten.

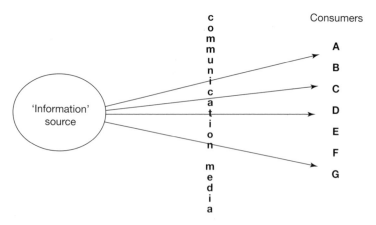

Figure 7.8 **The one-step flow model of interpersonal communication**

The two-step flow model is an elaboration that tries to explain better what happens when people talk to each other about products and providers (Figure 7.9). Person C is an opinion leader. Persons A and B have been exposed to a promotional message and look to C for further information in the form of opinion and advice. Person C reinforces the impact of the information received directly from the provider. For persons D and E, however, person C is the original source (they did not see the advertisement or meet the sales representative).

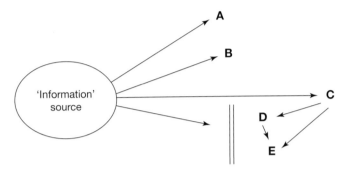

Figure 7.9 **A model of two-step interaction**

Of course, this is still an oversimplification. The 'flow' of information (which is really the co-construction of meanings, identities and knowledge) or pattern of interaction may arise through several stages. Williams (1981) suggested the need for a multi-stage model.

People in society are at once individuals and in transaction with their environment (just like corporations). Thus marketers, and other managers of communication, must avoid seeing an 'audience' as simply a 'lump of humanity', and focus attention on individual mental states (attitudes, beliefs, past experiences, self-concept), typical responses (activity levels, sense of humour, learned modes of adjustment, locus of control), and role-related behaviour.

We must also consider those circumstances of marketing-dominated communication (advertising) and those that are consumer-dominated (face-to-face conversation). In planning persuasive communication (remember, by this we mean taking-into-account as well as being taken-into-account), it is apparent that personal influence can be a major factor in determining the outcome of interactions.

CONSUMER VS. BUSINESS TO BUSINESS

Throughout this book, we refer to 'consumers' and 'buyers' to make the distinction between those who purchase for their own use and those who purchase on behalf of others, while recognizing that it is in both cases always people who purchase products. The major differences in marketing communication approaches is in recognizing the differing environments and tasks of the decision-makers and purchasers that create different information needs. Whereas consumer advertising can appeal directly to consumers who make their own purchases, business-to-business information provision leads to contact between a buyer and a seller. The content, style, etc. of communication activities must be designed to match the needs of people who will communicate in order to find satisfying exchanges (Table 7.9). Marketing communication managers must develop a sensitive understanding of consumers and buyers as purposive communicators.

Table 7.9 **Characteristics of marketing communication management**

Programme feature	Consumer relationship	Business-to-business relationship
Communication context	Informal	Formal
Number of decision-makers	One or few	Many
Dominant tool	Advertising and sales promotion	Personal selling
Content	Emotions and imagery	Rational, logical – information
Decision period	Short	Long and involved
Scope of impact of dissatisfaction	Limited to a few people close to the purchaser/consumer	A range of people in the value system
Marketing approach	Targeting and segmentation	Limited targeting and segmentation
Budget priority	Brand management	Sales management
Evaluation and measurement	Extended range of techniques	Limited use of techniques

Table 7.10 illustrates the need to allocate expenditure to appropriate activities for the nature of the buying–selling situation, and that this judgement is dependent on the type of product.

CHOOSING COMMUNICATION ACTIVITIES

Today, more than at any other time, we have a proliferating cornucopia of tools and connections for communicating. For the manager, this presents both a wide choice and a dilemma: which of all possible means of communicating are appropriate and affordable? Table 7.11 attempts to

Table 7.10 **Illustrative budget allocation by type of goods**

	Advertising	Publicity	Sales promotion	Personal selling
Consumer: low value – chocolate bar	50%	10%	25%	15%
Consumer: high value – car	35%	10%	25%	30%
Industrial: low value – office supplies	20%	10%	25%	25%
Industrial: high value – machinery	10%	10%	25%	55%

suggest some important bases for judging the effectiveness and efficiency of marketing communication means (note that many are also used in public relations, including communication among employees of the providing corporation, and also among consumers and buyers).

The manager needs to ask and answer a set of questions from a communication perspective before making decisions about activities that will intervene in purchase and consumption:

- How well do we hear the voice of our customers, and other consumers and buyers?
- Can these people talk to us about their interests and ours in a manner that is attractive to them and to us?
- What is our style of communicating?
- What do our designs, brand name, literature, advertising, information, etc. say to these people about us?
- Do we excessively dominate and control through our communication activities?
- Are we assertive, aggressive, or passive?
- How consistent are the messages we intend with those that our customers, other consumers and buyers, and other stakeholders construct from our words and deeds?
- Do we have an efficient, coherent system for communicating?

Box 7.3 provides an example of communication as interaction.

Table 7.11 **Relative suitability of communication means**

	Advantages[a]	Disadvantages
Generative activities		
Market research	Fosters interaction with consumers and buyers. Generates new ideas	May produce minor product changes in competition with other offerings
New product development	Can involve customers. Develops productive capacity of the provider. Can lead to differentiated offerings	May result in product proliferation. Can be risky for first provider of innovative product
Representative activities		
Advertising	Simultaneous communication with many people – multiplicity of media channels allows greater precision in targeting	Simultaneous communication with many people. Media are expensive, especially broadcast TV
Publicity	Low cost, relative to advertising. Can be received credibly	Diffuse and indirect
Sales promotion	Boosts short-term sales performance	Erodes profits and undermines brand value through lowered price
Personal selling	Complex co-constructions of problem definition and solution can be negotiated in direct interaction, with personal commitment	Expensive, although telesales (rather less personal) is increasingly used
Demonstration/exhibition	Tangibilizes (makes tangible) the product benefits	Attendees may not be prepared to purchase. Can be costly
Direct mail	With detailed and accurate databases, advertising is unnecessary	Some people see it as intrusive
Sponsorship	Promotes the interests of the provider by associating with an event or cause	Can be expensive, with no direct measurable payback. May backfire if the event or cause comes under criticism

Brand identity	Brand name, logo and slogan can create a mental bond between the product and the problem or unsatisfied need	Can confuse consumers and buyers
Packaging	Can reinforce corporate and product identity and add value	Can be wasteful
Point-of-purchase materials	Can influence consumers	Can be expensive and may have only single episodic impact
Merchandising	Can generate income in its own right – customers pay for your advertising	Can be seen by consumers as exploitative
Word-of-mouth	Doesn't cost anything (usually because it is not invested in!)	A failure can be very costly to reputation and purchases
Corporate identity	Can differentiate provider so as to stand out from the crowd	May conflict with product values
Internal communication	Coordination of the value chain system for designing, producing, and delivering customer value	May distract attention from customer value
New media – the Internet	Personal media obviate the need for advertising	May be a fad that excludes some important stakeholders

Note: [a] To both marketers – providers and consumers

BOX 7.3   TAKE A SPIN ONLINE[a]

Introduced in early 2000, the interactive personal website is designed to provide a 'one-stop shop' for all the motoring needs of Peugeot owners. Registered users can access their own 'My car' profiled site to:

- receive e-mail notices in advance of service due dates;
- be notified of renewal dates for car tax, insurance, and MOT;
- order information on the latest finance deals and product offers;
- request car brochures and current prices;
- arrange a test drive;
- buy accessories online;
- get a valuation of their car from *Glass's Guide*
- get tailored information on a range of topics, including traffic news, hotel guide, etc.;
- request a call from the call centre.

Rapport is mailed to Peugeot owners four times during the year. A supporting 'Peugeot Open-line' is provided on 0345 565556.

(See the Peugeot Owner's website @ www.peugeot.co.uk)

Note: [a] This headline appeared in the New Year 2000 edition of the *Rapport* magazine for Peugeot owners

BEYOND THE 4 Ps

See Grönroos (2000) for an explanation of why the 4 Ps framework is no longer adequate for many marketing situations and the shift from thinking of communication as promotion, towards a conception of communication as a particular kind of interaction – that produces meanings.

CASE STUDY 7   MARKETING AT THE RNIB

When the goal of an enterprise is not profit, market share, or return on investment, the marketing mix takes on a particular form as a framework for directing marketing decisions and resulting activities towards achieving the goal. The charity sector is demonstrating considerable growth in adopting (and adapting) marketing for social purposes. This social marketing has the overall aim of serving the needs and wants of clients and donors – the wider society can also benefit from the resolution of problems. The exchange of financial support, time and support of the donors for the satisfaction of solving a social problem or promoting a cause is the basis of the business. One party comes to give up something they value in exchange for something else through negotiation and persuasion. Whereas for a profit-driven business, the main beneficiary is usually the shareholders, for charity the only beneficiary is supposed to be their clients.

An audit of the marketing activities can create marketing awareness among the members. The 'product' is usually ideas and/or services (although some charities now have high-street shops selling products to raise funds). The place decision relates to how these ideas and services will be made available to clients. When the basis of the marketing programme is an idea, then this merges the product, place (distribution), and promotion (communication) decisions together. In terms of distribution, there are usually no intermediaries and the production and consumption of ideas and services is often simultaneous. Note the parallel here between co-production of ideas and services and the co-construction of meaning, identity, and knowledge – what we have defined, in this book, as communication. Advertising has become a major means of communicating, with many advertising agencies donating their work in support of charitable causes. Direct mail is a major component of most programmes of information and persuasion, and personal selling in the form of door-to-door collections and recruitment is common. The major difference of the charity marketing mix from commercial business decisions, is pricing. A much broader concept of price is necessary – the valuation of the exchange (although this is often true in commercial exchanges, but is not readily recognized by managers). For many donors and volunteers, the cost is a lost opportunity in selecting one benefit over another (i.e. choosing what to spend money, time, and effort on). Professional low-cost administration, timely information, and competent, sympathetic, and trustworthy fundraisers, helpers, and administrators may also be valued by donors and helpers, when the consideration is the maximizing of social benefits.

The Royal National Institute for the Blind (RNIB) is the leading charity providing practical support, advice, and information for the one million blind and partially sighted people in the UK. For the RNIB, marketing is a philosophy of meeting needs in a businesslike manner in a highly competitive volunteer and fundraising sector. RNIB employs more than 3,000 staff and 750,000 volunteers at 40 sites, generating around £75m of income and providing around 60 services in the UK. RNIB has a strong brand in the UK and this is capitalized upon in printed and TV editorial coverage. The major marketing task is the building of long-term relationships, targeting limited promotional expenditure and service capacity through market research and market segmentation. Trust is essential – both with the blind and partially sighted people who are the beneficiaries and with the donors, so the RNIB brand is critical. There is a very strong philosophy of service as the end, whereas businesses pursue products and service only as a means to the end of profit, market share, and so on. It is important to raise awareness of visual impairment and blindness and the role of the RNIB in dealing with these conditions. Fundraising and getting people involved are the other purposes. A comprehensive multifaceted website has linked the RNIB into the world market for information, products, fundraising, and voluntary services. The website is a crucial means for market education. Today, when succeeding, as they do, to get press coverage, RNIB people need to ask interviewing journalists to mention the website in their article, and to make sure that statements made on issues can be followed up on the website.

Marketing is growing in use, but marketers in the charity sector have to face particular problems. First, those people depicted and represented in their advertising are not client, audience, product, or customer. Do they thus have a voice or are they exploited objects? The problems faced by a charity's client group are those that society creates. In commercial marketing, the offer is a way to be better off through getting (product benefits). In charity advertising, the viewer is presented with the idea of becoming worse off by giving (donations, etc). Charity advertising may not always be the bearer of a very attractive offer!

WHAT DO YOU THINK?

1 Review a product with which you are familiar. How do you 'read' the marketing mix as a communicating system for that product? What suggestions do you have for the managers responsible for marketing communication?

2 If marketing communication managers attend to the 'promotion mix' and leave the rest of the marketing mix to managers in other departments, what might be the consequences?

3 It has been said that marketing is everybody's job; analyse the significance of the coherent marketing mix from the customer's perspective.

4 Outline a programme of marketing communication activities that would not be intended to persuade customers to purchase.

5 Consider the notion of a marketing communication life cycle in which activities change to meet the communication needs of customers. Map an outline to illustrate this.

6 If a corporation has both consumer and industrial products, to what extent can their marketing communication activities be consolidated? Illustrate with examples.

7 Write a brief specification for a marketing communication system that supports the generative subsystem of the business.

8 Examine Table 7.11. Carry out a more detailed analysis of the advantages and disadvantages of different means for communicating, using specific information wherever possible.

9 Write a succinct statement that distinguishes marketing communication from marketing communications.

10 Where might significant differences arise in the communication needs of the provider and the consumer or buyer? How might managers deal with this problem?

FURTHER READING

Bradley, F. (1995) *Marketing Management: Providing, Communicating, and Delivering Value*, London: Prentice-Hall.

Davidson, M. P. (1992) *The Consumerist Manifesto: Advertising in Postmodern Times*, London: Routledge.

Dibb, S., Simkin, L., Pride, W. M. and Ferrell, O. C. (1999) *Marketing: Concepts and Strategies*, 3rd edn, Boston, MA: Houghton Mifflin Company.

Grönroos, C. (2000) *Service Management and Marketing: A Customer Relationship Management Approach*, Chichester: John Wiley & Sons.

Kotler, P. (2000) *Marketing Management*, The Millennium (10th) edn, Upper Saddle River, NJ: Prentice-Hall International.

Leiss, W., Kline, S. and Jhally, S. (1986) *Social Communication in Advertising: Persons, Products, and Images of Well-Being*, London: Methuen.

O'Shaughnessy J. (1992) *Competitive Marketing: A Strategic Approach*, 2nd edn, London: Routledge.

Smith, P. R., Berry, C. and Pulford, A. (1997) *Strategic Marketing Communications: New Ways to Build and Integrate Communications*, London: Kogan Page.

chapter eight

THE BRAND COMMUNICATOR

LEARNING POINTS

Careful study of this chapter will help you to:

- examine the nature and role of product brand management
- appreciate the communicative nature of a brand
- connect brand design with marketing communication objectives
- think of a brand as akin to a product–provider reputation

Shall I compare thee to a summer's day?
Thou art more lovely and more temperate
                              Shakespeare, Sonnet 18, ll. 1–2

People do not perceive the world as it really is
                              Robert Ornstein

The brand can defeat reality
                              Stuart Crainer

INTRODUCTION

Cognitive effects may influence behaviour – experience is interpreted and used to change attitudes and knowledge, which control our behaviour. Behaviour may be modified when people communicate. This can explain how some advertising and word-of-mouth interaction affect consumer choices. This is counter to the behavioural perspective. Behaviourists rejected the idea that thought and feeling initiate actions. They saw thought and feeling as effects not causes. The stimulus–response (S–R) is now widely considered to be outmoded (see chapters two and three).

The cumulative effect of advertising is to associate commodities with meanings. Thus in Britain a Valentine card stands for romantic love, a roast turkey stands for Christmas. As we saw in chapter six, cultural differences produce various meanings for products and related expressions and representations.

Product purchase is an expression of a preference among a fixed range of options (those offered by providers). This is product or brand selection rather than choice.

Strong brands seem to live forever! A Boston Consulting Group study showed that in 19 of the 22 categories studied, the brand leader in 1925 was still the leader in 1985. In the other categories the 1925 brand leader was either second or fifth in 1985.

Why will customers pay over $400 more for an IBM PC than for a similar performance and specification PC from Dell or Compaq?

COGNITIVE RESPONSE TO MARKETING INTERVENTIONS

We are interested here in the communicative role of a brand. How can we encourage consumers and buyers to purchase our brand in preference to others, and to maintain this desirable behaviour for a long period? Brand loyalty (or allegiance) reduces the need for costly promotion (by fostering familiarity and connection) and excludes competitors' products from the consumption patterns of our preferred customers. Promotional activity also warns off potential competing providers, thus acting as a market entry barrier. The question for communication managers is: 'How might consumers respond to the offer of a brand? We need to revisit the concepts of brand awareness, brand image, and brand strength (or equity) from a communication perspective.

Cognition is about 'knowing' – the collective mental processes (memory, language, consciousness) that we use to combine information into knowledge structures for decision-making. These knowledge-based processes enable meaning-making from sense data. We could refer to this activity as thinking.

An attitude is a lasting evaluation of an issue, thing, or person. Attitudes consist of an affect, behaviour, and cognition. Thus, an attitude to a particular provider's product offering has an affective component (like or dislike), a behavioural tendency (consume or avoid), and a cognitive component (belief that the brand is desirable or repulsive).

Attitudes can and do cause actions, but this is influenced by other factors, such as whether or not the person believes that they can act and the social norms operating, i.e. whether or not it is believed that it is acceptable to act in a particular way. How well the attitude is remembered (i.e. memory) also affects whether or not it is expressed in action.

A person experiences cognitive dissonance arousal (Festinger, 1957) whenever he/she holds two cognitions – beliefs, attitudes, or knowledge – that are inconsistent with each other. This is a disharmony between an attitude we hold and our knowledge of something we have done or intend to do. This is uncomfortable and there is a motivation to reduce the dissonance either by changing the conditions or by changing behaviours. Dissonance usually arises when there is insufficient justification for an action. For example, we might sign a loan agreement for a new car without being certain that the deal is affordable or best value.

Cognitive learning is purposeful. We engage in this whenever we want to communicate ideas, obtain information, solve problems, or become competent in some endeavour. Cognitive modifiability is the ability to change our mental structure and contents. Learning involves a change in contents. Thinking rearranges the structure of information in consciousness. All mental processes are for adaptation to the environment.

Recognition is the re-cognition or recall or some idea from memory into conscious thinking.

We are alike and different in our thinking styles. We all think, but we think differently. It would be hopelessly naïve to assume that the way the marketing manager thinks is the way that all targeted consumers or buyers think. Cognitive balance is sought as internal consistency or consonance among our beliefs, attitudes, values, and decisions.

As pointed out by East (1997), the manner in which consumers behave is often not the predictable outcome of rational processes of systematic comparison of purchase options. We may simply act on established habit or merely satisfice on the first adequate option encountered. Our cognitive processes may be better explained as heuristics (structured trials) rather than as logical processes. Our behaviour is often more rooted in the immediate environment. Our sensing of this, rather than any marketing intervention, initiates many of our cognitive processes.

WHAT IS A BRAND?

A brand 'marks' a product on a consumer's consciousness. In days gone by, hot brands were applied to cattle, slaves, and criminals to burn a sign onto the skin as a permanent indication of identity and ownership. Thus, a branded commodity is afforded identity of ownership and difference. Products have extra value added in being branded. Brand management is part of the quest for profitable difference.

A brand is more than a merely functional product – there are other values to be considered: for example, a product is made in a factory; a brand is bought by a customer; products can be copied by competitors, whereas a brand is unique. Thus, a washing powder is a product, but Persil is a brand. The brand is the interface of the provider and consumer perspectives on what constitutes a valuable product.

Perhaps, we must think of brands as special, from a communication point of view, because the relationship of the product to the consumer or buyer and the provider is highly significant.

A brand identity is the distinct offer, comprising consistency, character, appropriateness, and performance. The brand secures a desired place in the consumer or buyer's mind. Brand image, on the other hand, is what is raised in the mind of each consumer or buyer when he/she interprets and judges his/her environment, which of course includes competing brands, concerns, and differing values and opinions. We will look further at identity, image, and reputation in chapter eighteen. Box 8.1 affords an illustration of rebranding.

BOX 8.1   REBRANDING THE LITTLEWOODS PORTFOLIO

Last year, Littlewoods announced that they are to use the Littlewoods name on all of their £1bn per year retail businesses. Brands to be dropped are Peter Craig, Brian Mills, Janet Frazer, John Moores, and Burlington. Market research has shown that the Littlewoods brand remains strong among lower-income families, and is strongly associated with trust, integrity, and value. The rebranding programme will cost £50m.

A brand is differentiated from a commodity by having associated with it, as an integral part of the total offering, values that are significant to the consumer and buyer. The commodity has only use value and is unattractive to producers because it traps them into high volume and economies of scale. The brand is attractive to the provider because it offers the possibility of a premium price and larger profit margin. See Figure 8.1 for an illustration of brand elements, and note how we are all capable of communicating something of the desirability of trading with the corporation.

Research by de Chernatony (1993) revealed seven 'brand building blocks' which can be stressed in different ways and degrees to differentiate a product from competitive offerings (Figure 8.2). We are particularly interested in the building blocks that communicate value in the brand, so that consumers and buyers identify either similar benefits to others brands but available at a lower cost from your brand, or unique benefits of your brand.

A brand may be capable of performing a number of functions:

- **identity**: the brand name guides consumers when making their choice
- **practicality**: the brand name summarizes information, allowing retention

A legal company	The corporate entity
A product	A journey
A service	Personal attention during the journey
Added value	A guarantee of superior reliability, etc.
A logo	Simple and distinctive, easily seen and recognized
An identity	Recognizable uniforms, plan livery, office style, etc.
A slogan	'The world's favourite airline'
A means of identification	Easily picked out in the airport terminal
A source of information	A statement of affluence?
An advertising image	Bringing the world's people together
An image	Stylish, reliable, international, high quality
A person	Lord King, Sir Colin Marshall, or the cabin steward?

Figure 8.1 **Elements of the British Airways brand**
Source: Based on Crainer, 1995

Fuctional capability	The brand–purchaser relationship is based on trust that the brand will meet performance expectations
Sign of ownership	The link to the parent corporate reputation
Legal protection	Trademark registration to counter counterfeiting
Strategic direction	Coherent combination of the six building blocks
Symbolic role	The emotional element, what the brand 'says' about the consumer/buyer
Name and logo	Stand-out identity by conveying strengths
Shorthand notation	The prompt of recall and evaluation of brand characteristics

Figure 8.2 **How does a brand mediate communication with consumers?**
Source: Based on de Chernatony, 1993

of information about the characteristics of the product by the association of the brand name with them

- **guarantee**: provides the 'signature' of the provider, reducing the sense of risk and uncertainty (of loss, disapproval, or other form of discomfort or dissonance)

- **personalization**: the brand name allows consumers to express their individuality and originality through their purchases
- **entertainment**: the brand allows the exercise of choice, thereby giving consumers satisfaction of their need for novelty, arousal, surprise, and so on (gratification)

Perhaps, simply, we can think of a brand as a shorthand or *aide mémoire* for a particular product–provider combination. The choice of brand name is considered in Box 8.2.

BOX 8.2   COMMUNICATING LOW RISK

Promise is an Internet-based mortgage lender that aims to overcome the problem of high-cost loans by operating without expensive overheads such as a branch network and application form administration. So how do they overcome the dual problem of the risk of a high involvement house purchase loan (perhaps with repayments over twenty-five years) and the further risk of trading with an 'invisible' company. Perhaps the choice of brand name is the key?

(See www.promise.co.uk)

In the modern 'science' of branding, products mean something by virtue of how they are used. Neither the meaning nor the use are fixed by the provider. These meanings may be rational and/or emotional, and are created within the context of ever-changing group affiliations of people as providers, consumers, and buyers. Thus, there arises a dialogue between people who learn from each other what a product means to them and to others.

Most brands have characteristics such as those listed in Table 8.1.

The communication of marketing mix elements, as we saw in chapter seven, provides consumers and buyers with information (context-specific data) from which they create meanings. Construed added values are distinguishers that are taken as brand personality. How well do these match with the self-image of the consumer/buyer? Is your product seen by your preferred customers as a brand that is like an old friend?

COMMUNICATION BEHAVIOUR AND BRAND OFFERS

An essential part of the marketing communication manager's job is to make offers of products to consumers and buyers that are taken by them as distinctive and attractive brand offers. But, crucially, the task of understanding how to deploy marketing communication resources for appropriate communication purposes and related objectives must precede this.

Promotional communication effort must be supported by knowledge of what will grab attention, create attraction, catalyse action, and foster

Table 8.1 **Brand personality factors**

Brand image	Characteristic	Example
Sincerity	Down to earth	Family-oriented, small-town, conventional
	Honest	Sincere, real, ethical, thoughtful
	Wholesome	Genuine, classic, old-fashioned
	Cheerful	Sentimental, friendly, warm, happy
Excitement	Daring	Trendy, exciting, flashy, provocative
	Spirited	Cool, young, lively, outgoing, adventurous
	Imaginative	Unique, humorous, surprising, artistic, fun
	Up to date	Independent, contemporary, innovative, aggressive
Competence	Reliable	Hard-working, secure, efficient, trustworthy, careful
	Intelligent	Technical, serious
	Successful	Leader, confident, influential
Sophisticated	Upper class	Glamorous, good-looking, pretentious, sophisticated
	Charming	Feminine, smooth, gentle, sexy
Ruggedness	Outdoor	Masculine, active, athletic
	Tough	Rugged, strong, no-nonsense

Source: Based on Aaker, 1995

allegiance to the product–provider. The strategic task is not merely to sell a unit of your product but to introduce it as a long-standing component of the consumer/buyer purchase habit (Figure 8.3).

We can think of a brand as an array of informational clues about value for money, suitability, reliability, and so on, associated with the purchase of the particular product from the particular provider. The communication behaviour of a consumer or buyer will be situationally determined (Grunig, 1992). Figure 8.4 shows that the purchasing behaviour of a consumer or buyer will depend on how they understand their situation in terms

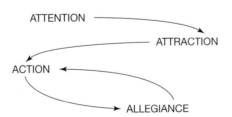

Figure 8.3 **Integrating your brand into a consumption pattern**

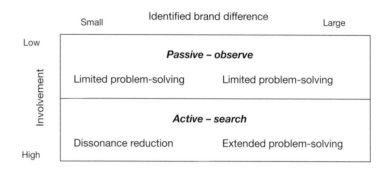

Figure 8.4 **The situation determines who initiates communication**
Source: Based on Grunig, 1992, and de Chernatony and McDonald, 1992: Figure 3.1

of level of involvement with the brand and the degree of differentiation of the brands considered for purchase.

The behaviour expected is situation specific. When a person recognizes an unsatisfied need or desire for gratification, they will consider how significant this is to them and how likely they are to accomplish this desirable outcome. He/she will actively seek a satisfier if he/she believes that one is available. The behaviour expected in acquiring a lunch to satisfy hunger differs considerably from that expected for the purchase of a house by means of a twenty-five-year mortgage loan.

THE SOCIAL SIGNIFICANCE OF BRANDS

Because we have taken the view that human communication is more about relating and meaning-making than about informing, we need to examine how the brand has a social role. Thus, a brand means something (as a sign) much more than it does something (with a function).

A brand is elected when it means something to a consumer that is consistent with that consumer's needs, values, and lifestyle. For example, Guinness is a rich, creamy, dark, bitter alcoholic drink. However, through advertising, it has become much more for some people. A brand personality of manliness, mature experience and wit has been developed, based on the symbolism of nourishing value, power, and energy. More recently, the main competitor, Murphy's, has been running advertisements featuring a team of glamorous protectors who take care of those select few who choose to buy that brand. These products have ceased to be tangible goods and have taken on emotional value.

Brands as symbols of lifestyles and expressions of personalities can be highly effective communicators. We can say something about ourselves through the brands we select, discard, and consume. We can enact rituals through selected brands. We can also 'read' other peoples' personalities and make judgements about relationships and situations that will make us feel 'good'. Some brands can even help us to communicate something to ourselves. Of

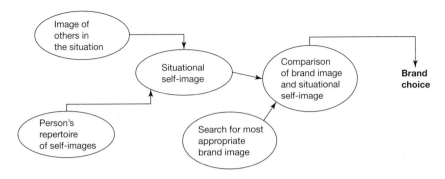

Figure 8.5 **How brand selection is specific to situations**
Source: Based on Schenk and Holman, 1980

course, as we saw in chapter six, these associations are specific to a particular culture.

The situational self-image (Schenk and Holman, 1980) is an important indicator of what brand choices a person might make. The situational self-image is that image that a person wishes others to have of them in a particular situation. This helps to explain why we probably would not wear the same clothes for a party as for a job interview or wedding (Figure 8.5). However, not only does a consumer's self-image influence the brands that they select, but also the brands that they select have a symbolic value and this influences the consumer's self-image. We also make inferences about people from observing which brands they own. Thus, brands are cultural signs. But how do certain meanings come to be associated with objects? Why is gold a symbol of wealth and authority? These are learned as we become socialized into a group or culture. Levels of meaning can be discerned (Table 8.2).

Table 8.2 **How culture links brands and consumers**

Level	Sign	Example
Basic	Utilitarian	Washing machine: reliable, effective, value-for-money
Second	Commercial value	Porsche vs. the old Skoda (recently they have gained credibility and some respect for their new models under the direction of owners Volkswagen)
Third	Socio-cultural	Club membership tie
Fourth	Mythical	Old Spice, Napoleon Brandy, Manchester United

Source: Based on de Chernatony and McDonald, 1992

BRAND LOYALTY

When a consumer or buyer believes that they obtain benefits from maintaining a relationship with a brand (product–provider combination), they will strive to purchase that brand repeatedly. Such an attachment to a brand may be associated with a conviction about its superiority compared to competing brands on functional, symbolic or psychological attributes. The marketer's problem is how to encourage and facilitate such consistent purchasing behaviour. Of course, true loyalty to brand is not the same as inertial repeat purchasing. High involvement leads to discernment of differences between brands, whereas high satisfaction leads to brand liking or attachment. The marketer gains doubly when true brand loyalty arises, because the consumer or buyer consistently purchases the brand and is highly likely to engage in positive word-of-mouth promotion. An example of a successful branding device is given in Box 8.3.

Some marketing communication agencies now specialize is continuity programmes that provide rewards to consumers and buyers for continuing loyalty to a brand.

BOX 8.3   COLEY PORTER BELL – BRAND DESIGNERS

This firm is one of a growing number of consulting groups that specializes in design and identity. Established in 1979, the firm uses a range of planning tools, including shopper selection mode analysis, to define visually the rational and emotional qualities of brand names. This makes them stand out and stimulate reactions from consumers. Visual clarity enhances the communicative power of the brand, and is especially important as more consumers are deciding what to buy in the store. Packaging is thus primarily important in conveying brand personality.

For example, CPB developed an identity for LEGO Duplo as a pre-school range that stimulates and educates through fun. They created a strong branding device – the yellow brand band – together with pack photography that stimulates the imagination and appeals to children, while reassuring parents of the product's educational values.

(See www.cpb.co.uk)

BRAND PREFERENCES

From the provider's point of view, the provider benefits when consumers buy their products in preference to others, especially if this is maintained over long periods. Brand loyalty offsets the need for promotion and is a barrier to market entry by other providers. An established brand can support the launch of new products by extending existing buying propensities. When consumers are willing to buy a brand, the provider may be able to charge a premium price. Brand loyalty seems to be the key factor in brand management, as a source of competitive advantage.

A consideration set is the brands that a person might or does buy (Roberts and Lattin, 1997). Since consumers are mostly polygamous and habitual in their choice of brand (i.e. are loyal to several brands in any product category), advertising mostly publicizes a brand to make the brand salient in the consideration set (Ehrenberg *et al.*, 1997). Brand saliency is much more than brand awareness and brand recall, which are the typical measures found in much market research on product advertising impact. A brand is salient when it is conspicuous, prominent, or noticeable – it is noted by the consumer or buyer for some particular reason, and stands out from other brands as one that they do or might buy.

For a brand to have salience, which may be subconscious, the consumer or buyer must have, for that brand:

- awareness
- some degree of interest
- assurance (quality, service, etc.)
- familiarity and acceptance
- consistency
- habituated choosing

'Always Coca-Cola'

In the launch of a new brand, the immediate communication task is informational and publicizing, rather than strong persuasion. Repeated exposure to a brand name has been shown to increase familiarity and liking for the brand. Perhaps a more realistic role for brand advertising is to maintain distinctiveness, and only exceptionally to increase sales. Indeed, many advertising designers do not seek to make persuasive messages but simply to attract attention and to generate interest. According to Ehrenberg *et al.* (1999), most advertising is really only publicizing brands and does not really persuade at all.

Advertising connects a product with a brand by providing the means to communicate, even create, the right added values, to make the brand more appealing and plausible, and relevant to the apprehending consumer. The personality of the brand is coupled with the illusion of a dialogue between the consumer and the brand. When successful, typically, a brand counters the 'feel bad' of most news reporting, with a 'feel good' factor (see Figure 8.6). This may lead to brand loyalty (see Box 8.4).

PERCEPTUAL (COGNITIVE) MAPPING

This is a widely used technique to engage brand designers and consumers/ buyers in surfacing the bases for their judgements about a brand.

People are asked to identify the characteristics and features of goods and services and their providers, and then to compare a brand with competing brands. For example, coffee brands may be compared on a cost dimension (cheap–expensive) and a flavour dimension (mellow–strong). Quality and

Self-expression	Prestige products show that the user or purchaser is somehow different, e.g. Daimler, Rolls Royce, Rolex, Gucci, Armani, etc.
Simplicity	Product choices are simplified in a cluttered marketplace. Apple Computers, for example, dropped technical jargon, behaving in a consumer-friendly fashion to provide practical solutions
Quality	A brand can convey a sense of quality, benefits, and value for money as a shorthand to past experiences – trust is a mediator for present and future purchase choices
Choice	Purchasers can discriminate between offers
Risk avoidance	Buying well-known or reputable product offers less risk than buying an unknown product – there is some assurance that it will live up to expectations

Figure 8.6 **Reasons why brands are attractive to consumers**

BOX 8.4   GREY'S BRAND LOYALTY+ INDEX

A survey of 10,000 people in 24 countries has found that consumers are not very loyal to single brands, and in fact in each category studied (coffee, beer, petrol, supermarket, credit card, yoghurt, and fast food) buy several brands and believe that own-label brands are as good as or better than national brands. Price is the major deciding factor for most people when choosing brands.

Advertising agency Grey Worldwide use the Index as part of their Brand Loyalty+ Program that evaluates the state of consumer–brand relationships and determines a marketing action programme to strengthen consumer loyalty to specific brands.

Grey interpret their findings as further evidence of shamelessly fickle consumer behaviour and the need for marketers to focus on relationship issues beyond product features, benefits, and performance. Partly, this is accounted for by the increasing number of products on offer.

Many marketers have concentrated spending on direct response activities in the past decade and have neglected brand-building efforts. Advertising is needed to capture 'share of mind'.

---

cost are often discriminators. Some complex mapping has three (or more) dimensions because consumers consider multiple characteristics, but this is impossible to illustrate clearly here on a flat page, so we have limited the example to the more usual two dimensions. Where would you locate (map) your course? How would you know where to locate other courses you could take? Perhaps this tells us something about how a brand might work? What

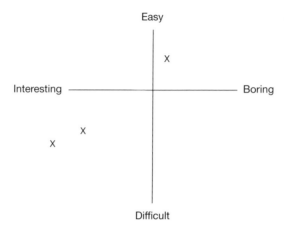

Figure 8.7 **An example of a perceptual map for a higher-education course**

other dimensions might be appropriate (relevance, employability of graduates, etc.)? This is represented by Figure 8.7.

Although termed 'perceptual' maps, these are really graphical representations of stated attitudes or judgements about brands. Of course, maps can also be constructed using actual descriptors, rather than opinions (price, size, duration, and so on). We can then talk in terms of relative positioning of a number of brands.

CASE STUDY 8   WHAT IS 'MANCHESTER UNITED'?

It's official! Manchester United is the world's biggest football team. The numbers tell the story. A survey by Team Marketing of 14 million UK homes in 1996–97 showed that 10 per cent of the population, including those who do not regard themselves as 'football fans', support United. There are 104 supporters clubs in Britain, 74 in Ireland, and at least 24 overseas. The club's monthly magazine *United* regularly sells more than 120,000 copies in Britain, and can even sell 40,000 copies in Thailand. A Malay version is also available. Old Trafford matches on average have had the largest home crowds in almost every season since 1968. In 1996–97 United became the first English team to attract at least 50,000 people to every home game. Of the 55,000 ground capacity, some 40,000 seats are held on season tickets. Every league game has been sold out for the past five years. The ground is being extended to 67,000 capacity and all expectations are that this will also be filled to capacity. The pinnacle of achievement was winning the English premier league title, the FA Cup and the European Cup in 1999.

In 1998, United's income, excluding payer transfers, was almost £88m, generating a £26m operating profit. The club was floated on the Stock Market in 1991 and is now one of Britain's 250 biggest quoted companies with a market value of £380m. The merchandising business alone generated sales of £28.5m. Sales were expected to top £100m, producing £30m in pre-tax profits, in 2000.

There is a mail-order business, a full-time office in Hong Kong, and a department specializing in developing new products and services under the Manchester United brand name. The commercial operation employs 115 people. In 1991, some 168 new trademarks were registered. In the nationwide Birthdays greeting card chain, some 40% of football merchandise sales are related to United. An international subsidiary has been established to build the business worldwide, including a major push into Asia, beginning with the People's Republic of China, Jakarta, Singapore, and Hong Kong. Old Trafford Megastores will stock merchandise, recruit new club members, run soccer schools, and operate Red Cafes to show matches live. Manufacturing of merchandise in China will follow. Sales of counterfeit United goods are estimated to already exceed $1bn per year. A chain of Red Cafes is to open throughout Britain and Ireland, too. United have their own subscription TV channel, MUTV, and an Internet facility called the Worldwide Manchester United Fans Webring. A new official hotel is opening as part of a leisure complex development in the shadow of the Old Trafford ground. Fans can pay for their stay with the official MU credit card. Pay-per-view TV coverage could be worth £1m per game to the club.

In recent years, the brand has secured several big commercial deals:

- Umbro sportswear – merchandising worth £40M over six years
- Sharp Electronics – sponsorship worth £10m, replaced by Vodafone in 2000 for £30m over four years
- VCI media – videos and fan magazines worth £10m
- Debenhams are adding MU merchandise to their stock throughout the UK
- Sun Microsystems has recently become a Platinum Sponsor

When News Corporation bid $1bn for the club, they saw football not as a sport, but as a consumable and as content for their broadcast systems. So what is MU? Certainly a pre-eminent football team, but also much more – a highly valued brand. Using Crainer's (1995) brand element analysis, we can try to understand what makes the MU brand so powerful.

- **a slogan**: 'The Theatre of Dreams'
- **an identity**: the club crest and players' strips, especially the red and white 'uniform'
- **a logo**: the distinctive red club crest
- **a company**: the 'Manchester United' corporate brand
- **a source of information**: supporting the club means the best of British
- **a means of identification**: the club crest and bright red and white team strip
- **an advertising image**: a successful football team
- **an added extra**: the brand is seen as guaranteeing success and ambition
- **a person**: currently David Beckham, but all players as personalities, including Alex Ferguson
- **an image**: successful, powerful, skilful, glamour, and a history
- **a product**: originally football as entertainment, competition, sport, success and winning, power, and patriotism, now also many products and increasing reputation
- **a service**: the website?

(See www.manutd.com and http://glorymanutd.cjb.net)

WHAT DO YOU THINK?

1 If Professor Ehrenberg is right, that mostly advertising is a means for brand publicity, how would the widespread adoption of the concept of saliency impact on the global advertising industry?

2 How would you characterize the brand personalities of Virgin Atlantic, EuroDisney, Nestlé, and British Airways?

3 Brands enable consumers to communicate something about themselves. Explain how this might work.

4 Try to explain human cognition processes using Vickers' idea of an appreciative system. In what ways does this help in understanding the product brand from the cognitive and communication perspectives?

5 Advertising transforms a product into a mirror of its consumer. Explain this in terms of branding.

6 Brands may be based on the following:

euphemism; metaphor; analogy; totem; fetish; metonym; substitute; catalyst; icon; synecdoche; symbol; corollary; syllogism.

Find a dictionary definition of each term that makes sense of branding.

7 Try this game. Write a list of ten familiar products. Ask your colleagues to name spontaneously a brand for each, including the manufacturer and a main provider. Why are these names so prominent?

8 If there were no brands, how would your life be affected?

9 Think of some people who are prominent in your life. List what you think might be their favourite brands. On what basis can you/do you make such judgements?

10 I have elsewhere suggested that a brand is a form of trope. Go back to your English lessons and work out what I might mean by this (why not send your answer to me by e-mail?).

FURTHER READING

Aaker, D. (1991) *Managing Brand Equity*, New York: The Free Press.

Crainer, S. (1995) *The Real Power of Brands: Making Brands Work for Competitive Advantage*, London: FT Pitman Publishing.

de Chernatony, L. and McDonald, M. H. B. (1992) *Creating Powerful Brands: The Strategic Route to Success in Consumer, Industrial and Service Markets*, Oxford: Butterworth-Heinemann.

East, R. (1997) *Consumer Behaviour: Advances and Applications in Marketing*, London: Prentice-Hall.

Festinger, L. and Maccoby, N. (1964) 'On resistence to persuasive communications', *Journal of Abnormal Social Psychology* 68: 359–66.

Haley, I. (1985) *Developing Effective Communication Strategy: A Benefit Segmentation Approach*, New York: John Wiley & Sons.

Ind, N. (1997) *The Corporate Brand*, London: Macmillan Business Books.

Jones, J. P. (1986) *What's in a Name?: Advertising and the Concept of Brands*, Lexington, MA: Lexington Books.

Ornstein, R. and Carstensen, L. (1991) *Psychology: The Study of Human Experience*, 3rd edn, San Diego, CA: Harcourt Brace Jovanovich.

Temporal, P. and Alder, H. (1998) *Corporate Charisma: How to Achieve World-Class Recognition by Maximising Your Company's Image, Brands and Culture*, London: Piatkus Books.

chapter
nine

SELECTING MEDIA
FOR COMMUNICATING

LEARNING POINTS

Careful study of this chapter will help you to:

- understand the range of media available

- examine ways of comparing media suitability

- take account of major changes in media options, without losing sight of central marketing communication objectives

> What we are facing with cable is a transformation of our
> world similar to the one brought about by the printing press
> George Gerbner

> The trouble with her is that she lacks the power of
> conversation but not the power of speech
> George Bernard Shaw

INTRODUCTION

Providers typically give their marketing communication brief to an advertising agency – for many managers, marketing communication is advertising. Traditional textbooks have always presented advertising (discussed at length in chapter fourteen) media selection as a scientific endeavour based on the measurement and analysis of 'opportunities to see', response rates, cost per exposure, 'impacts', and similar criteria for 'cost effectiveness'. Today, we are faced with a much greater challenge – how well do we understand how people use the various media and how they feel about their relationship?

The original concept of the market as a physical meeting place is further challenged by business mediated through electronic connections – the response requires more than simply applying orthodox theory. The problem is more than how to advertise in electronic marketspaces – the traditional dichotomy of producer vs. consumer may no longer be very helpful, marketing communication practices may no longer be fully understood as acts of sending and receiving information – even if that was ever really the case.

By the end of the 20th century, two-thirds of marketing communication spend was on 'below-the-line' (i.e. not advertising) activities such as direct mail, sponsorship, sales promotion, telemarketing, and 'infomercials', with conventional advertising taking up the rest ('above the line'). This is a reversal of the traditional allocation of budget.

While it is obvious to us that consumption is an activity of consumers and buyers, for some time marketing communication was considered as active for marketers and consumers were considered as passive recipients. Today, consumers are thought of as active media users. There is considerable cognitive activity in media consumption – attending to and making sense of the world. Thus, we must examine media use as both attending to and meaning-making. The intentional fallacy is the notion that what the message creator intended it to mean is what the audience members take it to mean. Research on what people do with media demonstrates that people are very creative, often doing surprising and unpredictable things with media products (Grossberg *et al.*, 1998).

With so many communication media options available, selection decisions must be based on judgements of both effectiveness (suitability) and efficiency (performance).

The Internet is considered a means of allowing buyers and consumers to participate in trading communities in which some corporations are members. We now have a many-to-many mediated selling and buying environment (Hoffman and Novak, 1996 – see also Tapp, 2000).

PRODUCT PLACEMENT: 'STEALTH ADVERTISING'

Because we have devoted the whole of chapter fourteen to an examination of the most widely used and familiar means of (promotional) marketing communication, we will not dwell on it at length here. However, a growing alternative to costly commercials is product placement.

As the costs of advertising through traditional commercial TV, magazines, newspapers, and radio escalates (partly due to conglomerate ownership), some marketers are turning to alternative vehicles to make contact with consumers and buyers. TV programme and film-makers are opening a further avenue to their audiences as consumers and buyers. The BBC, for example, does not carry advertising slots in their programming, but products can be spotted within drama, situation comedy, and serial programmes. Instead of fictional brands, characters appear alongside real products to foster greater authenticity.

In this integrated or embedded marketing, participating providers receive free product publicity in return for furnishing goods as free props for the film set. Viewers don't realize that they are, in effect, watching an advertisement.

The Rovers Return (Coronation Street) once pulled pints of fictitious Newton & Ridley bitter, but now features a prominent Guinness pump on the bar. Actually, a N & R beer was produced, as was 'Betty's Hotpot' from Holland's Pies. For the launch of a new Z3 convertible from BMW, a $3m placement was secured in the then new James Bond movie, *Goldeneye*, making the car the hero's preferred ride (and $240m in advance orders). The *Men Behaving Badly* lads often sip Stella Artois lager direct from the distinctive, easily recognizable cans. Actually, this promotional technique is not new. In 1955 James Dean clearly used an Ace Comb in *Rebel Without a Cause*. Perhaps the first (unintended) product placement was Gordon's Gin seen in *The African Queen*. More recently, and definitely planned, is the Ericsson mobile phone used by Agent Scully in *The X Files*. Ericsson even have a full-time product placements manager (curiously, part of the Corporate Citizenship and Sponsorship Management team, based in Toronto). (See Box 9.1 for a contemporary example of product placement in films.)

The pay-off for providers can be huge. During the early days of the aborted BBC soap opera *Eldorado*, a 10-second exposure in each episode could have been worth £2–3m in raising consumers' awareness of brand names. Yet Thorn-EMI, for example, paid merely £25,000 to construct its video rental

---

BOX 9.1   AUSTIN POWERS: THE SPY WHO SOLD LOTS OF STUFF

Perhaps the most sophisticated example of product placement to date is the *Austin Powers* film in which laughs and free advertising go hand in hand as the technique is at once made fun of and exploited for profit.

In return for placement, for example, Heineken has promoted the film in its 32,000 US in-store displays, providing the equivalent of millions of pounds in free promotion for the film. Marketing campaigns for products featured in the film use the Austin Powers character to sell products and, in doing so, increase awareness of the film.

So which brands are featured and how? Dr Evil calls Scott the 'Diet Coke' of evil. Austin receives e-mail via AOL, and lives next door to a Virgin store and a Phillips TV store. Dr Evil's HQ is a Starbuck's restaurant. Austin's Volkswagon car is a time-machine!

Of course, once the audience becomes aware of product placement, its impact may be compromised. The film *Back to the Future II* was overflowing with blatantly visible products such Nike, Pizza Hut, Black & Decker, and DeLorean.

shop-front on the programme set. This saved the production company the cost of constructing part of their film set, but expended only a small fraction of the company's promotional budget.

Some people are unhappy with this development, seeing this increased commercialism as a taint on TV and film audiences. In 1999, *The Truman Show* poked fun at the technique by including fake products. For some people, this promotional effort smacks of the scary idea of subliminal advertising – purchase suggestion hidden from our awareness – commercialism insidiously entering our lives, urging us to 'buy more stuff'.

Marketing managers are now employing product placement agents to offer their products (often with accompanying payments) to producers for use in their programmes. The BBC's guidelines on product use are strict. Payment is forbidden. No commitments or promises on screen appearances are allowed. The ITC is stricter. Makers can have free benefit of products only if they are an essential element of the programme, helping to develop the plot or enhance realism, and no undue prominence is given. Of course, apart from the question of legality, we can also ask whether stealth advertising is ethically acceptable?

It is claimed that the benefits (to the provider) of product placement extend well beyond on-screen exposure. A promotional campaign can create a positive association between the product and the film plot and/or its characters – a 'halo marketing' effect. This co-promotion and joint marketing is a growing business.

Typical objectives are:

- avoid the clutter of advertising media by placing the product in the entertainment media
- build awareness through establishment or reinforcement
- celebrity endorsement is implied – when the product is used, a preference or choice is suggested
- exposure to people who do not read and watch conventional broadcast media
- product use consistent with the desired image, i.e. in natural and believable situations, reinforcing the image
- attractive portrayal to increase desirability of purchase, perhaps boosting conventional advertising impact
- positive reinforcement of brand loyalty

What is the impact of product placement? Providers may raise brand awareness and employee morale, reinforcing the broader marketing programme.

ADVERTORIALS: STORYTELLING

For many years, articles written by marketers and their advertising and publicity agencies have appeared in the popular and trade press, and this is spreading to the journal and business press.

The writing of positive business stories that take the place of paid-for advertising is highly advantageous for marketers who have a complex issue to deal with in educating their market. However, editors have to remain loath to publishing articles that might be construed as having editorial support.

To ensure that readers are not misled, such material must be clearly marked as 'advertisement', 'advertising', or 'promotion'.

Often advertorials will be written by opinion formers such as eminent academics and politicians. The purpose is to show authoritatively the provider's products in a good light, perhaps as a solution to a social problem. They can have much more impact than a conventional advertisement. Research shows that people are more likely to read an advertorial because it raises interest in the way that editorial does, and is seen by many readers as added-value advertising – informative, rewarding, stimulating. (See the Virgin Direct example in Box 9.2.)

The cost can be high, because publishers will charge a premium when there is the additional benefit of implied endorsement. But response rates often are much higher than from conventional advertisements. The production and placement of an effective and efficient advertorial represents the cross-over point between marketing and public relations. We will consider this further in chapters ten, fourteen, and eighteen.

BOX 9.2 PEPPING UP PEP PROMOTION

Virgin Direct wanted to make contact with, and broaden the appeal of personal equity plans for people who do not regularly read the personal finance sections of national newspapers.

Agency Consolidated Communications created a series of advertorials that appeared in the news sections of several major daily and Sunday newspapers. These were written to given a more in-depth explanation of the benefits of Virgin's PEP products, and featured quirky photographs of Richard Branson in various related situations that would be immediately recognizable and with which people could identify and see as fun.

The style of the features was consistent with that of the respective publication but did not attempt to mimic editorial. Information was kept very basic so that readers could make up their own mind.

Through a direct-response telephone number, the 'On the track of the best PEP' article generated more than £1m in sales.

(*Source*: based on Purdom, 1996: 11)

MARKETING COMMUNICATION THROUGH NEW MEDIA

The traditional view that marketing management focuses on the market as an object is being challenged. Networks and interactions are at the core of the new marketing paradigm (Gummesson, 1999, for example). Value is constantly created in interaction with consumers, suppliers, employees and managers (Normann and Ramirez, 1994). In these interactions, people construct experiences (Holbrook and Hirschman, 1982). The value of the experiences is increased by customized marketing relationships. In this new way of thinking, consumption can no longer be seen as separate from communication, buying, post-purchase behaviour, and so on (Gatarski and Lundkvist, 1998).

Box 9.3 and 9.4 provide two illustrations of marketing communication through new media and by innovative methods.

BOX 9.3   MARKETSPACE

is a virtual realm where products and services exist as digital information and are deliverable through information-based channels. This is distinct from the traditional notion of the physical world with its real consumers and their single and fairly stable identities.

(See Rayport and Svikola, 1995).

BOX 9.4   THE RIGHT TO BRAND

When the *Telegraph* (newspaper) ran advertisements for certain products under their name rather than the name of the producer, sales of these *Telegraph*-endorsed products rose up to 36 per cent. By 1996, some 400 branded reader offers generated £15m in sales turnover. Today, you may well receive a *Telegraph* mail pack offering car and house insurance.

The newspaper has moved from being merely an intermediary distribution channel, i.e. a medium of communication, to become a retailer (product distributor) in their own right who own a share of the customer relationship by exercising their 'right to brand'.

The emergence of the media retailer, combining branding, media, and retailing, may spell disaster or opportunity for providers – depending on how they reassess their assumptions about market structure and modes of relating, competing, and cooperating.

The functional roles are changing. Entertainment is now a service and part of advertising. Information is a service and an element of advertising, as well as real-time research. Communication may never have been so crucial for commercial prosperity and social well-being.

(*Source*: Based on Mitchell, 1996).

We saw, in chapter two, that traditional marketing thinking presupposes that producers produce and communicate, while consumers receive and consume. In the marketing process, i.e. in taking a product into the marketplace, production, communication, and consumption are separate processes. The task of the marketer is seen to be to reach, and stay in, the minds of consumers. It is also presumed that consumers are (naturally) human and that marketplaces are geographically separated entities. New media have forced a change in our way of thinking. The key concept is interaction.

Interaction and interactivity

If we apply the concept of conversation to the process of communicating, we find that interactivity is critical. Communication, as we saw in chapter two, is not really merely about information sharing.

Interactivity arises when later exchanges in a process of communicating are related to the degree to which previous exchanges referred to earlier exchanges. Consumers engage in marketing relationships and in so doing co-produce. There is an integral memory in the process, and essentially it is the consumer who controls the content of the interaction.

Thus, interactive marketing is the **immediately iterative** process by which customers' needs and desires are uncovered and met by the providing firm (see Bezjian-Avery *et al.*, 1998). Both parties elicit information from the other in ongoing attempts to align interests and possibilities. The marketer is able to build databases that allow tailoring of subsequent purchase opportunities through customized information provision. Interactive marketing is discussed further in chapter eleven. In traditional advertising, a predetermined linear presentation is made to expose consumers passively to product information (for example in a TV advertisement segment or page sequence of a magazine). In interactive advertising, consumers actively choose, step by step, their 'journey' through the available information. Box 9.5 considers one such major alternative trading channel.

BOX 9.5   M-COMMERCE

Mobile telephone handsets launched in November 1999 have a mini Web browser (WAP) that can send e-mail, receive news and information, send orders for products, transact banking services, and download music. By 2004, around 95 per cent of mobile phones are likely to be WAP enabled. With around 50 per cent of UK adults owning a mobile phone by the end of 1999, this is going to be a major alternative trading channel.

(*Source*: *Retail Week*, 18 February 2000)

Interactive advertising vs. traditional advertising

Although there has been excitement among marketers, advertising agencies, and marketing educators alike, there is no universally agreed view that interactive advertising is superior in marketing performance than the traditional approaches to advertising. Bezjian-Avery *et al.* (1998) compared consumer reactions to products advertised through interactive media and through traditional, non-interactive formats. A formal test was made of thirty-one advertisements in terms of product appeal, appetite appeal (the test featured food and drink products), novelty, and verbal appearance of the advertisement. Some ninety-six people participated in the test. The researchers found that for certain products and certain consumers, interactive advertising interrupts the process of persuasion. Effectiveness is usually gauged in terms of engagement and persuasiveness. If persuasion is a process of presentation and attention, through comprehension, through generation and retrieval of related cognitions, to yielding and retention, then it is the link between retrieval and yielding that is broken by interactive systems. In the test purchase, intention and time spent viewing the advertisement were both lower for the interactive advertisements than for the traditional advertisements. Participants with a visual bias in their information processing were inhibited by the interactive system. Thus, the performance of interactive advertising seems to depend upon whether the consumer prefers information in a visual or verbal manner, and whether the advertising content is primarily visual or verbal in impression.

Box 9.6 focuses on a recent strategy in the music business that fuses the communication act and exchange.

BOX 9.6   A STAIRWAY TO HEAVEN.COM?

Following an unlikely pairing of the Black Crowes and Jimmy Page for a charity gig at London's Café de Paris, the collaborators set out on a mini tour of the USA. A spin-off, eighteen-track live album may well be the unexpected breakthrough that music fans have longed for and some parts of the music industry wish would go away.

The album *Live at the Greek* isn't available in any record stores. It can only be bought from a single website – musicmaker.com, but in a multitude of formats. By logging onto the website, fans can order the double CD for $17.90, or browse through the 30-second track samples before selecting which ones and in what order they will appear on a custom-made disk. For those who cannot wait for a mail package, MP3 format files can be downloaded for $1.00 each.

Musicmaker claim that this facility is 'a whole new paradigm shift' for the industry, representing the first Internet-only music release by a major act. Musicmaker isn't merely selling a few CDs online in parallel with traditional retail business, they have 'constructed a new business model that the industry is watching closely'.

First they released a single as a taster, which was provided only to those radio stations that had a website. They then linked those sites to the Musicmaker site. When a radio listener hears the single and buys the music through the respective websites, the radio station receives a commission on the sale, providing a clear incentive for them to play the record and to promote the website. The effect? The single entered the Top 10 US Radio and Records Rock chart, reached number 15 on Billboard's Rock Track chart and number 14 on the album network. Pretty impressive for a record made by an artist who is not associated with singles and for a product that is not available to browsers in high-street shops! *Music Week* predicts that many more deals will be made in this way – cutting out traditional retail network and record manufacturers, and putting the artist and fan one step closer together.

There are no competing discount deals among retailers to erode profit margins, and the product is never out of stock, while promotional expenditure is largely directly spent on making sales. Fans now know exactly where to find the products and can even be alerted automatically by e-mail messages when new releases are made. Many established acts have their own website – many sell their records direct to fans – this is the first to cut out the middle man. The communication act and exchange are no longer separated; the interaction is at once an interchange.

(*Source*: Based on Edwards, 2000 and the www.musicmaker.com website)

Table 9.1   **Relational dimensions of communication media**

Media	*One-to-many*	*One-to-one*
Directive	**Presentation** • Mass media advertising • Standard catalogue • Product demonstration	**Narrowcasting** • Direct mail • Selective catalogue
Interactive	**Consultation** • Trade shows • CD-ROM • List-based e-mail • Public relations and hospitality • Website	**Conversation** • Personal selling • Telesales • Personal e-mail • Personalized website • Consulting

Source: Based on van Raaij, 1998: 3

Table 9.1 shows four possible modes of relating and examples of the technologies that enable such means of communicating. The technological and social changes witnessed over the past thirty years has blurred the distinction between public and private communication and between senders and receivers (McQuail, 1987 – see Figure 9.1).

Interactive advertising can use interactive media to qualify sales leads, turn customer prospects into purchasers, lower marketing costs, and create new sales channels. This presents a challenge for marketing specialists, who have to become expert in advertising fundamentals and interactivity – see Boxes 9.7–9.12.

Public sender – Public receiver Traditional mass communication processes (allocution)	**Private sender – Public receiver** Advertising; advocacy; image-building activities of public relations
Public sender – Private receiver Interpersonal communication; intra-corporate communication (exchange)	**Private sender – Private receiver** Videotext; subscription cable television (search)

Figure 9.1 **McQuail's typology of communication events**

BOX 9.7   BROADCAST VS. INTERACTIVE

What do the post, telegraph, telephone, fax, and Internet have in common? They are all interactive connectors of people. But they only thrive in a network of users. The very first fax machine purchased was actually totally useless!

Traditional advertising differs from these interactive media: it has always been used in a fundamentally content-based communication strategy.

BOX 9.8   THE MYSKI BUSINESS CONVERSATION

Through the Internet, MySki Inc. enable consumers to design their own products by entering details of their height, skill level, style, and so on at www.myski.com. Visitors to the site can choose colours and provide text and logos that can be printed onto the upper surface of the skis, which are made to order. The website allows local customer support in twenty-five native languages, and an ever-growing consumer database of preferences, interests, orders, enquiries, etc. Consumers are co-producers in conversation with this supplier.

(*Source*: Based on Gatarski and Lundkvist, 1998)

BOX 9.9   SATURN CAR CLUBS

At the Saturn subsidiary of General Motors, brand managers encourage customers to join car clubs and support access to information about members via a searchable online service.

(*Source*: Based on Gatarski and Lundkvist, 1998)

BOX 9.10 HOT MODEM CONVERSATIONS FOR MEGAHERTZ

When a customer of modem supplier Megahertz offered his modem for sale in a CompuServe online forum, he was contacted by a company representative who asked him why he wanted to sell it. During the next week several people offered similar explanations – dissatisfaction due to some malfunctions with the equipment. Even when other people said that they had decided not to buy a Megahertz modem because of what they had read in the forum, the company kept out of the discussion. Several discussants subsequently offered recommendations to the company on what to expect in market conversation and behaviour in electronic media. Consumers were running the conversation. Perhaps managers were missing the point: sometimes marketing communication is unplanned, i.e. initiated by customers (who may be dissatisfied). They also failed to participate in the debate – this passive stance can be damaging.

(*Source*: Based on Gatarski and Lundkvist, 1998)

BOX 9.11 55,000 MEMBERS IN THE DIABETES FORUM

When a diabetes sufferer wanted to discuss his disease with other sufferers, he started a CompuServe forum – with no doctors and medical experts. Consumers of pharmaceutical products and public and private health service users exchange information and solutions to problems by discussing their experiences. Occasionally, external speakers are invited to participate – rarely are producers invited. There is here an alternative to a relationship with the producer.

(*Source*: Based on Gatarski and Lundkvist, 1998)

BOX 9.12 ARTIFICIAL CONSUMERS

As electronic media become more pervasive, **agents** are becoming more likely to act on behalf of consumers to provide reminders, to filter, to criticize, to match, to guide, or to shop. BargainFinder is a shopping partner that can search ten online catalogues for discounted CDs. When a title or artist's name is located, a link can be followed to the vendor's site. Despite the advantages to consumers, who can use agents as artificial representatives, they may not be popular with vendors, who limit the information provided. In other developments, agents can 'learn' and even converse with each other.

As an example, Barnes & Noble Inc. have adopted the Firefly Online system that allows consumers to enter a personal profile that is used to locate suitable products. Other systems go even further, being able to negotiate, buy, and sell goods as artificial consumers.

Interestingly, trials show that the technology available is already adequate for these services. What is, as yet, missing is sufficient trust by consumers in their artificial agents.

(*Source*: Based on Gatarski and Lundkvist, 1998)

For the value-provider, the Internet offers the potential benefits of:

- higher levels of customer service
- strengthened relationships with customers
- extension of the customer base through recruitment
- reduced communication costs, with customers and prospective customers
- effective awareness creation and positioning of brands
- an alternative or additional channel to market

PUBLICITY AND WORD OF MOUTH

Publicity is the bringing of what is otherwise private into the public sphere of awareness. Arguably, publicity is brought about through advertising that is not paid for by the initiator, and (at least potentially) provides benefit to both initiator and appreciator (see Vickers' appreciative system, chapter two). Thus publicity differs from other forms of marketing communication in that the identity of the sponsor is absent. Indeed, it is the intention of the marketer to remain unknown as the initiator, thereby gaining credibility for the informing and claiming content as if emanating from a third party (journalist, editor, reviewer, etc.). Publicity is generally regarded as more credible than advertising, in taking on the credibility of the media vehicle in which it appears.

For example, in 1996 the English National Opera planned to stage Zimmerman's *Die Soldaten* (Strong, 1997). This was potentially a controversial proposal because of the huge orchestral and technical requirements, but also more importantly because the opera contains strong language, nudity, and a rape scene.

The publicity team worked closely with the marketing team to play down the sensational aspects of the opera and instead chose to focus on the rarity of the performance.

The conductor Elgar Howarth made himself available to talk to journalists throughout the rehearsals, and advertising and direct mail was used to raise awareness and understanding of this comparatively unknown work. Rehearsal and preview photographs appeared in national newspapers, including a special piece in *The Independent*, and reviews were featured on several radio and TV arts programmes.

Many people attended the performances because they were intrigued by what they had read in the press. Ticket sales exceeded the target set and the company retained its artistic credibility.

For a growing number of people, being 'in the know' is part of their lifestyle (Robinson, 2000). An ethos of discretion is developing among clubs, hairdressers, bars, clothes boutiques, and so on. They operate their businesses on word of mouth alone. This trend is a reaction to the overhyped 'superbrands' that have dominated high-street shopping for the past twenty years. Exclusivity, where customers are invited to trade, often on recommendation from 'members', is the new business model. Word of mouth has replaced advertising. Customers are personally contacted by the proprietor with an exclusive offer derived from personal knowledge. Some business owners are actually shunning publicity – they do it because they want to be talked about for that very reason.

Word-of-mouth recommendation, by a satisfied customer, is one of the most effective, and cost-effective marketing communication means. Personal influence arises when people converse about products and providers. People ask for information from those others whose opinions and experiences they value and trust. People like to talk about their experiences (but not always to the advantage of the provider). According to research by Dichter (1966), involvement is the motivation for this 'market chatter'. We like to relive things that were particularly pleasant or unpleasant, and are attracted to prestige and status which can be acquired through establishing ownership. We can also attempt to reduce dissonance by seeking reassurance. We can also feel good by sharing the benefits of products with others. These are examples of market exchanges that extend beyond the initial offer made in advertising – we explained such multi-step communication in chapter seven.

EXHIBITIONS AND TRADE SHOWS

One quite popular venue for consumption conversations is the seminar, trade show, or exhibition. For many years, manufacturers, distributors, whole-salers, and retailers have felt the need to spend considerable amounts of marketing resource on presence at these events in order to 'meet the buyer'. Some events are intended for selling, i.e. orders are placed by buyers with suppliers, while others are purely promotional.

So how cost-effective are such attempts to reach potential customers face to face? As Bythe (2000) points out, these are rather like modern-day medieval markets. Blythe provides a rather helpful analysis of the problem of managing exhibitions and trade events.

Our question here is do exhibitors get value for effort in their attempts at selling, or are visitors merely 'surfing'? Recent research by Skerlos and Blythe (2000) shows some considerable and disturbing differences in visitor and exhibitor purposes. The expectations of visitors to exhibitions and trade fairs are largely to gather information about products and suppliers and to discuss technical problems. On the other hand, exhibitors wish to sell, meet customers, and show new products – a highly sales-oriented purpose (see Box 9.13). There is a fundamental mismatch of motives of participants that is costly to exhibitors. Setting clear communication objectives is a must. For some, this will centre on image-making.

SALES PROMOTIONS

Ask your mum about the Hoover 'free flights' débâcle! A classic example of a promise that could not be kept.

Ways of encouraging the purchase of products include competitions, discount vouchers, and salesforce prize incentives. Sales promotion activities help salespeople to do a better selling job through sales presentation support

---

BOX 9.13   DIGGING THE DIGGERS IN MALAGA

Take 200 UK distributors, their top customers, 30 JCB excavators of various shapes and sizes, and a plush armchair conference centre in southern Spain during March. What have you got? The launch of a range of new products and a marketing strategy that resulted in the restructuring of the business!

March is the start of the construction-equipment selling season and Spain has the nice weather at that time of year, while Malaga has a superior airport and the conference facilities of the Torrequebrada Hotel.

The launch took the format of a series of conferences over a two-week period with welcoming dinner followed by formal presentations supported by video. Temporary grandstands were used to house the equipment demonstrations, and delegates were treated to a display of horsemanship and flamenco dancing.

This format was judged to be more cost-effective than five or six national events throughout Europe. One customer commented, 'if the aim is to demonstrate quality and commitment, they've done very well'.

---

materials, and stimulate additional selling effort by offering prizes and other rewards. Retailers and wholesalers are encouraged to sell more through displays, direct mail, or specially prepared advertising. Selected prospective customers are influenced through video, trade shows, and direct mail. Advertising and selling impact is enhanced through samples, coupons, premiums, and competitions and draws.

According to Gardener and Trevidi (1998), sales promotions accounted for almost three-quarters of the advertising and promotions budget in the early part of the 1990s (see Box 9.14 for a look at character merchandising). At the same time, around eight out of ten people who responded to a sales

---

BOX 9.14   ADDED-VALUE CHARACTERS

The world-wide character merchandising business exceeds $100bn to retail prices. Licensed characters can appeal to young consumers and raise awareness for the launch of a film as well as prompt impulse purchase. For a big film, merchandising may exceed box-office revenue. Income will be huge, but short-lived.

But think about it for a moment. A tin of *Pokemon* baked beans tastes no different and the tin and label are discarded as soon as its contents are removed. Why then does this add value?

Collectibles are another matter. *Star Wars* tie-in products that transform the playgroup into Darth Maul, Anakin Skywalker, and soldiers of the Galactic Empire need little explanation (at least to my 5-year-old son), and some give-aways become collectors' items and increase in value.

It seems that invented people can be better at selling products than real people!

---

promotion offer were in fact already loyal customers who presumably would have bought the product anyway. Further, sales promotions do not only impact on sales but also on brand value. As we suggested in chapter seven, the price of a product has a lot to say about quality, value for money, prestige, etc. We also have seen that what such factors have to say depends on who is hearing it and in what context. Clearly, sales promotion is not simply another promotion option – it underlies all of the marketing mix effects.

Gardener and Trevidi provide a framework that allows the marketing communication manager to judge sales promotions activity in terms of the effectiveness in accomplishing the various communication objectives that may be desirable to the marketing management. Table 9.2 summarizes their conclusions.

Table 9.2 **What can sales promotions achieve?**

	Free-standing insert coupon	On-shelf coupon	On-pack (gifts)	Bonus packs (% free or 3-for-2, etc.)	Everyday low prices
Grab attention and create an impression	M	H	L	H	L
Generate understanding	H	H	L	M	M
Persuade	M	H	M	M	M
Influence purchase behaviour	M	H	L	M	L

Source: Based on Gardener and Trevidi, 1998

Sales promotions work best when all of the four levels of communication objective are accomplished. It seems that the on-shelf coupon does this best. Consumers receive a value-added incentive that is easy to take advantage of without incurring costs. They do not have to clip the coupon, save it, and take it to the store. The redemption of coupons differs markedly between countries. North Americans redeem around 6 times as many as British consumers, and 60 times as many as Spaniards. Managers must design promotions that communicatively link the consumer with the value of purchase.

A variety of sales promotions are dealt with in Boxes 9.15–9.17.

BOX 9.15   THE SPIN SELLING SYSTEM

Rackham (1988) developed a four-stage selling approach that develops commitment and relationship marketing. A precisely defined sequence of four questions enables the salesperson to move a conversation with a buyer/consumer logically from exploring the customers' (implied) needs to designing solutions by surfacing explicit needs that can be met. The type of questions are as follows:

- **Situation questions**: these are essential to clarify the current position;
- **Problem questions**: these uncover difficulties that present the provider with an opportunity to serve;
- **Implication questions**: these make the problem seem more acute to the buyer and raise the possibility of consequences of not resolving the problem;
- **Need-payoff questions**: these focus attention on the solution.

Although it is recognized that this technique can be abused, it does offer the possibility of jointly creating a shared understanding. This cooperative selling–buying interaction can be described as strategic talk (Heyman, 1994) when mutual understanding is negotiated through summary and explanation, questions and answers, paraphrasing, examples, and storytelling.

BOX 9.16   BOOTS PUT THEIR FOOT IN IT!

When City of Ely Community College pupils collected 943 vouchers (one voucher per £5 spent), they were astounded to find that this bonus from retail expenditure of £4,715 could be exchanged for only one gym mat. Even when Boots doubled the exchange value of their scheme, the school still only got two mats!

Such promotional schemes encourage children to nag their parents into buying specific brands. Parents want to support their child's school, but if not properly researched, such schemes can be resented by consumers who may feel that the provider is more interested in a sales promotion opportunity than giving service to its customers and stakeholders.

(Based on O'Sullivan, 1993)

BOX 9.17   POINT-OF-PURCHASE MATERIALS

Research by the Point of Purchase Advertising Institute (The Consumer Buying Habits Study) has shown that four out of five purchase decisions are made in-store. Grocery shoppers are exposed to three hundred products a minute in a large supermarket, and two-thirds of them have no shopping list while shopping. The impact of p-o-p advertising on impulse sales can be dramatic. The UK p-o-p industry accounts for more than £500m in marketing expenditure. Retail displays can prompt large increases in sales. In-store marketing is a specialized field based on the communicative capability of design of packaging and display materials.

MEDIA SELECTION

With no shortage of media options available, but within the scope of a limited budget, how can selection decisions be made? Figure 9.2 suggests a number of essential considerations when considering a particular medium.

Reach	Number of people who pay attention, geographic coverage, and penetration of the total population
Audience type	Profile of those who can and do pay attention – values, lifestyle, etc.
Audience size	How many people to be contacted
Budget	Production costs and media purchase
Communication objective	What can be accomplished and what response is required?
Time	Timescale for intended response, relation to other media use, etc.
Media-buying constraints	Air time is sold through competitive bidding and requires booking many weeks in advance
Restrictions	Regulations exclude certain products from certain media
Competitor activity	Where, when, and why are competing providers advertising?

Figure 9.2 **Systematic selection of media**

To make best use of the limited budget available and to ensure that a genuinely dialogic relationship is maintained with consumers and buyers as potential and current customers, media should be selected for their effectiveness (suitability) and efficiency (performance). The effectiveness of a medium is its capacity to generate a desired outcome or condition in a particular situation or context, i.e. to accomplish a desirable communication objective. The efficiency of a medium is the amount of resource (time, money, effort, etc.) expended in striving for the accomplishment of the desired communication objective. Table 9.3 indicates performance characteristics of various media options, and these must be considered in relation to the communication objectives set and the cost of using the medium.

Against the performance characteristics of the media options set out in Table 9.3, the following questions must be asked:

1 Is the medium interactive or not?
2 What is the cost of reaching the target consumer/buyer?

Table 9.3   **Media characteristics**

Medium	+ Reasons for using	− Reasons for not using
News press	Relatively inexpensive way to generate news; short lead time; wide reach; reader determines consumption rate; good for technical detail and third-party endorsement	Passive; reproduction of photographs may be poor; no dynamics – attention-getting fairly poor; reading is a declining pastime
Magazine	Quality of reproduction provides high impact; readers want advertisements; longevity; can associate a brand with cultural icons among a mass audience	Visual only; long lead times; cannot make a sale; does not foster a relationship
TV	Realism – sight, sound and movement; repetition; regional zoning; entertaining; gives credibility to the product	Poor selectivity; detail often missed; cluttered; relatively high cost; long lead times; highly regulated content; thinly spread fragmented audiences (proliferating channels); inflexible
Radio	Widespread use; active; local targeting; targeting in time slots; relatively inexpensive; intimate and immediate; topical; can involve listeners	No visual content; transient; often used only as background, so attention is low; small audiences; low prestige
Cinema	High impact; captive audience	Expensive, especially production; lacks detail
Billboard/poster	Low cost; localized; easily changed; short runs are economical	Low-attention capacity; limited segmentation possible; vulnerable to vandalism; lots of distraction; relatively poor image
Direct mail	Low-production cost; can be kept for reference; allows details; targeted and testable	(Relatively) expensive to execute; a 2% response rate is typical! Junk mail and telesales calls are unpopular!
Sales promotions	Direct impact on sales; encourages trial	Turns brands into commodities
Internet website banner	Inexpensive presence; active; allows movement, sound and colour to attract; fast information provision; can have a sales facility	No national coverage; limited access and not relevant for perishable and 'sensory' goods such as perfume and food

3 How much flexibility is available?
4 What state of mind is the consumer/buyer likely to be in?
5 Can you afford the minimum cost of media space?
6 How will each option work with or against the brand values?
7 What is the level of accountability for performance, in terms of cost v. return?

Table 9.4 summarizes the relative effectiveness of the three main modes of marketing communication in the accomplishment of communication objectives.

Table 9.4   Relative effectiveness of communication approaches

Factor	Advertising	Personal selling	Sales promotion
Awareness	high	low	medium
Interest	medium	medium	medium
Conviction	low	high	high
Purchase	low	high	high
Post-purchase	high	low	low

How would a marketing website compare with traditional advertising (impersonal) and personal selling (personal)? See Box 9.18 for an example of an alternative channel of distribution.

Of course, the website is available relatively easily and inexpensively as an international marketing communication tool and has the potential to be a major influencer of the various communicators that can be managed, in the following ways:

BOX 9.18   TUNING IN TO ALTERNATIVE CHANNELS OF DISTRIBUTION

Getting your music heard is no longer a matter of being in the right place at the right time. Peoplesound.com is a revolutionary new way to get your music heard – on the Internet.

Covering more than twenty genres of popular music, this distribution system promotes and sells music direct from the artist via CD and downloadable MP3-format files. Peoplesound.com promote the music via charts in the weekly music magazines and through reviews posted on their website. Staff are experienced former employees of major record companies.

(*Source*: Peoplesound brochure and www.peoplesound.com)

- new product development and testing in dialogue with buyers and users
- sale and delivery of products (software downloading and virtual shop-front, shopping malls, electronic shopping trollies)
- pricing administration – frequently updated paperless price lists and customized pricing

NEED–SATISFACTION THEORY

Consumers and buyers, presumably, mostly make purchases to satisfy unmet needs. The salesperson must, therefore, discover the person's needs and show how their own products will fulfil those needs. This customer-oriented approach contrasts with alternative salesperson-oriented approaches (stimulus–response and selling formula: **A**ttention, **I**nterest, **D**esire, **A**ction).

Unlike the selling formula that requires the salesperson to point out all of the features of the product, the customer-oriented approach starts by asking about the customer's needs. This is a communication problem because it requires the salesperson to be sufficiently self-confident to control the sales interview through questioning in conversation rather than by dominating through presentation. The salesperson's mental model of communicating is crucial in this situation. The investment in turning this more time-consuming and complex interaction into an interchange is rewarded by a greater likelihood of making a mutually satisfactory sale by matching the customer's needs with the appropriate product's features and benefits. If the distinction between exploitative and transactional interactions is unclear, refer back to the explanation of a social model of communication in chapter four.

THE CHANGING STRUCTURE OF MARKETING MEDIA

In the 1980s, desktop publishing became affordable, thus allowing low-cost entry into design and publishing of magazines and other printed publications. Today, almost all publishing firms use PC-based technologies to cost-effectively produce small runs of printed materials. Since the 1980s we have witnessed a massive proliferation in the number of narrowly targeted magazines catering for specialized interests.

Deregulation in TV and radio broadcasting has shifted the industry from broadcast to 'narrowcast', with many channels and small audiences in place of few channels with 'mass' audiences. Sponsored programming has also become commonplace in media regions outside of the USA. ONDigital and cable services offer interactivity, with online banking and shopping, and e-mail facilities.

In the UK, around one-third of the adult population owns a PC. Almost two in three households have a PC.

The advent of the Internet has opened up a means of (two-way) interchange between providers and users, in place of the (one-way) sending of messages from providers to (assumed passive) receivers. This interchange may be initiated by either party and involves both listening and talking. Both shoppers and providers can ask questions. This form of 'corporate conversation' can provide both parties with information on a range of aspects of a much more negotiated relationship (trust, credibility, risk, etc). We will discuss this further in chapter eighteen when we consider the significance of identity, image, and reputation. Arguably, marketing via the Worldwide Web (WWW) is changing the dynamics of competition, since it is now website creativity rather than market power that matters – pressure is on marketing managers to differentiate their offerings on new terms – see Box 9.19 for an example of a potential disadvantage of website marketing. Particularly taxing is that the consumer/buyer has to find the provider rather than vice versa.

BOX 9.19   FALLING FOUL OF THE NEW TECHNOLOGY

In 1996, Virgin Atlantic Airways failed to update the prices shown on their website and were fined $14,000 for violation of advertising regulations, according to the *Wall Street Journal*, March.

THE IMPACT OF THE INTERNET

The Internet-centred business model, which requires reorganization of business activities around networked communities, is replacing the increasingly outmoded model of industrial organization. For a growing number of businesses in all market sectors, this redesign has produced increased efficiency, enhanced service capabilities, the empowerment of employees, improved response time, and greater customer satisfaction. All people involved in the purchase and supply of goods and services are connected, creating an integrated production–supply–consumption chain comprising communities of employees, customers, managers, and suppliers and partners. The technology adopted has to be capable of providing more than systems for passive information transmission and electronic brochures. Interactive networks have to be enabled. This is an issue that has yet to be fully addressed by those software vendors and consultants who have adopted the terminology of relationship strategy but not the substantive principles. This is considered further in chapter twelve when we examine relationship marketing and (the currently fashionable) customer relationship management (CRM).

IMPLICATIONS FOR MARKETING COMMUNICATIONS MANAGEMENT

With the continuing development of multimedia, mediated marketing communication activity will merge into a TV/PC environment that will see TV, the Internet, radio, telephone, etc. operating as a single connection. Marketing communication managers and their servicing agencies and advisors must recognize that marketing communication includes, but is not merely, advertising. Rather than thinking in terms of separate media, planners and designers will have to deal with the concept of a range of media environments.

Consumer experiences and emotions have been given a central role in consumer behaviour theory for some time. With the advent of artificial agents, how will such factors be dealt with?

One person may be represented by many agents, and many people may choose to have a single agent to do their shopping. Agent behaviour may become much more significant than consumer behaviour.

The traditional distinction between 'above-the-line' and 'below-the-line' promotion is far better recast as marketing communication, including various forms of advertising, direct marketing communication, interactive marketing communication, personal negotiation, publicity, sponsorship, and various forms of supporting sales promotion.

CASE STUDY 9   MARKETING CREDIT CARDS: DIRECT COMMUNICATION FOR THE LAUNCH OF RBS ADVANTA[a]

In the early to mid-1990s, the UK credit card market was believed, by the major card companies, to be mature. The number of new card issuers was stagnant and the value of account balances was growing slowly. The whole market worked on 'inertia' – the fact that once you'd attracted a customer to take 'your' card, they would stay loyal – mainly due to the hassles involved in 'switching'/cancelling one credit card and going through the credit approval process all over again for another one. Yet, across the Atlantic in the USA, the credit card market was buoyant with much activity: new cards were being launched and customers were switching to new accounts often in search of good and better deals (termed 'card surfing').

In the USA, around 75 per cent of adults held at least one credit card, while the uptake in the UK remained under 40 per cent. The major high-street banks saw the situation as unattractive, while other financial businesses eyed the UK with plans to exploit a substantial growth opportunity. In 1990, Save & Prosper (eventually taken over by Flemings) dipped into the 'low APR' market and launched a credit card with a low rate – around 14 per cent, when the market was at 23 per cent. This was backed with low-key advertising in London and the south-east of England. This was followed rapidly by Chase Manhattan who launched a low APR card in the UK – and put substantially more marketing and advertising behind their entry. This included national press advertising, direct mail and 'image advertising' in the weekend newspaper colour supplements. Just as this card was beginning to take off (200,000 cards issued within 18 months) Chase Manhattan experienced economic difficulties in its home markets and cut all 'overseas projects'. The card was sold on to Girobank and then onto Alliance & Leicester and has not been promoted since. Save & Prosper and Chase Manhattan had been the first to launch low-cost credit cards in the UK – neither had significant sustained success at that time. In 1993, MBNA established a UK office in Chester, while other US companies began to look seriously at the UK, e.g. The Associates, Capital One, etc.

During 1994, senior executives from the Royal Bank of Scotland visited the USA to observe the market at first-hand. Meanwhile the Advanta Corporation of Pennsylvania had sent observers to the UK. A deal was struck with Advanta – who were already looking at moving into the UK market – for a joint venture in the UK. RBS Advanta was born.

Advanta was one of four small mono-line card service companies operating with the successful US business model that interested the Royal Bank of Scotland. In the USA, credit bureaux supply data to credit card companies who use derived credit profiles to select potential new customers. They offer introductory discounted credit account rates to attract new customers from the regional banks. Prospective customers are targeted exclusively with direct mail. The card companies have no strong brand in themselves, but are able to sell their services on the strength of their MasterCard and Visa affiliations.

The deal was struck between Advanta and the Royal Bank of Scotland in 1995. Although the US business model cannot be applied fully in the UK – we do not have the same opportunities to access credit bureaux information in the UK (house rules apply, so that banks are not allowed access to full consumer data) – the credit card usage profile of the UK was somewhat similar to that of the US, albeit lagging three to four fours years behind in terms of development.

Brand was key to the planned joint venture. Although smaller than the major high-street banks, the Royal Bank of Scotland has a strong brand. A new company, RBS Advanta was formed and launched in February 1996 as a specialist credit card marketer. Their new approach threatened the traditional banking sector. UK-based credit card issuers have seen their market share decline by about 4 per cent each year since 1994 when they completely controlled the market. In the period 1996–98, US issuers such as MBNA and CapitalOne took control of 15 per cent of the UK market, and since then several others such as Bank One – who moved from start-up to being one of the three biggest users of direct mail in the UK within eighteen months – have moved in and set up aggressive direct marketing, sophisticated market segmentation, and risk analysis systems.

RBS Advanta has been a leading player in upsetting the 'apple cart'. Even before the new company started trading, their new approach provoked objections from an established operator. A test mailing to 200,000 prospective customers in October 1995 included 15 'bullet points' that claimed to provide a direct comparison of product benefits and interest rates. This included comparative information about the Barclaycard offering. Barclays Bank, in seeking to defend against the new competition, took out a court action against RBS Advanta, claiming infringement of the recently introduced UK Trade Mark Act (1994), in that the Barclaycard trade name had been used without permission and in a derogatory way. The court ruled that this was a case of 'honest practices' and that a reasonable reader would not regard the particular use of the word 'Barclaycard' in the RBS Advanta advertising as dishonest. However, certain items in the direct mail packs were held to be not comparing like for like and it was highlighted that the pack made no reference to certain benefits which Barclaycard offered and which the RBS Advanta card did not. Comparative advertising can be problematic (as we discuss in chapter fourteen), but is ideal for use in established markets where a big brand, or several brands, 'own' the market and 'you' as a smaller brand have a demonstrably better product.

There are two categories of credit card customer: borrowers, who have debit balances on their accounts and thus pay interest, and transactors who use their card simply in place of cash. The RBS Advanta business model has been to attract only borrowers, through detailed analysis of the type of card usage, and termination of inactive accounts. They even measured the success of their direct marketing campaigns – not just by the number of new customers attracted but also by the number of borrowers (immediately) attracted. But in the UK, the capability to target through credit history profiling is much more limited than in the USA. Mostly, direct marketers use aggregated data to target segments, but RBS Advanta felt that postcode classification as used in market segmentation data systems (such as MOSAIC, ACORN, SUPERPROFILES, etc.) was inadequate for their needs. What was wanted was much more personal detail to target tightly direct mail. RBS Advanta did something radical – they asked consumers to answer questions directly about their credit card use, and did not rely on abstracted market research surveys. The company sponsored two questions on all UK consumer surveys: 'Are you considering changing your credit card?' and 'Do you pay off all of your credit balance every month?'. Only those who answered the questions with a 'yes' and a 'no', respectively, were included in the RBS Advanta database. Elsewhere, people who buy products and services by mail order were also identified. Regular mailings to bought-in consumer mailing lists have achieved desired response rates, otherwise lists have been dropped or modified. List testing is regularly carried out for the purpose of refining targeting. RBS Advanta have conducted over 700 tests of list data-pack execution combinations in their customer acquisition programmes.

In 1998, RBS Advanta become a wholly owned integrated part of RBS Cards Division. As an incentive to switch to an RBS Advanta account, a discounted introductory interest rate was offered. This has clearly been attractive to those selected to receive the mail offerings. By summer 1999, RBS Advanta had attracted 1,000,000 customers, entirely through direct mail, by offering lower-interest rates on outstanding account balances, and was profitable by its third year and has continued to be so. Currently the product portfolio comprises the Classic, Gold, and Platinum cards.

In looking back on the success of this communication strategy, Tim Lewis, Marketing Director, is clear that the key aspects of their successful approach have been pricing policy, targeting, creative execution (i.e. the building of a strong 'brand identity' and responsiveness through letter and brochure design), and expert analysis. Every mailing that went out contained a 'control' pack and there were at least ten to fifteen 'test mailings' run. If a test mailing beat the control – it would then be 'step-tested' and would normally become the control for the next run. By developing new and different 'test packs' – together with list testing and offer testing – RBS Advanta was able to improve response to its card mailings by over 100 per cent in two years. The introductory-rate offer launched in 1996 has been very successful. A survey was conducted to collect prospect names, and this has produced response rates of three to four times the norm for direct mail. The Platinum Card product was launched very early in the development of the market.

RBS Advanta have now tested over 300 price/creative combinations live in the market-place (rather than through market research), and over 6,000 segments of the total consumer base of the UK. Every mailing list has been measured for direct response rate, and the attrition rate and economic value-added (calculated as the total income over five years plus the terminal value of the portfolio of accounts depreciated to net present value, divided by the number of mail pieces). Regular analyses also examine customer behaviour after joining, in terms of: value of balance transfer; spending; how much is paid off the balance at the end of the month; how much left to 'roll over'; at the end of the 'introductory' low-rate period, how many 'borrowers' remain. Competitor mailings are tracked through specialized agencies whose selected consumer panels collect all the mail packs they receive in a week.

A further aspect that is seen as crucial is product development. Finally, card brand has been critical. Certainly, many people have responded to a strong, rational, value-for-money identity. Perhaps what is less certain is the emotional element of the brand. Tim Lewis is not convinced that emotion can be conveyed well through impersonal media such as direct mail. Royal Bank of Scotland has a strong business identity, but how can the success of the RBS Advanta card be explained, when recall of the name and logo is low and the brand value is weak on the emotion dimension? Just as did First Direct (which both Tim Lewis and Hawkins Innovation Network worked for at this critical time), who everyone 'assumes' spent a lot of money on 'above the line' advertising to create a brand and build their customer base, RBS Advanta did the same. They ensured that every mailing went towards creating a brand as well as establishing response. First Direct relied almost solely on direct mail and favourable 'word-of-mouth' advertising from their satisfied customers from 1991–95 to build their brand. RBS Advanta deliberately set out to build a brand that was 'straightforward; open; honest; modern' – part of the new world of finance and not part of the 'establishment'; one that was consumer friendly. RBS Advanta invested substantial amounts of both time and effort in internal brand seminars with continuous input from their agencies.

What next? Can a brand be built further on the Internet, as Prudential are trying to do with the Egg brand, with supporting traditional media (TV, press, public relations, etc.). Egg is undoubtedly positioned now as the 'high-tech' product (although launched as a 'direct' brand rather than as an Internet brand – they even recruited the original brand team from First Direct to do this). Once they had launched Egg, they used the Internet as part of their recruitment strategy. They attracted people at a lower cost through this medium and concentrated on it. They might also have noted that, even though they were 'giving away money' at rates that could not be sustained, there was an amazing effect going through to their share price. With a preferential rate available only to customers who use the service online, Prudential intended to control the extent of service uptake. Despite this, by June 1999, Egg was attracting over 1,000 new customers each day. The Internet continues to develop as an alternative communication and commerce channel. Barclays' online service has signed-up around 10,000 customers each week since launch, making it the largest online banking service in the UK.

Goldfish and Marbles are the 'wacky' cards – the latter is promoted as the way to pay for purchases on the Internet. The former has targeted transactors through an integrated marketing communication programme. The Goldfish brand was designed by British Gas (in association with HBC, as it then was), as a loyalty device against the Government's heavy regulatory push which started to empower competition. The Government's stated policy was to drive the British Gas share of the market from '100 per cent' down to 16 per cent. British Gas did everything they could to prevent this, including building the Goldfish brand. It was only with two months to launch that the Data Protection Registrar refused them permission to use their customer database for direct mail. The major 'attraction' of a Goldfish Card was – and is – a discount on your British Gas (Centrica) gas bill. The Goldfish concept was designed to capture consumer imagination and to portray personality through the picture of a goldfish and the heavy promotion of advertising campaigns (television, press, and direct mailing, including Billy Connolly as the celebrity face). By May 1999, some 920,000 cards had been issued as part of a widening portfolio of financial products.

For futher information see:
www.rbsadvanta.co.uk
www.cardforum.com
www.goldfish.com
www.hawk-in.co.uk

Discussion topics

1. Who else has built a product brand with only direct mail? (Names that come to mind include *Reader's Digest*, *Which? Magazine*, and the International Masters Publishers (IMP) series of specialist books. Pizza Express, for example, never advertise. Can you identify others?)
2. What is the impact on direct mail for the adoption of the Internet?
3. Royal Mail clearly have a vested interest in direct mail. What is their response to Internet advertising and trading?
4. What is the reason that the Royal Bank of Scotland is not able to build a strong brand?
5. What should they do next?
6. Does the consumer credit card finance market need regulating? (See the *Cruickshank Report*).
7. Why are people in the UK so inert to the onslaught of promotional marketing messages? (In 1999 more than 300 million mailing packs were sent to 21 million households).

Note: [a] The cooperation and assistance of Tim Lewis, the Royal Bank of Scotland, and Dave Hawkins, the Hawkins Innovation Network, in preparing this case history is gratefully acknowledged

WHAT DO YOU THINK?

1 Consider the advent of artificial agents ('intelligent search engines loaded with consumer preference data') in online shopping. What are the implications for the management of marketing communications?
2 With 'e-tail' (online retail shopping) accounting for only a tiny portion of total retail sales value, why all the attention?
3 What are the advantages and disadvantages for consumers/buyers and providers, respectively, of the proliferation of media options?
4 What might be the symbolic value to a marketer and to a consumer respectively, of a web presence for the provider?
5 As product and corporate branding efforts increase, arguably advertising will have to be increased in volume and impact to promote and protect brands against more competition in the minds of consumers and buyers. How will this affect media-selection judgements?
6 'New media generally do not replace "old" media, they simply offer another option.' What implications does this have for marketing communication managers?
7 Some selection criteria are degree of interactivity, content format, cost, and availability. Examine several rather different media options and identify realistic benefits and limitations for several communication objectives.
8 Why is media selection a critical part of the marketing manager's job?
9 What media options are available for the generative part of the marketing process? How would you evaluate their effectiveness and efficiency?
10 Some people are today arguing that the media are not merely 'communications channels'. What is meant by this?

FURTHER READING

Arnott, D. and Fitzgerald, M. (eds) (2000) *Marketing Communications Classics: An International Collection of Classic and Contemporary Papers*, London: International Thomson Business Press.

Berthon, P., Pitt, L. and Watson, R. T. (1996) 'Re-surfing W^3: research perspectives on marketing communication and buyer behaviour on the Worldwide Web' *International Journal of Advertising* 15: 287–301.

Crosier, K. (1994) 'Promotion', in Baker, M. J. (ed.) *The Marketing Book*, Oxford: Butterworth-Heinemann, pp. 48–86.

Fletcher, K. (1995) *Marketing Management and Information Technology*, 2nd edn, London: Prentice-Hall.

Gatarski, R. and Lundkvist, A. (1998) 'Interactive media face artificial consumers and marketing theory must re-think', *Journal of Marketing Communications* 4 (1): 45–59.

Heyman, R. (1994) *Why Didn't You Say That in the First Place?: How to Be Understood at Work*, San Francisco, CA: Jossey-Bass.

Rackham, N. (1988) *SPIN Selling*, Maidenhead: McGraw-Hill.

Smith, P. R. (1998) *Marketing Communications: An Integrated Approach*, 2nd edn, London: Kogan Page, chapter 7.

Tapp, A. (2000) *Principles of Direct and Database Marketing*, 2nd edn, London: FT Prentice-Hall.

van Raaij, F. (1998) 'Interactive communication: consumer power and initiative', *Journal of Marketing Communications* 4 (1): 1–8.

Waldeman's World of Web Ads at www.wwowa.co.uk.

chapter *ten*

IDENTITY, IMAGE, AND REPUTATION

LEARNING POINTS

Careful study of this chapter will help you to:

- identify the relevance of the concepts of corporate identity, corporate image, and corporate reputation to the management of marketing communication

- distinguish and relate the concepts of identity, image, and reputation

- distinguish and relate the respective roles of marketing and public relations

The first person to throw an insult rather than a rock was the true founder of civilization

Sigmund Freud

What's in a name?

William Shakespeare

INTRODUCTION

Many people value their reputation. Fewer understand the nature of their reputation. Reputation is considered by a growing number of management practitioners and scholars to be an intangible asset that enables the enactment of relationships among the corporation and their publics. (See Box 10.1 for an illustration of valuing one's name.)

BOX 10.1   WHAT'S IN A NAME?

The newly opened Prada Society Café in Manchester is today dumping its name, menu cards, tablecloths, and plates. After only nine days' trading, the proprietors have been forced to change the name of the café by the Milan fashion house Prada, which has claimed intellectual property ownership of the trading name with full legal backing.

A recent conference entitled 'A Most Admired Company' was subtitled 'Success builds reputation: Reputation builds success'. The promotional brochure stated that:

A company's reputation is a valuable asset, yet many companies are relatively unaware of how they are perceived, and how important this can be for their business.

This chapter on identity, image, and reputation seeks to show that the reputations of the corporation are both significant and, at least to some degree, manageable. Corporate reputation management should be part of a strategic communication agenda. This work will be part of organized stakeholder relationship management.

What makes and influences a company's reputation? Can corporate reputation be managed as an asset through enlightened investment? Some industries – financial services, chemicals, nuclear, utilities, etc. – suffer from a serious image problem. In the eyes of many they are seen as exploiters, inefficient, having fat-cat bosses, etc. Such views may be justified, but in many cases are uninformed. But this is not a new realization. Parkinson and Rowe (1977) voiced the need to communicate over twenty years ago – to be part of any debate about what matters to you – many executives and managers have yet to take heed.

Sound ethical and responsible behaviour is not enough. Performance improvement must be communicated if a positive reputation is to be built and defended.

Everyone may potentially hold some notion of a particular corporation or industry in mind. Corporate reputation is an all-encompassing term for what employees think about their employer, what customers think about their provider, what investors think about their shareholding, etc. A range of public-specific roles exist, defined by each member of those publics. Reputation is a stakeholder issue.

Reputation does not originate from the corporate communications office, or the marketing plan, or individual behaviour. It is not a fabricatable artefact that can be used to manipulate others' feelings, in the way that advertising can be (mis)used. Reputation springs from experiences, thought processes, and values of people who see themselves as stakeholders of a business. Reputation may be good or bad in the mind of an individual, and may not be based on direct knowledge of the corporation and its members and their actual behaviour and intentions. Reputation leads to liking and disliking and a sense of comfort or concern with what is perceived.

How about those corporations that have a reputation for being friendly, honest, and competent – are we really identifying a corporate personality? What kind of people do you feel at home with and which threaten you? Those who are in close contact are the ones we get on with, while others we try to avoid. So it is for business corporations.

We need to distinguish between industry reputation and corporate reputation. For example, there are reputable companies (Saga, for example) operating in the package tour industry (which is not well respected).

CORPORATE REPUTATION

What is the significance of reputation? How does a strong, positive reputation impact on business performance? What makes and influences a corporation's reputation? How can corporations protect and manage their reputation?

The Public Relations Consultancy Association's website defines corporate communications (see chapter eighteen for more on this) as: 'the deliberately planned management of the perceptions of an organization'.

Some people feel that public relations **is** reputation management. Is there more to it than publicity?

With so much said and printed about corporate reputation, why do we still need to think more about this problem? Put bluntly, most managers simply do not understand how reputation is created and communicated, conclude Smythe et al. (1992).

In everyday life, we do a lot of talking about reputation: when making friends, inviting people to speak at seminars, deciding which course to study, job searching, recommending products, and so on. Thus, reputation could be defined as what is generally said or believed about a person's or thing's character or standing.

We can also think of reputation as a state of being well reported on, or as a set of judgements a community makes about the personal qualities of one of its members (see Emler, 1990). But this is rarely a factual reporting of what is but rather of what people believe to be:

> Many a man would not recognize his reputation if they met on the street
>
> (proverb)

The dictionary is full of words that are similar in meaning to 'reputable': respectable; notable; honest; influential; of distinction. The term reputation (meaning public recognition) stems from the term *reputare* – meaning to think.

> Reputation is what you need to get a job;
> character is what you need to keep it.
>
> (Unattrib.)

Management efforts can be directed towards building a positive reputation, but, rest assured, a reputation will be out there in the public sphere, whether managed or not. Organizations may strive after an excellent reputation, but, it has been argued, in the final analysis, they'll get what they deserve (see Haywood, 1994).

> With a reputation you can do anything – without one, nothing.
> (Haywood, 1994, paraphrasing George Washington)

> Public relations is a long-term exercise; a reputation built over many years can be seriously damaged in seconds.
> (Sir Anthony Cleaver, Chairman of IBM UK, quoted in Haywood, 1994: 3)

Several closely related concepts need to be considered.

KEY CONCEPTS AND THEIR RELEVANCE TO MARKETING

In order to understand the key concepts, we visit the thinking of several academics and practitioners – see Box 10.2 for the results.

BOX 10.2   KEY CONCEPTS AND THEIR RELEVANCE TO MARKETING: AN OVERVIEW

Corporate identity

> the symbols (such as logos, colour scheme) an organisation uses to identify itself to people.
> (Dowling, 1994: 8).

> not merely a logo. It is about what the organisation is, its personality; the sum total of its expertise, history, philosophy, culture, strategy, and structure.
> (*Marketing Business*, February, 1994: 5)

> what the organisation thinks it is and likes to be seen as.
> (Unattrib.)

> who the person/organisation really is
> (Unattrib.)

> Corporate identity, the characteristics that distinguish one organization from another, is analogous to personal identity.
> (Bromley, 1993: 156)

Corporate image

> how an organisation's audiences (the public, staff, city financiers, customers . . .) perceive its corporate identity.
> (*Marketing Business*, February 1994: 5)

---

what the customer perceives the organisation to be.

(*Marketing Business*, February, 1994: 5)

the total impression (beliefs and feelings) an entity (an organisation, country or brand) makes on the minds of people.

(Dowling, 1994: 8)

First . . . the literal image (name or icon) . . . symbolises the organisation, product or service . . . Second, . . . the pattern of beliefs and feelings associated with the literal image that give it its meaning or psychological significance.

(Bromley, 1993: 158)

The relationships between an organisation's self-image, the image it wishes to portray, and the real public image that evolves are complicated.

(Bromley, 1993: 158)

Brand image is tied closely to marketing and consumer behaviour. Corporate image, on the other hand, especially in larger, more diversified organisations, is tied more closely to corporate identity than to brand images of its products or services.

(Bromley, 1993: 159)

visual identity refers to the visual features that identity an entity . . . a company's logo and livery, a product's packaging.

(Bromley, 1993: 160)

Corporate reputation

the collective *experience* of those who work for and deal with the organisation.

(Fearnley, 1992: 35–6)

the *evaluation* (respect, esteem, estimation) in which an organisation's image is held by people.

(Dowling, 1994)

we try to develop a particular sort of reputation by acting in ways we think will lead other people to form a particular sort of *impression*.

(Bromley, 1993)

what is generally believed

(Unattrib.)

A firm's reputation is partly a function of its behaviour (including its public relations performance), and partly a function of the behaviour of those sections of the public that take an interest in it or have some involvement in it.

(Bromley, 1993: 162)

a well-established reputation implies trust amongst various interest groups.

(Bromley, 1993)

Corporate communications

the way in which an organisation projects its identity (or what it would like its identity to be) to the outside world via the media.

(Marketing Business, February, 1994: 5)

corporate reputation, the management of which reaches far beyond the traditional black arts of the marketing department. This requires that external communications be seen in the broadest possible sense, including every personal contact and telephone call as well as the mass media . . . It also requires that internal communications, and how the organisation lives its brand promises – the development of its own 'brand of work' – become one and the same . . . pervading corporate 'ideologies' . . . which are expressed in everything the company does and which create an unmistakable identity.

(Mitchell, 1995: 33)

Corporate manifesto

the way an organisation presents itself through its visual identity, staff, buildings, sponsorship, etc.

(Marketing Business, February, 1994: 5)

Corporate personality

the perceived structure of preferences which are exhibited in the behaviour of members of the group/corporation/firm.

(March and Simon, 1958)

what the organization actually is.

that set of major attributes that truly characterises an organisation.

(Bromley, 1993)

Corporate brand

The company name . . . forms the epicentre of marketing activity . . . Corporate brand is part of something much larger: corporate reputation.

(Mitchell, 1995: 33)

So why are we interested in these concepts when studying the management of marketing communication?

THE SIGNIFICANCE OF REPUTATION TO BUSINESS PERFORMANCE

Reputation is only one of several factors in the general ecology in which a corporation operates – the others are social, political, technological, and economic in nature. In some circumstances reputation has only marginal effect on an enterprise's success; in other circumstances reputation has a critical effect (Bromley, 1993).

Kay (1993: chapter 6) describes reputation as a primary distinctive capability, which has differential value in various markets. In a narrow class of markets, building reputation can be a powerful source of competitive advantage.

In those markets in which consumers cannot inspect and compare goods and services and where experience of the good or service is only possible over a long period of time, the purchase is made only once, or where the purchase is on behalf of the consumer (pension plan, funeral service, cat food, car, computer software, company shares), consumers rely on other criteria in making their purchase and use choices. They rely on their knowledge of the manufacturer or supplier, on advice from an intermediary, or on recommendations from friends and magazines, rather than on their own experience with the goods or services.

If customers cannot tell the quality of a good or service by inspection or immediate experience, how can they make a proper choice between low and high price and low and high quality. Kay defines reputation as a 'reiterated high-quality strategy in a market for long-term experience goods' (1993: 92). The quality of a good or service is often judged not only on its cost but also with reference to the standing of the manufacturer or provider. Firms with a good reputation can charge a higher price for what is objectively an equivalent or inferior product. Reputation conveys public esteem and distinctiveness in competition for scarce resources

Every organization has a reputation whether actively managed or not (Edwards, 1997). Even if the corporation remains unchanged, a reputation can change simply because of changes in the related public/stakeholder group. Reputation is a scarce commodity, reflecting the effects of competition in a field. When one corporation gains reputation, another loses – something akin to a football league.

Reputation is an intangible asset which enables the enactment of relationships among an enterprise and its publics (Page and Kinsey, 1997). It is a more significant, powerful and holistic predictor of organizational excellence and success in the marketplace than either corporate image or identity (Page and Kinsey, 1997).

Kay (1993) asserts that reputation is only of major significance in markets where consumers cannot determine product quality through search or their own experience – then they will be swayed by reputation and reputation is profitable. Reputation provides the legitimizing basis for business – the 'licence to operate'. Thus, the concept of reputation spans the concerns of public relations, marketing, finance, and management (Sobol et al., 1992).

Management thinking is clearly moving towards greater emphasis on the development of relationships among stakeholders and wider acknowledgement of environmental influence on the 'bottom line' through the impact of reputation (Kent, 1996). Environmental monitoring is required to assess, enhance, and maintain corporate reputation as a measure of stakeholder expectations.

> if we don't have reputation, we don't have anything.
> (Steve Melcher, CEO, Allied Dunbar & Eagle Star,
> *PR Week*, 2 May 1997: 12)

Yet, many managers simply do not understand how corporate reputation arises or its effect on morale, profitability, and the ability of the corporation's people to achieve their goals and objectives in the long term.

A leading scholar in the field has stated that:

> A corporate reputation is a perceptual representation of a company's past actions and future prospects that describes the firm's overall appeal to all of its key constituents when compared with their leading rivals.
> (Fombrun, 1996: 72)

According to Kay (1993) reputation is the most important commercial mechanism for conveying information to consumers, but is not equally important in all markets.

Who says that reputation is an important criterion in determining purchasing decisions? Fearnley's study (1992) produced the findings that are represented by Figure 10.1.

The same survey showed that both consumers and purchasing managers believe that corporate reputation is a wasted asset. Yet, many academics and practitioners believe that it can be a source of sustainable competitive advantage. But in what terms?

- 79% of consumers
- 78% of marketing managers said that reputation influences their
- 56% of purchasing managers buying behaviour

- 45% of marketing managers believed that corporate citizenship efforts are repaid in the bottom line

- 87% of business-to-business marketing managers felt the need for a good reputation

- 63% of consumer marketing managers felt the need for a good reputation (compare this with the 79% of consumers who said that reputation did influence their buying behaviour)

Figure 10.1 **Reputation as a criterion in determining purchase decisions**

An aspect of service and product quality

Kay (1993) indicates that reputation is especially important in markets where product quality is important but can only be identified through long-term experience – i.e. for service users who have no (or few) tangible clues:

> Reputation is the market's method of dealing with attributes of product quality which customers cannot easily monitor for themselves.
>
> (Kay, 1993: 87)

Work by Choi and Kim (1996) suggests that consumers, when faced with uncertainty over the quality of certain products and especially services, employ surrogates to allow some choice to be made on rational criteria. Factors relating to the firm's reputation, such as size and age, may assist consumers to learn about their product quality.

The quality of product and service delivered is the ultimate determinant of reputation. Although the modern consumer and purchasing officer is increasingly looking to buy a package which includes the company standing, their primary focus remains the output of the managing system – the products and services which are promised. The management problem remains the design, production, communication and delivery of value to the customer (Bradley, 1995).

Image of the service provider

Image exists on more than one level – the corporate image influences the local image. Grönroos (1990) argues that because local business environments and local societies differ, it may be self-defeating to try to streamline local image to fall in line with corporate image. This issue of differentiation or standardization may depend on the strengths of disparate local images.

A favourable and well-known image is an asset because image has an impact on customer appreciation of the communication and operations of the corporation, by:

- communicating expectations
- filtering and influencing the perception of technical and functional quality
- combining and reflecting the experiences and expectations of each customer
- impacting on employee attitudes by communicating values

In the marketing of professional services, for example, personal selling and other interpersonal interactions are crucial to judgements of competence in delivering the service.

'Most Admired Companies' rankings

The biggest and best known study of admiration for companies has been conducted annually for many years by the *Fortune* magazine.

In Britain, *The Economist* carried out, with the help of Professor John Saunders and other researchers from Loughborough University Business School, a similar exercise in 1989, 1990, and 1992. This was undertaken by sending 1,800 business people and analyst participants a list of publicly quoted firms in their own industry, selected on the basis of market capitalization. In total, 7 executives in each of some 260 companies in 26 industries were asked to participate. Participants were asked to rank the firms on their own industry (excluding their own) on eight criteria. More recently, the study has been published by *Management Today* in 1994, 1995, and 1996.

In 1994 Price Waterhouse was commissioned by *The Financial Times* to conduct a study in Europe to identify the most respected companies (see *The Financial Times*, 27 June, 1994). This study asked senior executives to nominate the most-respected companies in their industry on the basis of seven measures of business performance:

1 customer focus
2 people
3 products and services
4 business performance
5 leadership and management
6 strategy
7 environment

The *Fortune* study has been criticized for not capturing the views of all constituents (see for example, Fombrun, 1996). *Fortune*'s surveys have sought the evaluations of senior executives, directors, and analysts, but have misrepresented the company images with other constituents – employees, customers, and the local communities in which the companies operate. Instead of broadening the coverage of images, *Fortune* have merely increased the number of executives surveyed – well beyond the sample size required to get a representative view.

Closer to home, the *NorthWest Business Insider* annually reports a league table of the Top 250 (recently expanded to 300) best-performing companies based in the north-west of England. This is compiled using published annual reports and accounts, using:

• chief-executive salary
• dividend payments to directors
• profit
• profit per employee
• sales growth
• number of jobs
• change in net-cash holding
• donations to charity
• donations to political parties

These performance indicators in themselves do not address the question of reputation, so the author examined a number of annual reports of companies included in the survey. The text of the annual report was examined for explicit or implicit evidence of attention to corporate image and reputation.

THE CONSTITUTION OF CORPORATE REPUTATION

Fearnley (1992) asserts that reputation is in the eye of the beholder – it is the purchaser who interprets signals from the company. Companies do not communicate corporate reputation to the purchaser.

How is the corporate reputation constituted? Fearnley (1992) lists a range of components of a dynamic bundle of complex issues and considerations – both functional, the basic elements which are taken as given and allow entry and acceptance in the market, and emotional, which differentiate, including, in rank order of importance:

- community involvement
- environmental record
- employment record and practices
- quality of offering
- price
- recommendations from third parties
- media endorsements
- financial soundness
- well-established products and services

For Fearnley, corporate reputation is about what a firm is, as what a firm does is no longer sufficient for consumers.

The *Fortune* studies of corporate reputation have used eight attributes of a corporation as the basis for evaluation of standing:

1 quality of management
2 quality of products and services
3 innovativeness
4 value as long-term investment
5 financial soundness
6 ability to attract, develop, and keep talented people
7 community and environmental responsibility
8 use of corporate assets

As we shall see shortly, this list may be incomplete, and communication practices is a further key consideration.

Clearly, some of these attributes will be little known to some stakeholders. What could we expect customers to be knowledgeable about? Few are likely to have much information beyond personal experience and word-of-mouth reports of product and service quality. Shareholders might be keenly interested in all of these factors when considering the relative attractiveness of the shares as an investment.

Dowling (1994) suggests that corporate identity enhances corporate image by stimulating recall. The image conjured up in the person's mind combines with their prior values and attitudes towards appropriate roles and behaviour for the particular organization to form a reputation. Fombrun (1996) defines attributes of corporate reputation: credibility; reliability; trustworthiness; responsibility. Fombrun makes it clear that he believes that reputation cannot be defined in abstractions of the enterprise's publics. Managers must, to understand the nature and value of reputation, capture the judgements of their publics.

Grunig (1992) is clear that no one set of characteristics can be appropriate for the evaluation of reputation for all enterprises which face different situations among differing stakeholder groups. This reflects Grunig's situational theory of publics, and he goes on to suggest that perhaps management groups should set their own criteria for excellence (1992: 223). For example:

> communications behaviours of publics can be best understood by measuring how members of publics perceive situations in which they are affected by such organisational consequences as pollution, quality of products, hiring practices, or plant closing.
>
> (Grunig and Hunt, 1984: 148)

The presence and degree of symmetrical communication practice is significant in excellent companies who stay close to their customers, employees, and other 'strategic constituencies' (Grunig, 1992). Heath (1994) also identifies the importance of symmetrical communication criteria in considering reputation.

Hickman and Silva (1984) also counsel against standard formulas for evaluating excellence and reputation. They argue that both objective and subjective yardsticks are required. The *Fortune* criteria may need to be adapted to capture nuances of context. Studies must be situational. Gray (1986) defends the *Fortune* approach in identifying that corporations have been rated on reputation as the perception of important publics and that each attribute is associated with how the company looks to outsiders.

Varey (1996: 139) has noted that:

> Organizational communications management can be conceived as a core business competence. Communication is necessary for organizations to effect requisite collective work – through co-operation, experimentation and shared learning.

THE MANAGEMENT OF CORPORATE REPUTATION

Image development or improvement efforts have to be based on reality.

> If the image is false and our performance is good, it's our fault for being bad communicators. If the image is true and reflects our bad performance, it's our fault for being bad managers.
>
> (Bernstein, 1984)

Every organization has a range of reputations, whether managed or not. Each observer holds some attitude towards the corporation and this assessment of standing and personality may differ markedly from that intended by conscious cultivation through public relations, marketing, and selling efforts.

There are two possible reasons for an image problem (Grönroos, 1990):

1 the organization is known but has a negative image (and the experiences of customers are probably bad)
2 the organization is not well known, and thus has an unclear image or image based on out-of-date customer experiences

The creation of a strong reputation requires a continuing investment of management time and other resources, and must reflect the company if it is to be successful. Reputations fade if they are not continually renewed (Emler, 1990). Reputation needs to be managed, and cultivation of a distinctive reputation needs to be active. Problems may be real image problems or image communication problems.

When problems of technical and/or functional quality exist, a communication campaign alone is not going to work. At best it will be a waste of money. Reality always wins in the long run. An image advertising campaign that is not based on reality only creates expectations. If expectations are higher as a result, but the experiences of reality are unchanged, the perceived service quality is affected in a negative way, and the image is damaged. Problems with service performance (technical and/or functional quality) cause an image problem, and internal actions that improve the performance of the firm are needed if the bad image is to be improved.

If the image is unknown, there is a communication problem. There is no in-depth image based on experience. Perhaps the performance has changed but insufficient interaction has taken place for the new reality to be experienced. Advertising can speed up the process of image improvement. It is important to realize that image is not what is communicated if the communicated image does not correspond with reality. When there is an inconsistency, reality wins and the corporation is perceived as untrustworthy – this damages image even more.

A dialogue between the firm and its stakeholders must communicate ethics, mission, and values. Presentation of image will never suffice. The spheres of experience of all people with rights and responsibilities to the business must be understood. In managing reputation, it is necessary to cultivate different reputations in different groups, and to use appropriate methods in each.

Reasons given for attempting to manage corporate image and identity centre principally on trying to make clear to stakeholders what the values and beliefs of the corporation are and how it is striving to achieve its objectives. When managers are asked, their reasons include:

- there is general promotional value
- it encourages favourable behaviour towards the company
- there is likely to be an effect on product sales
- products can be differentiated
- shareholders and employees can be recruited
- it helps good relations with the community and government
- it influences attitudes
- it creates familiarity to foster favourability
- it reflects the company as it is
- it services corporate objectives
- it aids management decisions
- it operates as a competitive tool
- it affects attitude survey findings

When BMRB/Mintel (*Marketing Business*, 1994) asked 930 adults about their attitudes towards corporate identity, they found the following reasons given for promoting corporate image:

- to improve sales
- to tell people they are better than the competition
- to appeal to a new set of customers
- to tell people they have new products
- to give a caring image
- to improve people's feelings towards them
- to encourage the purchase of shares in the company
- to look more modern/fashionable
- to counteract bad press
- to appear more international

Self-monitoring is the process of evaluating own performance, taking account of the likely reactions of others, especially key others, in order to reach accommodation between the self-concept and reputation.

The problem of reputation monitoring and reputation management to protect and enhance it requires a wide range of public relations techniques. A damaged reputation can sometimes be repaired by reputation management and public relations efforts. If the effect of reputation on performance is, however, marginal, the resources required for public relations can be kept small. Resources have to be geared to the level of threat posed by a damaged reputation.

A realistic understanding of the corporation's identity, the direction of its development, its publics, and the means by which they can be informed and influenced, is required. These requirements are separate from, but linked in with, the central functions and operations of the corporation.

A false reputation can be built by convincing publics that the corporation possesses certain desirable characteristics which it does not have. The danger of discovery is that the whole reputation is damaged, not just the attribute that was simulated or hidden.

Reputation management is not an annual event! A communication planning process must be part of the managing system so that it involves managers and communication facilitators daily as part of their basic work.

According to Kay (1993) reputation, in the long run, can only be based on the provision of high quality in repeated trials. Consumers come to recognize high quality through much experience and further experience to recognize that it is consistently high. Reputation is spread most rapidly in markets in which consumers are inclined to share their experience – reputations are created and destroyed relatively quickly in such markets as retail stores, restaurants, and cinema. In markets such as personal hygiene, financial services, and health, consumers are less likely to wish to discuss their needs and interest because of embarrassment, and these present great opportunity for profitable and enduring reputations, once established.

Often reputation may arise from another source of competitive advantage, such as innovation.

At a point in time a corporate reputation may be absolutely stable (the nature and extent of its public image or 'social identity') and relatively stable (compared to other corporations). At other times it may be unstable – its distribution of attributes assigned to it by interested parties changes. Attributes of reputation become more salient under certain conditions.

Corporations make different impressions on different groups for two reasons:

1 they present themselves differently to each group
2 the groups are interested in different aspects of the corporation and their values, policies, activities, and so on

The corporation's reputation is a set of reputations in various interest groups (stakeholders or publics), or the intersection of these reputations. A clear public image requires a clear corporate identity. However, a clear public image may be stereotyped and false when idiosyncratic behaviour of members is taken as representative. Because a particular reputation is specific to a public, the policy-making of a corporation can be difficult when different publics may perceive the policy of benefit or harmful.

PUBLIC RELATIONS AS IMPRESSION MANAGEMENT

Self-presentation, the attempt at conveying information to others in order to influence, always presents an 'edited' version of the personality to a particular audience.

Most people rely on opinion leaders, experts, and 'popularizers' (?) for information and advice about a corporation, since information emanating directly may be difficult to understand or too extensive or technical, or it may be deliberately incomplete. Bromley (1993) describes public relations as the corporate equivalent of impression management.

As we will see in chapter seventeen, we need to consider the ethics of impression management. The motivation behind it **may** be immoral, since it may be intended to mislead and deceive, e.g. lying to gain personal advantage. But, of course, most self-presentation behaviour is not intended to deceive but to increase the likelihood of success in some endeavour. Belief in (rather than pretence of belief) and action (rather than pretence of action) in accordance with the desired public image, in order to protect or enhance reputation, is what discriminates ethical from unethical behaviour.

Reflexive impression management is behaviour that aims to change the impression we have of ourselves (self-image) to bring it closer to our ideal self. Management to improve the public image of a corporation – its reputation – requires more than simply using public relations techniques to change public opinion. The nature of the corporation and its individual members must be changed. Change is organizational policy, and practices, social skills training, alteration of ethos, and perhaps even identity may be required. Awareness of a disparity between self-image and public image often provides a signal that action is needed to remedy the situation.

Impression management may be:

- **promotional**: to consolidate or enhance social standing, aspirations and achievements or the benefits we can provide for others because of our abilities and circumstance
- **defensive**: positive or negative response to threats to a reputation

Impression management may call for forceful action to maintain credibility and may require substantial shifts in behaviour. The adoption of methods used to enhance corporate reputation may require the corporation to engage in activities and relationships that go well beyond the core functions of producing goods and services:

- visual identification
- policy statements
- public relations activities: including charitable donations, sponsorship, competitions, exhibitions, lobbying, etc.
- personal impression management
- bathing in 'reflected glory'
- avoidance of 'guilt by association'
- derogation and denigration of competitors

External audience reactions may reveal whether the reputation is enhanced or not by a particular method of promotion used, while internal audience reactions may reveal whether the image being promoted is in the best interests of organizational morale.

While impression management is immediate and tactical ('putting on an act'), reputation management is pre-planned and strategic (long term) in trying to convey personal identity or self-concept (Bromley, 1993). The personal or corporate reputation is a social identity and is clearly a communication issue that marketing managers cannot ignore.

MARKETING IMAGE

Barich and Kotler (1991) introduced the notion of 'marketing image' in an attempt to deal with the apparent conflict of interest between marketers and public relations specialists. This provides the marketer with a role in managing the corporate identity in order to foster the desired corporate image. Kotler (1986) argued that public relations should be part of 'megamarketing' (social marketing), along with power – the 6Ps! The marketer takes responsibility for the supply of benefits to parties other than target consumers, for example, government, unions, or other interested third parties, who may act as gatekeepers. It is sometimes necessary to arrange additional incentives, inducements or sanctions to gain desired responses from groups other than customers.

This approach is the strategically coordinated application of economic, psychological, political, and public relations skills to gain the cooperation of a number of parties in order to enter and/or operate in a given 'protected' market. This approach requires cooperation and coordination between marketers, company officers, public relations and public affairs specialists, and legal specialists in the corporation. But public relations is seen as primarily a communication tool for influencing attitudes, whereas marketing aims to elicit specific behaviours and includes not only communication but needs assessment, product development, price setting, and the creation of distribution channels (Ehling *et al.*, 1992). Thus, public relations is not seen as involved in defining the goals of the corporation, but merely in making it easier to sell products and services.

White (1991) disagrees, arguing that public relations is a central management concern which complements marketing communications, and is firmly strategic, forward-looking, and coordinating in scope and nature.

MARKETING PUBLIC RELATIONS

It is helpful to distinguish corporate public relations from marketing public relations, the latter of which, like financial public relations and community public relations, serves a specific group – in this case, the marketing department. Kotler sees marketing public relations as a development of 'publicity' which moves beyond 'editorial column inches' to assistance in product launches, repositioning mature products, promoting product categories, influencing target groups, defending products under threat, and building corporate image – i.e. creating an effect, and not just output. Bradley (1995: 666) defines public relations as 'any non-personal communication in the form of news about the company or its products which is carried by the mass media'. In a book of some 990 pages, public relations gets little more than three pages. (This is disappointing for a book with such an alluring title!) What Bradley describes is closer to marketing public relations (MPR), but it should be pointed out that MPR is not all 'non-personal' communication, nor is it only about promotion. Fill (1995) appears to present marketing communications are part of organizational communication.

Cutlip *et al.* (1994/1999) distinguish corporate public relations as a function of management seeking to identify, establish and maintain mutually beneficial relationships between an organisation and the various publics on whom its success and failure depend, whereas marketing public relations is not only concerned with organisational success and failure but also with specific publics: customers, consumers, and clients with whom exchange transactions take place.

Mercer (1992) sees public relations as the means by which the various significant 'publics' of the corporation are identified and communicated with, to the advantage of the corporation, through personal and impersonal media. This publicizes a positive image of the company's achievements and leads to a good reputation. Mercer feels that publicity is the dominant form of public relations activity in practice. Others have argued that public relations is merely a form of consumer-oriented sales promotion. Then, marketing public relations is simply part of sales promotion – an information dissemination activity.

CASE STUDY 10   ENGAGING STAKEHOLDERS: THE SHELL INTERNATIONAL CORPORATE IDENTITY PROGRAMME[a]

Objectives

The objectives of the Royal Dutch/Shell Group of companies are to engage efficiently, responsibly and profitably in the oil, gas, chemicals and other selected businesses and participate in the research for and development of other sources of energy. Shell companies are committed to contributing to sustainable development.

The Corporate Identity Programme was conceived to communicate Shell's commitment to these objectives to Shell's stakeholder groups and, thereby, to earn increased licence to operate through altering any negative stakeholder perceptions of the way that Shell – and other multinationals – go about their business.

Strategy

After some highly visible environment and human rights based issues in the 1990s, Shell conducted research in more than sixty countries among opinion formers and members of the general public. Results indicated alongside 50 per cent positive associations with Shell, a minority (10 per cent) of negative opinions and a further 40 per cent ambivalence towards the company. Furthermore, on a number of issues, stakeholders were increasingly unwilling to accept Shell's assurances of best practice because of perceived aloofness, indifference, and arrogance. Little was known about Shell's published business principles and about its commitment to sustainable development.

Shell decided therefore to enter a dialogue with stakeholder groups to raise awareness of issues surrounding the energy industry and to present Shell's point of view as a way of stimulating debate around the issues. Critical to this process was a policy of open and honest presentation of facts and the adoption of an adult-to-adult tone of voice. No attempt has been made to bypass opinion-former audiences by adopting a direct-to-customer approach.

Implementation

The process of engagement started with the publication of the *Shell Report* – a yearly investigation of Group performance from an economic, environmental and social perspective, first published in 1999. The *Report* – widely acknowledged as best practice in the field of corporate reporting – is distributed to key stakeholder groups and aims to inform and invite feedback on issues that impact on Shell's business and the energy industry in general.

This initiative to promote transparency and accountability was then supported by a number of other stakeholder engagement initiatives:

- **stakeholder forums**: in a number of key markets between different interest groups and key Shell personnel
- **press and Internet advertising**: designed to raise the profile of issues and invite open debate with stakeholders
- **television advertising and proactive media relations**: to provide evidence of positive Shell action on all the issues
- **a direct mail, insert and database management programme**: designed to ensure maximum awareness of the whole range of communication tools in the programme

Results

Early tracking of target audience opinions of Shell conducted by the research agency BPRI indicate that of the fifteen long-term performance metrics identified by the group, five have already been achieved by the campaign. The remaining ten metrics have all shown significant improvement.

In brief, overall favourability towards Shell increased by 40 per cent, positive advocacy increased by 66 per cent and confidence in Shell's ability to meet the world's energy needs in 2050 increased by 40 per cent.

(See www.shell.com)

Note: [a] The assistance of Froydis Cameron in providing this summary is gratefully acknowledged

---

WHAT DO YOU THINK?

1   In 1997 British Airways famously changed the livery of their aircraft with 50 new designs portraying the airline as British and modern, rooted in their UK heritage but at home wherever they travel. What impact, do you think, this design intervention might have had on the marketing relationships of the corporation?

2   In 2000 BP announced a change of logo style for all their petrol stations. Speculate,

based on a review of available published material, on the management process that led to this decision.

3 How do you distinguish the concepts of identity, image, and reputation?

4 Given that Shell has been working on their corporate identity and reputation for several years, what benefits seem to have accrued to the corporation and their customers and other stakeholders?

5 Try to explain the nature of a corporate personality. Why is this significant for marketing communication?

6 How would you rate your local supermarket's reputation? At what level is the main influence on your judgement?

7 Consider the idea that image and reputation may arise for corporation, product, or person. How does this differ from the concept of brand?

8 It has been said that corporations can do well by doing good. What might be meant by this?

9 How does marketing communication impact upon brand name?

10 Consider the notion of the marketing communication system enabling and fostering impressions of both marketer (provider) and marketer (buyer/consumer). How might this be managed in practice?

FURTHER READING

Barich, H. and Kotler, P. (1991) 'A framework for marketing image management', *Sloan Management Review* 32 (2): 94–104.

Barich, H. and Srinivasan, V. (1993) 'Prioritising marketing image goals under resource constraints', *Sloan Management Review* 34 (4): 69–76.

Bernstein, D. (1984) *Company Image and Reality: A Critique of Corporate Communications*, London: Cassell Educational.

Dowling, G. R. (1994) *Corporate Reputations: Strategies for Developing the Corporate Brand*, London: Kogan Page.

Fombrun, C. (1996) *Reputation: Realizing Value from the Corporate Image*, Cambridge, MA: Harvard Business School Press.

Gardner, N. (1996) 'See the advert, buy the bank', *The Sunday Times*, 21 January.

Ind, N. (1992) *The Corporate Image: Strategies for Effective Identity Programmes*, rev. edn, London: Kogan Page.

Ind, N. (1997) *The Corporate Brand*, London: Macmillan Business.

Kotler, P. (1986) 'Megamarketing', *Harvard Business Review* 64 (2): 117–24.

Markwick, N. and Fill, C. (1997) ' Towards a Framework for Managing Corporate Identity', *European Journal of Marketing* 31 (5): 396–409.

Olins, W. (1978/1990) *The Corporate Personality: An Inquiry into the Nature of Corporate Identity*, London: The Design Council.

Olins, W. (1989) *Corporate Identity: Making Business Strategy Visible Through Design*, London: Thames & Hudson.

Parkinson, C. N. and Rowe, N. (1977) *Communicate: Parkinson's Formula for Business Survival*, London: Pan Books/Prentice-Hall.

Weigelt, K. and Camerer, C. (1988) 'Reputation and corporate strategy: a review of recent theory and applications', *Strategic Management Journal* 9: 443–54.

chapter eleven

INTERNAL MARKETING COMMUNICATION

LEARNING POINTS

Careful study of this chapter will help you to:

- explore the concept of internal marketing

- consider internal marketing as a responsible, responsive approach to managing communication for the management of marketing communication

- connect communication and marketing through the concept of exchange

Every company has two organizational structures: the formal one is written on the charts; the other is the living relationship of the men and women in the organization.
Harold Geneen, former Chairman of ITT

Not only is there no God, but try getting a plumber at weekends.

Woody Allen

INTRODUCTION

Increasingly, consumers and buyers judge quality and value for money in terms of not only what they are able to buy, but also the exchange experience. People are an essential part of the value package.

Developments in the management of the communication required to generate produce, and represent valued products have brought concepts of internal communication, employee communication, and organizational communication into the realm of internal public relations, i.e. employee relationship management.

Marketing and human resource management groups work much more closely together to build and maintain brand equity by breaking down departmental barriers that disrupt the value-creation system, to institutionalize learning and interaction.

The integrated value-making system requires that people are seen not simply as factors of production, but as marketing resources. Clearly, production and provision requires coordinated effort. At the start of the process, market-sensing (Day, 1992) requires connectedness.

In recent years, the principles of marketing have become even more central to management thinking and practice.

WHAT IS INTERNAL MARKETING?

The literature on marketing, services marketing, corporate strategy, total quality management, operations management, human resource management, organizational communication, and organizational development refers to an internal-marketing concept, an internal-market concept, or an internal customer–supplier relationship concept.

The internal-marketing concept has its origins in the writings on service management and service quality improvement which have flourished since the mid-1970s. More recently, the concept has been given wider application as the belief that all corporations provide some degree of service has gained acceptance. The notion of an internal supplier–customer chain can be traced to the early literature of the resurgence in interest in quality. Another perspective is that of internal organizational communications.

It is increasingly recognized that in order to sustain a competitive position, the corporation must develop a customer service culture that both allows and encourages employees to give good service. While the possibility of differing goals between managers and employees is recognized, nevertheless internal customers have to be served well as part of the service to the ultimate external customer. Employees who believe that their corporation facilitates their performance, aids their career aspirations, and provides 'positive' supervision, will feel free or 'enabled' to carry out the corporation's main work of serving customers.

> In the service business, you can't make happy customers with unhappy employees.
>
> (Unattrib.)

An internal market consists of people with moods, needs, and wants, which must be continuously assessed, and satisfied.

The need for real improvement in organizational capability for, and the delivery of, valuable customer service, which matches customer needs, as a basis for competitive strategy and competitive advantage, has received widespread attention in the academic and professional management literature in recent years. Bennis (1989) has spoken of the need for a 'social architecture capable of generating intellectual capital' as a key to competitive advantage. The 'servitization' of business (Vandermerwe and Rada, 1988) is resulting in more employees becoming recognized as service providers, to each other and to (external) customers.

Their individual accumulated know-how within the corporation can turn knowledge into applications that add value to the product or service offered to customers. This is a service-centred business philosophy. Fisk *et al.* (1993) argue that internal customers and employee satisfaction are prerequisite management concepts for (external) customer satisfaction. A service-centred business philosophy is called for and competitive advantage is increasingly achieved through the mobilization of the accumulated know-how of individual employees to create value for customers through processes (service activities) and relationships which are not easily copied. Competitive advantage comes from recruiting and retaining more capable and better-motivated staff than those of competitors. Studies have shown that employee commitment requires that they have opportunities to participate in company decisions and a clear understanding of company values.

Managers are urged to create actively the conditions under which people will tend to be motivated (Weiss, 1989). This requires managers to focus on:

- finding the right person (abilities, skills, knowledge, but also behaviour and understanding of others – Weiss terms this personal style)
- structuring the role to add value to organization activity and future direction
- establishing proper mechanisms to ensure superior performance, requiring flexibility, support, and feedback

However, there is continuing internal resistance to marketing in some corporations, particularly when the pursuit of a marketing organization would require major organizational or procedural change. Managers may also be required to assume greater responsibilities through direct involvement in the marketing process. This, potentially at least, may be a dilemma for managers. Internal marketing has been suggested as a means to develop employee awareness of their roles and help them to commit to active participation in the marketing or exchange process, i.e. to make the corporation more marketing-oriented. Yet, the marketing concept itself is often resisted!

Internal marketing can be seen as a management approach that enables and motivates all members of the corporation to examine their own role and communication competence and to adopt a customer consciousness and

---

BOX 11.1   THE MARKETING OF MARKETING

Compton (1987: 17–20) urged employees of the American Red Cross to treat 'marketing' as 'a way of thinking and acting about what we do based on the concept of exchange' rather than as PR, advertising, selling, and a management tool. The approach taken to achieve this way of thinking was to market marketing internally among employees.

---

service orientation (which requires an interest in the problems of customers), whether front-line service performers or back-office service support workers, to meet the needs of external customers through a commitment to the corporation's goals. Everyone, then, must participate and share in the responsibility for dealings with customers. This is achieved through the development of a service climate with service-mindedness, customer-consciousness, and sales-mindedness pervading the corporation. Indeed, internal marketing can focus on employee development. If corporation members see themselves as part of a service delivery system, they can be educated and persuaded that they are contributing to a customer-satisfying, market-responsive system which should and can adapt.

Thus internal marketing provides a focus on a philosophy for customer satisfaction. Grönroos (1990) also describes internal marketing as a management philosophy that provides managers with an understanding and appreciation for the roles of employees in the corporation, requiring that they have a holistic view of their jobs. Managers then attend to service attitude and communications. The idea that internal marketing is a philosophy has been questioned – it may simply be, in practice, a set of techniques or a sequence of activities.

One view of internal marketing has marketers using the marketing process to communicate customer needs and requirements and associated implications throughout the corporation to ensure consistent focused decision-making and action, and to motivate corrective action and method improvements when design, production and delivery responsibilities for fulfilling these needs are not met. This in turn requires the adoption of a customer paradigm to explain internal-market relations in which a corporation-wide positive service attitude can be engendered by management action. Thus customers become managers of the service supply and this is a form of participative management. Internal marketing should therefore be viewed as a management philosophy for both motivation and support, rather than as a short-lived exhortation programme or campaign to boost attention to customers. Staff experience the business (and not only their own job) – their business and market consciousness is increased – and are prepared for a service orientation by being conscious of customer relationships and their own role in achieving customer satisfaction. However, the effectiveness of this internal-marketing approach is dependent on the effectiveness of conventional marketing in the 'inner market'.

Marketers may have different roles in different parts of the corporation, which should be market-driven (i.e. responsive to customers) but not necessarily always marketing-driven (i.e. controlled by marketers using marketing tools such as advertising). Essentially, then, internal marketing is concerned with engendering market-oriented management (Grönroos, 1983) in which marketing is not a function but rather a way of doing business (McKenna, 1991).

Gilmore and Carson (1995: 300) offer a helpful definition of internal marketing as:

> the spreading of the responsibility for all marketing activity across all functions of the organisation, and the proactive application of marketing principles to 'selling the staff' on their role in providing customer satisfaction within a supportive organisational environment.

A ROUTE TO MARKETING ORIENTATION

The problem of implementing strategic change plans has been increasingly recognized and has received major attention in the literature by both general management and, more specifically, marketers. There are a number of recurring difficulties in the effective implementation of major new plans, which inevitably imply and require change:

- the changes proposed may not fit with organizational culture or resource constraints and capability, i.e. the plan is not implementable
- decisions are made on data which subsequently proves to have failed to indicate changes in the environment, such as competitor moves or changes in consumer preferences
- rigid plans which are too analytical are adhered to even when performance variances should signal problems
- there is a lack of ownership and therefore commitment on the part of managers
- differences between senior management and issues of power and vested interest are often not addressed
- strategy changes are often decided out of context without due consideration of the corporation's prevailing culture, hence the way of implementing decisions remains unchanged and becomes incompatible with the required way of working
- customers and their specific needs are not clearly identified
- other failures in information flow and decision-making

Much of this can be accounted for by the continuing widespread practice of treating planning and implementation as separate, the failure of planners to involve those who will be required to take the necessary action, and the prevalent failure of managers to communicate the content and rationale of their plans to the rest of the members of the corporation.

The formulation and coordination of internal and external marketing plans is necessary, with the effective application of the former providing a bridge between the formulation and implementation of the latter by creating knowledge, understanding, involvement and consensus for marketing strategy and plans. Ballantyne (1991) in particular has highlighted the need for marketers to influence and motivate staff to change collaboratively the internal processes required for the effective implementation of marketing plans. Internal marketing is the overlap between marketing management and human resource management. The changes required for good service can be facilitated if employees see the corporation as their customers see it. This in turn leads to marketing strategy having increased impact on corporate strategy as a marketing orientation and marketing capability is developed throughout the corporation. However, marketing is often seen from too narrow a perspective and it is necessary to market the marketing concept, function, and the necessary change. Problems can arise from employees' attitudes towards the essential purposes of marketing. Morgan (1991) has suggested that strategic internal marketing can effect incremental culture change towards market responsiveness, i.e. operationalize the marketing of marketing and a marketing orientation. Mercer (1992) has also highlighted the marketer's role as a change agent. Internal marketing is continuous training to enhance the service providers' knowledge of their services and capabilities, their awareness of market opportunities and their marketing skills. The mobilization of corporate knowledge as an inimitable customer-value creator.

Marketing planning must take account of organizational culture by considering it equivalent to consumer lifestyles. Then employees can be given specific attractive guidelines and incentives that promote a system of strongly held and shared values which emphasize customer consciousness and quality. We need to consider the role, involvement and influence of marketing, training, and even some personnel and recruitment matters. These are areas which have a bearing on, or direct contact with, the market and therefore, in effect, are part of the product.

The view that internal marketing enables external marketing is echoed by Wilson *et al.* (1992: 144):

> the internal stakeholders . . . undoubtedly exert the greatest and most immediate effect upon the mission and subsequently upon the objectives pursued, since it is their expectations and patterns of behaviour which influence the organisation most directly on a day-to-day basis.

Kotler and Andreasen (1991) consider the purpose of internal marketing to create and maintain customer orientation and service-mindedness by ensuring that all in the corporation realize that every interaction with a customer is a 'moment of truth' (Carlzon, 1987). In doing so, managers must manage indirectly to influence service quality by creating a customer-friendly system which reinforces the above concerns and empowers employees to take appropriate discretionary action to satisfy each customer as long as they believe that it is in the corporation's long-run best interests. What is required is the intentional building of a working climate which fosters improvement and innovation – the learning corporation.

Internal marketing can be seen as a means of promoting marketing orientation. Logically, as in McKenna's compelling view, marketing orientation of the corporation can lead to competitive advantage through:

> company and customer working so closely together that selling, no longer a discrete function, is subsumed in problem solving.
> (McKenna, 1991: 49)

Internal marketing is important as a tool for legitimizing strategic actions. A framework for action is created by 'framing' the company and its context (opportunities, constraints, and market segments), and communicating the mission to the employees. There is a conscious attempt to infuse the corporation with the dominant values, or the values of the dominant coalition of the corporation. In this way a 'marketing culture' may be encouraged.

CORPORATE IDENTIFICATION, IDENTITY, IMAGE, AND REPUTATION

Most, if not all, employees are in a position to affect customers' behaviour and their beliefs about the corporation and their products. Corporate identity and corporate reputation are increasingly seen as major strategic issues to be managed. Corporate communications management is integral to the marketer's responsibilities and links to the core management function as impression management. The proportion of customer-oriented employees in the corporation's workforce can make a significant difference to its competitive position in the marketplace.

Humans need involvement and identification with other humans. In the past, community was based on proximal relationships of cooperation – strength in numbers, and in the sharing of tasks such as hunting, tending livestock, and cooking. Today, cooperative community (Halal, 1996) is rooted in much more psychologically open factors, such as feelings of acceptance and approval (status, etc.), and this requires some willingness to conform and to adapt to the needs of others in return for being considered an 'insider' and not an 'outsider'.

People need to identify with others and motivating causes or purposes. They need to feel that they can realize personal goals through a commitment to contributing to collective goals. Otherwise, why cooperate? Affiliation in work is now a basic human need as the social institutions of community involvement – organized religion and extended family – have declined.

Communication is the basis of identification. We evaluate our position in relation to the values of others and may come to accept the goals of others as our own, thus bringing them into close proximity, or overlapping, or even merging our selves/identities. We come to our working arrangements (jobs, roles, employment contract, etc.) with a 'prior structure of preferences – a personality'.

Identification is a means of gaining personal status. In many cases, prestige may come from subgroups rather than from the whole enterprise. This encourages subgroup identification, but not identification with the total 'group' (business enterprise). Most people identify with their occupation and each other more than with their employing corporation. Thus, they interpret the meaning of their corporate environment in terms of their occupation and work group more than the corporation per se. How then can a sufficient degree of commonality and alignment be achieved to enable the business performance required of the total enterprise through active participation in the required tasks at the necessary level of effectiveness and efficiency (i.e. the production of excellent service)? How can wasteful and frustrating 'tribal warfare' be avoided?

To what degree are we as employees in general involved in the goals of the corporation? That is, genuinely identifying with the purpose and objectives of the corporation, rather than just displaying a 'necessary' instrumentalization of personality traits? We are interested here in the person's identification with tasks, subgroups, and the enterprise as a whole, as well as identification with customers (as part of a discernible 'special' subgroup which comprises insiders (colleagues) as well as 'outsiders' who have to be treated as 'insiders' in a given sell–buy situation). Strength of identification with the group influences the degree to which our goals conform to our perception of group norms. Identification can explain how alternatives are recognized by a member.

> A decision maker identifies with an organisation [sic] when he or she desires to choose the alternative that best promotes the perceived interests of that organisation.
>
> (Heath, 1994: 194)

The strength of identification with the group is determined by the:

1. perceived prestige of the group
2. extent to which goals are perceived as shared among members
3. frequency of interaction between members (also related to 2)
4. number of personal needs satisfied in the group (also related to 3)
5. amount of competition between members

Forms of involvement to be found in the corporate situation are: pay; skilled and professional achievement; aesthetics; community spirit; social value. These are each contingent on identification with the working process and/or strategic concept of the particular corporation. Identification may be with the corporation, the job or work, a profession, other members, and/or with people external to the corporation. This may arise through symbols that bond, or through feelings of membership (e.g. employment, qualifications, financial relationships such as purchasing, etc.).

Productivity is the standard by which subgroup (work group, division, department, team, etc.) prestige is judged, and high performance leads to strong identification of a person with the subgroup. Groups that facilitate interaction and satisfaction of personal goals are more cohesive. Small work groups allow closure of interpersonal relations and this provides for greater identification.

Identification produces adoption of premises and assumptions. Subgroup identification implies the acceptance of, and conformity to, subgroup norms. Task group identification may be with a subgroup or extra-organizational group (such as a professional association). If a task is perceived as training or preparation of some other task(s), the identification with it will be weaker. Characteristics of the job (commonality of needs, level of technical skill required for the task, degree of autonomy in making decisions, range of skill needed), length of service, and mobility are also contributors.

Coordinated internal and external communication is an aspect of service quality in its broadest sense, since it is concerned with managing customer and other stakeholder expectations into line with organizational capability, and in ensuring that employees are knowledgeable in, and prepared for meeting, those expectations.

Corporate communication is the integration of human resource management, corporate strategy development, organization development, public relations, and marketing management. We will discuss this further in chapter eighteen. Communication is managed from an organizational, managerial, and marketing perspective as a corporate competence. The perceptions of corporation members of their corporation, based on their attitudes and values, has an impact on the perceptions of external stakeholder groups – through the service deliverer's behaviour and values. In part, corporate image comes from the total experiences of dealing with the corporation's people. Image management is intended to take some control of the reputations held of the corporation in the minds of significant key publics who can influence the performance of the corporation. Corporate communication, including internal marketing, provides the means and policy for members to look in on the corporation as well as out to customers and other stakeholder groups. Corporate communication shows the corporation to itself as well as to others.

A corporation develops a 'corporate personality', through non-visual characteristics, when a set of interrelated factors are organized towards internal integration in psychological terms, i.e.:

> the organisation of various traits, feelings, attitudes, etc., into one harmonious personality . . . the significance of some reasonably intuitive relationships between such factors as employee satisfaction, employee motivation, service quality, customer satisfaction, and, indeed, increased volume of business or profitability.
>
> (Heskett in Congram *et al.*, 1987)

For some corporations and markets the corporate image may be more important than the products or services provided, and human resources (people, skills, commitment, etc.) create and convey the image to the outside environment. Corporate image is the outcome of an expressive strategy.

Corporations actively seek to create an 'image' of themselves that can also be used in managing internal processes. Corporate identity is the symbolic–affective aspects of the collective human resources.

INTERNAL MARKETING AS A CORPORATE INTEGRATOR

Internal marketing has a role in reducing conflict between the functional groups of the corporation by eroding barriers through improved sharing of information and alignment of objectives around external customer satisfaction and marketing principles. Internal partnering is an overt approach to reducing internal conflict and for improving organizational effectiveness and efficiency.

When functional groups perform specialized portions of the totality of business tasks of an enterprise, this may be a convenient form of organization for the company. The impact on the customer's judgement of service may be little understood or underemphasized. This traditional approach to organization design is the epicentre for much intra-organizational conflict and the source of many strategy implementation problems. Cross-functional coordination requires attention to organization design, improved communication, and decision-support systems. Improvements in the degree of collaboration can lead to better products that enter the market faster. Groups with either demand-generation (e.g. sales and marketing) or supply-meeting (e.g. production, logistics, customer billing, training and development) responsibilities recognize their interdependence in working together to meet all targeted customer needs.

The sales force is often the first 'customer' of the designer, producer, and engineering and technical support staff (for pre-sale and post-sale support). Technical support staff need to understand the service needs of both the sales force and the end customer. There is an assumption here that improved internal coordination can lead to improved service quality and thus to strengthened relationships with end-customers (see Figure 11.1).

Congram *et al.* (1987) urge managers to work for internal integration to achieve unity of wholeness because responsibility for service delivery and response to customers is shared throughout the service organization.

Grönroos (1990: 223) defined his internal marketing concept as:

> a unifying concept for more effectively managing a variety of inter-functional, and frequently well-established activities, as part of an overall framework aiming at a common objective.

It is increasingly being recognized that corporations are networks of interacting and interdependent groups. Organizational structure alone is insufficient to deal with power dependencies and relationships, and here

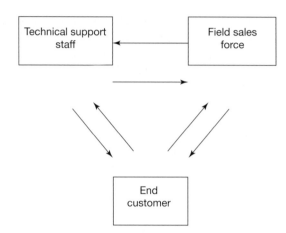

Figure 11.1 **Reciprocal determinism among functions**

internal marketing can help by providing a perspective in which responsibility for marketing interaction is widespread throughout the corporation, transcending functional or departmental boundaries (Gilmore and Carson, 1995). Internal-marketing management must be seen as a holistic, systemic and corporation-wide concept, and not solely in the interests of the marketing department.

Internal marketing can build supportive working relationships between departments, who come to understand each other's needs, instead of focusing solely on building a roster of customers. This requires mutual trust and respect, which comes from demonstrated commitment, keeping promises, and interactive open communication, and can result in better customer service. Each party must be willing to take account of mutual expectations, and training is required, since teamwork requires a team.

Bowen and Schneider (1985) have pointed out that the management group has a dual problem of motivating employees and customers. Traditionally, these tasks have been separated between human resource management and marketing departments. However, employees and customers share many motivations and interact, therefore the need for integration seems logical (see Box 11.2).

A shared set of beliefs about the meaning of customer orientation is required. This will require the promotion of a particular interpretation of the marketing concept and the systems and tools to achieve its objective, i.e.

BOX 11.2   RECOGNIZING AND SUPPORTING INFLUENCES

When US food retailer Ukrop's found that their check-out clerks and baggers had the most influence on customer relationships, they reassigned funds from advertising and sales promotion into training to improve impact at this point of brand contact.

(Duncan and Moriarty, 1998)

delivering value to customers at a profit. The managers of such an approach will focus on the understanding and acceptance of a 'corporate ideology', while planning locally for appropriate activities to operationalize it. Skills and attitudes for communication and service will be central requisites.

The role of the manager will be shifted from that of overseer and controller to that of organizer and supporter. Employees and managers will have to understand and agree on what is in the corporation's long-run best interests and how they individually gain from this.

Communication will be seen as the **mode** of organization, rather than the means (Drucker, 1973). The achievement of goals will be seen as occurring within relationships rather than in discrete transactions of discrete individuals or groups. This interactional perspective will balance economic (monetary) and non-economic values through a cooperative management system. Above all, there will be a removal of the submissive, subordinate working relationship at least at the local (team) level. Collaboration will mean the self-regulation of relationships and obligations at work. People will no longer be required to work under the duress of directing, order-bestowing force, and because the system is ambition-driven, their work will be a free act of obedience to their own purposes, which will be widely understood and balanced with the collective purposes.

Internal marketing seen as internal relationship management is an integrative process within a system for fostering positive working relationships in a developmental way in a climate of cooperation and achievement. The internal customer relationship management system has a number of key features:

- the 'voice' of the customer is incorporated into product/service decisions
- customer commitment is earned in a 'social' contract
- there is open exchange of ideas for mutual gain
- customers are involved in product design, production, and service
- there is close partnership between suppliers and customers
- customers are viewed as individual people and so are 'value' providers
- there is continuous interaction and dialogue between suppliers and customers
- there is a focus on discovering, creating, arousing and responding to customer needs
- relationships are viewed as enterprise assets
- there is systematic collection and dissemination of customer information (detailing and negotiating requirements, expectations, needs, attitudes, and satisfaction)

Subscription to the managerial perspective on marketing management allows the ring-fencing of 'marketing' as a set of activities to be carried out by a department – a number of variables simply have to be selected and manipulated – but no commitment to a value-creation philosophy is required. This simplifies the perceived complexity of enterprise organization and direction, and permits tribal empire-building. The resulting intra-organization communication problems are perpetuated through attempts to manage via such a fragmented approach to organization and management.

The broader approach discussed here robs the functionalist/specialist of sole ownership of the territory, but the gain to the system when each individual is able to contribute to the whole enterprise is realizable in terms greater than mere 'market efficiency'. The needs and wants of the individual can be met as the means to achieving the corporation's success in conducting the business of the enterprise.

The structure for this is a network of self-managing teams (or mini-businesses) who serve each other, develop specialist knowledge, execute projects, and sell to 'outsiders'. Internal marketing is the relationship and knowledge management required for the 'new organization'. The internal–external boundary becomes blurred as the traditional organization form is dissolved in this move towards 'marketization', which is characterized as having:

- a flattened organization
- fluid arrangements
- projectized work
- temporary network membership
- individual units aiming to own a market through better service
- symbiosis with customers
- pursuit of mutually satisfying employment relationships

We can now examine – see Boxes 11.3–11.4 – some applications of the internal marketing way of managing.

BOX 11.3   DELIVERING CUSTOMER SERVICE IMPROVEMENT AT PARCELFORCE

An internal-marketing way of working was introduced in a business unit of a national network parcel carrier.

The idea of introducing this approach into the business unit came about through a convergence of thinking and experience. An extensive study of the principles and practice of internal marketing in service businesses had been completed by an advisor to the communications manager, who had attended presentations by a number of communications professionals, including a talk about the introduction of internal marketing in a large public sector government agency. This coming together in thinking was facilitated by their cooperation on an informal review of organizational communication practices within the business unit. Both realized that internal marketing offered a systematic realignment of practices with the nature and purpose of the business and that this would provide the infrastructure and climate for a number of other major business improvement initiatives (known in Parcelforce as transformational projects).

The results of a national employee opinion attitude survey, conducted in May 1995, showed that morale was low in the company. Perhaps indicative of the communication climate in the North East business unit was the participation rate for their own employee opinion survey – just 32%. Many people aspired to an excellent-service culture, but many felt unable to deliver due to obstacles in the way that the business unit operated and was managed.

One of the transformational projects, an integrated communications programme, branded 'Understanding the Business', was being launched as part of a programme of improvement in communication activities, aimed at increasing the knowledge of employees, at all levels, especially in the areas of:

- products and services for external customers
- commercial awareness
- competitor activity
- important customers
- advertising plans and campaigns

Other developments at that time were in response to a growing recognition that what was needed was a much more open and dynamic communication climate and system. The internal-marketing approach offered an integrating system of interactive communication that focused working practices and decisions on customer service in a competitive marketplace.

BOX 11.4   LAVISH COMMUNICATION IN THE HERMAN MILLER COMMUNITY

In order to ensure that employees feel part of a community and can make responsible choices, Herman Miller Inc., a famous US upmarket office and healthcare furniture-maker corporation based in Zeeland, Michigan, has striven to create a rich bath of 'lavish communication', with minimum requirements:

✓ full financial information for all employees and training in how to read financial statements
✓ regularly posted measurements for all activities
✓ open discussion of strategic options and competitive situations, as well as problems and concerns
✓ frequent discussion of how each part fits with the whole
✓ freedom of internal speech
✓ freedom of internal website postings and e-mail
✓ right of inquiry and learning in order to pursue the mission and best serve customers and the corporation

The company was one of the first to adopt the Scanlon Plan for 'gainsharing' management by integration and self-control, and is one of the most widely known successes. This involves participative management practices, structured employee participation, and a method for sharing productivity gains (and profits) between the company and employees. Managers have consistently paid attention to values that build community. Max DePree, Chairman and CEO, has called this the 'intelligent organisation' and leadership an art. The Scanlon Plan has been described formally in the company as not simply a compensation system, but rather as a 'way of life' for the company, and significant gains in productivity have been achieved. Staff, under the Scanlon Plan, set objectives, work to improve performance, and receive typically 7 per cent of the gains. Herman Miller Inc. is one of at least 25 per cent of US firms that have a gainsharing plan (Belasco, 1990).

DePree believes that leaders owe their workers 'a rational environment [that] values trust and human dignity and provides the opportunity for personal development and self-fulfilment' (DePree, 1989: 16). He also talks of giving employees 'space so that we can both give and receive such beautiful things as ideas, openness, dignity, joy, healing and inclusion' (DePree, 1989: 17). DePree, following his father D. J. DePree (who founded the company), never takes people below him in the chain of command for granted.

Workers are seen as whole human beings – community, unlike bureaucracy, begins by recognizing the equal value of each human, and caring about their lives, their growth, their competencies, and their happiness as inherent values.

'Videotapes of monthly officers' and directors' meetings reviewing all the business operations are shown to all employees at work-team meetings. Seemingly everyone in the company – from factory floor to the very top – talks about values and has intimate knowledge of the successes and problems of the corporation' (Nelson-Horchler, 1991). Today, the corporation comprises almost 8,000 'employee-owners'.

(See www.hermanmiller.com)

CASE STUDY 11   KOCH INDUSTRIES AND THE DEATH OF COMMAND-AND-CONTROL MANAGEMENT[a]

Koch Industries has grown from a small firm to one of the largest private corporations in the world as a result of its system of 'market-based management.' The CEO, Charles Koch, defines all corporate functions in terms of market equivalents.

The corporation can be thought of as a social system that must accomplish transformation as well as reformation in its processes (Ackoff, 1998) if it is to survive and prosper. Market-based management focuses on the form of organization and knowledge as a way of managing that adopts free enterprise principles, as outlined by Gable (1998), requiring: market-process analysis; comparative advantage; just conduct; property rights; market incentives; free flow of ideas; and a price system.

This 'internal' perspective deals with the operation of the system. To ensure that the system is adaptive requires that it is open, i.e. that it appreciates its environment, including the network of relationships within which it operates.

Koch Industries managers have gone beyond the familiar notion of corporate culture to build an operating philosophy and set of values that heavily influence the way they do business. They call this system Market-Based Management, ® or MBM.® This alternative to traditional command-and-control thinking is the creation of Charles Koch. He, along with others, developed this management philosophy based on market-process economics, the philosophies of science and knowledge, and many years of practical business experience.

MBM is much more than a set of management tools. It involves a vision of our rapidly changing world, a set of core commitments, and an aim to enhance the potential of each employee. MBM stands against the traditional command-and-control approach to corporate governance, with its command hierarchy and incentive systems designed to ensure that orders are followed and the hierarchy preserved. MBM promotes, by contrast, a spontaneous order of employee-entrepreneurs. These individuals work within a framework of appropriate incentives and decision rights, and create value for customers by applying powerful knowledge systems.

People at Koch Industries believe that MBM improves company performance by helping people to realize their potential. In essence, MBM helps employees act like owners.

Where and how we look determines what we see. What we see determines what we think and how we act. Our vision either limits or enlarges our potential. The revision of Koch Industries from a commodities company to an operating, processing, purchasing, selling, and trading company is one example. Similarly, when individuals see their jobs as creating value rather than following instruction, and as satisfying customers rather than the boss, they begin to act and feel like entrepreneurs.

Change is one of the few constants in our professional lives. People at Koch Industries try to minimize resistance to it and reduce the hardship it can bring by emphasizing certain core commitments:

- **humility**: acknowledging weaknesses and learning from others are essential to social progress and economic growth
- **integrity**: a 'discovery culture' based on honesty, openness, and constructive challenge improves and expands our knowledge and vision
- **tolerance**: unless we treat others with dignity and respect, actively cooperate with and learn from those with different kinds of knowledge and perspective, we cannot realize the possibilities of a discovery culture, far less build a truly civil society
- **responsibility**: only if we have the self-discipline to accept responsibility for our mistakes will we learn from them
- **desire to contribute**: employees must want to contribute, believe that they have the potential to do so, and believe that they will be rewarded accordingly

Incentive systems must be geared toward contributions to long-term success as well as to short-term profits, and include contributions to our culture and communities. As individuals make contributions to long-term success, they acquire decision rights – that is, a greater level of responsibility and authority to allocate the firm's resources. The concept simulates the market process whereby profitable entrepreneurs accumulate property rights or the ability to direct more scarce resources. MBM moves control of resources to those who successfully satisfy customer needs.

Companies must have profit signals, or discovery measures, so that employees can see what does and does not create value. These measures will expand employees' vision, change their thinking, and enable them to make new discoveries. Again, the signals must include contributions to the whole, not to just one part. Moreover, the most efficient knowledge system in the world is useless unless shaped by the core commitments of the decision-makers.

(www.koch-industries.com)

Note: [a] The assistance of Dick Anderson, Director of Market-based Management Capability, Koch Industries, is acknowledged with thanks

WHAT DO YOU THINK?

1 Do you have any internal-marketing practices in your workplace or college?
2 What would obstruct the adoption of a market-based management process in your corporation?
3 How might the absence of an internal-marketing system hinder the development of marketing communication?
4 How might internal marketing be used at Koch Industries to further their Market-based Management Capability?
5 Why, traditionally, would employee communication not be seen as based on exchanges?
6 Imagine that all of your colleagues could be regarded as marketing resources. What specific actions might be necessary to realize this notion?
7 Internal-marketing outcomes are the necessary inputs for effective external marketing. What is meant by this assertion?
8 Professor Grönroos summarizes internal marketing as attitude and communication management. What does he mean?
9 How well does the 'marketing mix' managerial framework explain what is required for internal marketing?
10 As marketing manager, how can you apply the concept of internal marketing to enhance the outcomes of your work?

FURTHER READING

Carlzon, J. (1987) *Moments of Truth: New Strategies for Today's Customer-Driven Economy*, New York: Ballinger Publishing Corp.

Day, G. S. (1992) 'Marketing's contribution to the strategic dialogue', *Journal of the Academy of Marketing Science* 20: 323–29.

DePree, M. (1989) *Leadership is an Art*, New York: Doubleday. (Documents the leadership and commitment necessary for responsive and responsible business.)

Drucker, P. F. (1973) *Management: Tasks, Responsibilities, Practices*, London: Heinemann.

Gilmore, A. and Carson, D. (1995) 'Managing and marketing to internal customers', in Glynn, W. J. and Barnes, J. G. (eds) *Understanding Services Management*, Chichester: John Wiley & Sons, pp. 295–321.

Grönroos, C. (1990) *Service Management and Marketing: Managing the Moments of Truth in Service Competition*, Lexington, MA: Lexington Books.

Halal, W. E. (1996) *The New Management: Democracy and Enterprise Are Transforming Organizations*, San Francisco, CA: Berrett-Koehler.

McKenna, R. (1991) *Relationship Marketing: Own the Market Through Strategic Customer Relationships*, London: Century Business Books.

Morgan, N. A. (1991) *Professional Services Marketing*, Oxford: Butterworth-Heinemann/CIM.

Varey, R. J. (1995) 'A model of internal marketing for building and sustaining a competitive service advantage', *Journal of Marketing Management*, 11 (1–3): 25–40.

Varey, R. J. (1995) 'Internal marketing: a review and some inter-disciplinary research challenges', *International Journal of Service Industry Management*, 6 (1): 40–63.

Varey, R. J. and Gilligan, C. T. (1996) 'Internal marketing: interfacing the internal and external environments', in Kunst, P. and Lemmink, J. (eds) *Managing Service Quality*, Vol. 2, London: Paul Chapman Publishing, pp. 59–77.

Varey, R. J. and Lewis, B. R. (1999) 'A broadened conception of internal marketing', *European Journal of Marketing* 33 (9–10): 926–44.

Varey, R. J. and Lewis, B. R. (eds) (2000) *Internal Marketing: Directions for Management*, London: Routledge.

chapter twelve

RELATIONSHIP MARKETING

LEARNING POINTS

Careful study of this chapter will help you to:

- examine why relationship marketing has become of major importance in marketing management

- connect the concept of relationship to the concept of communication

- realize some implications for marketing planners

- consider the importance of communicating before, during and after a value exchange

> Marriage is one long conversation, chequered by disputes. Two persons more and more adapt their notions to suit the other, and in the process of time, without sound of trumpets they conduct each other into new worlds of thought.
>
> Robert Louis Stevenson

INTRODUCTION

As traditional marketing becomes more and more obsolete, the idea relationship marketing highlights the centrality of communication – not as a means of informing, but as the mode of organizing exchanges. Relating requires communication, and communicating arises within a relationship.

Thus, in a book on marketing communication, we have to see relationship management as fundamental. Consider, again, for a moment, the shift in conceiving communication as a participatory social phenomenon rather than as a neutral tool for objective informing. As we have seen in the discussions of the preceding chapters, communicating is what is done with people, rather than to or from them. This is the very basis of relationship marketing.

Communication is the mode of inter-action, and a relationship is the shared context for meaning-making. Thus, whereas recent writers have begun to speak of 'interactive communication', a more helpful way of defining a framework for responsive and responsible management is to think of communicative interaction (as part of the corporate communication system of managing that sees marketing and public relations converging) (see Varey, forthcoming).

Grönroos (1990) highlighted that traditional marketing activity treats all people the same – there is little or no distinction between first-time and repeat/long-standing customers – in traditional marketing, everyone is treated as a prospect for recruitment, even if they have already traded and established a relationship. Interactive marketing, on the other hand, is what arises when customers and providers cooperate to co-produce the value they need and want.

The cost of recruiting a new customer may be several times the cost of retaining an existing customer. It can be much more cost-effective, profitable, and satisfying in other ways to maintain trading relationships with customers than to allow them (through neglect) to exit and then have to exert effort in trying to attract them back or to recruit replacement customers.

Trust and commitment are key requirements for lasting trading relationships, and are the outcome of communicating. The management of communication is key to managing relationships with customers and other stakeholders.

The problem for marketing managers is how to treat consumers, buyers, and customers personally. This aim is nothing new. Treating different customers differently should be seen as a reason for institutionalizing managed interaction with consumers and buyers.

MANAGING DIALOGUE

Dialogue has been defined as reasoning together in trust-based interactions (Ballantyne, 1999). This theory is highly significant for marketing communication managers since dialogue and knowledge generation in relationship marketing create and contribute value for stakeholders – customers, suppliers, and other people.

It is worthwhile revisiting our earlier question on what we imagine human communication is like – and thus how we might try to manage communication for a purpose. Nowadays, we often see the phrase 'interactive communication'. This is misleading. To be conceptually clear, interaction is any action that generates a response. In marketing systems, interaction is mutual and requires participation. Communication is a special kind of interaction that enables communicators to construct meaning by speaking and listening (remember the idea of intentional strategic talk mentioned in chapter nine?). These reflective conversations are entered into in order to get beyond the understanding of any one person (a 'third way of knowing') – thus, dialogue moves from interaction to participation. This is where past textbook authors have gone wrong – relationship marketing is much more about partnering (dialoguing) in cooperative relationships, than it is about managing information. We need the term communicative interaction to provide the necessary emphasis for the management task. Marketing managers manage communication systems.

RELATIONSHIPS AS VALUE ADDED

Products are increasingly commodities, but relationships will always be unique. But why would a consumer or buyer wish to relate to a provider? A trading relationship saves time, ensures some consistency in value for money, and provides a sense of comfort and security. For the provider, a loyal customer buys more and generates more profit.

Strong relationships are built on trust, whereas profitable relationships are built on knowledge. The trading partners need to know each other's preferred ways of being treated and what is available for exchange. Yahoo!, for example, offers the proposition that the user will save time and get help in finding the information they want (see Box 12.1). Being the Internet site of first choice is the basis for a strong relationship.

BOX 12.1   PROBABLY THE WORLD'S BEST INTERNET SEARCH EXPERIENCE?

Google Inc. indexes more than 1 billion URLs, thus providing access to the full text of 560 million web pages. This means that I can search the equivalent of a stack of paper more than 70 miles high in less than half a second! With searches available in 10 languages and highly relevant search results, I have become an enthusiastic advocate for using this search engine for all Internet searches. Google almost always finds what I want. Google is my first choice when using the www for communication, learning, and entertainment.

The people at Yahoo! are so impressed with Google's technology that they have struck a deal that makes Google their default search results provider to complement their Web directory and navigational guide.

We will meet Google again in a later chapter.

(See www.google.com and www.yahoo.com)

Communication and culture guru Marshall McLuhan observed in the 1960s that commercial competition creates resemblance. This has serious implications for marketing managers in pursuit of competitive advantage! Providers competing over a market niche or position tend to grow more alike. This leads to escalation in competitive effort. Thus, market share becomes harder to gain. The only way out is to change the rules of the game. McLuhan termed this the competitive exclusion principle (McLuhan and Powers, 1989).

The relationship may be valued when product performance and quality is taken for granted and there is little differentiation on that basis alone.

RELATIONSHIP STATUS

Consumers, buyers, and providers (sellers) seek to establish and maintain trading relationships when they believe that such an investment will enable them to accomplish the goals of their 'life projects'. The buyer–seller relationship has been likened to a marriage (Tynan, 1997). These ways of thinking about such relationships are drawn from the study of interpersonal relationships by social psychologists. Dwyer *et al.* (1987), on the other hand, used a life-cycle approach to model the buyer–seller relationship (Figure 12.1).

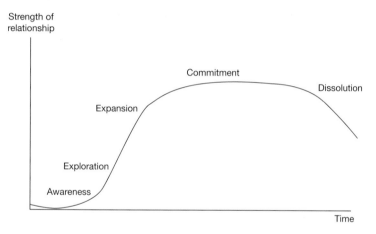

Figure 12.1 **A buyer–seller relationship life cycle**
Source: Based on Dwyer *et al.*, 1987

In the exploration stage, parties try to attract the attention of the other, to bargain, and to understand the expectations, norms, and power of the other. Expansion occurs when the initial exploration succeeds in establishing the basis for a continuing relationship. Exchange outcomes provide clues about the suitability of this. Commitment reduces the need for searching for alternatives. The possibility of termination is always present, and the consequences are greatest once the parties have made significant investments in the relationship. The relationship-marketing task is to sustain and maintain the trading relationship for as long as it provides benefits to the parties – see Box 12.2. If we refer back to the marketing mix discussion of chapter seven, we can see that relationship development requires a fully integrated approach to managing the wide-ranging marketing communication situations (see chapter thirteen for elaboration of this key idea).

BOX 12.2   CARING FOR CUSTOMERS – GUARANTEED!

In 1993, SONY UK launched a customer care-line and a product insurance policy as part of its move into relationship marketing (Toor, 1993). Customers register at the point of sale for access to the information telephone service and are offered an extended-service warranty. SONY's quality development manager, Paul Campbell, identified customer desire for a relationship with the manufacturer that extends beyond the initial purchase: 'It's important that we have the opportunity to communicate directly with our customers', he commented. This becomes more difficult, and the market for consumer electronics products becomes more fragmented and broadcast advertising then becomes less cost-effective. Broadcast advertising will focus on brand exposure, while direct mail is used to generate sales leads. For example, owners of 7-year-old TV sets were mailed with brochures on new technology sets.

Ironically, in the early 1980s, SONY was one of many consumer electronics manufacturers who dropped the guarantee card because they were overwhelmed with thousands of cards that they could not find resource to deal with. Today, electronic registration at point of sale and on the Internet has solved that headache! The customer care programme has become a major element of the marketing communication system.

We will see in chapter fifteen how the nature of the relationship and any gap between this and the desired relationship can be addressed by setting appropriate communication objectives. Later in this chapter, we will examine marketing communication approaches to establishing commitment as loyalty.

Several levels of commitment can be identified. A prospect has yet to establish a relationship, whereas a strong advocate is fully committed not only to product purchase for themselves but also to recommending to associates, friends, and family – see Figure 12.2.

Advocate

Supporter

Client

Customer

Prospect

Figure 12.2 **The ladder of consumer/buyer commitment**

TRANSACTION VS. RELATIONSHIP APPROACH

Whereas market exchanges are casual short-term discrete (transactional) episodic encounters primarily motivated by self-interest, relational exchanges develop when people wish to develop long-term exclusive and supportive relationships on the basis of mutual knowledge that simplifies their trading environment. Whereas traditional marketing, operating through market exchanges, manages the preparation and promotion of an offering in order to consummate an exchange, relationship or interactive marketing also works to maintain the relationship between product-based exchange episodes.

Rather than pursue a market relationship to bring a product and a consumer/buyer together, relationship marketing attempts to establish and cultivate a marketing relationship that enables cooperative problem-solving (Table 12.1). Communication is participated in for the purpose of informing, answering, listening, aligning, and matching.

Characteristics of relationship marketing:

- Retention of selected customers, rather than recruiting new ones to replace valued defectors.
- A focus on long-term associations, with an orientation to identifying and meeting future customer needs.

Table 12.1 **How does relationship marketing differ from the traditional approach?**

Transaction marketing	Relationship marketing
Focus on recruitment of customers for a single sale	Focus on customer retention
Orientation on product features	Orientation to product benefits and system solutions
Short-time horizon	Long(er) time horizon
Little attention to customer service	Customer service considered very important
Limited commitment to customer	Commitment to customer is high
Moderate contact with customer	Customer contact is frequent and rich
Quality is primarily a concern of production	Quality is the concern of all
Communication is for persuasion	Communication is for meaning-making
Information is the content of communications	Information is the product of communicating
Business model is functional, mechanistic, production-oriented	Model is humanistic, relationship based

- A focus on service benefits, rather than features – a system orientation which customizes offerings, including communication, through interaction (Grönroos, 1983).
- Emphasis on high levels of customer service through repetitive interaction.
- High levels of commitment based on promises to and from selected customers.
- High level of customer contact (frequency and number of people involved) – many transactions merged together.
- Interactive-marketing function connected with all other business functions, not separated like the traditional marketing function.
- Interactive marketing supported by marketing mix activities – customers involved in design of solutions, rather than unilateral attempts to change attitudes.
- Customers less sensitive to price.
- People in the supplier organization become critical marketing resources as 'part-time marketers'.
- Direct management of the customer portfolio, rather than concern for market share.
- Continuous real-time dialogue with customers, rather than ad hoc satisfaction surveys.
- Anticipated conflicts of interest and future trouble are counterbalanced by trust and efforts at unity – a mutual learning interaction.
- Joint efforts related to both performance and planning over time.
- The seller regards relationship marketing as a strategic issue, mainly because the profit centre is increasingly the customer rather than individual transactions.
- The buyer considers relationship marketing as a communication process that should enhance the relevance of the seller's offering.
- A balanced formal/informal communication strategy with measurement of satisfaction in relational terms.
- What is offered in the relationship – the service content – may be undifferentiated. Then it is the relationship itself which provides the benefits, rather than what is delivered.

Box 12.3 provides an unusual example of relationship marketing.

The relationship approach requires that business managers responsible for matching, producing, and representing value exchange opportunities need to adopt a service orientation to the manner in which the business is operated, with a process perspective that recognizes the manner in which value is created and provided to consumers and buyers. This requires active involvement of partners in a value-creating network of suppliers, producers, intermediaries, and so on.

Relationship marketing focuses on the individual customer, but also other stakeholders, and seeks to manage the relationships to add value for each person.

BOX 12.3   ORGANIC COOPERATIVE PUNCHES ABOVE OWN WEIGHT

Richard Counsell of Somerset Levels Organic Foods has just been voted UK e-commerce operation of the year. This is some considerable achievement for a small Somerset farm that only recently acquired a second-hand PC by swapping it for an Aberdeen Angus heifer and established an Internet site using free software from a magazine.

The site sells organic lamb, beef, cider, Cheddar cheese, and fresh vegetables to 800 customers, and orders are growing by 5 to 10 per cent per month, averaging £90 each. Trading with supermarket chains was robbing the farm of much of its profit. Today, the proprietors can deal directly with consumers, many of whom would otherwise never have heard about the firm's produce. Orders come in from as far afield as the Orkneys and the Channel Islands, many from high-class restaurants. Customers can pay online and take a virtual tour of the farm, as well as select produce for their order, and get a recipe of the month.

ONE-TO-ONE MARKETING

Don Peppers promotes the notion of a shift, enabled by electronic telecommunications systems, to customer relationship management from the traditional product management of mass marketing. In this strategy, the aim is to establish and build enduring trading relationships in which customer relationship managers find products for their customers. This is very different to the product manager's task of finding customers for the corporation's products. Consider the examples illustrated in Boxes 12.4 and 12.5.

BOX 12.4   SELLING A HOUSE IS EASIER WITH EASIER.CO.UK

A new business model is displayed in this situation where an Internet site removes the need for a traditional house sale agent as the go-between seller and buyer. The Internet connection allows direct interaction between vendor and potential purchasers, without the need for an intermediary.

Interestingly, what are traditional estate agents doing about this development?

The first requirement is the ability to identify each customer individually and to classify them in terms of their purchase and consumption habits and preferences. Then, customers must be differentiated in terms of why they buy so as to gain a greater share of their total purchasing power. Thirdly, interaction with the customers is a crucial part of the business strategy. Asking about needs, interests, uses, preferences, and experiences – then listening to the answers and acting upon them – is the basis for one-to-one marketing. Finally, the value production process must be capable of delivering customized

---

BOX 12.5   INFORMATION TECHNOLOGY OR RELATIONSHIP TECHNOLOGY?

How do marketers use the Internet to build relationships with their customers and consumers and buyers who are prospective customers?

There is more to it than merely connecting a website to a database. A variety of new means for posing questions, listening to responses, and, in turn, responding to them are available. It is not sufficient to take a broadcast approach, a direct response approach, or a publishing approach. What is required is a dialogue approach – i.e. a website and associated features, such as e-mail, as a conversation tool.

---

products to valued customers. The relationship must be continually producing learning, and requires customer relationship management.

THE RETENTION STRATEGY

Traditional 'marketing' practice aims to recruit new customers who will make purchases that contribute profit margin with a short-term performance framework. The concept of the most valuable customers is ignored or given low priority. Also the influence of one customer on another is largely ignored.

Current customers should be encouraged to participate in retention and expansion. Lapsed customers need reconciliation activities. Prospective customers need to be engaged by attractive offerings that transcend mere product and price. One way of identifying the people who are important for the business of the provider is to analyse the lifetime value (LTV) of a customer's patronage. For example, a house mortgage can be thought of either as a £500 per month revenue stream or as a £250,000 contract over twenty-five years. Similarly, a car purchase may be thought of as a single £10,000 transaction or part of a fifty-year stream of car purchases worth £150,000. The weekly supermarket shopping bill may total £50. Over the next fifty years this will amount to £125,000!

Another crucial question is why do 10 to 30 per cent of our customers move on to other providers each year? Apart from ceasing to need a particular product, mostly people switch because they feel neglected or misunderstood. Even worse, they feel that their interests are not central to the way providers operates their business system.

Providers can act to retain customer patronage by:

• adding value to the relationship
• operating a loyalty programme that rewards a continuing relationship
• barring exit from the relationship

Any attempt to make a customer dependent upon a provider is an act of aggression and is going to fail eventually. Once a customer feels that they are being 'held hostage', then the basis of the trading relationship is unhealthy and may prove costly for both parties. We will not consider such an approach any further.

CUSTOMER RELATIONSHIP MANAGEMENT

The creation of customer satisfaction with the product and their treatment is a sure way to earn repeat business. This is not, of course, solely the responsibility of the marketing team. We have seen that generative, productive, and representative work is necessary. We will consider the problem of integrating this in chapter thirteen. The starting point of a relationship marketing strategy is a deep understanding of why customers would want a relationship with you as a provider of value? The answer, stated simply, is that a sustained relationship with you must itself provide additional value to the customer. Such a developing committed relationship will come from:

Knowledge, privilege, cooperation

Information that is interpreted and transformed into satisfying products is essential. Increasingly, it is this transformation of knowledge from one form to another that is the basis of the business: i.e. the customer–product relationship. Then, customers have to be treated differently from prospects. Commitment must be reciprocated if the provider is to be rewarded for their relationship management efforts with profitable sales and favourable word-of-mouth publicity and promotion.

The growing adoption of a Customer Relationship Management (CRM) system is evidence that more and more providers are trying to put the customer's interest at the heart of their business by integrating marketing, customer support, and other functions to maximize added value in a dialogical relationship. Instead of finding customers for products, providers are managing relationships in which they find products for customers (Peppers and Roger, 1993, 1997). Marketing communication no longer simply tries to create and refresh product awareness and identification. Instead of saying 'we are here, look what we have got', providers are saying 'we are here with you, continually providing value'.

CRM is a holistic approach to the generation, production and representation of a value-creation system, i.e. marketing, customer service, and logistics. The aim is to move the supply chain nearer to the customer to link customer needs more directly into the management of supplies, design, manufacturing, packaging, transport, and the ultimate purpose of all of this – profitable exchange. This enterprise view is a shift away from a departmental view. The technology captures and provides information about interaction history, enabling a consistency of experience for valuable customers in all interactions – inquiry, order, delivery, maintenance, upgrade, and so on. (See Box 12.6 for an example of exploiting technology to effect.)

CRM systems can send customers reminders about essential servicing and tailored offerings based on past trading history and personal information profiles. Customers can self-select assistance through the provider's website, and gather information about products, billing, order progress, and so on.

This development should challenge the marketing communications manager because it includes knowledge management, marketing automation, customer care, call centres, and sales force automation. This is obviously much more than promotional advertising design.

BOX 12.6   E-COMMERCE TAKES OFF AT AIRTOURS

The launch of mytravelco.com provides a global branded integrated travel service through which holiday and travel products can be bought through multiple channels including the Internet, interactive TV, WAP phones, telephone call centres, and high-street offices.

The integration of customer relationship management and distribution systems is founded on strategic technology partnerships with BT, Oracle, Sun Microsystem, the Landmark Travel Channel, Lonely Planet, Telewest, and others. This recognizes that the distribution structure that puts value into the 'hands' of consumers and buyers is part of the total communication environment. Marketing communication management is a critical aspect of supply chain management, and not separate from it.

The mytravelco loyalty programme rewards customers with points throughout the holiday experience.

Chairman David Crossland believes that this £100m investment will 'revolutionize our relationships with our customers, enhance our revenues and provide significant opportunities to further increase efficiency'.

(www.airtours.com/emedia)

AFFINITY MARKETING

For the provider, customer loyalty means that customers continue to repeat their purchases over an extended period of time. This means that at some point in time they are not switching their purchases to brands that offer more benefits and/or lower prices. This continuity in purchase behaviour may be due to lethargy or a fear of the risk of changing product and/or supplier. Looked at from the marketing communication manager's perspective, loyalty to another brand can be broken by sales promotion and created by advertising (NB: if it works for you, it may work for competing providers too!).

Loyalty schemes provide rewards to customers in return for their continued patronage. The value provider is able to gather personal information that is much more valuable for customized product offerings than is any of the aggregate data about the 'average' customer or market segment typically used in traditional marketing practices. Thus, data can be gathered from enquiries, purchases at store checkouts, and so on. However, because the enabling technologies are being heavily promoted by their vendors, such schemes may not provide competitive differentiation for long. Arguably, it is the relationship that matters, rather than rewards that can be copied and bettered by other providers.

Some examples of popular loyalty schemes are: the Tesco Clubcard with nine million holders, of which six million are very active spenders with the card and are considered to be loyal; and Sainsbury's Reward Card.

Shell Smart card partners with ten retailers, enabling the four million people who hold the card to earn points when shopping for a range of goods and services. The aim is to increase the number of partner retailers to around thirty to cater for consumers' everyday needs – in some cases with a smartcard that can be used through a digital TV set-top box to make purchases online.

The affinity card, which links a business with a charity or cause, has become a popular way for consumers to identify with a particular cause and to make a donation to charity based on spending. This form of innovative fund-raising has been adopted by charities such as the RSPCA and Save the Children. It has also become part of the commercial fundraising activities of football clubs (a 'grown-up T-shirt', according to Nick Begy, sport account manager at US affinity marketing corporation TransNational).

The reward card carries redeemable points for spending, and generates consumer purchase behaviour information for the provider. A number of co-branded cards have been launched, and a number of consortia of retail, financial services, and utilities have been formed to share marketing resources, distribution channels, and information about customer purchasing.

Marketing objectives for these schemes are to: generate income; add value for, and build affinity with, (credit)card holders; develop loyalty; and develop brand awareness.

Ultimately, if loyalty schemes are to be sources of sustainable competitive advantage, they have to catalyse an alternative way of thinking about the business of the value provider. Instead of a 'what can I make and how can I sell it?' mentality, this approach drives a 'who are my customers and what can I sell them?' mentality. And, as a bonus, loyalty schemes generate information that has value in its own right (Mitchell, 1996); see Box 12.7. Thus, the task at hand is for marketing communication managers to think in terms of their contribution to relationship management.

One implication of a relationship-marketing strategy is the need for consistency in marketing communication activities so that trust is built through coherence in stakeholder relationships. We explore the idea of integrated marketing communication in which a single voice and consistency in the expression of corporate values, product performance, and brand identity and position is designed into communication processes that are appropriate for each category of product–market combination in chapter thirteen. Box 12.8 deals with the question of when relationship marketing might not be a viable option.

BOX 12.7   COMING ON STRONG WITH THE HOG

Once, a Harley-Davidson motorcycle was the symbol of rebellion – today it is a status symbol and so popular that new orders take more than a year to deliver. Customers are certainly loyal! Some even tattoo the company name onto their bodies.

All new owners are given a one-year membership of the Harley Owners' Group (HOG), and receive regular mailings of literature and manuals. Dealers support the relationship by sponsoring local HOG chapters. A customer retention direct-mail programme was devised with help from the US Postal Service Tactical Marketing and Sales Development division. This aims to encourage HOG members to renew their $40 annual membership by mailing humorous reminder cards, member magazines, and easy-to-use renewal kits. When the HOG was launched in 1983 there were 33,000 members. With a 75 per cent renewal rate, this has grown to more than 500,000 members.

In 1999 the HOG.com website was launched to provide on-demand membership information and administration. As the site proudly proclaims, 'some HOG benefits you hold in your hand – some you hold in your heart'.

(www.harley-davidson.com, www.hog.com and www.harley-davidson.co.uk)

BOX 12.8   WHEN RELATIONSHIP MARKETING IS NOT APPROPRIATE

Commodity product providers cannot adopt a relationship-marketing strategy because their customers have no reason to remain loyal to a single provider. They routinely search for the most accessible lowest-cost product supplier. The suitability of a relationship marketing strategy depends on the nature of: the product (risky products in turbulent markets and where benefits accrue over a period of time, e.g. personal services and medical care); the customers (valuing of economic and social exchanges of relationships, orientation towards transactions or relationships, and trust and commitment); and the provider (emphasis on differentiation and value-creation manifest in corporate structure, processes, and core values).

Relationship marketing can pay off handsomely with customers who have long time horizons and high switching costs.

(Kotler, 1991: 197)

REVERSE MARKETING

In some situations, the buyer takes the initiative in seeking suitable suppliers. This situation has been termed reverse marketing, buyer initiative, or proactive procurement (Leenders and Blenkhorn, 1988). When this occurs, the provider has to respond through a reactive-marketing process. However, this is a passive strategy that will not attract buyers to form trading relationships with the corporation.

Although this situation has been recognized, particularly in industrial and business-to-business marketing management, it has largely been taken to be the adoption of a marketing system by buyers in order to persuade an attractive supplier to supply.

What has largely been missed is that this concept of reverse marketing suggests that marketing communication systems must be able to cater for buyer-initiated interaction. Often, this responsibility for communicative interaction has been located with a customer service group and treated as an administrative task. Thus, the marketing communication system must be receptive as well as expressive – and providers need to expect that in some situations buyers will be hunting for suitable suppliers. Surely, this presents an (often unrecognized) opportunity for many supposedly customer-oriented corporations. Promise-making may have to be more receptive, accommodating, and responsive. These are all questions of communication system capability.

EFFICIENT MARKETING COMMUNICATION

Wernerfelt (1996) proposes that providers should treat their customers as partners when they make decisions about marketing communication. Efficient marketing communication adopts partnership criteria to help customers to learn in order to avoid unfavourable uninformed expectations without misleading them, and to construct positive beliefs about benefits of purchase. Persuasion is seen as a short-term strategy (is it then really only a recruitment tactic?). It is better in the long run to help consumers/ buyers and customers to assess whether a product is a good choice for them. Disappointed customers are harder (more costly) to persuade! Wernerfelt compares, in general terms, benefits available to customers and the related costs to customers and providers for each means of communication (Table 12.2).

Wernerfelt reminds us that these characterizations are general and benefits, cost of acquisition, and cost of supply will vary among consumer, product attributes, and market conditions.

Table 12.2 **How efficient is your marketing communication?**

Means of communication	Benefits to customer	Cost for customer	Cost for provider
Sales force	Sales person can determine suitability of complex products, and can customize information	Planning, meeting and travelling time	One-to-one communication is expensive
Retail showroom	Evaluation through seeing and/or handling the product, paying attention to what matters to them	Travel, including time	Expensive, but economies of scope are possible with multiple brand stock
Catalogue	Less reliable and customizable information is provided, with only pictures and description	Cheap to use at any time, no travel necessary, but requires concentrated attention	Relatively cheap with economies of scale in production, but delivery precision is critical
Print advertising	Similar to catalogues	Located among newspaper articles and reports	Variable targeting efficiency and costs, and simultaneously carry numerous advertisements
Television advertising	Easy to access	Easy to watch	Large economies of scale – cheap on a per-consumer basis, but cannot customize information
Samples by mail	Good information provider for experience products (e.g. coffee, shampoo)	No information is provided if the sample is not used, and an opportunity cost is incurred if tried instead of pursuing other activities	Depends on the nature of the product – most useful when market segments are difficult to identify
Word of mouth	Beneficial information at negligible cost, but what incentive to users?	Negligible	Negligible – reliability of information is reduced by incentives

CASE STUDY 12　BUILDING A RELATIONSHIP BUSINESS

Established in 1993 in Westwood, Massachusetts, Streamline Inc. has gone a step further than the growing number of online grocers who offer Internet-based ordering and home delivery. In order to improve quality of life by alleviating some of the most mundane hassles facing overworked and stressed people, customers in the Boston, Chicago, and Washington, DC, areas pay a monthly fee for the use of a refrigerator, a freezer, and storage shelves. A ring bar-code reader, worn on the finger and linked to a wrist-worn computer radio-frequency data communication unit, is used to record what each customer keeps in these, in their medicine cupboard, and in their kitchen cupboards. A personal shopping list is then posted to the Streamline website. This allows editing by the customer. Over a period of weeks, the list is refined, allowing ordering, via the web or fax, of a selection from over 10,000 grocery items, video rental, dry cleaning, parcel delivery, shoe repairs, picture processing, ready-made meals, and bottle and can recycling. Typical orders are placed forty-seven weeks a year for seventy-five or so items totalling $110 and paid for by credit card or electronic funds transfer. Thus the annual value in the relationship is around $5,000.

Rather than being based on leading-edge technology, the Streamline offer is a home-based relationship that attends to necessity, frequency, and reliability. The corporation has carefully selected who they want to trade with. 'It's easy to get customers. It's harder to get the right customers', argues Gina Wilcox, Director of Strategic Relations. In choosing to do business with young and middle-aged couples with high incomes and at least one child, 'we collaborate with families that want to run better', explains Vice President of Marketing and Merchandising, Frank Britt. Consumers are coming to depend on the corporation to help them make their lives simpler and better, thereby freeing up time to do the things that really matter. For example, almost 50 per cent of customers use the 'Don't Run Out' service that has Streamline staff regularly replenish the items that the family identifies as 'must-have'. This redefines loyalty and marketing, suggests Gina Wilcox. They are pioneering new supply chain strategies with their customers and their suppliers to provide 'lifestyle simplification'. The relationship is very tangible and interactive. Apart from the weekly orders, Streamline representatives have permission to enter the customer's garage even when they are not at home. How many businesses have that level of trust? The website has 'smiley faces' that allow customers to rate the service at every interaction, and 'Streamline Screamline' provides telephone access for feedback and venting of any frustrations.

The Streamline business model follows the notion of a 'products for customers' strategy as explained by Don Peppers. There is fast learning during the installation phase, then a strong understanding of the customer's purchasing patterns arises and needs can be very effectively anticipated. Using sophisticated databases and telecommunications, the customer response centre tracks orders and maintains a customer profile. There are immediate benefits to everyone. Only competitors, who find it hard to attract customers away from the service, are disadvantaged. A number of partnerships are being built to provide the kind of products and services that customers watt. UPS collect and deliver parcels, while Kodak process pictures in a variety of formats. Marketing and advertising partnerships are being developed with leading packaged goods companies (i.e. fast-moving consumer goods or FMCG) to provide revenue from fees, merchandising, and other direct-marketing activities. Fresh foods, such a fish, are supplied just-in-time direct to the consumer.

Founder Tim DeMello is clear that 'We are not in the grocery business. We are in the lifestyle-solutions business. We are not a product business. We are not a service business. We are a relationship business'. The asset is the consumer relationship. What prompted the launch of the business was the 'commoditization' of time and the introduction of technology that enables people to interact with service providers. Streamline becomes a consolidator and gatekeeper to its customers. Bills, delivery, and problem-solving are easily accessed together, while the corporation recognizes each customer's needs, learns from them, and responds accordingly.

Streamline Inc. plan to roll out their service to twenty US metropolitan areas by 2004. The business publicly issued shares in June 1999. More than 75 per cent of orders are received over the web. By August 1998, the company was ringing its office bell to welcome another new family every hour or so. The annual customer retention rate is about 90 per cent. DeMello claims that in the categories of consumer spending served his corporation get around 85 per cent of the money that their customers spend each year. The referral rate is also very high.

CASE STUDY 12A   NATIONAL GEOGRAPHIC'S SUBSCRIBERS HAVE ALWAYS BEEN MEMBERS[a]

We all recognize instantly the distinctive *National Geographic Magazine*. But did you know that it was first produced as a benefit for the members of the learned society founded at the Cosmos Club (across the street from the White House) in Washington in 1888 by thirty-three men from diverse backgrounds to increase and diffuse geographical knowledge. The first issue of the National Geographic Society's magazine was provided to 265 member subscribers as a journal. Today, some 9 million people receive the magazine in 17 languages. Furthermore, 60 million members in 62 countries and 14 languages receive the National Geographic TV channels via BSkyB, NBC, and Fox. Some 147 book titles are published in 24 languages, and a thriving video, CD-ROM, and DVD business operates internationally with several production and distribution partners. *The Complete National Geographic*: 109 Years of *National Geographic Magazine* on CD-ROM (retailing at $130) brings 180,00 photographs and 9,300 articles together in a searchable format that could never have been imagined by those early members of the Society. There are two websites and a gateway through CompuServe. Online delivery provides members with not only super-fast distribution, but further added-value from special editorial-content.

To bring the corporation up to contemporary performance, membership is being re-emphasized over subscriptions. The relationship-marketing programme has been developed to manage expectations, in terms of fulfilling member needs and keeping promises. New products are being developed to diversify the business into additional markets. This has been managed through partnerships based on licences, affinities, and some joint ventures.

National Geographic is sold to new members through direct-marketing activities of direct mail, door-to-door, direct-response TV and radio, and affinity programmes. Some press and TV advertising (particularly on the NG channel via cable and satellite) and sales promotion supports this effort. Customers are retained through emphasis on efficient and friendly service, a number of added-value benefits, and a recently enhanced renewal management strategy.

Partnering with other providers enables National Geographic to capitalize on local market expertise and to build huge databases that provide the information that enhances knowledge about interests and values. For example, in 1998 WebRep LLC forged an advertising and sales partnership with the Society.

Today, the Society is concerned over the alarming lack of geographical knowledge among young people and the pressing need to protect natural resources. New vehicles are under development for broadening their reach and enhancing their ability to bring the world to millions of members. At the same time, the magazine faces a continuously declining circulation, and must increase sales and reduce operating and production overheads if it is to avoid extinction.

The National Geographic Society is the largest non-profit scientific and educational institution with around 1,400 employees and income of £323m in 1998. To date, over 7,000 expeditions have been funded. The for-profit subsidiary, National Geographic Ventures, is developing the TV, Internet, map-making, and retail businesses, owning 25 per cent of the National Geographic Channel.

Relationship marketing requires that manages provide suitable different ways of treating consumers who are to be recruited as customers, and those customers who are members of the network. There must be both traditional and interactive marketing – recruitment marketing plus retention marketing. The crucial way of seeing this is as the initiation of a relationship, then the nurturing of the relationship. Increasingly, other types of business system are being turned into relationship-management networks.

(See www.nationalgeographic.com and www.ngstore.com)

Note: [a] The assistance of Jenny Mosley, Vice-President of Marketing, National Geographic Society, is gratefully acknowledged.

WHAT DO YOU THINK?

1 How might database (or data-driven) marketing support a relationship-marketing strategy?

2 How do affinity cards add value for the co-branders and for customers who use them?

3 Is there any need (and justification) now for mass communications?

4 How does the marketing communication system contribute to total customer satisfaction?

5 Relationship marketing requires a continuing conversation between provider and consumer/buyer. How can/do customers benefit from this?

6 Try to identify some examples of providers rewarding people for providing information to them that is subsequently transformed into satisfying products (Dell Computers is but one example!).

7 Are 'loyalty' and 'affinity' synonymous with close continuing relationship?

8   How could loyalty programmes undermine brands?

9   Marketing communication has both planned and unplanned (word-of-mouth) elements. How can favourable WOM be planned for in a Relationship Marketing programme?

10   As the newly appointed Marketing Communication Manager at National Geographic, what will be your priority for further developments?

FURTHER READING

Barabba, V. P. and Zaltman, G. (1991) *Hearing the Voice of the Market*, Cambridge, MA: Harvard Business School Press.

Duncan, T. and Moriarty, S. E. (1998) 'A communication-based marketing model for managing relationships', *Journal of Marketing* 63: 1–13.

Gordon, I. (1998) *Relationship Marketing: New Strategies, Techniques and Technologies to Win the Customers You Want and Keep Them Forever*, Toronto: John Wiley & Sons Canada.

Grönroos, C. (1990) *Service Management and Marketing: Managing the Moments of Truth in Service Competition*, Lexington, MA: Lexington Books.

Grönroos, C. (1996) 'Relationship marketing: strategic and tactical implications', *Management Decision* 34 (3): 5–14.

Leenders, M. R. and Blenkhorn, D. L. (1988) *Reverse Marketing: The New Buyer–Supplier Relationship*, London: Collier Macmillan.

Palmer, A. (2000) *Principles of Marketing*, Oxford: Oxford University Press.

Peppers, D. and Rogers, M. (1993) *The One-to-One Future: Building Business Relationships One Customer at a Time*, New York: Doubleday.

Peppers, D. and Rogers, M. (1997) *Enterprise One-to-One: Tools for Building Unbreakable Customer Relationships in the Interactive Age*, London: Piatkus Books.

Prus, R. (1989) *Making Sales and Pursuing Customers*, London: Sage Publications.

Sheth, J. N., Mittal, B. and Newman, B. I. (1999) *Customer Behavior: Consumer Behavior and Beyond*, Fort Worth, TX: The Dryden Press.

Tynan, C. (1997) 'A Review of the Marriage Analogy in Relationship Marketing', *Journal of Marketing Management*, 13 (7): 695–704.

Varey, R. J. (forthcoming) *Relationship Marketing: Dialogue and Networks in the E-commerce Era*, Chichester: John Wiley & Sons.

chapter thirteen

INTEGRATED MARKETING COMMUNICATION

LEARNING POINTS

Careful study of this chapter will help you to:

- appreciate the development of the integrated marketing communication (IMC) concept and managerial approach to marketing communication

- consider the added value for provider and consumer/buyer of an IMC strategy

- identify obstacles to practical IMC

The din of modern advertising and the clamour of the mass media.

Anon

Consumers see the one brand but often hear it speaking different tongues, let alone in a variety of tones of voice.

C. Robertson, advertising executive

INTRODUCTION

For the majority of consumers, their attention is saturated with information, signs (images) and messages – these are both confused and impotent in their profusion and inconsistency. In contemporary society, mass media advertising rarely works well on its own.

Relationship marketing is more communication intensive than traditional transaction-based marketing. Integrated marketing communication is a shift towards more personalized, customer-oriented, technology-supported marketing systems. This is managed by a brand-level, cross-functional team to integrate marketing and marketing communication activities. Brand management requires integration of systems of communication, especially when, as we saw in chapter twelve, a relationship-marketing strategy requires that customers are treated differently to prospective customers.

Internal and external communicative activities/actions communicate whether or not they are done with the intention of communicating. Thus, planning for the comprehensive use of a range of activities that provide communication opportunities and coherent messages, recognizes that consumers and buyers do not see discrete advertising, public relations, and sales promotion.

This theme of integration will be carried through our discussion of planning and evaluation in this book. The adoption of a true integrated marketing strategy requires, in many cases, a redesign of the business system to ensure that the making of promises and efforts to keep promises are coordinated.

WHAT DOES INTEGRATION MEAN?

The value provider operates within a network of stakeholder relationships in which these relationships are influenced by meanings for the communication participants that are produced in their interactions. There is interaction among stakeholders and the marketing manager can never control this for their own purposes, but merely participate.

There are numerous persons and groups who have something to tell or ask. For example, advertising may promise quality, a sales promotion may promise bargains, and product publicity may discuss product safety. Stakeholders who apprehend these differing topics of conversation may be confused or uncertain. This can lead to an erosion of confidence that may seriously affect the ability of the provider to convert exchanges into desired inputs (such as profit, for example). Consistency may be absent, leading to inappropriate outcomes for marketing communication efforts, and conflict with what is being told and asked by other people in the corporation, customers, news media, and competing providers. Everything the people of the proving corporation do (and sometimes do not do) can generate meanings for stakeholders. These can strengthen or weaken the relationships upon which the business enterprise is founded.

Comprehensive coherent communication

Duncan and Moriarty (1998) identify three aspects of management that should be attended to with the concept of integration. Corporate focus should be on relationships with stakeholders rather than on transactions with customers. Conflicting messages can be avoided, and resources redeployed to meet particular business and communication objectives as corporate and stakeholder priorities change. Processes that facilitate purposeful dialogue must be established and managed. The dialogue should be purposeful for both provider and stakeholder. A further process should ensure consistency in brand message design. Another process is needed to remind all stakeholders what the corporation stands for. Finally, a process of priority-driven planning is needed to operate those marketing communication efforts that capitalize on critical strengths and opportunities, while addressing significant weaknesses and threats. An appropriate infrastructure is required that is based on integration competence, partnering with communication specialists, and cross-functional management. We can appreciate now, perhaps, how important internal marketing (IM) is to enabling IMC, and how effectiveness in this can make the provider competent in relationship marketing.

Table 13.1 summarizes some of the points at which the provider interacts with stakeholders, and at which meanings (intended or unintended will arise for either participant).

IMC is, then, the strategic analysis, selection, execution, evaluation, and control of all communicative actions that can effectively and efficiently enable and facilitate productive exchanges in the provider's stakeholder relationship network.

Smith *et al.* (1997) offer a seven-level examination of IMC management which can be used as a basis for assessing the extent to which stakeholder relationships are impacted through communicative marketing actions (Table 13.2).

STARTING WITH THE CUSTOMER

Schultz *et al.* (1993) proposed that any model of marketing communication should analyse what happens with the customer rather than starting with the marketer. This receiver perspective is much more in line with the marketing concept than is the traditional marketer perspective. Thus a model of IMC is built around the customer at the focal point (Figure 13.1).

This approach ensures that the marketing communication mix is developed on the basis of (actual, 'natural') customer activity in relation to the brand and (necessary) marketer activity in relation to the brand.

Table 13.1 **The total communication system from the marketing perspective**

Point of interaction between provider and consumer/buyer or other stakeholder	*What is it that can communicate?*
Customer service	Telephonist and receptionist, reception area, brochures, security clearance, sales office and telephone line
Salesforce	Brochures, appointments, manuals
Retail merchandising	Display and shelf-facings, point-of-sale materials
Dealer/distributor	Brochures, manuals, training
Production	Quality assurance, training, quality management
Brand management	Standard-setting, after-sales service
After-sales service	Manuals, training, brochures, online information sources, helpline
Internal communication	Newsletters, briefings, team-working, grapevine
Corporate identity	Design and policy, logo, signage, livery, uniforms, letterheads, business cards, gifts, annual report, packaging, office location and ambience
Advertising	Messages, information content, style, vehicle
Distribution	Location of outlets, vehicle condition, driver courtesy and safety, packaging
Pricing	Value-for-money relative to competitors – quality and status
Products	Quality consistent with price and advertising messages
People	Attitude, behaviour, orientation, and preparedness of sales, technical, delivery and reception staff
Processes	Technology and methods of product and co-production, convenience, reliability, safety
Market research	Hearing what customers, consumers, and buyers want and like/dislike
Complaints, comments, and requests	Access to responsible, responsive people
Public relations	Sponsorship, events, information sources, public profile of people and products, corporate performance

Source: Based on Smith *et al.*, 1997

Table 13.2 **Is your marketing communication system integrated?**

Level of integration	Concern of the manager
Objectives	Are the communication objectives appropriate for the marketing and corporate business objectives?
Functions	Do the marketing communication activities fit with production, staffing, training, etc.
Marketing	Are price, quality, specification, and distribution decisions consistent with the communication objectives?
Communication	Are all communicators effectively guiding stakeholders to productive exchanges?
Design	Are design and creative execution consistent with the chosen product positioning?
Organization	Are all agencies working together to a single plan with regular progress checks?
Investment	Is the budget being used wisely for long-term investment impact and efficiency?

Source: Adapted from Smith *et al.*, 1997

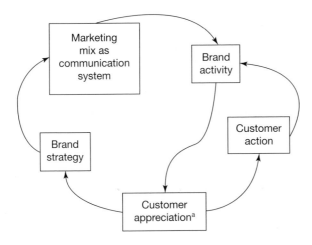

Figure 13.1 **The brand as integrator**

Source: Based on Smith *et al.*, 1997

Note: [a] Denotes the appreciative system that perceives (aspects of the environment), interprets (makes meaning), judges (values against a standard), and then decides how to act

WHY HAS IMC BECOME SO PROMINENT IN RECENT YEARS?

The significance of integration in managing communication for marketing purposes has been heightened in recent years by a number of changes. We will briefly consider these here, bearing in mind that they will affect corporations differently because their circumstances will be different, and that they are not all discrete and independent .

Changes in our society

As consumers become less deferential and more proactive and discerning, as well as more aware of alternative offerings and the 'real' cost of products, marketing systems have to be both responsive and responsible. There is a continuing move away from blanket mass media advertising to more segmented and targeted effort, ultimately leading to one-to-one marketing enabled by direct addressing through electronic media. Marketing has become more professional as more managers formalize their knowledge. Integration is becoming more recognized for its benefits and there is growing evidence that systems and programmes organized in this fashion are sufficiently beneficial to warrant the investment required. Consumers and buyers are now seen as active users of communication media rather than passive subjects. More of us are concerned with the impact of the products we consume on the natural environment.

Changes in our economy

Rising costs of broadcast media and increased pressure on budgets require both cost savings and increased performance. Economies of scale in media use remains a constraint (some would argue a positive force for improvement) on marketing communication systems. Consumers and buyers no longer see a necessary trade-off between quality and price – reliable, high-performance products can be obtained at low cost. Low price and high quality are no longer differentiators on their own.

Changes in the available technology

The media for communication are proliferating and diversifying and are usually not replacing but supplementing established media. Networks are increasingly at least international, if not global in their reach (e.g. satellite TV). The World WideWeb and Internet are huge webs of connected personal computers. Software applications are themselves being integrated to provide online data capture, data warehousing, and data mining, all of which help to manage knowledge as the underpinning of a relationship-management strategy.

THE BENEFITS OF IMC

We can connect the concepts of internal marketing, integrated marketing communication, and relationship marketing, so as not to imagine them as separate or alternative managerial strategies for customer relationship management (see Figure 13.2). As Levitt put it in 1962, management of communication with stakeholders should aim to create one compelling, self-reinforcing, simple and persuasive story – a total communication system with a coherent output. However, we should beware – Levitt's frame of reference was almost certainly Schramm's sender–receiver model of communication. Of course, we need to reinterpret the sentiment of his thinking – communication is meaning-making interaction, so the story is, in a sense, negotiated.

If we do this, what might be the benefits to provider and consumer/buyer?

For the provider, integration of marketing communication activities can avoid confusion and disaffection in the minds of consumers and buyers, offering a comfortable identity to customers and staff. Agencies who support the marketing communication process can take a more holistic and thus strategic stance to their client's business, concentrating on strategic development rather than separate agendas.

Unintegrated communicative actions can appear disjointed to stakeholders, resulting in confusion, frustration, and anxiety.

Figure 13.2 **The three concepts connected**

OBSTACLES TO ADOPTION OF IMC

Of course, it would be naïve to expect that IMC is universally understood, accepted, and adopted, or even that where adoption has been attempted, there is no resistance to the changes in processes, infrastructure, priorities, and attitudes required. We briefly highlight some obstacles that will be faced by the marketing communication manager. Again, we should not imagine that these obstacles are not interrelated and mutually influencing.

Attitude

We often experience real resistance to change, especially when the idea for innovation does not 'belong' to those people who are asked to participate and cooperate. There is a further political obstacle, 'tribal warfare', in that specialist groups may resist the change if they believe that it will weaken their struggle for ascendancy of power in the corporation ('turf wars').

Autocratic management style, premised on the need to control, can inhibit integration and resulting flexibility. If marketing is seen as persuasive (i.e. selling products to customers), then only a traditional marketing programme will be pursued and integration will seem unnecessary. If, however, a relationship-marketing system is managed, integration of efforts in a coordinated traditional **and** interactive marketing system will seem necessary. This will be enabled within an internal-marketing framework. There is also considerable misunderstanding and lack of clarity about the concept of integration. Some managers, for example, see it as no more than 'one-stop' shopping among agencies or as coordinated creative executions.

Organization

Functional division of responsibilities and tasks can block systemic changes, and established planning processes can work against integration by maintaining the status quo (fragmentation can favour some interests, but suboptimize the system as a whole). Often, functional specialists are appointed and rewarded on the basis of technical skills needed to execute programmes rather than the conceptual skills needed to plan them. Agencies and service providers, and even trade associations, remain largely fragmented around specialisms, arguing that only particular tools can achieve impacts and effects.

Resources

Ownership of resources is a way of demonstrating power and status. Also, integration requires the reinvention of the corporation as a responsive, responsible value-creating system. This requires a major investment in time and effort for review, analysis, thinking, decision-making, and revision of processes, infrastructure, and possibly strategic focus and values. Budgeting is often decided on a historic basis – what was spent last year – rather than on a careful assessment of what is required to accomplish specific objectives. Budgets are allocated separately to each sub-function, often on a competitive 'slice-of-the-pie' basis.

If communication systems and programmes have to be integrated, it is plain to see that marketing has to be an integrated facet of any business.

CASE STUDY 13   LAUNCHING THE TOYOTA YARIS[a]

Toyota is a car manufacturer with an impressive track record for producing exceptionally high-quality products. However, few people realize that it is also the world's third-largest car manufacturer. As a global player, its statistics are staggering:

- in 1999 Toyota built over 5.4 million vehicles – that's one new car produced every six seconds of every day
- Toyotas are sold in more than 160 countries around the world

- the Corolla is the world's best-selling car with more than 23 million sold around the globe since the model was launched in the mid-1960s
- every year Toyota spend over £1.5 billion on research and development, the most of any of the major car manufacturers.

By the mid-1990s, Toyota was the market leader in Japan and a major player in the North American market. The next area targeted for expansion was Europe, where the company had had a historical market share of approximately 3 per cent, considerably behind the 45 per cent share enjoyed in Japan. In part, this performance resulted from the historical voluntary quota arrangements Toyota operated under, restricting the number of vehicles that would be imported into the European market. With the impending removal of quotas in January 2000, the foundation was set for real expansion in this market. The strategy for Europe focused around two key points:

1 To develop class-leading cars tailored to European tastes. This was a recognition that European customers had separate needs from Japanese or American buyers.
2 To develop an emotional and aspirational brand. Market research identified that reliability, Toyota's historical strength, was not in itself enough to motivate consumers to buy Toyota cars. Instead, purchasers were increasingly relying on brands as a statement of themselves in all their buying behaviour. As such, Toyota needed to make its brand values relevant to the target customers in the segments the different models sold in.

The model that marked the implementation of this strategy in Europe was the Yaris, a supermini launched in the UK in April 1999, replacing the Starlet. Having a competitive model in this volume-selling sector was a significant part of Toyota's strategy for European growth. Therefore, for this model, Toyota totally reassessed its launch activity to reflect its new strategic direction. This case study considers the European level of this strategy before focusing on the specific communications activity in the UK.

The product

From the outset, the Yaris was targeted specifically at the European market, the first Toyota to have been conceived this way:

- the Yaris was designed by a European team led by the Greek designer Sotiris Kovos based in the European design centre
- the design concepts were continually tested with clinics of European customers to get their reactions and input to the process
- from 2001, the car will be primarily produced at the new factory at Valenciennes, near Paris

As well as a European-specific styling and design process, the Yaris was designed to be class leading in all the major functional areas:

- The Yaris is powered by brand new 1.0 and 1.3 litre VVT-i (variable valve timing intelligent) engines whose technology means that they produce more power than other engines of the same size, but also deliver better fuel economy and lower emissions.

- New construction methods meant that lightweight steel could be used without compromising safety, contributing to the outstanding fuel economy and good driving performance.
- In the sector, the Yaris is the smallest car but has the largest interior space.
- The Yaris also has many innovative features including a 3-D centrally mounted speedometer display and a sliding rear seat. The 3-D display is a design and safety feature, reducing the amount of time necessary to look at the read-out and then refocus on the road again. The rear seat slides backwards and forwards to maximize rear legroom or boot space as required.

The brand: the Yaris and Toyota

This section will cover the steps in delivering the Yaris message to the market. These steps involved:

- identifying the target market – who are Yaris buyers?
- internal communications – coordinating the message within Toyota
- external communications:
  - the Yaris communications task
  - pre-launch activity
  - launch activity

The target market

Concurrent to the research and design process to ensure the product was right, Toyota re-examined its marketing approach to the small-car sector. The previous car, the Starlet, had been a strong product from the traditional reliability aspect, but had failed to grip the imagination of customers. It was essential that the Yaris was seen in a different light and fulfilled the objective of starting to move the Toyota brand towards a more emotional and aspirational ideal.

The key part of taking the car to the market was to understand the lifestyle of the Yaris target audience. Figure 13.3 shows the general segmentation within the small-car sector.

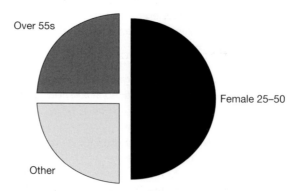

Figure 13.3 **Demographic segmentation of the small-car market**
Source: Based on NCO, 1997

The two key segments of females 25–50 and the over 55s were identified as the main areas of opportunity and strategies were developed for them. Studies showed that Toyota had a strong following in the over 55 market, driven by the traditional strengths of reliability and quality, while Toyota was considerably weaker in the female 25–50 segment. Therefore launch communications were targeted at these two groups but with the emphasis on the second sector as this represented the major opportunity but was where the Toyota brand needed the most work.

All activities below were based on information gained through extensive secondary- and primary-market research on these groups.

Internal communications: coordinating the message

Aside from designing the product, the actual planning process for the launch of the Yaris in the UK took fourteen months to organize, with over nine different departments from Toyota's UK operation involved. In these circumstances, it was vital that one consistent message was delivered to the market from every potential point of contact. Therefore internal coordination of the message was essential between these internal departments, the Toyota dealer network, and the Toyota field team who managed the dealers.

Interdepartmental coordination was achieved via a launch committee which met every two weeks and whose meetings were always attended by the major departments. Through regular dialogue, the launch committee ensured that all activities across functions were coordinated, deadlines were met, and relevant issues were resolved as they arose.

The communications message for the customer was shared with the launch committee at an early stage and all subsequent communications from advertising to training for dealerships, to finance communications, to press releases followed and reinforced the basic messages.

Ten weeks before launch the entire launch programme was presented to the Toyota field team to ensure they understood the strategy. This was critical as the field team would be instrumental in ensuring dealers also delivered the same Yaris message. Two separate meetings were subsequently held with dealers two months and one month before the national launch to cascade the information to them so they could plan local launches effectively.

Therefore with a consistent foundation, the external communications strategy could be devised and specific activities developed.

External communications: the communications message

The launch of the new Yaris was the most significant communications event for Toyota in 1999. Over £10 million was spent on advertising alone, with further investment in direct marketing, promotions, the Internet, and literature. The investment not only launched the new model in a very impactful integrated campaign, but, as outlined, was also an important step in the ongoing development of the Toyota brand.

1 **The Yaris communications task**: research showed that the decision to buy a small car is often influenced by emotional factors, more than in any other sector of the market. The decisions are made based not only on specification and price, but image, style, personality, character, and individuality.

This appeal to the heart rather than the head can be seen in many of the successful advertising campaigns in this sector, so the key task was to ensure that rational product information was presented in a style that was relevant to the target audiences and that would serve as a foundation to deliver focused messages. Therefore the product strengths of the Yaris were summarized into six key attributes embracing the Yaris offering. These formed the tone for communications with the objective that this was the overall impression customers should have of the Yaris. These were:

- extraordinary
- stylish
- accessible premium brand
- intelligent
- substantial
- a car with character

These were the bedrock of all communications activity.

With one of the main target groups being not overly familiar with Toyota, delivery of this message relied on ensuring that the Yaris was positioned in the right place and in the right manner over a long period of time. This process started in November 1999 following the Birmingham Motorshow and continued up to and through the launch date.

The activity was split into pre-launch and launch – pre-launch to develop awareness among a targeted group and start word-of-mouth activity, and launch to communicate to the general audience.

2 **Pre-launch**: This was driven by direct mail and the Internet and started with the 1998 Birmingham Motorshow. Activity followed two streams, as shown in Figures 13.4.

3 **Launch communications**: Communications were designed to work in three phases, as represented by Figure 13.5.

Phase one: introducing the Yaris

The objectives were to ensure people got the pronunciation right, while alerting them to the fact that Toyota had a new small car.

In the two days before the launch of the Yaris, a 10-second teaser advert ran on ITV and Channel 4 which purely communicated the launch of 'the new Toyota Yaris'.

To maximize the effectiveness the top-ten programmes watched by the target audience on those two evenings were chosen to carry the advertising, ensuring the message reached the right people.

At the same time, the Yaris was incorporated into the main Toyota website.

Phase two: full-scale TV launch – 8 April 1999

The main TV launch for the Yaris started on 8 April 1999. This was a high-visibility campaign starting with a 40-second commercial for the first four weeks and then using a 30-second version for the following four weeks.

This heavyweight launch targeted ABC1 adults, with 86 per cent having the opportunity to see the campaign eight times during these two months.

The following three months used an 'event TV' strategy. This was a lower-weight campaign of selected high-profile programmes specifically watched by the target markets. By choosing high-profile programmes as opposed to a high volume of programmes, Toyota was able to

Prospects generated from the 1998 Motorshow were segmented into two groups depending on the information that was captured

All prospects who had an intended replacement date within twelve months or less were placed on the regular-contact scheme, those who had a date of greater than twelve months were given a reduced-fulfilment pack and were contacted separately nearer their replacement date

The contact strategy for the immediate prospects was based on a number of books that were building blocks to providing information on the development of the Yaris:

- Book of Character/Book of Facts: mailed November 1998. An introduction to the Yaris
- Book of Space: mailed December 1998. This covered interior space and storage
- Book of Beauty: mailed January–February 1999, covering styling and design features
- Book of Reason: mailed February–March 1999, covering safety, fuel economy

90,000 conquest prospects were mailed in the first two weeks of February 1999

By engaging prospects at this point in time, Toyota aimed to start a relationship, and provide relevant information at the right time

The mailing was aimed at the two distinct target groups:

1 Women aged 25–50
2 Men and women aged 55+

Internet
An Internet microsite was established where the car could be viewed. The use of a microsite ahead of launch gave visitors a sense that this was a special preview of the Yaris

A final launch mailing was sent to all respondees from these two streams to drop on the launch date of 8 April 1999 and was designed to create a link with the above-the-line launch campaign. This provided the final pieces of information to the prospects and generated showroom activity for each dealership.

Following this mailing, respondees from the pre-launch communications who had indicated a particular replacement date were sent Yaris information packs ahead of that date

Figure 13.4 **The two streams of pre-launch activity of the Yaris launch**

increase the impact and memorability of the campaign and still ensure that 60 per cent of the audience had an average of five opportunities to see the ad.

Figure 13.6 summarizes how the TV medium was used.

Phase One: First Three Weeks – Introduce the Yaris

The initial launch phase for the Yaris mainly used the traditional media of TV and press in a large-scale launch to build familiarity with the new Yaris name, establish its segment credentials and raise awareness of the new Toyota small car

Phase Two: The Next Five Weeks – Nurture the relationship

After the initial-awareness phase, the task was to build the involvement of the target audience with Toyota and the Yaris by further establishing the character of the car and providing more in-depth communication

Phase Three: The Next Six Months – Develop consideration

Six months is the average time it takes for a new car to establish its position in the market. After the large-scale activity at launch, the Yaris was kept front of mind during this vital period with a continuous presence in high-profile, high-quality media. Specific TV programmes and specific press titles were chosen to reach the two target audiences. This activity was supplemented with cinema advertising and promotions to create a varied and integrated campaign

Figure 13.5 **The three phases of the launch communications**

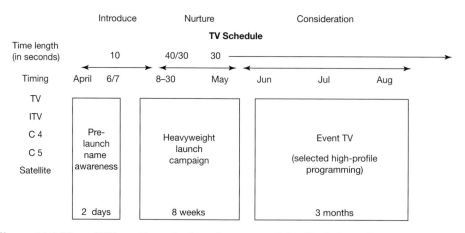

Figure 13.6 **Use of TV medium during phase two of the Yaris launch**

Phase three: develop consideration

Activity here covered several media channels.

Cinema advertising: extending the targeting

Cinema advertising was a first for Toyota, but the recent increase in popularity of cinema-going, especially among the younger audience, made it an excellent opportunity for the Yaris.

Cinema was used during June, July, and August 1999, after the main burst of TV activity, with advertisements appearing in films most relevant to the target audience, such as *Notting Hill*.

At the same time, two promotions ran with UCI and Warner Brothers cinema chains which placed cars and point of sale in the foyers of selected cinemas and featured competitions for the audience to win holidays.

Building the relationship with the press

Press and magazine advertising were an essential part of the Yaris communications strategy, not only in the initial launch phase to help build awareness and familiarity, but also in the relationship-building process. The press advertising provided a focused and long-term presence and the use of upmarket, glossy women's press and style magazines contributed to the stylish, premium-brand positioning of the model.

The main launch campaign in the press started with weekend review sections and magazines and continued with a steady presence from April to October. It used a mixture of double and single pages all in colour; Table 13.3 lists the type of publications used:

Table 13.3 **Press and magazine advertising coverage for the Yaris communications strategy**

Review sections	Magazines
Guardian Weekend	Marie-Claire
Independent on Saturday Magazine	Cosmopolitan
Mail on Sunday – You	New Woman
Times Magazine	She
Sunday Times – Style	Red
Telegraph Magazine	Ideal Homes
Daily Mail Weekend	Elle Decoration
Observer Life	Living, etc.
	Hello!

Building the relationship with promotions

The main strategy to promote the Yaris outside the advertising capitalized on the existing relationships customers have with other brands they buy to gain endorsement of the Yaris and therefore acceptance by the core target market.

The strategy operated on three levels:

1 Toyota activity: tie-ups with partners on a national basis.
2 Toyota/Toyota dealer-combined activity: tie-ups where Toyota arranged the promotion, but there were elements where local dealer participation was possible.
3 Dealer activity: individual tie-ups with relevant partners in dealers' local areas.

Toyota activity covered:

*   Ideal Home Exhibition, Earls Court from 17 March to 11 April 1999. The show attracted over 525,000 visitors with a profile that matched that of Yaris's core market. Toyota sponsored the main refreshment area, Café Yaris, had vehicles on display in the Café and ran a competition giving the opportunity to win a trip to see the midnight sun in Greenland.
*   BBC Fashion Week Live, Wembley Arena 22–25 April 1999. Yaris sponsored the designer catwalk at the show and a separate vehicle display was constructed.
*   Shopping centre roadshows. There were three shopping centre roadshows during 1999, which toured the major shopping centres around the UK. The tour was heavily branded Toyota and the Yaris was again displayed.
*   Magazine promotions. Five magazines ran promotions that featured Yaris from June to September 1999. In line with the overall strategy, the titles chosen were aimed at the target audience and also reflected the six core values of the Yaris message. Titles included *She*, *Red*, *Living*, etc.

Joint Toyota and dealer activity included the cinema promotions above, where the display cars were supplied by the local dealer, who also took the opportunity in supervising the displays to introduce themselves to the customers. In addition, a tie-up with Principals involved a dedicated insert into the Principals statement mailing together with a £10 Principals discount voucher which the customer had to get stamped by visiting their local Toyota dealer.

Dealer activity included individual shopping centre displays, and displays at local supermarkets and garden centres. Dealers were provided with their own promotional kits to facilitate this – see Figure 13.7.

In addition to this activity, dealers were supplied with point-of-sale displays and literature which also supported the main messages.

This covered the initial launch of the Yaris. Additional activity was also planned to continue throughout 2000 and 2001 to ensure the message was communicated.

Results

The Yaris launch was the most successful launch of a new Toyota up until that date.

*   Toyota Yaris was named European Car of the Year for 2000, the first time for Toyota and the second time that any non-European manufacturer had won the award.

	Nov	Dec	Jan	Feb	Mar	Apr	May	Jun	Jul	Aug	Sep
Internet	Microsite					Integration into main site					
Direct mail		Motorshow follow-up									
		Character		Space	Beauty	Reason					
				Awareness Mailer		Launch Mailer					
Advertising						TV					
						Press and magazines					
Promotions					Ideal Home						
						BBC Fashion Week Live					
						Shopping Centre Roadshow		Shopping Centre Roadshow		Shopping Centre Roadshow	
							UCI	Warner Village		Principals	
						Dealer Activity					

Figure 13.7 **Schedule of promotional activities**

- The Yaris campaign was declared runner-up in the Launch Strategy of the Year category at the 1999 *Media Week* awards.
- Post-campaign research showed that:
  - exposure to the advertising considerably increased people's strength of relationship with the Toyota brand;
  - consideration of Toyota among both target audiences doubled in 1999 compared with 1998;

- when comparing 1998 with 1999, Toyota showed the largest increase in conversion of showroom visitors into sales of any manufacturer.
- Sales of the Yaris achieved 108 per cent of target in 1999 in the most competitive segment in the car market.
- In just eight months of sales activity, the Yaris was the eleventh bestselling car in the supermini sector, making significant inroads against the established brands in this market.

Note: [a] A special thank you is extended to Eifion Jones for writing this case study. Eifion was Advertising Manager, Toyota, at the time of writing

WHAT DO YOU THINK?

1 Explain how IMC provides the managerial bridge between internal marketing and relationship marketing.
2 How do you, as a consumer, actually benefit from the management of an IMC system of a provider from whom you regularly purchase a product?
3 There is an excellent case study on the IMC programme of the Fruit of the Loom corporation on the WWW. Find it by using the Google search engine, review the plan and discuss it with your class.
4 If you were the Marketing Communication Manager at Toyota, what would you prioritize for enhancement to their communication system?
5 At the regular Toyota launch-planning meetings, what topics and issues would be discussed?
6 Some corporations are operating a form of IMC that is little more than consolidation for cost reduction. What benefits are they missing?
7 How could a provider incrementally adopt IMC?
8 How does IMC link to corporate strategy and organization design?
9 How might IMC fail, and what counter measures could be taken?
10 What, specifically, would you advise the Toyota marketing team to do next?

FURTHER READING

Duncan, T. and Moriarty, S. E. (1998) 'A communication-based marketing model for managing relationships', *Journal of Marketing*, 62: 1–13.

Kitchen, P. (1993) 'Marketing communications renaissance', *International Journal of Advertising* 12: 367–386.

Linton, I. and Morley, K. (1995) *Integrated Marketing Communications*, Oxford: Butterworth-Heinemann.

Miles, L. (1991) 'Mix and match', *Marketing Business*, October, pp. 32–34.

Moriarty, S. E. (1994) 'PR and IMC: the benefits of integration', *Public Relations Quarterly*, autumn, pp. 38–44.

Schultz, D. E. and Schultz, H. F. (1998) 'Transitioning marketing communication into the twenty-first century', *Journal of Marketing Communications* 4: 9–26.

Schultz, D. E., Tannenbaum, S. I. and Lauterborn, R. F. (1993) *Integrated Marketing Communications: Putting It Together and Making It Work*, Lincolnwood, IL: NTC Business Books.

Schultz, D. E., Tannenbaum, S. I. and Lauterborn, R. F. (1995) *The Marketing Paradigm: Integrated Marketing Communications*, Lincolnwood, IL: NTC Business Books.

Yeshin, T. (1999) *Integrated Marketing Communications: The Holistic Approach*, Oxford: Butterworth-Heinemann.

chapter fourteen

ADVERTISING AS COMMUNICATING

LEARNING POINTS

Careful study of this chapter will help you to:

- appreciate the contemporary use of advertising in its many forms

- critically examine advertising as a corporate, supposedly credible and creative phenomenon that pervades our lives in attempting to link products with satisfactions

- understand how and why the form and use of advertising is changing

Man more often needs to be reminded rather than informed.
(Dr Samuel Johnson)

Advertising is fundamentally persuasion and persuasion happens to be not a science, but an art.
(Bill Bernbach, Doyle Dane Bernbach agency)

Advertising draws a straight line from the manufacturer to the consumer.
('Blue Book' definition, J. Walter Thompson agency, 1909)

You can't have good advertising for a bad product.
(Marcel Bleustein-Blanchet, founder of the Publicis agency, France, 1926)

Advertising: the poetry of euphemism.

(Anthony Trollope)

INTRODUCTION

Advertising is an institutional model of communication that is deeply rooted in daily interests and has continued to contribute to the reproduction of the social conditions and values of a mode of living and a social system.

Advertising is an integral part of 'free-market' economies that enables consumers and buyers to locate and compare brands and to understand distinctions and innovations among proliferating product offerings. Thus, advertising has a vital role in helping to inform purchase decisions. Today, advertising has a social role in connecting persons with products and images of well-being, reaching into our personal concerns about personal identity, interpersonal relationships, happiness, affluence, stereotypes, sex roles, cultural traditions, persuasion, personal autonomy, the role of business in society, and so on. Advertising is not simply a conveyor of information and persuasive messages, it is a massive and pervasive industry, afforded great prominence in our lives, that provides social communication. Today, much of our communication of attitudes, expectations, and sense of identity, is about and through objects (consumer products). In 1999, according to the Advertising Association, advertising spend in the UK topped £15.3 billion – that's £250 for every person living in the UK, and almost 2 per cent of our GDP. This was an increase of 6.4 per cent on the previous year and the eighth consecutive annual increase. Newspaper advertising accounted for 51.1 per cent of the total.

Advertising is the art of making commodities communicate with us (Dichter, 1960). Arguably, much product advertising entices us to 'come and get me', but ignores the other part of the bargain, the obligation to pay (Gabriel and Lang, 1995). The market, and its commercial advertising, is not primarily a 'want-satisfying' mechanism: it is a 'want-creating' mechanism. Blythe (2000) has distinguished advertising that is wanted by consumers because it is useful to them (sought advertising) from advertisers' efforts to attract attention (unsought advertising). He suggests that classified advertising helps people to find the products they want, whereas display advertisements distract in order to attract.

The advent of the Internet is shaking the foundations of the advertising-media industry. The converging telecommunication and computer technologies can definitively tie the information that consumers apprehend to the purchases they make. The rapid growth in Internet use has stimulated competitive advertising by providing a new place, particularly for targeting young people (see Box 14.1). Also, new dotcom businesses are buying advertising to build their presence and customer bases. New technology is changing commercial television as an advertising medium. Cable TV, video-on-demand, and personal video recorders (PVR) are set to become commonplace. The last allows viewers to skip past advertising to their favourite programmes. Personalized virtual television programming will shift viewing from timed schedules to a content-driven basis. This will have a dramatic effect on channels that are funded by advertising (Doward, 2000), leading to linear mass-market advertising schedules. Perhaps soon we will watch only those advertisements that are relevant to our lifestyles.

BOX 14.1   WHEN IS ADVERTISING NOT ADVERTISING?

The newly launched online public catalogue of The British Library carries a link to Amazon.co.uk on the homepage. This carries the words 'Buy books NOW from our sponsor'. According to a spokesperson from The British Library, Amazon have sponsored the site for three years, thus helping to offset the costs of providing the online catalogue. The text does not constitute an advertisement but a special link that allows users who search on one service to search automatically on the other. Another librarian thinks that by carrying an advertisement, the Library's public service remit is subverted.

(*Source: Times Higher Education Supplement*, 16 February 2001: 4)

See also Box 14.3, which deals with advertorials.

ORIGINS OF ADVERTISING

In 1477 an advertisement appeared in an English newsletter (Fang, 1997). As early as 1630 an advertising 'agency' model was operating in France as a public service with the role of providing social assistance to people. As a clearing house, those with needs were brought together in a 'harmonious regime'. This activity was termed 'publicity', and formed the foundation of today's 'public relations' (Mattelart, 1996). In 1655, the word 'advertising' was introduced (Fang, 1997). By 1785 *The Times* was founded, combining news and opinions with commercial presentations. This differed fundamentally from the earlier model, being based on a competitive model with commercial intentions and exchanges predominating. Thus, the 'conflictual advertising' that is so familiar today was born. A year earlier, the *Pennsylvania Packet and Advertiser* was founded in North America. Of the sixteen columns printed, ten were advertisements!

By the 1830s, the press had become a high-circulation commercial enterprise in England, France, and North America. For example, by 1836 the French newspapers *La Presse* and *Le Siècle* relied systematically on advertising for their commercial prosperity. In 1841 the first commercial US advertising agency was established (Fang, 1997). As we saw in chapter one, by the end of the nineteenth century, marketing needs were strongly influencing developments in tools for communication. What was necessary was a means of 'welding together' large-scale repetitive production with mass consumption, work with entertainment (Mattelart, 1996). Formalized advertising, practised as the means of persuasion to the advantage of the advertiser, came to be the answer. In 1897 the General Electric company created a publicity department, while in 1898 New York State felt it was time to pass a law against misleading advertising (Fang, 1997).

WHAT IS ADVERTISING?

Is advertising superfluous distracting puffery, or a vital informer and persuader? Is advertising no more than coercive persuasion, or does it allow argumentation? Is advertising informational or transformational? Is the attendant consumer or buyer a bewildered manipulant, or the rational evaluator in search of solutions to problems of dissatisfaction?

Typically, 'publicity' is cast as unpaid advertising (with added credibility). May it not perhaps be the other way around? Advertising can be thought of as bought publicity.

In the development of advertising, as a marketing tool and as an industry in its own right, Leiss *et al.* (1986) can discern four communicative formats (explained more fully in Figure 14.2 below). The original informational role (i.e. about the product and its utility) gave way to product image, brand name, and packaging that gave special qualities by means of symbolic relationships. Post-war, product image was personalized. In recent years, consumption style has come to the fore. Advertising has become representational.

In UK society, advertising has become part of our everyday experience, and largely aspirational. In Germany, France, and Italy, however, this is not the case. In the UK and USA, advertisements teach consumers their preferences. This is not true elsewhere, where advertising has remained merely informational (Lannon and Cooper, 1983). We discussed the cultural dimension to marketing communication in chapter six.

We should not lose sight of two further facts. Marketers, who advertise, are customers of a growing and powerful media industry who sell advertising for profit. Audiences are gathered as gateways, by media operators, for marketers into markets. Thus, as a member of a gathered audience, we are offered to marketers as product (see Box 14.2). Further, advertising imagery can stir up social discontent that has only social remedies – then products are irrelevant (we will consider the ethical responsibilities of marketing communication managers in chapter seventeen).

ADVERTISING KNOWLEDGE

The process of creating value from intangible assets is termed knowledge management. Of course, knowledge is not the only intangible asset of a market mechanism. This is a formalized approach to the creation, acquisition, combination, deployment, and distribution of knowledge. Today, this 'building' work can be facilitated by intranet and extranet connections.

In advertising practice, the ability to bring together apparently disconnected ideas is what is often referred to as creative input. Research data, problem definitions, and this associative ability combine to create communication solutions to the marketer's problems.

Codified knowledge can be classified and stored in databases for future retrieval. A book is an example of codification of knowledge. Market segmentation and benchmarking data are documented and can be drawn upon by several people in project work. Tacit knowledge is available to a person, and those with whom they interact, in working, but may not be communicable through speech and writing. It is 'out of awareness', but nonetheless in dialogue with others, that the holder of such knowledge can make a significant contribution to design, problem-solving, and other creative tasks. Teamworking is a way of deploying tacit knowledge.

Advertising and design agencies are knowledge brokers. The problem is identified and a match (similarities and differences) is sought with previously solved problems. Solutions are adapted and adopted accordingly. Skills are essential, but marketers need knowledge and experience in combination.

BOX 14.2   THAT'LL GET THE NEIGHBOURS TALKING . . .

A direct mail pack drops through the letterbox one Saturday morning. It has a photograph of a new car and is headed *The Telegraph*. But what could the newspaper have to say about cars?

Intrigued, I open it to find out what it is about. The letter thanks me for recently completing a reader questionnaire. I expressed interest in car financing, and the enclosed brochure details the Freeway scheme. 'You expect a diverse range of news and comment from *The Telegraph*, and I hope we've opened your eyes to an exciting way to drive a new car' ends the letter.

The pack connects my stated interest with a product. Arguably, this helps both the provider and the buyer.

WHAT CAN ADVERTISING ACCOMPLISH?

Advertising can contribute to profits by: encouraging people to buy a particular brand and thus to pay higher prices; increasing consumption; increasing opportunity to purchase by increasing distribution; improving targeting (reducing costs); and obstructing market entry by competitors (East, 1997).

Five basic desirable effects from advertising effort can be thought of as communication objectives (these will be discussed more fully in chapter fifteen):

1 Arouse need by forging connections between the product category (e.g. instant coffee or car) and consumer/buyer values.
2 Contribute to brand awareness (e.g. Maxwell House instant coffee).
3 Enhance the liking of the brand so that it is preferred over other brands.
4 Encourage people to 'instruct themselves to buy'.
5 Facilitate purchase by answering such questions as 'how much will it cost?', 'where can I get one?', and 'how can I pay?'.

Ambitious advertisers can also attempt brand conversion – converting loyal users of other brands into loyal users of the brand advertised.

Thus mostly advertising works to contribute to something being added to (or not dropped from) a consumer's repertoire, or causing purchase to be more frequent (or preventing less frequent purchase). A consumer's brand repertoire consists of several brands in a particular category, purchased with varying frequency. In recent years, supermarket checkout barcode data has shown that few of us stick to just one brand of coffee, beer, or breakfast cereal – continual temptation by competing promotion turns us into promiscuous shoppers.

Few marketers today still believe that buyers and consumers are merely passive receivers of messages. Social psychology has shown us, as we discussed at length in chapters two, three, and four, that communication is a far more dynamic and essentially interactive process than the old idea would suggest. We have to accept that people take away from advertising (and other forms of communicating activity) largely what they choose to, and also bring existing preconceptions with them. Pre-existing images of brands influence the perception of product offer presentations.

Today, conventional step-by-step, hierarchical and transmissive models that imply a rational consumer being moved, by the advertiser, through a sequence of steps to product purchase are being reviewed critically. The DAGMAR model, for example, provided a simple framework for defining advertising goals for measured advertising results. Research has shown that far from attitude change causing behaviour change, it is more likely that attitude change may be caused by behaviour change, at least in part. Further, there is evidence that advertising can affect behaviour directly without intermediately affecting attitudes.

In the short-term, advertising works by establishing presence (Moran, 1990). Ehrenberg (1997) has referred to this as 'salience'. When a product is present and salient (i.e. stands out), it is more likely to be purchased. In the longer term, advertising is part of the presentation of the product – a fundamental part of manufacturing the product (Joyce, 1991).

The Foote, Cone and Belding (FCB) grid (Figure 14.1) relates type of product to an appropriate particular type of advertising strategy and sequential model of the advertising process. This shows that advertising has a different function for different types of products.

Essentially, advertisements are representations of a product that bring people and products into meaningful relationship. The task of the viewer is to interpret advertisements in order to make sense of them, and this occurs within four basic communicative formats (Leiss *et al.*, 1986 – see Figure 14.2). The four types have appeared in chronological order as the dominant type in use by advertisers, although all types may be in use in a market sector.

Sought advertising content is that which is actively looked for during the information search phase of purchase activity. This requires design that includes all salient aspects for the purchase decision. Unsought advertising content may not be actively looked for but may nonetheless trigger recognition of a need or become part of the information search at a later stage.

	Think	Feel
High involvement	Informative (economic) Learn–Feel–Do Car, appliance, insurance	Affective (psychological) Feel–Learn–Do Cosmetics, jewellery, fashion clothing
Low involvement	Habitual (responsive) Do–Learn–Feel Petrol, groceries	Satisfaction (social) Do–Feel–Learn Beer, cigarettes, sweets

Figure 14.1 **The Foote, Cone and Belding grid**

Product information	All elements explain the product: characteristics, benefits, performance, construction. There is little reference to the use or context of use of the product. Rational argument is used to emphasize the effectiveness of the product or benefits of use
Product image (symbolism)	The product is embedded in a symbolic context that provides meaning for the product beyond simple benefits and its component parts – work, the home, a historic moment, a landscape, etc. The setting provides a frame of reference for interpreting the product's qualities
Personalized	Tries to create a direct relationship between a product and a human personality. People are explicitly and directly interpreted in their relationship to the product: social admiration, pride of ownership, satisfaction in consumption, and so on. The product is displayed as an integral part of human existence and interaction
Lifestyle	This format combines elements of the previous two formats to produce a more balanced relationship between person, product, and setting. Consumption behaviour is the unifying framework for interpretation, rather than use, satisfaction, or utility

Figure 14.2 **Advertising formats**
Source: Based on Leiss *et al.*, 1986

BOX 14.3   ADVERTORIALS

These joint ventures with publishers of newspapers and magazines are especially effective for product launches, when special introductory offers can be made alongside an editorial feature. They can inform and change attitudes to products, involve readers, and lead to product sampling.

This is a form of advertising that seeks to present the advertisement in the style of editorial. However, when the text is not a genuine editorial but advertising space paid for at a special rate, then it is not legitimate publicity and may fall foul of the Sales Promotion Code. This requires advertisers, publishers, and media owners to ensure that advertisements can be clearly distinguished from editorial (for example, by including the advertiser's name and address and a heading 'Advertisement'.)

ADVERTISING OBJECTIVES, STRATEGY, AND TACTICS

The purpose of an advertisement is to build a particular impression of a brand and/or to produce sales – in a particular situation. Thus, it must be seen, read, or heard by those among whom influence is desired, and, as a result, these people should come to think that the claims made are, at least: important, exclusive, pleasant, believable, interesting, understandable.

Advertising can remind us to keep buying, reassure us that the things we like are acceptable (socially), and direct us to a specific brand. Theorists are increasingly sceptical of the power of advertising to persuade or brainwash. Brands are now a trusted part of our lives, therefore emotional appeals tell us that the brand advertised will make us feel good (the pleasure principle). Advertisements can be entertaining, especially when not overly repeated, although costly repetition is widely used in the USA, but the impact on sales and profits has not been universally proved to be positive. Today, advertising is accepted as just one step away from propaganda (see Box 14.3).

Advertising objectives

To say that we want to advertise in order to sell products is, on the one hand, obviously sensible. On the other hand, it is a gross simplification of what is a complex human activity. So for what reason might we go to all of the trouble of planning, designing, and executing an advertising campaign? Some aspects of human cognition and action that we may wish to affect in a progressive sequence are represented by Figure 14.3.

The long-term objective is to influence those people whose decisions and actions determine corporate performance. This is brought about by establishing a distinctive and memorable identity for the product.

Advertising must be 'upsetting' if it is to be effective. By this I mean that advertising (and sales promotion) is used in trying to get people to do something that they might not have done otherwise.

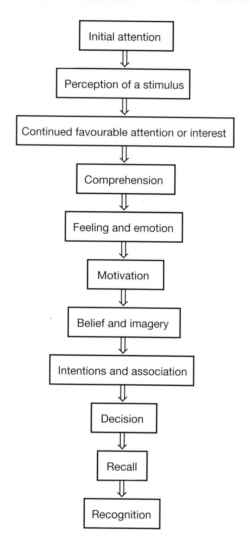

Figure 14.3 **Aspects of human cognition that advertising seeks to affect**

Advertising strategies

In directive advertising, the advertiser tells the person to buy the product because purchase will give benefit. The person is told his/her problem and how to solve it (with the brand) through a direct appeal. In non-directive advertising, the advertiser creates a friendly, sincere, and understanding atmosphere which shows the benefits of the product with direct intention to sell. The person is able to consider new ideas without threat to old ideas. The appeal is inferred. To what extent is the choice of appeal dependent upon the personality of the advertisement creator?

Advertising tactics

The advertising designer must be guided by the communication objectives of the business enterprise. A range of tactics or communicative styles should be considered. Figure 14.4 briefly examines ten available tactics for advertisers.

Inform	Present news of the product without explanation or argument
Argue	Relate reasons why a purchase is desirable
Motivate	Explicitly state benefits, using emotional appeals to self-interest
Repeatedly assert	Repetition of a central point, generally unsupported by proof
Command	Reminder which may be reinforced by an authoritative figure
Familiarize the brand	Friendly conversation with few facts, suggesting loyalty to, and trustworthiness of the advertiser
Symbolically associate	Subtle presentation of a simple fact linking the product with a person, event, or symbol
Imitate	Celebrity testimonial or person(s) with whom consumers can readily identify due to recognized characteristics
Obligate	Offer of free gift or information for which the consumers will feel grateful
Initiate a habit	Offer a sample or introductory discount to start routine behaviour

Figure 14.4 **Advertiser's communication act design tactics**
Source: Based on Simon, 1971

Cereal Partners Worldwide (CPW) is a European joint venture of Nestlé (the world's number one food manufacturer) and General Mills Inc. Through their advertising agency, McCann Eriksen Coley Porter Bell (who bill themselves as 'brand designers'), CPW have been running a 'kid-oriented' premium promotion with merchandise tie-in for the hugely successful Disney/Pixar film *Toy Story 2*. Packs of selected CPW breakfast cereals (Shreddies, for example) have carried a PC CD-ROM sampler that includes a screensaver, game, video clip, and several novelty features. What better way for children to get a taste (excuse the pun) of the film and the cereal. This is an example of habit initiation or even obligation in what is presently a novel advertisement. Such new avenues are opening to supplement and in some cases replace traditional print and TV advertising.

O'Shaughnessy (1988) identifies four tasks for advertising that will usually be used in combination and should relate to the overall goal of creating a distinctive and memorable identity for the product (i.e. a brand) (Figure 14.5).

Retain	Promote want-satisfaction to resist change (i.e. brand switching)
Attract	Promote want-conception by getting people to appreciate the potential of the product to meet their needs
Increase use	Promote want-development by showing further uses of the product
Convert	Promote want-focus by showing how the product better meets the consumer's goals, wants, and choice criteria than rival offerings

Figure 14.5 **Advertising goals**
Source: Based on O'Shaughnessy, 1988

Goal setting for advertising is contingent upon market conditions and provider–product situation. Often, sub-goals have to be specified as means of accomplishing the goals. We will examine goal-setting further in the next chapter.

CREATIVE STRATEGIES

Message strategy or creative strategy is concerned with what is to be said in an advertisement. Laskey *et al.* (1989) produced a typology of informational or transformational advertising concepts (Table 14.1).

Simon (1971) reviewed copywriters' work to classify advertisements based on the view that product–brand characteristics each require particular methods of 'activating' the customer to buy through exposure to advertising. Table 14.1 summarizes nine creative strategies.

EXECUTIONAL FORMATS

The executional format is the technique used by an advertiser for presenting messages. This is concerned with how something is said to someone, i.e. the content of an advertisement. McEwen and Leavitt's (1976) framework for describing television advertisements in terms of stylistic features shows a range of ways of saying something that has been observed through content analysis in TV advertising (Table 14.2).

Another typology of formats was developed by Hefzallah and Maloney (1979) to classify TV advertisements (Table 14.3).

Advertising comes in many forms: some more obvious than others – see Boxes 14.4–14.6 for contemporary examples.

Shimp's (1976) typology of executional formats offers another way of classifying advertisement content (Table 14.4).

Of course, we might expect that decisions about which format to use will be related to the type of product and the market within which it is to be offered.

Table 14.1 **Types of creative strategies found in advertising**

Strategy type	Form of strategy
Informational	
Comparative	Explicitly mentions competing offers
Unique selling proposition	Explicitly claims uniqueness of offer
Pre-emptive	Makes a testable claim of superiority based on an attribute or benefit
Hyperbole	Makes an untestable claim of superiority based on an attribute or benefit
Generic	Focuses on the product class
Transformational	
User image	Focuses on the user
Brand image	Focuses on the personality of the brand
Use occasion	Focuses on occasions when the product is or might be used
Generic	Focuses on the product class

BOX 14.4   WISE WORDS

The Marketing and Communications Group at York City Council engaged Radio 1 cult celebrity gurus Mark Radcliffe and Boy Lard to present a twelve-minute CD guide to City Council services for young people in the style of a daytime radio programme:

> Now that you're 18 you're a fully paid-up member of the adult race, and many perplexing choices lie before you: which clothes make the right fashion statement, which musical trend will last longer than the next six months . . . And then there are your rewards for becoming a grown-up. Now you get to pay Council Tax. And you can vote.

The CD is offered as an essential guide through the maze of life. This is advertising that is entertaining, 'hip', and 'cool', and engages attention through the medium of celebrity personalities, and the popular medium of CD (not directly associated with advertising as persuasion). Arguably, this is a contemporary take on the usually boring public information service.

(See www.york.gov.uk)

Table 14.2 **A typology of advertisement content**

Content factor	Example
Empathic product integration	The product setting has people in it who are portrayed as close – as friends or neighbours – and as product users. There is clearly a main character
Integrated announcer	A celebrity demonstrates or tastes the product
Demonstration by people	People demonstrate the product to reveal consumer benefit
Pleasant liveliness	There is activity, music, children – like a variety show
Confusion	There are more than five situations portrayed, perhaps with unusual camera techniques – the advertisement seems cluttered
New-product introduction	A new product is introduced, perhaps with a mother figure present
Problem solution	A problem is solved by people in an ordinary setting, perhaps with a connection to some other familiar situation
Animation	An instantly recognizable cartoon or animate figure is used
Unpleasant stimulation	A demonstration uses graphs or charts with red emphasized – the end is surprising and the advertisement looks like a new report and may be irritating
Persuasive stimulation	Distinctive music and colour causes viewers to think of previous use of the product, to feel that it can be smelled or felt, and that they should buy it
Opening suspense	At first another product is brought to mind, then the lead-in creates a surprise

Table 14.3 **Executional formats developed by Hefzallah and Maloney**

Strategy	Execution
Association	The product is associated with pleasant past or present experiences
Demonstration	The appearance and function of the product is shown
Information	An impression of quality is sought
Plot	The product is shown solving a problem
Stage	An activity shows the product in use and people satisfied
Testimonial	A famous person praises the product

Table 14.4   Executional formats according to Shimp

Individual oriented	Story oriented	Product oriented	Technique oriented
Celebrity endorser	Off-camera video drama	Demonstration	Fantasy
Typical person endorser	On-camera video drama	Product display	Analogy
Spokesperson	Narration		
Personality			

BOX 14.5   'WE HAVE OVER £6,000 WORTH OF GOODIES TO GIVE AWAY'

Ever wondered why magazines give away products? To qualify for the free goodies, you return a postcard or dial the special telephone number – and you give your name and address. The sponsors then have current, directly generated, qualified mailing lists. You have told them what products you want to own. The telephone line may well be a premium-charge line, which also generates income for the sponsor. The magazine publisher may well sell more copies because the offer is available, too. Even if you don't ask for a free one, you have seen the product promoted in the magazine. You may get the product you know you can't live without. Everyone is a winner! Free give-aways are actually highly focused advertising campaigns.

BOX 14.6 COMPETITIONS

To generate interest in a new product, why not run a competition that is easy, so that many people will send in their names and addresses on postcards, enter personal details on your website, or dial a premium-charge telephone number. The magazine will wish to run the event because it helps to boost their sales. Everyone's a winner (not quite everyone, you understand!). This is advertising – but you don't pay for page space.

COMPARATIVE ADVERTISING

Some advertisers set out to refer to the price or quality of a competitor's products directly or indirectly. This is an increasingly popular and effective tool for drawing attention to claims of advantage over competing offers.

The legal profession has also benefited from this development in the use of 'knocking copy'. The clash of interests is obvious. Brand owners and managers are concerned that their product, corporate reputation, and goodwill can be damaged. Consumers, however, can gain by the additional information they can gather and the stimulation of competition that arises from comparative advertising – see Box 14.7.

BOX 14.7 ADVERTISING THAT ISN'T ADVERTISING

How can *PC KnowHow* sell for £1.75, *Internet Advisor* for £1.99, or *Computer Buyer* for £2.99? Each carries a CD-ROM on the cover and provides several full versions of popular and new software programs with clipart, fonts, and screensavers, as well as trial and demo versions of games, utilities, and free Internet access. This spells a great deal for the buyer, but how is it worthwhile for the publishers and software providers?

Could it be that because PC software is an intangible until operated and can be transported at almost no cost on CD-ROMs or through download from the WWW, this 'free give-away' is a viable alternative to traditional print, TV or radio advertising? People can try the product for themselves and register to buy upgrades, usually via the WWW. Marketing budgets can be focused on creating awareness and experience of use, instead of being diluted into packaging and distribution costs. And in many cases, the potential customer actually pays for the privilege.

INTERNET ADVERTISING

In 1994, advertising on the World Wide Web was virtually non-existent. By 2000, worldwide Internet advertising was estimated to be worth around £3.5bn according to various commentators (see Tapp, 2000, for related estimates). Perhaps more important to appreciate is the lightening pace of growth in the adoption of Internet advertising. It has been estimated that the time taken following introduction to reach 50m consumers in the USA for radio was 38 years. TV took just 13 years, and cable TV just 10 years. Astonishingly, the Internet has done this in only 5 years.

Perhaps the most familiar form is the banner advertisement that sits on the top 20 per cent of the web page. Clicking this can take the interested person to either the advertiser's website, or, more usefully, a microsite that expands on the banner. Banner advertisements can appear that relate to the search topic. The advertiser can buy a relevant search term at a particular search engine (e.g. GoTo.com).

An Internet advertisement is much more than simply an additional visual space (i.e. replicating the printed page of the newspaper or magazine). Advertisers get direct data on how many people view their banner and how many click through to their homepage or micro-website pages. Advertising campaigns can be much more flexible and responsive. Advertisers can test several variants and modify their strategy using daily response data. This is known as 'hot-testing', which is impossible with print-runs that have lead times of several weeks or days.

Advertising has traditionally been bought on an opportunity-to-see (OTS) basis (calculated from the print circulation, number of readers per copy, and number of times the page is viewed). Internet advertisers typically charge on a 'pay-per-click-through' basis. This is real performance data for the advertisement since it gauges directly how many people respond, whereas print advertisements can never do this except if there are telephone and voucher responses. As an alternative to the rate card way of pricing advertising space, Internet advertising may be priced on the value of the product advertised and the degree of interactivity required (i.e. the communication objectives for the advertisement), rather than per impression – see Box 14.8. We will examine ways of calculating return on investment in chapter sixteen.

The traditional distinctions between marketing communication activities and other aspects of corporate communication are becoming blurred by the adoption of the Internet as a medium for communication. Publicity, public relations, direct marketing, direct-response advertising, internal marketing, and personal selling are being mixed together in ways previously unimagined and unsupported.

An example of proactive Internet advertising is the ValueMad service that operates in the UK. Registered users receive e-mail messages that describe special offers on a wide range of products. Inducements to purchase are mostly exceptionally low prices with links to the supplier's own website. Users' clicking creates databases of e-mail addresses to which further targeted offers can be made.

At present, it is mostly technology companies who are advertising on the Internet (Microsoft, IBM, and Excite led the way in 1997 expenditure). A survey by CMR/InterMedia showed that the average spend in 1997 was just 0.74 per cent of total consumer advertising spend. On the other hand, online and Internet service providers spent 28 per cent of their budget online. Computers and software accounted for 50 per cent of all Internet advertising. Financial services was second, and telecommunications third. In 1998, P&G was the only packaged-goods marketer in the Top 50 Internet advertisers (by spend), placed at number 30.

BOX 14.8   INTERACTIVE MARKETER OF THE YEAR

Advertising Age rated Proctor & Gamble (P&G) as the leading Internet advertiser in 1998. Criteria were leadership, online spending, innovation, and successful advertising campaigns. The world's largest advertiser has also been able to make good progress in addressing the major issues facing the emerging Internet advertising industry, as part of the Future of Advertising Stakeholders (FAST) summit:

- consumer acceptance
- standardized measurement
- models of interactive advertising
- ease of purchase of online media

With some thirty-three brands involved in some form of Internet advertising, a marketing investment fund called 'Incent' was established for testing online advertisements to encourage more activity in this burgeoning field. They even have a 'digital brand manager'. By 2001, all interactive funding will be part of brand budgets. In 1998, P&G's interactive team created and ran 200 interactive advertisements. The Internet is also part of product launch, where TV advertising directs consumers to a website where they can request product samples in advance of stockists receiving shipments. One campaign achieved a click-through rate of 20 per cent.

They are now reviewing whether the advertising impression is the best measure for brand building.

CASE STUDY 14   GOOGLE ON THE WEB

Google Inc. uses their own advanced keyword-matching search technology to help users to find the information they are looking for quickly and effectively. They deliver their services through their own public website and by licensing their web-wide search services, which they host, to commercial sites. Web directory service provider Yahoo!® is one recent high-profile new partner who selected Google® as their default search results provider. Google powers eighty portal and destination websites in more than twenty countries. Current other implementors of the service include Netscape, the *Washington Post*, RedHat, and Virgin Net.

Google offers advertisers a high-traffic web location to attract customers. The total number of searches served by Google exceeded 17 million per day in 2000 – this is projected to grow to 30 million per day with a growth rate of 20 to 30 per cent per month. Advertising on the Google service is precisely targeted and designed graphically to enhance each user's overall search experience. Users can find the relevant information they need easily and speedily. Google thus delivers a matched goal-driven audience to advertisers who have something to say – the service is 'sticky' – once users are attracted they tend to stick with the service.

One example of the advertising feature of the Google site is the displaying of Amazon.com book titles at the top of search results pages, related to the queries entered by users. Google intends to match consumer searches with many other products for advertisers. Thus, Google provides targeted advertising opportunities in the form of direct matching of keywords and key phrases, and relevant Internet categories. An enhanced text-link appears at the top of a Google results page whenever the keyword or phase purchased by the advertiser is queried by a Google user. Alternatively, advertisers can select from a range of Internet categories created by the PageRank algorithmn (see below). Google then matches the advertisement to appear on the search results page if that category is relevant to the searcher's query.

In June 2000, Google's WWW index listed more than 1 billion web pages (equivalent to searching a stack of paper more than 70 miles high in less than half a second!) that can be searched in ten languages. In effect, Google's 4,000+ server machines index the entire Web, which has grown from about 50 million pages in 1995. The patented PageRank technology examines the number of people viewing each web page and 500 million variables and 2 billion terms to rank each page. The algorithm calculates the 'authority' of the pages – if the site is good, it is reasoned, many other websites will link to it. Other features examined include the placement of links on the page, font sizes and capitalization, and so on. As the Web gets bigger, the Google service scales up with it, making Google's competitive advantage simply that their service gets smarter.

So who is part of the audience that Google delivers to their advertisers? They have distinct demographics: 65 per cent are male with at least a first degree; 73 per cent have professional occupations. Average income is $71,000. Online experience exceeds four years for 58 per cent of users; 48 per cent access the Internet from work; 71 per cent report 'high' or 'very high' for their computer skills. A user satisfaction survey by NPD Research Group (New Media Services) ranked Google first overall of search engines and WWW portals for site effectiveness, user opinion of the site, and loyalty. Some 94 per cent of users expressed their willingness to recommend the site to a friend; 98 per cent rated Google as better than the other sites, while 97 per cent find what they are searching for all or most of the time. Google is chosen for their searches by 70 per cent because the service delivers the best results. The business is being built on a foundation of providing users with the best search experience that makes the service indispensable. What a basis for selling matched advertising resources! Google can claim added value and can show the data to prove it.

The Google phenomenon is growing apace. In a recent search engine report[a] the author commented

> reviewers continue to rave about Google, as does the general public. When I speak about search engines to groups and mention Google, something unusual happens to some members of the audience. They smile and nod, in the way you do when you feel like you've found a secret little getaway that no one else knows about. And each time I speak, I see more and more people smiling and nodding this way, pleased to have discovered Google.

Google Inc. was established as a spin-out from the Stanford Research Institute with $25m in start-up funding in 1998.

(See www.google.com, www.yahoo.com and www.npd.com)
Note: [a] www.searchenginewatch.com/ereport/00/07-yahoo.html

WHAT DO YOU THINK?

1 Even supermarkets now capture customers' details and mail out product catalogues. ASDA, for example, recently ran a George clothing competition and have built a mailing list. How do you see this developing?

2 To what extent are knowledge and experience really the same thing? How do advertising agencies manage their knowledge capital?

3 Likeable advertisements seem to sell more products. Try to explain this finding from advertising research.

4 Advertising has been called the 'strategy of desire'. What is meant by this?

5 William Randolph Hearst once said: 'News is something someone is trying to hide. Everything else is just advertising'. What did he mean?

6 Despite US advertising spend increasing by almost 75 per cent in the period 1986–96, more people than ever believe that most products in most categories are exactly alike. How can this be? What does this say about the role of advertising media?

7 Internet advertising accountability is being measured by 'click-throughs'. How is this threatening traditional media?

8 When advertising can be linked directly to purchases, it is termed 'retail'. When, and how, is 'image' advertising justifiable?

9 We should not concern ourselves with what advertising does to people, but rather with what people do with advertising? What is meant by this?

10 Advertising is used for propaganda and persuasion in commercial and political arenas. One encourages product consumption, while the other encourages conformity to ideology. How do these perspectives differ?

FURTHER READING

Blythe, J. (2000) *Marketing Communications*, London: FT Prentice-Hall.

East, R. (1997) *Consumer Behaviour: Advances and Applications in Marketing*, London: Prentice-Hall.

Fill, C. (1999) *Marketing Communications: Contexts, Contents, and Strategies*, 2nd edn, London: Prentice-Hall Europe, chapters 13 and 14.

Jefkins, F. and Yadin, D. (2000) *Advertising*, 4th edn, London: FT Prentice-Hall.

Leiss, W., Kline, S. and Jhally, S. (1986) *Social Communication in Advertising: Persons, Products, and Images of Well-Being*, London: Methuen Books.

Moran, W. T. (1990) 'Brand presence and the perceptual frame', *Journal of Advertising Research* 30 (5), October–November, pp. 9–16.

Rust, R. T. and Oliver, R W. (1994) 'The death of advertising', *Journal of Advertising* 23 (4): 71–7.

Smith, P. R., Berry, C. and Pulford, A. (1997) *Strategic Marketing Communications: New Ways to Build and Integrate Communications*, London: Kogan Page, chapter 11.

Sutherland, M. (1993) *Advertising and the Mind of the Consumer*, St Leonards, NSW: Allen & Unwin.

Tapp, A. (2000) *Principles of Direct and Database Marketing*, 2nd edn, London: FT Prentice-Hall.

chapter
fifteen

COMMUNICATION STRATEGIES AND OBJECTIVES

LEARNING POINTS

Careful study of this chapter will help you to:

- recognize the role of strategy-making and communication objective-setting

- distinguish marketing objectives, marketing communication objectives, and communication objectives

- broaden your thinking beyond promotional intentions to consider objectives for total communication systems

---

Most success comes from ignoring the obvious.
(Trevor Holdsworth)

INTRODUCTION

Marketing strategy is the plan that marketers use to guide their efforts to provide particular products to specified market segments through exchanges. Communication strategy is the plan developed and used by marketing communication managers to provide the necessary communication environment for such exchanges to become possible and to be consummated. It should be noted that these objectives and even the concept of communication are in most marketing practice defined outside the social system to which they are targeted. That is, both the definition of the problem (i.e. customer satisfaction) and the communication solution are defined by providers but not consumers and buyers. This is a significant point in considering the management of the social system of exchange we call marketing – consider Figure 15.1.

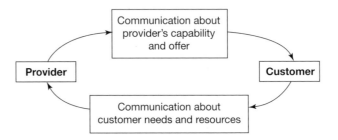

Figure 15.1 **The role of communication in marketing**

Market segmentation divides the total market into groupings (based on similarities in consumption pattern, identified need, media usage, and so on, i.e. their likely similarity in response to marketing interventions) and then offers specific products to selected segments (see Box 15.1). These groupings of consumers and buyers require separate marketing mixes, which might entail differing communication systems and activities. Product positioning conveys to consumers and buyers in the selected segment that a product is more appropriate and desirable for them than other offerings and signals to people in other segments that it will not meet their needs.

BOX 15.1   COMMENT: ON NEED CREATION

Some people claim that marketers strive to create needs by developing and promoting products that are not really needed – that a consumer culture has been created that commends consumption and defines identities by the things we consume.

If you adopt the model of motivation we have described in chapter three, it is people who recognize needs and seek satisfiers, not marketers who create needs. Marketers attempt to influence the choice of goals, but goals do not motivate product purchase unless a person believes that this will satisfy his/her need.

Need creation is perhaps best thought of as a cooperative process.

We will examine the planning process in fuller detail in chapter sixteen, but we need an outline here in order to appreciate the place of communication strategies and communication objectives in the marketing plan.

Wilson *et al.* (1992) provide us with a straightforward, yet comprehensive, framework for appreciating how we arrive at a coherent, relevant, rigorously thought-through plan (Figure 15.2).

Figure 15.2 **A systematic process for planning, implementation, and control**
Source: Based on Wilson *et al.*, 1992

Note that strategy comes before tactics in this planning process. Although much practice seems to begin with tactics and then selects objectives to pull things together, the more professional and effective and efficient managerial approach is to match intentions with situation and capability.

MARKETING COMMUNICATION OBJECTIVES

The basic aspects of the marketing communication strategy are, as insightfully observed by Schultz *et al.* (1993):

* start and end generative, productive, and representative (i.e. marketing system) intentions, decision-making, and choice-making with the consumer or buyer – they need a buying incentive and responsive and responsible points of contact
* work to establish a relationship – loyal customers are cooperative antagonists who themselves will bargain, inform, persuade, argue, and dialogue – this is to be encouraged and facilitated
* differentiate the brand (i.e. the product–provider offer) by establishing rapport, empathy, and dialogue

The task, then, argue Schultz *et al.* (1993), is to avoid the mixed-up, mass-directed, incompatible communication from a multitude of sources that confuses, bores, and scares away consumers, buyers, and customers.

When efforts to communicate are directed towards the accomplishment of marketing objectives, the process is termed a campaign. The marketing communication campaign may have one or several objectives, such as to:

- create awareness of the company and its products
- inform and educate consumers and buyers
- encourage a preference for the company's products over those of competing providers (a brand specifies the product and the provider)
- encourage product trial among potential new customers
- boost sales in the short term by stimulating action
- reassure customers and reinforce their particular desirable buying behaviour
- generate information from customers
- create sales leads

The campaign may be short term and tactical or long term and strategic. Communicating with customers has two primary purposes in managing marketing.

1 **Deciding on the offer (promise)**: We are clear now that the marketing process strictly does not begin with promotion. Consumers and buyers may be asked directly about their needs, interests, wants, satisfactions and disappointments. Their buying behaviour may be monitored so as to lead to modifications to offerings. The voice of the customer is brought into the product development process, perhaps through a designated manager who is responsible for bringing market and marketing information to the R&D team. In such an integrated system, new product and enhancement and termination decisions will be made with core capabilities and limitations, and customer views, taken into consideration.

2 **Making the promise**: At this stage of the marketing process, the major objective is to influence those consumers and buyers with whom an exchange is desired. The hierarchy of effects model (Figure 15.3) shows phases through which the thinking and behaviour of these people have to be shifted if sales are to be made. Marketers are then attempting to create an image and to support relationship building with customers and other stakeholders: initiators, users, decision-makers, influencers, buyers, and gatekeepers. It should be noted that universal acceptance of this model has dwindled in recent years, and more sophisticated models of advertising effects are now available. Professor Andrew Ehrenberg, for one, has been a vociferous critic. However, this model does give a sensible grounding to our understanding of what marketing communication managers may be trying to accomplish when planning the operation of their communication systems.

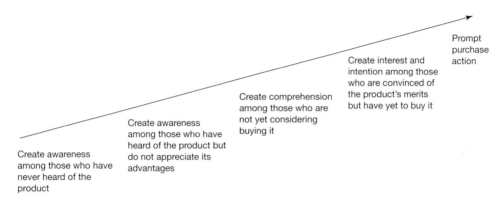

Figure 15.3 **The classification of buyer awareness levels**

Communication goals must be set if the activities and resource usage of the marketing department are to be best deployed in contributing to corporate business goals. Figure 15.4 outlines a number of goals from which the two priorities of an integrated marketing communication programme should be selected. This concentrated effort will ensure that goals can be accomplished and overstretching of limited resources avoided.

The wider marketing campaign may have social-change goals (Kotler, 1982):

- **cognitive** change: to inform about, or increase recognition of, a cause
- **action** change: to call for demonstration or petition-signing against some behaviour or action of others

Build brand equity	Communication activities are used to reinforce brand values and identity. This encourages stronger band preference and can strengthen trading relationships in a competitive situation
Provide information	Detail product uses, availability, incentives for purchase, technical specification, and so on
Manage demand	Stimulate demand for new and innovative products, boost sales of mature products, or dampen demand for out-of-stock items
Differentiate and position	Emphasize significant factors of difference, and position relative to competing offers
Influence attitudes and behaviour	Promote favourable thinking about a product and encourage some resulting action

Figure 15.4 **Marketing communication goals**

- **behaviour** change: to urge adoption or abandonment of a routine way of doing something
- **value** change: to convince of the value of certain actions or conditions in the environment

Further, marketing communication systems should facilitate the keeping of the promise(s) made to customers and other buyers/consumers. Especially in service environments, front-line customer contact people are a vital source of intelligence on preferences, likes and dislikes, competitor offerings, and so on – direct from customers.

COMMUNICATION STRATEGY

A marketing strategy is essentially a design for the use of the marketing mix for selected markets: customers, consumers, and buyers. A marketing communication strategy is that element of the marketing plan that provides the communication systems to enable and facilitate the planning, implementation, and control of the marketing system. A communication strategy is a design for enabling and facilitating appropriate forms of interaction, relationship, and so on.

There is much more to human communication than promotional messages. Vickers (1984) distinguished seven overlapping and coexisting ascending levels of trust and shared appreciation (see Figure 15.5 and the discussion in earlier chapters). This is a taxonomy that can be applied to many marketing situations, when the practices of one party dominate the other person.

We can, with some thought here, identify several levels at which the marketing system must be effectively communicative. For example, apart from outright violence and threat, an interaction between 'marketers' could aim to reach a bargain (exchange), inform, persuade, argue, or dialogue.

Of course, both consumer/buyer and provider, each as marketer, will have a communication objective and strategy (even if only implicit). A householder receives a telephone call and answers some questions about various products. They buy some products later in the week. There is a dialogue. Each purchase is a message to the producer and supplier. The provider advertises, promotes, distributes, and displays. The consumer answers back by buying or not buying the various product options (prices, sizes, brands, etc.). The consumer or buyer can communicate with the producer by answering questions in a survey or by asking questions or making complaints. The provider then responds by creating new products and modifying the others.

THE STRATEGY DOCUMENT

The investment in time and effort to develop a strategy has a number of benefits:

- integrates communication systems
- greater impact from clearer communication

Violence	Erodes trust and evokes a response to contain it and to abate it, but has no specific communicative purpose – violence does not have to be physical – it is mistreatment that violates rights
Threat	The conditional 'do it or else' coercion – involves trust only to the extent that the threatened party needs to believe both that the threatener can and will carry out a threat unless the condition is fulfilled and that to fulfil the condition will avert the threat
Bargain	Involves a greater shared assumption – each party has to be confident that the other regards the situation as a bargain – the attempt to negotiate an exchange on terms acceptable to all the parties – each must believe that the other parties can and will carry out their undertakings if agreement is reached – each is free to make not merely an acceptable bargain but the best they can, or to withdraw from the negotiation
Information	The receiver must not only trust the giver's competence and reliability, they must also be assured that the giver's appreciative system corresponds sufficiently with their own to ensure that what is received fits the receiver's needs. Even if it does, it will, to some extent, alter the setting of their appreciative system
Persuasion	The giver actively seeks to change the way in which the other perceives some situation and thus to change the setting of his/her appreciative system more radically
Argument	When the process is mutual, each party strives to alter the other's view while maintaining his/her own
Dialogue	Each party seeks to share, perhaps only hypothetically, the other's appreciation and to open his/her own to the other's persuasion with a view to enlarging the approaching mutual understanding, if not also shared appreciation

Figure 15.5 **Levels of communication**

- broadens decision and judgement perspectives (i.e. appreciation)
- provides a clear strategic direction within which tactical planning is conducted
- tactical activities support and complement each other
- encourages reflection
- reduced stress from the hassles of error, omission, and uncertainty
- cost savings

One fatal mistake made by so many marketers is to write a massive tome that has more value as a doorstop that as a business tool. Schultz *et al.* (1993)

provide an outline for an integrated marketing communication strategy that fosters thinking about the key issues and a concise manner in which to capture the resulting strategy guide (this has been summarized in Figure 15.6). Note that the answers to these questions should be considered by all who participate in the generative–productive–representative marketing system. These issues are not the sole concern of the marketing team.

What is the specific buying incentive for this group?

Does the product match the group (reality and appreciation)?

What do our competitors accomplish through their communication with this group? How will this affect our capacity to accomplish our objectives?

What is our competitive benefit for the consumer?

How will our marketing communication make the benefit believable?

What should the personality of the brand be?

What main idea should the consumer/buyer take from our communication, and what do we want them to do as a result?

In X months from now these consumers/buyers appreciate our product as what compared with competing offers, if we are to deem our communication to be successful?

What are the appropriate contact points (media) for believable, persuasive communication?

What future research should we undertake to develop our communication strategy further?

Figure 15.6 **Outline proforma marketing communication strategy**
Source: Based on Schultz *et al.*, 1993

Each group (loyal users, occasional users, wholesalers, retailers, specifiers, etc.) has their own buying incentive and thus require a distinct competitive benefit. Integration ensures that the result is a unified personality for the brand.

PUSH-AND-PULL COMMUNICATION SYSTEMS

Not all marketing communication effort is directed at end-users and buyers. A large proportion of the budget will be allocated to communication activities with intermediaries, although the proportion will depend on the nature of the market served; increasingly, businesses are moving to direct electronic connections with customers. Pull-through communication builds awareness, attraction, and loyalty, and reduces search costs. Customers are influenced to seek out certain products, thus pulling them through the distribution channels. Messages are delivered to consumers and buyers to encourage them to request products from intermediaries. Push-through communication is directly with intermediaries and intended to encourage and support resellers to make certain products available to customers, and thus to make resales. Most marketers will combine these strategies for effective influence on customers and impact on market position.

See Table 15.1 and Box 15.2.

Table 15.1   Push-and-pull techniques for offer creation and offer-making

Technique	Generate	Represent
Push	Sampling	Trade advertising
	Survey	Sales team
	Focus group	POS materials
		Exhibition
Pull	Concept testing	Press/TV advertising
	Sampling	Direct mail
	Survey	Sales promotion

BOX 15.2   PULLING THE CHIP INSIDE

In 1991, Intel, the world's largest computer chip manufacturer lost a court case that opened up the personal computer (PC) microprocessor market to low-cost competition. Marketing managers realized that they had to encourage PC buyers that the most important factor in their choice was not the brand of PC they bought, but the chip inside it. The campaign cost something like $100m in the first two years.

By branding the component parts, Intel was attempting to differentiate their product and the PC from commodity products bought mainly on price.

Intel thus sought to exert a 'pull' on manufacturers of PCs to use Intel chips by persuading consumers to buy a PC with an Intel chip inside. In 1994 more than 1,000 manufacturers used Intel chips and received cooperative funding from Intel for co-brand advertising.

THE TWO-PART STRATEGY

The marketing communication strategy deals with much more than what is said and to whom. It ensures that coherent systems are developed to:

* identify consumer/buyer segments based on behaviour and needs
* offer a competitive benefit relevant to the specific and particular buying incentive

- understand how the consumer/buyer positions your brand
- establish a unique, unified brand personality that helps the consumer/buyer to define and distinguish your brand from competing offers
- create real and appreciated reasons why the consumer/buyer should believe the brand promise
- identify key points of interaction where relating and communicating can arise
- establish criteria for the performance of the strategy and accountability
- determine requirements for continuing knowledge update and enhancement

The strategy also details where and how to interact constructively with the various people who can affect the ultimate sale of the product. Thus detailed decisions are made about how much, what and when various (communicating) media or 'marketing assets' are to be deployed:

Targeted direct marketing	Selective advertising
Stakeholder relations	Corporate identity
Product form and function	After-sales support
Exhibitions, trade shows, etc.	Distribution arrangements
Pricing structure	Sales promotion
Internal marketing communications	Packaging design
Sales literature	Displays
Interpersonal interaction	

Figure 15.7 **Detailed decisions of a marketing community strategy**

One organizational effect of such an integrated marketing strategy is the rethinking of departmental divisions in the provider value-creating system. If customer needs are the focus of the provider, then the way that business is conducted must be integrated for responsive and responsible generation, production, and representation. Putting out cleverly crafted selling messages simply isn't enough!

Boxes 15.3 and 15.4 both take a look at how information/product is offered to us.

BOX 15.3   THE CORPORATE WEBSITE AS AN INFORMATION RESOURCE

Siemens reorganized their UK website around industry categories rather than internal company divisions. This facilitates customer browsing through appropriate industry-related pages and the use of the search function to find Siemens' products appropriate for solving their problems. Requests can be sent via e-mail for sales meetings and product literature.

BOX 15.4   COMMENT: ON CRAFTY SELLING MESSAGES

Much that is offered to us is intended to whet our appetite. Even if we aren't aware of feeling hungry, we are encouraged to eat, so that we will discover a hunger we didn't know we had. We are offered free samples for this reason. From our point of view, however, a free sample may simply be received as a gift!

ADVERTISING STRATEGIES

Although in many markets advertising is by far the major element of the marketing communication budget (in others it will be the salesforce operation), we should take care not to confuse an advertising strategy with a marketing communication strategy. Advertising campaigns and budget allocations should be a subsidiary part of the marketing communication strategy.

Leiss *et al.* (1986) identify two basic approaches to the use of advertising:

1 **Hard sell**: provides a reason to buy, suggests a unique selling proposition, appeals to fear, and may offer a tie-in; this rationalistic process is designed to persuade
2 **soft sell**: stories of consumers consuming as mini 'soap opera', testimonials, strongly emotive and creative; this irrational process is designed to suggest and appeal to the consumer/buyer

Advertising objectives are summarized in Figure 15.8.

COMMUNICATION STRATEGIES AND PRODUCT LIFE CYCLE

Although a simplistic model of what is really much more complex, the product life cycle is a useful conceptual tool for recognizing that communication objectives must be carefully matched to the situation of the consumer/buyer (Table 15.2 and Box 15.4).

Category need	Connect the product category to audience values
Brand awareness	Create recall of the brand name or recognition of the product
Brand attitude	Enhance the liking of the brand so that it is preferred over others
Brand purchase intention	Encourage people to instruct themselves to buy
Purchase facilitation	Answer questions such as 'how much does it cost?', 'which shops stock it?', and 'how can I pay for it?'

Figure 15.8 **The objectives of advertising: a summary**
Source: Rossiter and Percy, 1997

Table 15.2 **Planned evolution of communication strategy**

Objective	Introduction	Growth	Maturity	Decline
Marketing objectives	Help early adopters to try the product	Gain market share of X per cent and establish distribution system	Strengthen market share and build customer and loyalty	Maintain dominant market position and consider brand extensions
Communication objectives	Create awareness. Create interest and desire among innovators	Create and strengthen brand preference by intermediaries and end-users. Encourage wider trial and use	Increase frequency of use and connect with possible new uses	Minimum promotion while retaining brand values and create specialist niche
Communication strategy (prioritized use of tools)	Publicity. Personal selling. Advertising. Launch offers	Advertising. Personal selling. Sales promotions. Publicity	Advertising. Dealer promotions. Sales promotions. Publicity	Reduced media expenditure, with sales promotions

Source: Based on Smith *et al.*, 1997

BOX 15.5 LAUNCHING CHICETTAS AS A DAYTIME SNACK

Derwent Valley Foods became a major provider of spicy exotic snacks with their Phileas Fogg brand range. In order to appeal to a wider range of tastes, a new corn-based snack in milder flavours was designed.

The marketing communication task at launch in the spring of 1995 was to establish a clear product identity among consumers and trade intermediaries (wholesalers, retailers, pubs, etc.) without alienating customers for the other products. A primary objective was to create widespread sampling of the snack.

A number of high-profile events were attended and cultural sponsorships organized so that samples could be handed out to the 'educated taste leaders' (25–44 year olds who dine out and travel) identified by previous market research. The advertising campaign was launched at a series of lunchtime concerts and performance artists were 'exhibited' at a specially organized 'art gallery' event.

The sponsorship of fringe arts events raised much publicity on regional TV and in national newspapers and magazines. Some 150,000 sample snacks were given to people. Around 350,000 other people heard about the product through literature about the sponsored events. Sales of Chicettas reached 10 per cent of total Phileas Fogg brand sales in the summer launch period. Next time, sampling will be even broader and not just limited to the sponsored events.

CASE STUDY 15   VHI SAYS GO FOR IT![a]

October 1999 saw the launch of the five-year VHI Says Go For It lifestyles education programme in Ireland. With a total budget of £1,560,000 this is a serious effort to position VHI as Ireland's champion of healthy lifestyles.

The Dublin-based Voluntary Health Insurance Board (An Bord Árachais Sláinte Shaorálaigh) (VHI for short) was established in the 1950s as a not-for-profit service to encourage Irish residents to become more self-reliant in providing for their healthcare needs. Their market monopoly was ended by legislation in 1994. Today, VHI has 1.43 million members, including 6,500 group schemes (this is 40 per cent of the Irish population, whereas only 11 per cent have opted for private insurance in the UK!). A further 1,000 people are joining the VHI membership every week, with an average age of 28 years. The defection rate (to competing healthcare insurance schemes, such as BUPA) is only 1 per cent. VHI strongly support community rating, in which all members pay the same premium irrespective of age, as an alternative to the UK's risk-rated premiums that increase as the member gets older. Income in 1999–2000 was around £400m.

The VHI Says Go For It brand is being developed through a series of lifestyle education programmes, targeting the five life stages, and based on national and international research and sound medical advice, that promote a positive, practical and light-hearted approach to healthy living. The brand is to be incorporated into all communication strategies, and will be an important asset in positioning VHI as an innovative provider of integrated healthcare products that meet all members' healthcare needs. VHI Says Go For It will be the focused vehicle for:

- direct positive contact with members
- enhancing emotional ties to VHI
- providing added value, especially for those members who do not claim
- attracting positive media attention
- meeting VHI's commitment to invest a portion of profits in promoting healthy living

Following an extensive review of sponsorship opportunities, a VHI-initiated and wholly owned project was designed, with the following strategic communication objectives:

- to establish VHI as Ireland's champion of healthy living
- to provide new positive communication opportunities that offer practical advice on healthy lifestyles, particularly to the 18–40 age group, families, and corporate customers
- to present VHI as innovative, efficient, and member oriented
- to provide a significant national profile for VHI
- to build emotional ties with VHI
- to support brand, sales, marketing, advertising and public relations strategies

In the first year, the project has been concentrated on lifestyle education for 5–10-year-old children. In subsequent years of the five-year project, programmes will be tailored to each life stage segment (niche group) by selecting the relevant lifestyle research findings and appropriate media for communication. For example, the Healthy Children programme has mailed 80,000 posters to those VHI members with young children, and a further 195,000 posters were circulated by the RTE Guide, and to schools, GPs, and other requests via a freephone line. More than 3,500 people responded to VHI Says Go For It competitions in the local and national press. A Go For It page was added to the VHI website. Following a comprehensive circulation of press releases, the programme was covered in almost all of the national and regional press and radio, with a twenty-minute feature on TV3. A promotional video was produced for use in VHI presentations.

The new brand is being used to rebrand VHI's healthy living activities and to initiate some new activities, including:

- *Go For It Magazine*
- Go For It public seminars
- Go For It on the Web, including joint-marketing ventures
- Go For It Health Columns in local newspapers
- Go For It magazine-style programmes for syndication to local radio stations and as audio content on the website
- *Irish Times Business 2000* case study as part of this multi media education pack
- supporting outdoor advertising at sports events and on 48-sheet billboards, and on prime-time TV
- sponsorship of the time checks on national and local radio

The impact of the project will be measured annually by independent omnibus research and the VHI customer satisfaction survey. Annual budgets will be reviewed when content and implementation of the life stage programmes is decided.

The marketing budget is not always deployed only for promotional purposes. At VHI, there is an investment in engaging people in issues that if successful, will change the way the market operates.

(See www.vhi.ie)

Note: [a] The assistance of Mark Cohen, Marketing Director, VHI, and Tara Buckley, General Manager for Corporate Communications, VHI, is gratefully acknowledged.

WHAT DO YOU THINK?

1 According to Vickers' levels of communication analysis, we could imagine such communication objectives as: connect, inform, persuade, learn, invent. Think through other appropriate objectives and list them with a brief explanation of the associated circumstances in which they might become part of the marketing communication plan.

2 Schultz *et al.* (1993) suggest that marketers spend far too much time talking about themselves. What do they mean by this?

3 What distinguishes a communication objective from a marketing objective?

4 Why is 'marketing' taken to be synonymous with promoting product sales by so many people?

5 'Strategy follows objectives.' Explain.

6 Why is VHI investing so much money and effort into their new brand campaign? Who will benefit from this?

7 How, in practice, can marketing communication strategies be linked to marketing strategies that contribute constructively to business strategy?

8 Write an outline task list for marketing planning in a business with which you have contact.

9 List as many marketing communication objectives as you can think of and separate out those that are really specific to advertising. What does this tell you about the scope of marketing communication?

10 Design a communication objectives statement for those communication subsystems that are necessary to contribute to the marketing system in terms other than immediate sales.

FURTHER READING

Best, R. J. (2000) *Market-Based Management: Strategies for Growing Customer Value and Profitability*, 2nd edn, Upper Saddle River, NJ: Prentice-Hall, chapter 10.

Kotler, P. (1982) *Marketing for Non-Profit Organizations*, 2nd edn, Englewood Cliffs, NJ: Prentice-Hall.

Leiss, W., Kline, S. and Jhally, S. (1986) *Social Communication in Advertising: Persons, Products, and Images of Well-Being*, London: Methuen.

Schultz, D. E., Tannenbaum, S. I. and Lauterborn, R. F. (1993) *Integrated Marketing Communications: Putting It Together and Making It Work*, Lincolnwood, IL: NTC Business Books, especially chapter 4.

Vickers, G. (1984) *Human Systems Are Different*, London: Harper & Row.

Wilson, R. M. S., Gilligan, C. T. and Pearson, D. J. (1992) *Strategic Marketing Management: Planning, Implementation and Control*, Oxford: Butterworth-Heinemann/CIM. This book comprehensively (and readably) deals with many issues of planning marketing system operation.

chapter sixteen

PLANNING, EVALUATING, AND CONTROLLING THE MARKETING COMMUNICATION SYSTEM AND PROGRAMME

LEARNING POINTS

Careful study of this chapter will help you to:

- conceptualize marketing communication planning in terms of the appreciative system

- consider planning in relation to the overall marketing communication system and communication programme requirements for marketing performance

- structure your thinking about planning around a simple, coherent planning framework that is based on evaluation and control as essential management functions, but not merely as an annual cycle of decision-making

The mark of a good action is that it appears inevitable in retrospect.

(Robert Louis Stevenson)

Everything should be made as simple as possible, but not simpler.

(Albert Einstein)

INTRODUCTION

Not all marketing communication occurs in a planned programme, but management implies setting out a schedule of actions and resource allocations to be deployed for the accomplishment of a specified goal and objectives.

The marketing plan is an essential aspect of the communication management process. It is, however, only one aspect, and is an input to the process rather than a product of it. The design of the marketing communication system and its programmes of generation, production, and representation should be based on a knowledge-driven rationale and contributory judgements and decisions.

Rarely was the operation of the marketing communication system planned in its won right until relatively recently. Traditionally, communication management for marketing purposes was limited to the 'promotion mix'. Many corporations still do not have a Marketing Communication Manager, but rather a marketing manager, advertising manager, and/or communication manager and public relations manager.

Professional marketing communication planning has to deal with three aspects of the communication required for responsive and responsible marketing relationships.

First, there must be an effective and efficient communication system comprising policies, resources, and performance criteria. Second, there must be specific, measurable, achievable, relevant and timely communication objectives set. Third, the execution of planned strategies must be controlled. The role of marketing research as a provider of knowledge into the appreciative system cannot be stressed too much. Knowledge is required for decision-making, evaluation, and selection.

The planning process must result in the design and operation of a marketing system that is appropriate for providers and their preferred customers (Figure 16.1).

The task of the manager of marketing communication is to evaluate the strategic roles of a variety of communication activities and to use discipline in applying them in such combination as to provide participation, clarity, consistency, and impact. In contemporary marketing, responsiveness with responsibility is paramount (we shall consider responsibility, in ethical terms, in chapter seventeen).

1	Product cues	Packaging (shape & colour, styling), presentation, brand image, guarantee
2	Price cues	List price, credit, discounts, other financial factors
3	Place cues	Quality, location and number of retail outlets; direct-response media, delivery times, distribution
4	Paid-for advertising	Newspapers, magazines, TV, radio, outdoor – all 'above the line' – permanent media
5	Promotion	Direct mail, exhibitions, competitions, financial offers, samples, literature, stationery – all 'below the line'
6	Personal selling and service	Field sales force, service depots and engineers, merchandisers enquiry and complaints hotlines
7	Publicity	Press relations and activities leading to editorial coverage – news and features/stories
8	Third-party messages	What other people outside the organization say about the company and/or its products – word of mouth, opinion formers
9	People as message sources	All the verbal and non-verbal signals from employees (manner, dress, language) – intended or not
10	Passive message sources	Those which were never intended to send messages to customers, but nonetheless do so!

Figure 16.1 **The 10 Ps of marketing communication planning**
Source: Based on Hart, 1995

BEYOND TRADITIONAL MARKETING COMMUNICATIONS

In our contemporary update, we have accepted that mass media persuasive advertising and personal selling are not the limit of marketing communication. Today, with the development of sophisticated electronic media, we can take advantage of a social and relational (or associational) nature of marketing (Duncan and Moriarty, 1998).

To build brand value for everyone's benefit requires planning tools that identify aspects of the complexity of brand communication that have hitherto been ignored or unrecognized. Analyses such as brand message audit, contact point review, and stakeholder mapping can reveal gaps and breakdowns in the communication systems and programmes that cause uncertainty, confusion, and mistrust.

Several simple principles need to be followed:

- Examine marketing relationships from your co-communicator's point of view – what does he/she need and expect? If you cannot answer these questions, ask them!
- Appreciate how customers position your product – features, benefits, value, etc. – if you are not sure, ask them!
- Appreciate the influence of competitors – if unsure, ask your customers and colleagues, trade sources, etc.
- Establish communication objectives.
- Identify your resources.
- Design a balanced portfolio of appropriate marketing communication activities (interactions).
- Monitor the performance of all subsystems.

A quick word about the traditional notion of market research is warranted in our contemporary (communication theory) view of the marketing system as a chain of generative, productive, and representative value-making/value-providing processes. Market research has been viewed as the link between the marketer and the wider public, of which consumers, some of whom become customers, are part. Here we should extend the view: marketing research is the preferred term for the organized activities that draw data into the appreciative system that we call marketing. Thus, just as we saw that an IT-supported knowledge system is needed for customer relationship management, this system ideally also captures data about all interactions with stakeholders, especially customers (and is not limited to only purchase acts), and captures decisions and performance data for continuous evaluation of the performance and the communication and marketing systems. This is an extension of the idea of a marketing information system.

THE PLANNING PROCESS

Intellectually, the planning of resource deployment in an effort to accomplish desirable objectives is sensible. So why do so many managers not manage (by manage, I mean proactively pursue appropriate objectives by deciding how to acquire and use resources)? All too often, marketing communication practice is overly determined by the initiatives of media sales people.

The most basic planning mechanism is an annual plan that describes the objectives that the provider intends to accomplish in the coming year and the budget required to realize these objectives. The annual marketing plan is the mechanism by which the objectives, activities, and budgets for the product development, advertising, sales promotion, and sales and distribution programmes are **integrated**.

The plan serves three basic purposes:

1 Like the various programme plans, annual plans serve as a communication device. They indicate clearly to the personnel involved in marketing what the planned objectives and programmes are, and thus should provide guidance on what activities to pursue.

2 In an organization with a range of products, markets, or other divisions, annual plans serve as important inputs to the resource allocation process. Top management usually will review each annual plan within an organization, assess the corporate resources available, and approve or modify budgets based on an assessment of each unit's needs and contributions.

3 Finally, once approved, the annual plan serves as a mechanism for control. The annual plan establishes standards of performance against which the organization's units' progress can be evaluated. Periodic checks of the gap between actual and planned performance can be useful in making timely modifications to the plan. The overall achievement of the unit is assessed largely on annual performance relative to the plan.

Depending on the diversity of the provider's products and markets and the organization of the corporation, it may be necessary to write a number of plans of varying scope and level:

• business level annual marketing plan
• annual product or department plan
• annual sales plan

We can identify five purposes of the operational marketing plan:

1 to explain the marketing situation now and that expected in the plan period
2 to specify the results expected so that the corporation can anticipate what their situation will be at the end of the plan period
3 to identify the resources needed to carry out the planned actions
4 to describe the actions that are to take place so that responsibility for implementation can be assigned
5 to permit monitoring of the ensuing actions and results

Planning in marketing communication, as in public relations, and especially in advertising, is synonymous with research-based strategy-making. In marketing, the value-creating system should be driven by managers' understanding of the product–market–media relationships. Knowledge and information are essential inputs to strategy-making and action-taking.

Marketing planners have some key questions to answer:

• Who are the people we want as our customers?
• What do they need?
• How can we make it, and profit by this activity?
• How do we tell them?
• How do we deliver it?
• How do we keep ourselves, and them, up to date?

Today, marketing is ever more about service as well as production. Staff have to have answers for customers. As Kevin Gavaghan (1993) said, we cannot afford to be the 'I dunno' society.

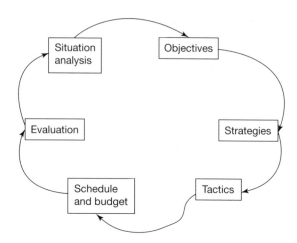

Figure 16.2 **Planning for marketing communication**

Figure 16.2 shows the basic dynamic process of marketing communication planning.

Implementation is that part of the planning process that turns the marketing plan into a programme of actions and ensures that the actions are executed in a manner that can accomplish the plan's stated objectives. Thus, evaluation is part of implementation (but is often omitted or underemphasized in practice).

REMEMBER INTERNAL MARKETING?

The effective implementation of marketing plans is often hampered by insufficient and/or inappropriate interaction among those responsible for formulating plans and those competent and responsible for implementing them. When customers and marketing relationships are placed at the centre of corporate decision-making in order to accomplish corporate and marketing objectives, resentment and hostility can arise from functional managers who see marketing as usurping their authority and power. This can be avoided or abated by interaction that leads to cooperation.

All too often, plans are formulated without participation of the people within the marketing system who can most affect its performance. Commitment to the accomplishment of marketing objectives requires motivation, leadership, and conflict resolution within the value-creation system. Traditional notions of departmental division of responsibility and work can be unhelpful in this respect. Customers simply do not see their interactions in this fashion. Such specializations are convenient for the managers who organize provider resources, but may fragment contact points with customers, thus causing frustration for customers and the value providers themselves (and often for the managers too!).

Successful planning requires a plan for planning, and managers must communicate widely on why a planning system is necessary. They must also recruit top management support and participation, and train line managers in the use of the planning system. The system should be tested on a limited basis to demonstrate its effectiveness and to identify opportunities for enhancement, and ensure that sufficient, timely data are available.

The resulting plan should be designed with both form and function in mind (Figure 16.3).

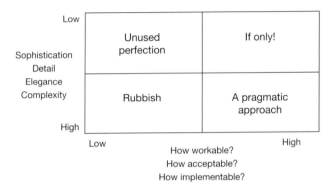

Figure 16.3 **The valuable plan**

Reasons for poor implementation include:

- isolated planning excludes key contributors to implementation or judgement
- long-term and short-term objectives are in conflict
- resistance to change among key contributors
- inadequate resources are provided
- corporate capability is not taken into account
- changes in the trading environment are not detected in a timely fashion
- lack of commitment

These shortcomings can be addressed by ensuring that the management system is marketing oriented, responsive and flexible (i.e. decisions and choices are driven by stakeholder needs and not simply habitual or comfortable), and fully committed to performance monitoring and evaluation. Further, the planning and implementation of a marketing communication system should not be seen as separate (i.e. implementers should also participate in planning); they should be appreciative of the operation and performance of the marketing system).

CORPORATE MEMORY AS A PLANNING AID

Nostalgia is just collective amnesia.

(Dominic Green)

Participative planning through internal marketing allows all to learn by doing. A 'corporate memory' should be created to record successes, mistakes, and omissions, in the evaluation of the effectiveness of plans, of the marketing communication system as a whole, and of the planning process. The corporation can then use this knowledge base to modify and improve procedure and knowledge as required.

At Parcelforce, for example, a live corporate memory was created using simple PC database software. In order to create a record of learning opportunities and results, and to facilitate the spread of best practices throughout the business unit, a database of issues, assignment for action, and outcomes was created. Assignment for action, progress chasing, and identification of past solutions was coordinated by the communications manager.

General Electric facilitated their cross-functional process management of their relationship with key customer Southern California Electric with a database management system that provides universal customer information and a corporate memory (Duncan and Moriarty, 1998).

The concept of a system of planned, measured communication efforts is akin to the creation of a 'corporate intelligence'. Kelley (1968) proposed the introduction of a marketing intelligence system, with major benefits, which include:

* help in expanding time horizons in decision-making and planning
* recognizes and responds to increasing complexity in decision-making as known and unknown factors and their interdependent relationships multiply
* handles the proliferation of data in the information age
* protects management from specialists' distortions, filtering, etc.
* offsets the tendency for top management to become divorced from reality
* opens up new and better sources of information
* allows creative intelligence functions
* provides responsibility for communication and aids the corporation in its communication

See Box 16.1.

Suitability of the marketing communication plan, as it is implemented in a campaign or communication system, can be determined by examining the following factors:

* customer and market data – response
* marketing goals – relevance
* product data – market performance
* tactics – efficiency and effectiveness
* measurement – sensitivity and relevance of data
* communications objectives – contribution of communication outcomes to marketing and wider business goals

---

BOX 16.1   VAGUELY RIGHT OR PRECISELY WRONG?

Clem Sunter's 'scenario thinking' tries to shift managers' thinking of the future as an extension of the past towards analysis of what the corporation can and cannot change, thinking of what now seems trivial as potentially crucial, and holding multiple scenarios in mind as real possibilities.

> The test of a first-rate intelligence is the ability to hold two opposed ideas in the mind at the same time and still retain the ability to function.
>
> (F. Scott Fitzgerald)

> It is the mark of an educated mind to be able to entertain a thought without accepting it.
>
> (Aristotle)

Clem Sunter was Head of Scenario Planning at Anglo American Corporation of South Africa, the world's largest mining group.

The performance of a communication system can be determined through a communication audit. This is a systematic review of the systems for communicating, and their performance.

We should also beware of the inherent delays in any knowledge system that can affect the integrity and coherence of a marketing planning system (Figure 16.4).

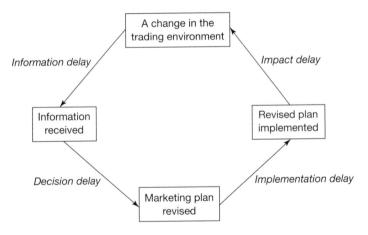

Figure 16.4 **Feedback is often not incorporated in real time**

INTEGRATION OF COMMUNICATION ACTIVITIES

Managers need to appreciate and take account of the core competencies – strengths and weaknesses of the corporation's value-creation system (generation, production, and representation), as well as how the marketing communication activities affect corporate competencies, and the strengths and limitations of the various marketing and marketing communication activities. Integration is itself a core competence (see chapter thirteen for further discussion of integration).

Integration may be created at system or programme level, i.e. integrated marketing system or integrated media deployment. Technologies are now available that allow an intelligence system to be used in decision-making (see CRM in chapter twelve). Information from a wide range of customer contact points can be shared throughout the value-creation system to support learning and decision-making (i.e. appreciation) in the generation, production, and representation of the various forms of knowledge valued by a range of internal and external customers and other stakeholders. Marketing management is today even more about creating an environment within which the voice of the customer is appreciated (i.e. heard, interpreted, valued, and acted upon). This becomes the focus of integration. Teams of specialists from the value-creating chain work together to deliver value to groupings of similar customers (market segments).

EFFECTIVE STRATEGY

To be effective, marketing communication strategy must have certain characteristics:

CONSISTENCY
No inconsistent objectives

CONSONANCE
A genuinely adaptive response to the trading and wider social environment

ADVANTAGE
Providing for the maintenance of competitive advantage

FEASIBILITY
Must not create unsolvable problems or overtax available resources

---

Figure 16.5 **Indispensable characteristics of effective marketing strategy**

Hughes (1980) explains why many plans are never properly carried out. Many marketing plans fail because the planner does not realise that the organisation is not capable of implementing the plan. Short-range plans will require adaptation to the existing organisation, whereas long-range plans may require redesigning the organisation.

Table 16.1 **Roles of stakeholders in the marketing system**

Role	Significance to planners (managers)
As market	People are potential customers (even those who have bought previously may not do so again) for both the medium and the message (e.g. the advertised product, or information), empowered by choice
As dialogue partners	A more dynamic, interaction process among active, contributive people, that aims for understanding, negotiation, and problem-solving, rather than informing
As clients	People are beneficiaries of communicating, with their interests given precedence over those of the planner, and influencers of the communication system operation and content
As communicators	People are active in finding ways to have their voice heard and as mediators

Marketing managers also need to consider the role of the people with whom they are communicating. Windahl *et al.* (1992) identify four possible 'types' of role (Table 16.1).

Of course, we would recognize that all of these roles are stakeholder roles in which either party may initiate the interaction. In the sense that communication is an exchange in interaction, all people are communicators when they interact with the marketing system. This is a subtle, but significant bias in our thinking. Marketing management can gain by taking this wider perspective that recognizes consumers and buyers as real people in all of these social system roles.

EVALUATION OF COMMUNICATIVE ACTION

The myth of efficiency lies in the assumption that the most efficient manager is *ipso facto* the most effective; actually the most efficient manager working on the wrong task will not be effective.

(R. Alec Mackenzie, management consultant and author of *The Time Trap*)

A common problem in planned communication is that the choice of medium is made too early in the process. This is beginning the communication planning process at the wrong end (Windhal *et al.*, 1992). It is essential in ensuring that effective and efficient communication is also responsive and responsible that the strategic role of communication activities (means/mode) is examined and judged prior to the tactical selection of media.

The analysis should focus on the impact of communicating in particular modes, using particular means (methods and tools), and in particular styles, at the points of interaction. In measuring results of communication activities, the total communication system has to be considered, i.e. the linear hierarchy of communication effects – awareness, attitude change, behavioural change – does not always occur (Ray, 1973).

The measurement of performance requires examination of both efficiency and effectiveness (Figure 16.6).

Low efficiency with low effectiveness = sudden death	High efficiency with low effectiveness = disappointment
Low efficiency with high effectiveness = improvement opportunity	*High performance management*

Figure 16.6 **Strategic and tactical performanc**

Efficiency measures examine the cost of communication efforts (in financial and other terms), while effectiveness measures examine the extent to which intended effects are accomplished (see Figure 16.7).

	Intended/foreseen	Unintended/unforeseen
Constructive	'We've successfully accomplished our objectives'	'Don't you just love it when a plan comes together?'
Destructive	'The price of success!'	'What went wrong?'

Figure 16.7 **Types of communication effect**

Imagine you are one of a party of tourists that is lost in a forest. As a tactician, you will choose a direction and march in search of escape. The strategist will, on the other hand, climb a tree so as to determine the best direction to walk.

In practice, evaluation is not as common as the logic would suggest it should be. Reasons for the absence of the evaluation element of the communication management system are:

- evaluation is too demanding of limited resources
- the planner/manager dare not find out the truth about the effectiveness of the system and his/her plan
- communication campaigns are treated as ends in themselves such that the aim is accomplished only when the campaign is completed

Actually, marketing managers can afford to be somewhat more confident of their professional value than can public relations managers. The latter are even less likely to invest in a full management system incorporating evaluation. But beware, this should certainly not be taken as an excuse or justification for failing to manage.

Evaluation is demanding and burdens the manager, but benefits both the system and the programme.

EVALUATING MARKETING COMMUNICATION ACTIVITY

The evaluation aspect of the marketing management process involves making carefully judged objectives and media selections and measuring performance results against predetermined goals. Evaluation enables managers to determine the effectiveness of their implementation and to plan corrective action where necessary.

We can imagine evaluation operating at four levels in the marketing system, as shown in Figure 16.8.

Communication audit	Concerned with the overall performance of the corporate systems for communicating
Marketing research	Attention to the performance of the overall marketing system
Media research	Supports the selection of modes for communication and media for communicating
Promotion (advertising) research	Examines the effects of messages and content

Figure 16.8 **Evaluating the marketing system**

Summative evaluation is research carried out after execution to explain whether or not the objectives of the system or campaign have been met and allows a proper decision about continuation. Formative evaluation is much more valuable as a planning tool. This effort produces knowledge that is fed back into the process to assist managers in making improvement decisions. The professional communication manager will assess all effects of their activities – both functional and dysfunctional (see Figure 16.7 above).

A marketing audit is a key element in a total marketing evaluation programme. Most companies are victims of at least some misdirected marketing effort. The 80–20 principle suggests that a large proportion of total orders, customers, sales territories, or products accounts for only a small share of total sales or profit. Conversely, a small proportion produces a large share of sales or profit. Thus marketing efforts tend to be proportional to the number of territories, customers, or products, rather than to their actual sales volume or profit. The iceberg principle suggests that only a small part of the detail of figures for sales, costs, and other performance measures are readily visible to managers. Total sales or cost figures are too general to be of use in evaluation, and may actually be misleading. Thus managers are required to make decisions based on inadequate information about costs and paybacks.

The evaluation process has 3 steps:

1 find out what has happened
2 find out why it happened
3 decide what to do about it

Tools for identifying misdirected marketing efforts are:

• sales volume analysis
• market-share analysis
• market cost analysis

These can be studied by product lines and market segments (sales territories or customer groups).

General marketing performance measures to be monitored for control purposes are:

• unit sales
• sales value (£)
• sales in specific market segments
• marketing costs
• production costs
• market share
• customer ratings of product quality
• customer ratings of service provided

What might be measured to control marketing communication activities?

ADVERTISING EFFECTIVENESS

The Knowability Paradox: The less we have known about how advertising and the media work, the more advertising and media there have been.

(Rothenberg, 1998)

Most discussion of evaluation is centred on advertising because it is the most tangible of marketing communication activities in our general experience. Examination of advertising evaluation will provide us with a basis for considering the wider need for judging the most appropriate mode of communication and the effectiveness and efficiency of subsequent activities.

Although it has long been believed that the aim of advertising effort is to increase sales, sustained growth is apparently rare. Jones (1998), for example, suggests that short-term results are the exception and long-term results are no more than a lottery. The scope for strongly persuasive advertising, in reality, to persuade people to make a purchase seems very limited or even nil due to competition. As for the future, see Box 16.2.

BOX 16.2   KNOWING WHAT GETS A RESPONSE

A barcode scanner and smartcard reader is to be incorporated into a TV remote control unit. When you see an advertisement you like, you use the unit to read a product offer and download a coupon into a smartcard to be used next time you go shopping. The manufacturer and retailer have no doubt about the response to their advertisement.

Evaluation may be carried out formally or on an ad hoc basis as part of the management process. The control of resource use is essential if planned communication is to have a desirable impact among a diverse group of stakeholders. Review and evaluation also provides an opportunity for learning, problem-solving, development, and refinement. Managers primarily evaluate communication activities and programmes to check that communication objectives have been met and that communication strategies deployed have had the desired effect(s) – see Figure 16.9. Secondarily, evaluation ensures a check on the efficiency with which resources have been used.

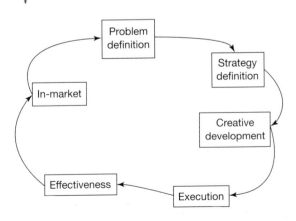

Figure 16.9 **The promotion research process**

Media selection decisions will include the extent of reach among the target social group and the cost of accomplishing this (cost per thousand reached). Pre-testing aims to predict the likely effectiveness of an advertisement. Panels are brought together to examine product concepts and communication proposals for meanings and weaknesses (especially copy testing), while motivation research tries to identify unconscious associations of ideas and words in the advertisement.

Once an advertisement has been run, evaluation can be conducted in the environment in which it is intended to accomplish results. The number of enquiries directly generated can be gauged from response cards, returned coupons, and 0800 telephone calls, as well as from the number of orders placed (see Boxes 16.3 and 16.4). Recall and comprehension tests examine the impression on consumer memory by interviewing several hundred people, often on the day after the advertisement ran. Although the validity of these tests is relatively low, they are reliable, and are commonly used to benchmark performance against other products and advertisements. However, they tend to be poor predictors of sales. Recognition of advertising is the most commonly tested, since it is more reliable and valid, as well as cheaper. Krugman's (1988) research suggests that readers of magazines are making a consumer vote when they indicate recognition, since they are identifying those advertisements that they find attractive and thus this may indicate likeability.

Sales tests are poor indicators since sales can only come from past actions and are only partly the result of these. Only direct-response sales and enquiries can show the result of advertising, and only then if properly monitored. Financial analysis is essential for those products for which advertising expenditure is a major resource. Variance analysis, for example, shows deviation from planned expenditure.

Tracking studies (consumer panels) use regular interviews among consumers to gauge impact on their attitude to a brand during a campaign, thus allowing adjustments to be made quickly if necessary. Questions are asked about awareness, brand image, products attributes, and consumer preferences. Stock held by retailers can also be monitored during a period of planned advertising. As mentioned earlier, the likeability of an advertisement has been shown to be a particularly good predictor of sales, but this is not as simple as it sounds. To be well liked, the advertisement has to be for a product that has personally significant value (i.e. it has to be thought by the person to be relevant, believable, credible, useful, interesting, and so on).

BOX 16.3   NIELSEN'S PEOPLE METER

As a more accurate viewer-sampling technology than the Audimeter it replaced, this has shown that far fewer people are watching television than was previously believed by TV executives.

BOX 16.4 GAUGING THE INTERNET

With the advent of Internet advertising, many marketers are wondering if advertisement impression remains the most appropriate measure of effectiveness. Some, like the interactive team at Proctor & Gamble, are rethinking what constitutes 'effective', and then how to pay for it. Options include: cost-per-thousand impressions, sponsorships, performance-based payment, and hybrids of these.

Because the Internet is essentially an interactive addressable medium, advertising impressions are no longer the sole (and rather abstract) means of measuring performance. Click-throughs, customer leads generated, and sales made are more tangible indicators of performance.

Of course, it is the consumer/buyer who has the real power to determine what is 'successful' advertising. Effective advertisements are those that are liked, that is, they are judged to be meaningful, pertinent, believable, and worthwhile – not merely entertaining. Brand advertising mobilizes the symbolic, rather than the literal. Increasingly brand properties are linked with lifestyle – motivations, needs, attitudes.

Measures of the impact of advertising include: brand name recognition, brand recall, attitude to provider. Attempts are also being made to apply psychological testing to gauge net positive cognitive responses. A range of techniques are used to study the effects of advertising (East, 1997). Some techniques are summarized in Figure 16.10.

Focus group and interview	A quick, relatively cheap way to assess response and meanings, but lacks validity and reliability
Case study	An illustrative, but not representative, way to understand campaign development and its effects
Experiment	Allow inference of causal relationships by controlling extraneous influences, but laboratory findings may not apply in normal conditions
Survey	Particularly valuable when data about consumer/buyer characteristics are generated, allowing demographic, usage and viewing pattern analysis to be added
Consumer data panel	Diaries and bar code scanning can reveal purchase patterns that can be related to advertising schedules
Econometric analysis	Various mathematical techniques can be applied to survey and panel data
Data fusion	Combines data from two sources using common elements, for example television viewing from one panel and purchases from another

Figure 16.10 **Techniques for measuring advertising response**

Each marketing communication activity (subsystem) can be assigned a customer response index, based on historic data on impact and predictions of future cost-effectiveness. This would provide a dynamic decision-support tool for prioritizing the allocation of effort to specific communication objectives.

CONTROLLING COMMUNICATION EFFORT

The control responsibility of the management system commissions evaluation research and takes the findings into the decision-making process.

The basic process for controlling the communication system is common with that for all management functions. Specific and appropriate performance standards have to be set and responsibility assigned for accomplishing the level of performance determined. Actual performance has to be evaluated and compared with the standards and corrective action taken if deemed necessary. Of course, this is the appreciative system we have also applied to the marketing system as a whole. This basic process is illustrated in Figure 16.11.

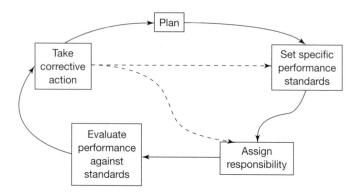

Figure 16.11 **The basic process of control**

Many 'creative' people will resist the notion of control. The purpose is not to constrain overly marketing management, but to ensure 'good housekeeping' for the benefit of all stakeholders.

The marketing plan is a tool for coordination but also a control device. This is designed to ensure that the organization of activities takes account of changes in: competitor actions; buyers' willingness and ability to buy; and other environment factors such as developments in communication systems, media, and evaluation techniques. It must also provide data to help to answer the question: how productive are the marketing communication programmes in accomplishing marketing objectives?

Post-action control occurs at the end of the planning period when the degree of success achieved is reviewed and the causes of any gaps between planned and actual performance are isolated. The new knowledge is used to develop future plans.

Steering control applies where performance deviations can be identified early, and managers can take corrective action; the plan can be adjusted to meet the original or modified objectives.

The corrective-action approach requires the manager to:

- select the performance measures to be monitored
- compare actual and planned performance at appropriate time intervals
- specify the acceptable degree of deviation
- identify implications of the deviations
- modify the plan to steer it towards the objectives

Both internal performance monitoring and trading environment monitoring should be attempted, and this requires:

- a plan for planning
- a planning system
- and a marketing intelligence system

THE COST OF COMMUNICATION EFFORT

The means for communicating and the possibilities for impact and effect are determined largely by the resources that are applied. How is the budget allocation determined, then? Typically, a fixed proportion of sales is allocated, or the spending of competing providers is monitored. Alternatively, whatever is available is deployed. Ideally, the level of resource application needed to accomplish the stated objectives is decided.

In a sense, all actions are read as communicating by those who attend to the people, products, company, industry, and market. Perhaps another crucial question is: what does it cost us when we try not to communicate with our customers and other stakeholders, or do not pay sufficient attention to our own and their communication needs?

When we think of marketing communication budgets, we tend to think of the purchase of advertising space, printing of product brochures, and charges for trade shows, and so on. However, the cost of building and effectively operating the total communication system, including the planning system, is a major investment that can reap great rewards for all stakeholders.

THE ALLOCATION OF FUNDS

Once marketing objectives have been set, a corresponding set of communication objectives can be decided. Only then can an overall budget be decided and an appropriate allocation among advertising, personal selling, publicity, sales promotion, exhibitions, and so on.

But how do you decide which of the various communication activities to spend your limited budget on and how much to spend? The budget decision needs some kind of judgement about the likely impact of the numerous options. This will be a complex of the nature of the product–market relationship, the stage of the life cycle, the financial resources available, and the cost of services available to the provider. Several approaches to budget allocation are outlined in Table 16.2.

Table 16.2 **Budget-setting approaches**

Budgeting approach	Comment
Percentage of sales	A fixed portion of sales income is allocated (ignores objectives and strategy)
Share of market	Implies that offerings are not differentiated
Investment (pay-out planning)	Takes the view that impact can be reasonably estimated on volume
Competitive parity	No account of effect is taken in simply trying to match competing activity
Maximum affordable	Ignores impact and assumes that greater benefit is gained from higher spending
Zero-based planning (objective and task)	Based on prioritized SWOT analysis, to identify those activities that are the most cost-effective ways to capitalize on critical strengths and opportunities, while addressing significant weaknesses and threats

Perhaps the reader can sense the preferred method for the author! Funds are required for the purchase of media (print space, brochures, postage, website maintenance, etc.), but also for marketing communication system management, evaluation research, training and development of staff, and so on.

WHAT DO YOU THINK?

1 Write a concise rationale for managing a marketing communication planning system.
2 How can the communication plan contribute to integration of communication policies, decisions, and activities?
3 Planning may be no more than mindless ritual. How might this arise, and what are the benefits to be gained from managing a sound strategic thinking process?
4 'Marketing communication planning is itself a form of marketing communication.' Explain this notion.
5 How does planning motivate?
6 Plans often languish in desk drawers and are not used to make decisions that have strategic consequences for marketing. Why might this happen, and what can be done to overcome this management weakness?

7 Discuss the strategic importance of research in designing the marketing communication system.

8 Revisit the concept of the appreciative system. Use this to explain the planning process in marketing communication management.

9 Evaluation is the control function of marketing communication management. How is this so?

10 Carry out a small survey of recent marketing literature. What are the 'new' evaluation methods offered by consultants and agencies, and what benefits are claimed for them by their vendors?

FURTHER READING

Bonoma, T. (1989) 'Marketing performance – what do you expect?', *Harvard Business Review*, September–October: 44–7.

Eadie, D. R. and Kitchen, P. J. (1999) 'Measuring the success rate: evaluating the marketing communications process and marcomm programmes', in Kitchen, P. J. (ed.) *Marketing Communications: Principles and Practice*, London: International Thomson Business Press, pp. 459–76.

Gilligan, C. (1995) *Marketing Communications: Planning, Implementation and Control*, Oxford: Butterworth-Heinemann.

Hargie, O. and Tourish, D. (eds) (2000) *Handbook of Communication Audits for Organisations*, London: Routledge.

McDonald, M. H. B. (1992) *The Marketing Planner*, Oxford: Butterworth-Heinemann/CIM.

Smith, P. R., Berry, C. and Pulford, A. (1997) *Strategic Marketing Communications: New Ways to Build and Integrate Communications*, London: Kogan Page.

Wilson, R. M. S., Gilligan, C. T. and Pearson, D. J. (1992) *Strategic Marketing Management: Planning, Implementation and Control*, Oxford: Butterworth-Heinemann/CIM.

Windahl, S., Signitzer, B. and Olson, J. T. (1992) *Using Communication Theory: An Introduction to Planned Communication*, London: Sage Publications.

chapter
seventeen

PROFESSIONALISM

LEARNING POINTS

Careful study of this chapter will help you to:

- anticipate the nature of the job of marketing communication manager in terms of role and responsibilities within the management system as communication catalyst, interpreter, mediator, and communicator

- consider the need for, and obligations of, the responsible and responsive communicator (i.e. the ethics of communicating)

This communicating of a Man's Selfe to his Frend works two contrarie effects; for it redoubleth Joys, and cutteth Griefs in halves.

(Francis Bacon)

Tolerance is the virtue of those who do not believe much.

(G. K. Chesterton)

The hottest places in hell are reserved for those who in times of great moral crisis maintain their neutrality.

(Dante)

In that first age of mankind, men knew neither laws nor revenge.

(Ransmayr, 1991)

Market discipline is a good servant, but a dangerous master.

(Michael Grade)

INTRODUCTION

Is ethics the forbidden topic for capitalist hegemonists – managers, shareholders, and politicians?

Consuming now dominates all other modes of social activity: producing, using, appreciating, participating. This has serious impact on how we appropriate our world. People as individual persons are socially constructed, but not merely as consumers. Is the attainment of a 'good life' synonymous to rising living standards, through better and bigger consumption?

Ethical questions deal with diversity and difference, when conflict arises between those who are 'other than'. What ethical concerns are significant to the manager of marketing communication? Consider:

- Do marketers reflect on the externalized costs of their decisions and actions?
- What forms of consumption are ethically questionable and damaging to the environment?
- Is the market-based system of consumerism ethically terminally unhealthy?
- Do consumers consider the origins of the commodities they simply have to have?

The marketing communication manager has to be an amateur (reflective) cultural critic. Ethical standards ensure that representation and expression are not misleading, deceitful, exploitative, demeaning, irritating, wasteful, arrogant, or servile.

MANAGING ETHICALLY

Snell (1999) points out four basic objections to the idea of ethics for business. Psychological egotism sees people as only ever pursuing their own immediate interests. But our experience shows us that this is fairly rare since people are successful in business when acting altruistically, with benevolence, in the service of others as 'good citizens'. A Machiavellian analysis of power suggests that to get to the top requires manipulation, controlling and altering information, lobbying, impression management, ingratiation, controlling scarce resources, and so on. Attention to business ethics would then require the surrender of these power-gaining and power-wielding tactics. Some people believe that business has its own form of rules. However, this is unsatisfactory since it implies that business does not impact on wider society. Another objection is that legally acceptable action is also morally acceptable. But much that is unethical in the working environment never comes under legal scrutiny. Milton Friedman (1970) condemned the 'doctrine of social responsibility' in his agency argument. Corporate employees are contractually obliged, he argued, to serve the interests of the employer within the law. Anything else is effectively stealing from the employer. Investment in wider community interest should not go beyond what will return a pay-off in corporate image, consumer loyalty, share price, limitations on regulatory interference, and so on. But business decisions can impose great cost (harm, damage, etc.) on others. Friedman's view is exclusionary, self-serving ideology that regards people as worth little.

Snell (1999) highlights the essentials of ethical thought and argument. Utilitarianism judges the moral worth of actions in terms of the utility of their foreseeable consequences for everyone affected (cost versus benefit). Actions leading to the greatest net benefit for the greatest number of people are favoured. This approach examines what is produced and its consequences but not the process. A complementary approach is deontology. This assumes that we are morally obliged to follow fundamental principles in our inter-actions. Thus, act only as you would wish to be universal for everyone and how you want others to treat you. Also, never treat a person as a means to an end but rather as an end in himself or herself. This protects against egotism. A middle-ground position is the five forms of justice: compensatory compen-sates for harm or violation; retributive punishes bad deeds; procedural requires fair procedures, practices, and agreements; distributive concerns the handing out of benefits and burdens; and interactional is concerned with the quality of treatment received from a decision-maker and the extent to which formal decision procedures are properly adhered to. Finally, the service of stakeholders is counter to Friedman's 'business as a game', taking into account the many people who are affected by or affect business decisions and actions. This approach emphasizes the building of trust and cooperation among all stakeholders – requiring political sensitivity and communicative/ interactional competence.

We will consider the need for ethical communication systems as the basis for ethical marketing communication later in this chapter.

THE CORE ASSUMPTIONS OF CONSUMERISM

One force that managers cannot ignore is the basic right of consumers and buyers to be able to use accurate and full information, to receive safe products, to have adequate product choices, and to use products that do not harm the physical and psychological environment. A trend, begun in the 1960s, is consumer and buyer rebellion against marketing hyperbole and corporations that purposefully mislead, offer restricted choice of alternatives, or sell unsafe products. This trend is manifest in consumerism. Actions may be taken by consumer activist groups, government agencies, and (sometimes) corpora-tions to protect consumers in the process of exchange.

Marketing communication managers have a responsibility to ensure that their communication systems are providing information about products in an ethical fashion:

- markets alone cannot deal with the consumer's need for free and fair information
- consumers need information if they are to avoid unscrupulous and inefficient suppliers
- inadequate goods will survive unless consumers have adequate information

- companies are not the only suppliers of such information

We have emphasized that marketing managers must try to understand consumer behaviour (see chapter three), but the consumer/buyer perspective can be very different. How do the respective perspectives differ? Table 17.1 summarizes three important differences.

Table 17.1 **Potential sources of 'marketing' abuse**

Managerial perspective	Consumer perspective
Most marketing strategies are specific to a single product	Consumers make decisions across a range of brand alternatives, and see a particular product as part of a larger constellation that reflects their lifestyle – thus products are related that are not related by the respective marketers
Managers have a vested interest in presenting their own products in the best light and are motivated to do so for their own profit – information is a material for influencing	Consumers are interested in evaluating information for their own needs – information helps make better decisions
Competition is viewed as a threat	Competition provides additional alternatives, often at lower cost

Source: Based on Assael, 1995

What are the implications of these differing views on the marketing exchange? Marketer's decisions and actions could lead to deceptive advertising, limited product choices, inadequate attention to product safety, and avoidance of ecological responsibilities. Consumerism has arisen to protect against the few instances of abuse when the free market fails. The term consumerism has four distinct meanings:

1 a set of values
2 a way of life
3 a political ideology
4 the process of advancing the cause of consumers in their role as purchasers and users of goods and services, through organized reaction to real or imagined inadequacies of marketers, markets, market mechanisms, government, and consumer policy

Marketers can best accomplish profit goals in solid exchange relationships with customers by offering high-quality products and accurate information.

THE ETHICAL CONSUMER

Earlier in this book, we saw that consumers may behave in a wholly unmanageable manner, as rebels and as activists – this is a problem for the manager who wants to manage consumption-based exchanges (see Gabriel and Lang, 1995: chapters 8 and 9).

It would be desirable to marketing managers with sales and profit objectives to accomplish to imagine consumers as malleable, seducible, and manageable – and convenient if they were so. But much contemporary consumption is unexpected, creative, and unmanageable. It is not so much that people reject consumer products or consumption, but rather that appropriations and uses of products are unorthodox.

Many centuries ago, the Greek philosopher Epicurus recognized that advertisers were to blame for people's unhappiness. The bombardment of offers of satisfaction blurs people's sense of true needs and desires. For example, Alain de Botton (2000), claims of a contemporary coffee commercial, it is the friends we want to buy, not the coffee. Much unreflective marketing activity does not provide us with the means for happiness as is often claimed. It is choice that brings happiness, it is friends, freedom, and reflection, says Epicurian philosophy.

Some principles for a different type of consumption are:

- consume less
- consume local products
- avoid products produced and merchandised by big business
- avoid cash and use alternative modes of economic transaction (for example, the Local Exchange Trading Schemes – see Box 17.1)

BOX 17.1   LOCAL EXCHANGE TRADING SCHEMES (LETS)

These are local community-based mutual aid networks in which people exchange goods and services, without the need for money.

Since the first experimental scheme was established in British Columbia in 1982, the system has spread to the USA, New Zealand, Australia, the UK, and elsewhere. At least 40,000 people are involved in the 450 schemes currently operating in the UK. Each is established on a democratic and cooperative model.

The LETS principle is simple – what is needed is a medium for communication for those who produce and supply and those who need and want – a personal relationship without mediation!

(See www.letslinkuk.org)

Some have taken to reaffirming the moral and political dimensions of consumer choice in ethical consumerism. Consumers are urged by activists to make providers socially responsible by recognizing brand purchase as a vote that is heard by corporations. Criteria of choice would include: charitable donations; the advancement of women; the advancement of minorities; military contracts; animal testing; disclosure of information; community outreach, nuclear power; fair trade; the environment; land rights; donations to political parties; and so on. Consumers are asked to consider not only the product, but the environmental impact of its production, use, and disposal, as well as the working conditions of its producers and distributors.

Consumers are also asked to become activists. Boycotts (saying 'no' to certain providers and their products) are not simply threats to or punishments for unscrupulous marketers. Such consumer actions against particular exchanges are manifestations of relationship breakdowns. The core assumptions of consumerism may be questioned and new alternatives surfaced. The effectiveness of consumer boycotts depends on their visibility. These 'moral acts' by consumers can affect public consciousness and corporate policies, at least in the short term, and are especially damaging to share prices.

MANAGERIALISM AND SYSTEMATIC DISTORTION OF COMMUNICATION

> Communication is distorted whenever genuine
> conversation is precluded.
>
> (Deetz)

There is a rather limiting and counterproductive practice that is not management. Deetz (1992) has defined this managerialism as 'a kind of systemic logic, a set of routine practices, and an ideology'. He goes on to specify that it is 'a way of conceptualising, reasoning through, and discussing events', but it also involves 'a set of routine practices, real structures of rewards, and a code of representation. It is a way of doing and being in corporations that partially structures all groups and conflicts with, and at times suppresses, each group's other modes of thinking' (Deetz, 1992: 222).

According to Deetz (1992), managerialism is characterized by:

- The desire for control and economic goals.
- A will to dominate, where the means to accomplish organizational goals (efficiency, rationality, conflict resolution or suppression) become ends in themselves.
- The managerial prerogative to decide what is to be done, when, where, and by whom. This is an arbitrary privilege for articulating life/world issues in terms of corporate costs, shifting the decisional responsibility from other corporate members to the manager.
- A cognitive–instrumental mode of reasoning, based on the belief that if one can completely understand all work processes, one can completely control them. Instrumental–technical reasoning aims at control, mastery, growth and material gain. It claims that values are in ends and that means are neutral.

- Power and money are the means to translate practical reasoning (pursuit of meaningful existence; satisfaction of social and symbolic needs; attempt to reach understanding; ends orientation) into instrumental reasoning. Everything that cannot be adequately translated into money, or has elements beyond managerial control is suppressed. For example, conflicts over values that are difficult to mediate tend to be suppressed through naturalization, neutralization, or subjectification.
- Efficiency remains above moral reproach. Coordination is achieved by distorting or suppressing some conflicts, especially those that defy the routinization and present alternative forms of rationality.
- The pursuit of pleasure in the service of efficiency. Meaningful work, participation in decision-making, and the enhancement of the autonomy of personnel are goods if they are strategic means to technical–instrumental control. There is no genuine concern for others' rights.
- The formal organization is its favoured site of reproduction. Authority and subordination are the preferred ways to represent the functional relations in corporations because this hierarchical basis assures managerial superiority.
- Managerialism is legitimated by all the members of the corporation, who accept it as natural and necessary without questioning its practice.

Deetz (1992) argued that in managerialism lay the ground for the systematic distortion of communication within organizations. This is because, from a participative perspective, communication problems arise as a consequence of value discussion and conflict preclusion. Systems of domination usually preclude genuine conversation. In managerialistic performance, consensus is reached only through authority and relations of power.

Genuine conversation entails for all the participants:

1 Symmetrical distribution of the opportunities to express one's ideas and opinions, and to choose what to say. Access to meaningful forums and channels of communication; equal access to communication technologies and distribution of training opportunities, etc.
2 Freedom from privileged preconceptions concerning the understanding and representation of the external world, i.e. from ideologies that would privilege one form of discourse, disqualify certain possible participants, and universalize any particular sectional interest.
3 The opportunity to establish legitimate social relations and norms for conduct and interaction. Rights and responsibilities are negotiated through interaction. Authority legitimation is earned with trust and natural leadership.
4 Freedom from coercive and hegemonic processes, to allow participants to express their own authentic interests, needs, and feelings.

Furthermore, a participatory communication practice requires an ongoing production of mutual understanding through the common formation of meaning and normative values. Conversely, the mechanistic, one-sided, 'arrow' managerial vision of effective communication is based primarily on reproductive fidelity, on the successful presentation of one's own meaning or point of view. In addition, the natural asymmetry and subordination of the manager–employee relationship makes arbitrariness possible, and could foster explicit strategic manipulation and instrumental uses of communication, for example, precluding conflict that challenges 'the institutional view'.

However, as Deetz emphasized, 'the more serious issues' rely on 'the invisible constraints to richer understanding', where 'strategy and manipulation are disguised, and control is exercised through manipulations of the natural, neutral, and self-evident'. 'Systematically distorted communication operates like strategic manipulation, but without overt awareness.' For example, the members of a corporation do not see the adopted methods of control as a violation of basic moral rights or misrepresentation of interests (Deetz, 1992). In fact, they accept them as natural, thus providing a false consensus.

Human communication is full of dysfunctional systematic distortions as well as modern organizations. 'We see people unwittingly act in opposition to their own values and needs' (Deetz, 1992). Habermas (1984), described this situation thus:

> Such communication pathologies [systematic distortion] can be conceived of as the result of a confusion between actions oriented to reaching understanding [communicative action] and actions oriented to success [strategic actions]. In situations of concealed strategic action [manipulation], at least one of the parties operates with an orientation to success, but leaves others to believe that all the presuppositions of communicative action are satisfied. On the other hand, [in systematically distorted communication] at least one of the parties is deceiving himself [sic] about the fact that he is acting with an appearance of communicative action.
>
> (Quoted in Deetz, 1992:)

Systematic communication distortions are produced by the structural and legitimated way of being and doing in corporations, and are thus protected from assessment (Deetz, 1992). They are by-products of the monopolization of exchanges, and of the opportunities to define the organization and its goals as well as the latent strategic normalization and routinization of potential conflict suppression. For example, corporation members do not elect directors, but nobody questions their authority.

Active processes of 'discursive closure' (Deetz, 1992) take place to avoid the expression of different ideas, interests, and opinions and its open negotiation, although individuals believe they are engaging in communication action for the pursuit of mutual understanding. In all of them, the latent prejudice, preconception, predefined personal identity or one-sidedness in the reproduction of meaning precludes responsiveness to an exterior, and therefore, scarce learning.

To improve the quality of working life, there is a need of a more democratic and 'moral communicative practice' fundamentally rooted in corporate citizenship. Freed from the domination of arbitrary privileged considerations, it should enable equal participation in the construction of meaning and identity, and in the definition of the good and the right. This implies the open presentation of the values and criteria used in decision-making, and the recovery of conflicts that have been suppressed through systematic distortion of communication (see Deetz, 1992) so as not to have to confront hard questions and diversity.

Jacobs (1992) has observed that there are often two contradicting cultures operating in a social group: government (usually an elected representation in bureaucratic administration – of course, managers are not elected by their constituency!), and management (the use of contrivance to effect some purpose. These 'cultures' are incommensurate, but both are necessary, reflecting the two basic ways of living a life:

1 **taking**: territorial responsibility (guardianship)
2 **trading**: commerce (exchange)

The guardian moral syndrome is concerned with, and characterized by:

* the work of protecting, acquiring, exploiting, administering, or controlling territories
* precepts: exert prowess; obedience and discipline; tradition; hierarchy; loyalty; ostentation; largesse; exclusion; fortitude; fatalism; honour – and shuns trading

The commercial moral syndrome is concerned with, and characterized by:

* commerce and the production of goods and services for commerce, and most scientific work
* precepts: voluntary agreements; honesty; easy collaboration; competition; contract; initiative and enterprise; open to novelty; efficiency; thrift; investment for productive purposes, optimism

The problem is not one of how to replace one with the other, but how to operate the two cultures together in supportive harmony. This requires of the manager a moral flexibility, in which managers:

* abandon 'scientific management', away from cynical management (exploitative, oppositional, obstructive, bureaucracy)
* work towards social technocracy for order, but not through mere control
* recognize managing as social and political activity $\Rightarrow$ stewardship, rather than ownership: balance guardian and commercial 'mindsets' to avoid 'rancid hybrids' (Jacobs, 1992).

Managers also have to resist: cynical management that is unreflective, unresponsive, self-referential, managerialistic – the fatal conceit of knowing what is to be known (Hayek, 1990); creating and operating systematically distorted communication systems (in which the conduit metaphor for 'communication' precludes participation; and our argument culture in which we persuade and argue, when dialogue and partnership are more constructive (remember Vickers' ladder of communication forms?). Thus, mere interaction becomes interchange (Tannen 1999).

ETHICAL COMMUNICATION

Management textbooks do not deal adequately with ethical questions, and even much of the growing literature on corporate communication management fails to engage with the issues. Avoidance of the question of ethical communicative behaviour presupposes the neutral social role or conservative or radical advocacy roles of communication management. Clampitt (1991) is an exception, and explains the paucity of ethical considerations in contemporary texts, as follows:

1 Many people believe that discussing ethics will inevitably lead to imposing one's morality on others, thus undermining their discretion and responsibility. Ironically, argues Clampitt, this stance is itself unethical.
2 Ethics is often seen as irrelevant to the basic purpose of business. The argument focuses only on the 'bottom line' and job satisfaction. But people are the heart and soul of business, and so any human community must be concerned with the human condition.
3 Ethical discussions are avoided because they are complex and 'it all depends on the situation'. Because every situation is unique, it is argued, any attempt at fundamental ethical principles is likely to fail. Clampitt does not accept such a relativistic view.

In debating the ethical conduct of communicators (i.e. those who communicate), Clampitt (1991) raises three fundamental assumptions:

1 Every communication decision has some ethical dimension, whether acknowledged or not. In choosing to speak, the communicator chooses to disclose information, motives, or feelings. Judging whether this communication should occur is partly an ethical decision, if only because silence signals acquiescence or tacit agreement. So are questions of how and when to communicate. People inevitably make ethical judgements in choosing the time, the subject, and the mode of the communication they initiate. In every act of listening we are also making a moral stand, by deciding whether we wish to know what the speaker can tell us.
2 Communication ethics inevitably involves both motives and impacts. When the motive for someone's behaviour is deceit, then the outcome is immoral. But what about good motives that produce bad impacts? Both actions and their ultimate impacts must be considered.
3 In considering the ethical nature of communication, we must consider simultaneously who communicates what with whom, where, and when.

Clampitt (1991) provides a catalogue of ethical dilemmas facing the manager, all of which concern behaviour and communicative actions:

- secrecy (intentional concealment)
- whistle-blowing (publication of information about corporate or fellow colleagues' abuses or negligence)
- leaks (anonymous whistle-blowing)
- rumours and gossip (speculation and unconfirmed reports)
- lying (a false statement intended to deceive)
- euphemisms (use of a less offensive expression to avoid causing distress)
- ambiguity (vagueness which can cause misinterpretation)
- apology (reforming or transforming perceptions of motive and reputation)

The problem is one of ensuring that people and corporations strive for ethical behaviour. Ethical organizations are created and sustained by individuals of personal integrity, operating in a culture of principle, and governed by conscientious policies. Policy is concerned with what and how information is gathered, and with how it is used. This information may be about, or be desired by, the individual, the corporation, and/or the community. In terms of individual character, Clampitt suggests five tests for engendering a spirit of honourable communication:

1 discretion: the intuitive ability to discern what is and is not intrusive and injurious, so as to be able to navigate in and between the worlds of personal and shared experience
2 relevancy: deals with the question of what to communicate and what information is necessary
3 accuracy: requires that communicators deal with truth and reliable information
4 fairness: requires that speaking and listening are judicious in avoiding ambiguity, correcting inaccuracy, defending reputation, and dealing with impropriety
5 timing: when to communicate is a question of judgement – of not restricting someone else's choices or undermining truth and trust

Leaders have to place significant trust in their stakeholders, to the extent that allowing 'their' values to be assimilated and contribute to the process of evolving and building 'our ethics'. Employees and managers need to be part of this evolution. The fragmentation of diversity places particular emphasis on ethics.

THE SOCIAL RESPONSIBILITIES OF THE MARKETER

We have seen that marketing managers are responsible for ensuring that the basic right of consumers and buyers to be able to use accurate and full information, to receive safe products, to have adequate product choices, and to use products that do not harm the physical and psychological environment is upheld in marketing decision-making and actions. They must also be sure to be aware of the impact of what they decide and do. Marketing communication management has a responsibility to ensure that communication systems are not distorted and are potentially participative, and that decisions and actions are morally founded.

Since the satisfaction of consumers' wants is the economic and social justification of a company's existence, then measures of marketing success have emphasized demand stimulation and provider profits. But is want satisfaction through the generation and nurture of material consumption a social welfare gain or just an economic gain by the provider? Effectiveness measures have too often gauged performance according to the degree of goal attainment and have thus not included the costs of securing the goals, which must be related to the costs incurred by others.

The notion of a 'social cost–benefit' requires corporations to consider the consequences of their marketing actions. While micro-marketing focuses attention on the performance of the corporation, macro-marketing requires a wider view of market transactions which may have foreseen and unforeseen effects. These effects may be direct to the parties to the exchanges, or indirect to all other parties (who are then unwitting stakeholders). These externalities can have positive or negative effects.

Consumption-based culture is in many respects dysfunctional, and marketing has encouraged and conditioned us with the desire for new and convenience goods (see Alvesson and Willmott, 1993, for a helpful critique). Some people are defining themselves more by what they consume than what they produce (by what they take rather than what they give). This is socially unsustainable. Further, some practices have detrimental social effects on individuals and society (negative externalities). An increasing recognition of the costs of technological advances will throw into question the balance between the social value and benefits of marketing technology and systems, and the resulting social costs, such as financial losses, dissatisfaction, health and safety problems, resource depletion, and discrimination.

The marketing literature has focused largely on environmental effects on the marketing exchange rather than the effects of the exchange on the environment. Future economic and political decisions will be controlled partly by concerns for our physical environment and, in turn, these will affect what we think we need in our daily lives.

Economic growth does not necessarily translate into better quality of life and self-interest may be incompatible with broader social objectives because it largely ignores long-term interests. Economic efficiency, consumer sovereignty, and business freedom of enterprise are implicitly assumed to be more important than public welfare and are based on material affluence goals. The future environmental goals will (have to) transcend economic goals and severely constrain them as resource allocation by the market mechanism continues to decline relative to the total of finite resources used.

WHAT CAN GO WRONG?

Sometimes marketing strategies can violate public trust. In particular, deceptive advertising and irresponsible advertising have social implications. Advertising that is in bad taste or is otherwise offensive can simply be seen as a bad thing.

Deceptive advertising

This gives false information or intentionally misleads buyers and consumers about product benefits. Attenders are deceived when they acquire false beliefs because of their exposure to the advertising. Regulators have codes of practice for advertising that they can apply to stop advertising from being run, to require amendment, or to require corrective advertising to counter deceptive claims. The common rule is that advertising should be legal, decent, honest, and truthful. Complaints are welcomed by the regulators on any advertising that is misleading, in bad taste, irresponsible, or encourages law-breaking or unsafe practices.

In the UK, the Advertising Standards Authority (ASA), with recourse to the Control of Misleading Advertisements Regulations (1988), deals with complaints about press, hoarding and cinema advertising, as well as computer and video games, software, and the Internet. There is a voluntary watchdog organization for UK press advertising – the Committee on Advertising Practice, but this has no statutory powers. The Independent Television Commission (ITC) regulates (through approval) TV, cable, satellite, and teletext broadcasts. Radio advertising is monitored by the Radio Authority, but the first line of complaint is always with the radio station manager. The Broadcasting Standards Council also receives complaints about radio and TV advertising. In the case of mail order, the local Trading Standards Office will deal with complaints about goods supplied that do not conform to their description or accepted standards.

Irresponsible advertising

This may not be deceptive, but it does depict or encourage irresponsible behaviour or portrays groups in an irresponsible manner. Women are often portrayed as stupid or dominated by men. Black people are often stereotyped as athletes or recipients of charity.

There has been a growing awareness among marketers in recent years of their responsibility to society. Socially responsible advertisers have a vested interest in providing accurate information to consumers – they gain trust and loyalty. As we saw in chapter four, an educated consumer may the marketer's best customer.

BOX 17.2   ISSUES, REGULATORS, AND LEGISLATION

Marketing managers have to keep abreast of legislation and other forms of regulation that can limit their actions or lead to claims of unprofessional conduct:

- marketer–agency contract
- intellectual property rights: copyright, trademarks, passing-off, confidentiality
- comparative advertising (Comparative Advertising Directive)
- the Internet: civil and criminal law on libel, copyright, proposed directive on electronic commerce, conditions and disclaimers on website content
- data protection (Data Protection and Privacy Regulations; Data Protection Act 1998)
- consumer protection: trade descriptions, coupons, unfair contract terms (Unfair Contract Terms Act 1977)
- advertising standards: codes of advertising and sales promotion practice
- telemarketing: telecommunications (data protection and privacy), Telephone and Fax Preference Service, ICSTIS
- direct marketing: mailing preference service, e-mail preference service
- prize promotions: competitions, lotteries, free draws

THE JOB OF THE MARKETING COMMUNICATION MANAGER

The explicit role of manager of marketing communication(s) is a recent development in management. Relatively few appointments have been made in the UK, but this job is commonplace in US corporations. Where a manager for this sub-function of the value-creation system is not employed, the responsibilities fall on the marketing manager or an advertising manager, often with a coordinator working to support them. This is a reflection of the importance placed on the management of communication in the corporation. There is, however, a definite and accelerating shift towards professionalizing the role of manager of marketing communication. This person will work with other roles, such as public relations, corporate communication, reputation management, customer relationship/service management, and so on.

We can ask: what is the role of the marketing communication manager? What will be the major responsibilities (see Box 17.2 for examples of relevant contemporary legislation and regulations)? What particular expertise (skills, competencies, knowledge, and experience) is required? What will be the key activities, and key relationships? Figure 17.1 shows a recent proforma job description suggested by The Chartered Institute of Marketing.

The role is most often managerial, taking responsibility for the development and implementation of marketing strategies and activities to build brand awareness, coordination of working relationships with public relations, design, and advertising agencies, and partnering with product development and communication specialists throughout the corporation. Ideally, the partnerships will extend to production and distribution to ensure a

---

MARKETING MANAGER

Description

Responsible for developing the marketing strategy and customer proposition, in order to deliver maximum value for business and grow customer traffic.

Plan and manage all promotional activity for the company, including the development of marketing media and general relationship management strategy with customers.

Responsibilities

Research target customers

Benchmarking approaches to the market and identifying/monitoring new product development

Developing product plans for key products and services based upon the market research and segmentation

Assist in new product development to maintain and build market share

Packaging of products and services for client and target markets

Briefing/managing external agencies providing marketing services

Briefing/training on products and services for industry groups, e.g. advertising, PR

Liaising with trade marketing in connection with client/account retention programmes

Developing mechanisms to measure marketing effectiveness and ensure appropriate follow-up actions

Costing marketing activities and working within marketing budget to deliver effective marketing against individual product/ service plans.

Person specifications

Minimum three years' experience in a senior role

Marketing qualification

Proven experience of undertaking and delivering of a wide range of marketing projects and initiatives

Ability to coordinate and deliver marketing initiatives on time, and to a given budget

Team-orientated

A thorough understanding of client marketplace

Previous financial control on client level

Working knowledge of PowerPoint, Microsoft Projects and Excel

Recommended qualifications

A graduate or of graduate calibre

CIM Diploma/Chartered Marketer

Average salary range

£35k–45k per annum

Figure 17.1 **Job and person specification**
Source: Chartered Institute of Marketing

contribution, through reporting to the head of marketing, to the management of the value-creating system: generating, producing and representing various forms of knowledge for the stakeholder network.

Programme responsibility may include contributions to, collaboration with, and/or management of:

- customer relationship management system
- internal marketing/partnering
- market assessment and customer requirements summary
- product definition and development
- product launch
- event management, including public speaking, exhibitions, etc.
- brand management, including an integrated marketing plan, enterprise positioning, and marketing evaluation
- generation-of-demand (promotional) campaigns, including copy, design, media purchase, website content, POS material, packaging, etc.
- channel management (distribution)
- online commerce

CASE STUDY 16 INTEGRATING MARKETING AND PUBLIC RELATIONS IN A PRODUCT RECALL SITUATION

Anderson Waterproofing is a Manchester-based manufacturer of bitumen-based products for the building trade. In 1997, they launched a high-performance waterproofing pitch polymer damp-proof course (DPC) product, which they bought from another manufacturer. DPC is used to restrict the ingress of moisture through mortar joints and porous structures. This product was chosen as a product line extension to enlarge their product-market portfolio.

The 'Pitch DPC' product had been on the market for 6 months when the managing director of Anderson, while visiting a building merchant, noticed brown stains around the product rolls in storage. Enquiries revealed that this was a common occurrence that other manufacturers explained was caused by polymer migration as the chemical compound of the product broke down and the polymer content rose to the surface to create a milky solution.

As a chemist, the MD knew that this could not be the case, so he sent samples to Strathclyde University for analysis, where a spectral analysis showed that it was pitch separating out, not polymer. The MD was concerned that this represented a health risk as he knew that pitch could be highly carcinogenic. The polymer was breaking down over time and allowing the pitch to migrate to the surface, thus presenting a potential skin hazard for anyone handling the product.

Further samples, including a number of other pitch polymer products currently available on the market, were sent to the Health and Safety Executive. Test findings confirmed the presence of some carcinogens in the product. The HSE pointed out that as a supplier and employer, the company directors had a duty under the Health and Safety At Work Act to provide adequate health and safety information to enable the product to be used safely. They gave guidance on how the product should be handled.

Anderson was now facing an ethical dilemma. They had already spent considerable launch costs and the product was now openly on the market in distributor stores and on building sites. Yet it now seemed certain that exposure to the product presented a potential hazard. The HSE recommended that their guidance be followed on every building site and in all merchants, but the company felt that it was highly unlikely that the HSE instructions would be fully followed in all situations.

Rather than providing health and safety information in a hazard safety data sheet, it was decided to withdraw the product. The company considered the legal and financial problems with possible future compensation claims that could be seriously damaging to the business, both financially and as a potential danger to the company reputation. However, withdrawal costs would also have to be met.

An integrated campaign of coherent and coordinated advertising and public relations actions was planned. A marketing communication campaign was designed to support the withdrawal of the product from the market and to actively promote alternative pitch-free products.

Two press conferences were organized, and two press releases were distributed for the trade press, to announce the problem and test findings, to explain the reasons for withdrawal of the product and to alert the trade to the problem of pitch-based products.

Anderson began labelling their other products as 'pitch free'.

Trade advertisements requested the return of unused product, and the trade association was informed to alert manufacturers, suppliers, and users. Staff were briefed about the withdrawal process and the reasons behind the move, and were provided with a comprehensive Q&A document to prepare them to deal effectively with enquiries. All stock was quarantined and collected from distributors for disposal.

Competitors initially dismissed the problem, then threatened legal action to resist, arguing that these products had been on sale for 20 years without any previous claims of risk or cases of skin cancer. In reply, Anderson pointed out that the previous test data had not been analysed in a way that would have identified clusters of cancer incidence among users, and there must be a risk because the pitch component is recognized as a carcinogen. The competitors obtained their own expert report which indicated that the level of carcinogens in the pitch residue was no higher than found generally in a number of commonly used products. The competitors then persuaded the HSE that there was no undue cause for concern, although the agency still maintains its guidance for the use of pitch polymers.

The product was withdrawn in 1998, resulting in an initial loss of about £100,000 when safe disposal costs were covered. Some £300,000 of other pitch-free products were sold, and now building specifiers are requesting pitch-free DPCs.

Anderson have been recognized as open and honest in the face of a potentially dangerous product – gaining credibility as a responsible manufacturer with specifiers and end-users.

The cooperation of Phil Richardson, Head of Marketing and Public Relations, Icopal Ltd, is gratefully acknowledged

---

WHAT DO YOU THINK?

1 Do people get, through marketing, what they want, or are they merely encouraged to want what they get?

2 What examples of deceptive and irresponsible advertising have you seen recently. Discuss these cases with your colleagues/fellow students. Do you all agree on the criteria for honest and responsible product promotion?

3 Production is dependent on consumption. The consumer is the lawful prey of the producer, and the job of the marketer is to seduce the consumer. Is this a fair and complete explanation of almost all behaviour in contemporary society?

4 When does marketing intervention cease to be persuasion and become seduction?

5 List externalities that may arise in a marketing communication campaign.

6 What other forms of regulation may be significant in the job of marketing communication manager?

7 In what circumstances may the marketing communication manager be faced with an ethical dilemma?

8 What is the connection of ethical communication with green marketing?

9 In preparing for a job application and interview for the newly created post of marketing communication manager, what would you offer to indicate your advantageous credentials for the role?

10 Distinguish guardian and trading actions in the management of marketing communication.

FURTHER READING

Alvesson, M. and Willmott, H. (1993) *Making Sense of Management: A Critical Introduction*, London: Sage Publications.

Clampitt, P. G. (1991) *Communicating for Managerial Effectiveness*, London: Sage Publications.

Deetz, S. A. (1992) *Democracy in an Age of Corporate Colonization: Developments in Communication and the Politics of Everyday Life*, Albany, NY: State University of New York Press.

Gabriel Y. and Lang, T. (1995) *The Unmanageable Consumer: Contemporary Consumption and Its Fragmentation*, London: Sage Publications.

Harris, R. and Carman, J. M. (1983) 'Public regulation of marketing activity', *Journal of Macromarketing*, 3 (1): 49–58.

McDonagh, P. (1998) 'Towards a theory of sustainable communication in risk society: relating issues of sustainability to marketing communications', *Journal of Marketing Management* 14: 591–622.

Snell, R. (1999) 'Managing ethically', in Fulop, L. and Linstead, S. (eds) *Management: A Critical Text*, London: Macmillan Business, pp. 335–63.

Tannen, D. (1999) *The Argument Culture: Changing the Way We Argue and Debate*, London: Virago.

chapter eighteen

CONTEMPORARY MARKETING COMMUNICATION, CORPORATE COMMUNICATION, AND . . . THE FUTURE?

LEARNING POINTS

Careful study of this chapter will help you to:

- appreciate how the marketing communication environment is changing

- appreciate how marketing communication practices are developing

- locate marketing communication within the corporate communication managing system

We are trying to leverage this interactive marketing phenomenon to reinvent our company's culture.
(Pete Blackshaw, digital brand manager, P&G)

INTRODUCTION

Although we don't notice everything around us, we live in a world that is in a continuous state of becoming. There is no such thing as stability, and there never has been. Today, change is more noticeable because the rate of change is accelerating. The timescale between noticeable changes is within our personal experience.

In only a few years, and certainly within the professional working lives of marketers, a number of key trends, centred on globalization, have emerged (Evans *et al.*, 1996):

- Society is continuing to polarize around economic and political interests, creating a two-speed economic and communication system (Mattelart, 1995).
- Mass markets are fragmenting.
- The market is increasingly a regulating factor of society.
- Retailers, because they meet consumers directly, have taken charge of market development, displacing producers to a subcontracting role.
- Markets have more production than consumption and have reached or are nearing saturation.
- A few multinational corporations control most production and distribution (by 1990–91, according to Lang and Hines (1993), the top 500 corporations controlled over half of world trade but employed only 0.05 per cent of the population. In 1991, the ten largest corporations had a collective revenue greater than the combined wealth of the 100 smallest countries (Hawken, 1993).
- New technologies in all spheres of human activity.
- The nature and status of 'communication' has changed: it became professionalized and its responsibilities profilerated (Mattelart, 1995).
- Commercial cosmopolitanism.

CHANGING CONSUMER BEHAVIOUR AND MARKETING SITUATION

As you might expect, we should identify changes in consumer attitude and behaviour, the marketplace, and providers. The number of people who defer to the offerings of providers is declining – more of us are active consumers who know what we want and what we will pay for it. We can expect further shift towards buyer-initiated relationships (the tradition has been to think of marketing as initiated by the seller). This phenomenon has been termed reverse marketing (Ottesen, 1995; Leenders and Blenkhorn, 1988) to recognize that once a relationship has been established, either party may initiate interaction in the expectation of a response from the other. Of course, had marketing (and management) thinking not been locked in the managerialistic 'conduit metaphor' mode of thinking about communication, this would have been more prominently recognized long ago. Communication, then, is the mode of creating mutual meaning(s). Marketing and communication systems will have to provide facilities for both parties to initiate exchange relationships.

Statt (1997) has suggested a number of significant areas of change that should concern the marketing manager. These should be considered by marketing communication managers in determining objectives, formulating strategy, and evaluating investments in systems and activities.

Direct action against providers' attempts to treat consumers as merely 'necessary profit-making fodder' (Statt, 1997: 293), through price increases, service cuts, or adulteration of quality, may lead to boycotts, organized complaints, and even legal action by consumers and buyers. Alternative lifestyles, such as green consumerism, ethical investment, and the exchange economy (see LETS, Box 17.1, p. 328) are at present marginal but growing movements.

In the marketplace, political moves to regulate and deregulate industries reflect official policy and ideology about what constitutes the most important values of our society. Shopping trends and buyer behaviour indicate the steady shift from satisfying 'needs' to gratification through satisfying wants in a society where for many, but not all, disposable income has increased. Thus brand choice is the motive in much buying today.

Providers of value, in its many forms, will focus much more on accomplishing efficient customer responsiveness. This will require the merging of marketing, quality, and customer service into an integrated managing system (for generating, producing, and representing valued forms of knowledge) that can effectively and efficiently respond to customers in a responsible manner (see Christopher et al., 1991, and Deetz, 1995, for discussions that should increasingly concern marketing managers). Business ethics will, it is hoped, become more prominent in decision-making and policy-setting as managers and customers become more socially responsible in the marketing of products.

Corporations have become the dominant institution and must address the social and environmental afflictions that we face in the world. Marketing functions to further human and business purpose by providing benefits to customers through products. Decisions on what products to make and how to offer them to customers is the substance of marketing strategy. But, decisions on what to make also determine what resources are required to make and market those products – both making and taking have costs to the ecosystem (wastes, pollution, damage, and so on). Increasingly, marketing managers will be required to adopt sustainable-marketing practices to ensure that the business is operated in a such a way that customers obtain genuine benefits, while the corporation accomplishes their financial objectives and the ecosystem functioning is preserved or enhanced (Fuller, 1999).

Managers are becoming the agents of social innovation (Drucker, 1986). Through innovation, much more than selling products can be accomplished if we treat the problem as more than people performing (i.e. getting the mob organized into an effective, purposeful, and productive group). This must be underpinned by ideas and symbols. Managers need a broader canvas – management can be intellectualized to good purpose. Managing **is** communicating.

CHANGING MARKETING COMMUNICATION PRACTICES

Leading marketing thinker Professor Philip Kotler (1999) sees the digital revolution as the driving force for markets and marketing to operate on fundamentally different principles than they have for the past 100 years. Marketing managers must adapt to the emerging electronic marketing – rethinking the processes by which customer value is identified, communicated about, and delivered – in many cases co-designing desired products. Advertising will be obtained by consumers and buyers on-demand, with information to aid product selection being found by intelligent agents and information brokers.

Kitchen and Wheeler (1997) identify seven developments in the way corporations develop and apply marketing in the contemporary world that are impacting on marketing communication thinking and practice:

1 growth in advertising and promotion
2 the emergence of the global consumer
3 development and importance of integrated marketing communication
4 direct marketing (using local rather than mass media) as a new promotional tool in targeting the likeliest customers for the particular brand
5 database marketing
6 internet advertising and e-commerce
7 process-oriented coordination and control

Marketers will become more aware of the ways in which customers behave in specialist roles of buyer, payer, and/or user, and will adapt their marketing effort to the type of role of the person with whom they wish to exchange (Sheth *et al.*, 1999). The marketing communication system must also be capable of treating the consumer/buyer differently from the way the customer is treated – not because they are inferior or less attractive, but because their needs are different. The communication system must be especially capable of supporting the retention of value-creating exchange relationships.

Recognition of interaction, relationship, and the need for integration are becoming the foundations for marketing communication management. A systems approach is becoming common practice.

COMMUNICATING IN E-COMMERCE

The accelerating proliferation of Internet-based (World Wide Web) commercial activity has two aspects: electronic transactions in which offer and purchase data flows between computer systems (e.g. product and price list, and credit card number and delivery address), and mediated human interactions (such as fault reporting, or service request). They differ as follows: electronic transactions do not have people (directly) participating, whereas human interactions are personal between two or more people. The challenge for the growing number of customer relationship management (CRM) vendors is how to move the capability of their technologies beyond merely enabling the former to enabling and facilitating both.

Hollensen (2001) identifies three levels of commitment to e-commerce that have significance for the communication manager (summarized in Table 18.1).

The 'new' business model requires that corporations manage relationships (see Fulop and Linstead, 1999, for example) through dialogue as the basis for value-based marketing that aims to make and keep negotiated promises through invested dialogue in the economic community. Traditional notions

Table 18.1 **Level of commitment to interaction**

Commitment	Interaction
Basic commitment **One-to-many information broadcast**	The Internet is used as an additional channel to represent the corporation and as a means of low-cost product brochure distribution. The aim is low-cost presence and a 'high-tech' image, often as a reaction to competitor moves. The emphasis is on providing information and the site design does not encourage anything beyond product enquiries, but improves the corporation's promotional budget efficiency.
Intermediate commitment **Selling though direct targeting**	At this level the degree of interactivity is greater, since communication is no longer limited (by the corporation) to sending out information to customers. Customers are able to play a part as they seek information and express their needs and interests. The site provides segmented information and gathers queries, requests, and suggestions – information is exchanged with stakeholders. The marketing manager has to provide a site that attracts people who have different interests.
Total commitment **One-to-one interaction in a networked e-commerce community**	The website is built to enable a high degree of interaction between buyer and seller, as part of the integration of e-commerce into the overall business strategies and processes of the corporation and its business partners (the value chain). This will almost certainly mean rethinking the design of the business through the adoption of a new model of business.

of competition will assume less prominence. Communication as dialogue, rather than simply informing, will continue to grow in importance.

THE CORPORATE COMMUNICATION SYSTEM OF MANAGING

Today we see increasing evidence for the convergence of the traditionally discrete marketing and public relations functions into a more strategic integrated management function known as corporate communication. This handles the totality of the corporation's links into the operating environment and well as the response to it. Debate continues about that part of the overall management task having to do with the management of important relationships, and with communicating with groups in these relationships. This 'subtask' may be argued over by marketing, customer relations, and human resource management, or public relations specialists. Its importance has been emphasized in recent years by the Royal Society of the Arts' study on the sustainable success of the company of the future (RSA, 1995).

The corporate enterprise has two primary communication systems that are interrelated. The internal system directs activities of organizing to accomplish goals that are based on the gathering and interpretation of data on expectations and attitudes, and on conditions, from the corporation's relevant environment through external channels of communication. External systems of communication are also used to present relevant information about the internal processes of the corporation to the relevant external environment to attempt to influence the behaviour of the various publics. Internal communication processes are directed towards establishment of structure and stability in organizing, while external communication processes are directed towards innovation by facilitating identification of directions for corporate development (Kreps, 1990). Managers and leaders seek cooperation for a productive balance between stability and innovation.

Rather than seeing traditional departments and narrow specialist groups operating in institutional silos in competition – for supremacy (see Lauzen, 1991), to protect their turf; to secure credibility, for a seat at the boardroom table, to secure the ear of the dominant coalition, or simply for resources – a model of integrated communication systems seeks to build bridges between the islands of communication (see Gayeski, 1993), and to establish eventually new task groupings, perhaps by way of cross-functional working in the interim. As organizations re-engineer working arrangements and formal structure around business processes, so they should re-engineer their communications management into a truly corporate (sub)system for managing.

Departments should not be allowed to seek independence and the concern of managers should not be encroachment, but how to remove barriers to real cooperative working so that communicating really can add value to business enterprise. The model we seek to build and deploy does not promote the engagement of non-specialists in competition with managing traditional communication departments. Rather we seek to foster greater recognition of corporate dependencies, the need for wider participation in constructing meanings, identity, and knowledge (Deetz, 1992), and shared organizational (business) goals. We urge stronger, direct linkages between those who need to communicate and those who are charged with enabling and facilitating these interactions. A value-creation perspective (of managing) on the departmentalization issue is required if the power–control assumptions and desires of the traditionalist manager (managerialism) are to be overcome for the benefit of the corporate community. This will require that managers recognize the corporate communication managing system as central to the work of the enterprise community. The corporate communication approach enables the reconciliation of social and economic interests, for business is in reality a socio-economic institution upon which we are all dependent, and may allow the vista of a 'life ethic' to temper the debilitating effects of the mutation of citizens into consumers. Figure 18.1 represents the determinants of corporate performance.

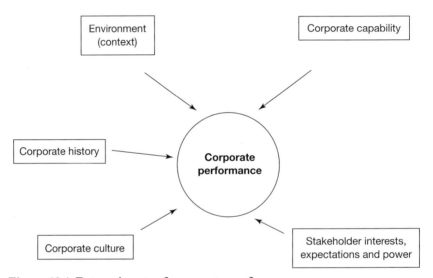

Figure 18.1 **Determinants of corporate performance**
Source: Based on Brown, 1995

The interests of the few (corporate owners, managers, and their customers) are no longer given greater value than the interests of the many (all other stakeholders). Arrogant managers who do not value relationships and stakeholders' interests (or even stakeholders themselves), and do not value leadership and other change-orientated actions (Brown, 1995) will find it more difficult to keep their licence to operate.

Carroll's (1993) stakeholder view of the firm requires that managers see stakeholders groups and their subgroups, at least until the legitimacy of claims and respective power have been examined, as both:

1. those who the management group thinks have some stake (an interest, right, or ownership) in the firm

2. those groups that themselves think they have some stake in the firm

It is then necessary to examine the nature of each relationship, as well as recognizing that some stakeholder groups also have relationships with each other. Stakeholder expectations cannot be ignored, but can be missed and/or misinterpreted.

Corporate community is the new form of organization governance that shifts emphasis from profit to democracy by unifying the goals of all parties – by focusing on the needs of the corporation's constituents (see Handy, 1995, for a discussion of federalism). The old profit-centred model of business is too limited and limiting because it ignores the reality that business is both an economic and a social institution. Corporate governance can evolve towards collaboration among all stakeholders. The shift from profit to democracy requires the creation of a coalition of investors, employees, customers, business partners, and the public. Such a corporate community can serve all interests better.

The onset of a knowledge-based economy has made cooperation efficient and thus there is no longer a need to consider business as a zero-sum game in which one party gains at the loss of another. The capitalist theory that profit is the driving force of economic progress is at last being practically challenged. The question is no longer whether to focus on making money or on serving society.

The old model required a focus on serving the interest of shareholders. The interests of employees, customers, and other stakeholders were not really goals of the company, but simply a means to meet the interests of shareholders – to make money. If the goal of enterprise is narrowly taken to be merely to make money (ignoring the wider costs), then the interest of business is opposed to the interests of society. Even the concept of 'corporate social responsibility' has not remedied the problem. It has proven useful in educating people in business about their social obligations, but in focusing on social service, the economic realities of productivity, revenues, and profits have been ignored.

In recent years, however, major changes in corporate governance have been underway. Collaboration with stakeholders is now occurring as they gain power and because managers need their support. Institutional investors have become more involved in the management of large corporations, including 'ethical investors'. Employee participation, often in the form of shareholding, has grown significantly, especially in the USA. Women and members of minority groups are becoming more influential in business. Other social constituencies have gained influence in recent years: relationship marketing to build trust and commitment with customers in long-term relationships; partnership agreements with suppliers and government; voluntary moves to protect the environment, and so on.

Halal proposes a stakeholder model of the corporation (1996) which views the corporation as a socio-economic system composed of various equally important constituencies: employees, customers, suppliers, the public and its government representatives, and investors. Each stakeholder has obligations to the corporation as well as rights. This view is gaining wide acceptance because managers realize that they need the support of these groups. Halal's return-on-resources model shows that all stakeholders invest financial and social resources, they incur costs and expect gains – these resources are their stake in the organization (see also Heath, 1994: chapter 6, for a discussion of negotiated enactment of stakeholder interests). Halal's analysis leads to a theory of the nature of the firm:

> Corporate managers are dependent on stakeholders because the economic role of the firm is to combine as effectively as possible the unique resources each stakeholder contributes: the risk capital of investors; the talents, training, and efforts of employees; the continued patronage of customers; the capabilities of business partners; and the economic infrastructure provided by government.
>
> (1996: 67)

In this view, managers act as stewards engaged in a 'social contract' to draw together this mix of resources and transform it into financial and social wealth, which they can distribute among stakeholders to reward their contributions. The closer the integration into a cohesive community, the greater is the wealth. Stakeholders have different interests according to their unique roles in the corporate community. These interests can be reconciled if they are organized to create a more successful enterprise. The goal of business, therefore, should be to serve the public welfare of all stakeholders.

There are some problems to be resolved in putting this into practice, but there are compelling reasons why the transition is occurring (Halal, 1996):

- the liberating power of information
- the benefits of cooperation
- the rising aspirations of people
- democratic ideals being extended into everyday life
- the new business model offers increasing productivity and social benefits, without clashing with the profit-centred model of business – it is a logical extension which helps to resolve the cultural contradictions of capitalism (Bell, 1974)

Marketing orientation

Drucker (1977) has argued that marketing is the business of creating customers, while everything else is a cost – much, but not all, of it necessary to enable and facilitate business enterprise to be productive. He has also revealed the political nature of modern business management (Drucker, 1980), showing that marketing alone cannot deal with all problems (see Ehling *et al.*, 1992). Public relations is a necessary and complementary overhead in a responsible enterprise.

The marketing concept views the business enterprise as an organized process designed to create and keep a customer (Levitt, 1969). Marketing is

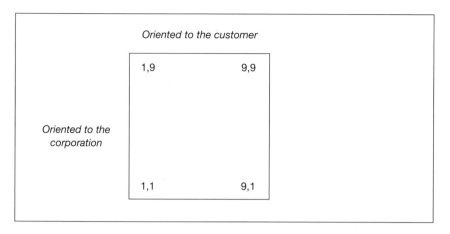

Figure 18.2 **Levitt's marketing matrix**
Source: Based on Blake and Mouton's managerial grid, 1964

a two-way mediating process between the customer and the corporation (see Figure 18.2). A balance is needed between management, which focuses on stabilizing the corporation's transformation processes, and leadership, which seeks to innovate by focusing attention on the external environment (Kreps, 1990).

Strategic marketing, according to Swayne and Ginter (1993) for example, maintains the desired relationship between the 'organization' and its environment. Attention is thus drawn to matters of production, finance, and human skills. The aim is to create competitive advantage. The impetus for significant change in the business environment, it is asserted, comes from many sources – government, domestic and international economic and market forces, demographic shifts and lifestyle changes, and the structural evolution of many industries. Anticipation and understanding of these changes, and the development of suitable marketing strategies, is the job of the marketer, we are told. But these authors, like many others, have failed to address the full picture. The actions, relationships, and expectations of many people will impact upon the performance of the business enterprise – many of them will not be customers. The 'marketing strategy' perspective can be too limited. Many marketing strategists urge managers to engage with the customer and the competitor. This trinity is often not even recognized as a set of reciprocal relationships or communication systems (as illustrated in Figure 18.3).

The adoption of strategic management is now widespread as executives try to control their environment and reduce uncertainty. Strategy – the art of bringing values and resources together to influence and shape the future (Moore, 1996) – is in common usage in the vocabulary of modern management. Strategic marketing is a company-wide (i.e. corporate) strategic management philosophy which guides the way of working (Brown, 1993). A managerial perspective may be insufficient to deal with the contemporary business and social environment.

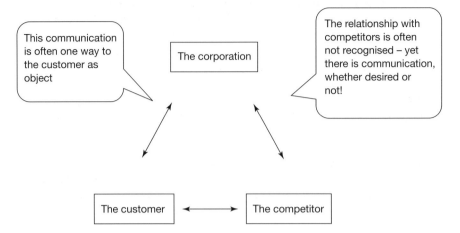

Figure 18.3 **Communicative relationships**

Gummesson (1991) has considered the problem of shifting attention from marketing management, i.e. the management of marketing, to marketing-oriented management, i.e. management based on marketing principles. Others have also urged the defragmentation of specialisms:

> marketing is not merely a cluster of related business functions. In a truly marketing-orientated business, marketing is a deeply ingrained attitude of mind, shared by everyone in that business.
>
> (Levitt, in Mesdag, 1991: v)

If marketing is seen as a boundary function that manages a continuing series of impersonal, discrete exchanges (transactions), a critical point is missed. Many markets have ceased to be essentially competitive and have been restructured on the basis of voluntary, long-term binding agreements among participating firms (Arndt, 1979). Moore (1996) speaks of seeking markets that are relatively free of competition in order to learn without this being appropriated by others. Examples of these 'new' arrangements can be found in joint ventures, franchises, subcontracting, vertical integration, joint-product development and joint-marketing contracts. In all cases, transactions are planned and administered on the basis of negotiated rules of exchange. Benefits realized for the 'community' include reduction of uncertainty in operations, reduced transaction costs, and economies from avoiding traditional (promotional) marketing arrangements. Such networks of long-term cooperation, or domesticated markets, have a degree of stability not envisaged in mainstream marketing theory.

Already under challenge in the 1970s and 1980s, the general paradigm of marketing premised on consumer choice and satisfaction and manipulation of the four Ps, has been criticized as not reflecting reality (see Day and Wensley, 1983, for example). Carman (1980) argued that exchange and related concepts such as transaction costs, information alternatives, and power may also be considered as central to marketing. Day and Wensley (1983) criticize the generally accepted theory of marketing as simplistic and incomplete in considering major elements of both practice and the discipline. The argument has been summarized in Table 18.2 by comparing the traditional perspective with a modern approach that is more in keeping with a relational and communication-based theory.

Day and Wensley (1983) integrate the shifts in thinking to form a growing consensus that:

> the marketing function initiates, negotiates, and manages acceptable exchange relationships with key interest groups, or constituencies, in pursuit of sustainable competitive advantages, within specific markets, on the basis of long-run consumer and channel franchises.

However, as Day and Wensley (1983) point out, the newer field of strategic management has addressed many of the issues that were part of the strategic-marketing orientation, that is, demand-based sources of competitive advantage. General managers mostly do not see themselves as marketers, but they should do just that, and corporate strategists must be marketing strategists (Baker, 1992). Without a market there is no purpose for the corporation

Table 18.2 **Marketing theory for the modern manager**

Traditional paradigm of marketing	Modern paradigm of marketing
A unidirectional stimulus ⇒ response mechanism implicit: customers react to management actions (Arndt, 1979)	Dyadic exchange: two-way transactional relations between sellers and buyers – outcomes depend on bargaining, negotiation, the balance of power, and the sources of conflict between the parties (Bagozzi, 1978)
Little explicit attention to competitive forces – customer orientation implies direct appeal to customers who are then won over	Competitor orientation views customers as the prize gained at the expense of rivals through advantage in distribution arrangements, preferential treatment, lower costs, and so on. Competitive advantage is pursued
Innovation results from the adoption of products by customers	Marketing is organized, rational innovation – marketers identify opportunity for, and initiate and monitor, change (Simmonds, 1982)
Neo-classical economic theory-based assumption of profit maximization	The task of organization is to maintain the enterprise by negotiating resource exchanges with external interests – internal coalitions adapt to enhance the efficiency and effectiveness of performing these negotiating functions (Anderson, 1982)

and no role for the corporate strategist. This denies claims that the latter takes a broader view than the corporation's activity in the marketplace.

But what of those who are destined never to be customers, or may be customers as well as holding other stakes in the actions and purpose of the corporation? Business is not primarily about products or profits – it is carried out by and for people. Several distinctly different groups have some form of relationship with business (Mesdag, 1991). Each group has an interest in the business, and some interests are (at least, apparently) directly opposed. Several groups expect to get money or value for money from the business enterprise of the corporation. This may be in the form of wages, salaries, taxes, environmental protection schemes, dividends, margins, or remittances. One further group is unique – it pays money to the corporation. While those tasked with generating profits, through direct or indirect activities, have a particular affinity with customers, the people with the other interests can make decisions and choices which may determine the fate of the business enterprise.

The initial *Tomorrow's Company* study (RSA, 1995) makes clear the extent to which successful companies depend on building relationships with important groups, to the extent that they are included, drawn into collaborative, 'win–win' (integrative negotiation) relationships with successful companies. The *Tomorrow's Company* study, which first reported in 1995, has led to the creation, by the Royal Society of Arts, of the Centre for Tomorrow's Company (see Goyder, 1998, for development of the 'agenda for action' and 'framework for success' which have been derived from the study findings).

The Centre is pushing debate further, setting out its vision for the company of the future, which moves beyond an emphasis on the creation of shareholder value. This goal remains of central importance, but the Tomorrow's Company approach creates value for other groups involved with the company. The successful company of the future aims to achieve more than mere acceptance in its key relationships, and its directors have obligations to give due weight to all stakeholders. Only by doing this will directors maximize the sustainable growth in value of their companies for the benefit of stake-holders, both present and future.

The interim study report was the result of an enquiry lasting more than two years and involving some of the most prominent UK companies. It aimed to stimulate competitiveness, offering a broad view of the possible sources of sustainable business success. The study concluded that an inclusive approach to business leadership, to investment needs, to people, and to society is needed for world-class business success. The approach requires companies to:

• clearly define purpose and values and communicate these consistently to all those people and groups who are important to success
• develop their own success models, drawing on stated purposes and values
• value reciprocal relationships, working actively to build these
• expect relationships to contribute to maintenance of a strong 'licence to operate'

The initial RSA study concluded that the successful company of the future will be inclusive, that is, it will recognize and respond to the interests of those with a stake in a company's success, and will 'include' all such groups.

The part of management concerned with the management of relationships is public relations, which may also be described as public affairs, corporate communications, and corporate affairs. These terms do have different meanings: public relations is the practice of managing important relationships, and public affairs deals with relationships involved in public policy development (with government, political parties, pressure groups and the media, as they contribute to public policy debate), and with issues of management. 'Corporate communications' recognizes the importance of managed communication in relationships and includes forms of communication used for corporate[1] purposes.

The *Tomorrow's Company* study advocates inclusion, and values the interest of stakeholder groups. Where important internal-stakeholder groups are involved, other studies have shown that they are more willing to come forward with ideas, feel able to express ideas, and trust the corporation to use rather than criticize the ideas that are put forward. Drawing in, and including stakeholders, means identifying them, and then using communication to establish a dialogue with them, which allows for:

* the expression of interests
* clarification of interests
* conciliation of what may be conflicting interests

Communication is central to the Tomorrow's Company approach, and communication between people is the core of business activity. The traditional emphasis of marketing, however, does not fit this philosophy.

Final comment

While the creation and retention of customers is crucial to business enterprise, the traditional implementation is too narrow. A relational marketing model, while it cannot resolve the many non-marketing problems of business in society, can work in tandem with public relations (managing relationships with publics to resolve conflicts) to form an integrative negotiation strategy. This integrated corporate communication strategy provides a necessary balance between innovation and stability, i.e. between leadership and management, within a stakeholder community.

And a final sobering thought, from a recent review of consumerism, for those of us who believe in the management of consumers. Consumers, in various ways, subvert, refuse, accept, interpret, surrender, or embrace. Despite efforts to control and manipulate them, consumers act in ways that are unpredictable, inconsistent, and contradictory. They (we) seem to be

---

1 The term 'corporate' here is taken to mean the total social collectivity, as distinct from the minority dominant coalition or shareholder groups. Thus, this is premised on a total social-system model of organizing.

steadfastly unmanageable. Further, there is no single uniform entity, the consumer. Consumers are distinct in income, aspiration, and culture. There is no such thing as 'the consumer'!

CASE STUDY 17   MARKETING COMMUNICATION MEETS CORPORATE COMMUNICATION AT AOL.COM

Metered telecommunications charges have a long and deep-rooted history in the UK. Charges on a per-minute basis have been the norm for so long that alternative charging schemes such as flat-rate monthly fees were not thought by consumers to be an option, despite US practice becoming common knowledge. As a result, time spent online in the UK was, in 1999, only one quarter of that typical in the USA.

America OnLine UK (AOL) found in an online poll of 11,000 of their more than 600,000 members (3.8m in Europe) that 92 per cent said, without prompting, that metered telephone charges was the only barrier to them spending more time online. Aspirations for major growth in e-commerce were being held back by the 'ticking clock'. BT, at the heart of the UK charging system, would have to be persuaded to respond to calls for reform.

AOL UK determined that they should campaign for unmetered Internet access in the UK. Thus, their 'Stop the Clock' campaign was conceived and initiated in June 1999. Five key audiences were addressed with the message that metered telephone charges severely penalized UK consumers and rendered our policy-makers' vision of the 'wired economy' fruitless. This was to be a solo mission for AOL – almost all of the UK's other so-called 'free' Internet service provider (ISP) services were dependent for revenues on per-minute charges. BT themselves made £500m in 1998 by charging at least one pence per minute to connect web users to their ISPs.

AOL commissioned economic analysis and conducted their own evaluation research to underpin their campaign. This data strengthened the validity and weight of their proposals as they briefed UK and European MPs, advisers, and ministers, and in discussions with the UK regulator at OFTEL. MPs debated the issue in Parliament in early June.

A series of press releases from AOL outlined the issue. Interviews with journalists called for, on behalf of UK consumers, an end to BT's outmoded pricing system. These views were amplified in AOL's alliance with the grassroots consumer action group, the Campaign for Unmetered Telecommunications (CUT). Some 400,000 members of the AOL community were urged to boycott the Internet on 6 June.

A key milestone came when on 12 October, *The Times* led its core news editorial with the headline 'Free the Net'. Several broadcasters used clips from AOL's TV advertisement to highlight high Internet telephone bills. In November, BT announced unmetered access – but at twice the price paid by US consumers. AOL UK prepared to escalate their campaign.

In December, MCI Worldwide asked OFTEL to require BT to provide an unmetered service. Other ISPs relented and started to attempt to launch free-access services, despite still being obliged to pay per-minute charges to BT for connections. Clearly, the UK Internet industry needed a timely ruling from the regulator! In May 2000, OFTEL ruled that BT must provide a wholesale version of their unmetered Internet tariffs (SurfTime) to their competitors. AOL is now working to accelerate the timescale for offering lower-cost flat-rate Internet access plans in the UK.

Media coverage of this historic ruling reflected the leading role of AOL UK. Evaluation research by Metrica showed that AOL had a dominant share of 'voice' media coverage) throughout the campaign and, at the peak of news coverage in March 2000 (more than 100 news articles published, thirty-nine in *The Times* alone), reached 72 per cent of UK adults with their message about overcharging. Consumer reactions to the campaign were evaluated using online notice boards and usage figures. In the four months since the launch of their one-pence-per-minute, flat-rate telephone tariff in September 1999, AOL's 'traffic' more than doubled. Metrica estimate that at the peak of news coverage, over 18m adults were exposed to reports mentioning AOL, with an average number of exposures per person of around five in October 1999 and March 2000 when key actions of the campaign took place.

Once the leading ISP in the UK, AOL has faced serious competition from Freeserve. Their successful efforts to persuade the public, the Internet industry, and OFTEL that there should be a switch to flat-rate telephone charges for Internet access have raised AOL's profile as an ISP and as campaigners for change against unfair charges. Thanks to the championing of this issue by AOL, UK Internet users now have what US users have had for years.

(See www.aol.co.uk/press/, www.the-times.co.uk and www.metrica.net

Note: [a] The cooperation of Matt Peacock, Corporate Communication Director, AOL UK, is gratefully acknowledged

FURTHER READING

Anderson, P. F. (1982) 'Marketing, strategic planning, and the theory of the firm', *Journal of Marketing* 46, spring, pp. 15–26.

Arndt, J. (1979) 'Toward a concept of domesticated markets', *Journal of Marketing* 43, autumn, pp. 69–75.

Bagozzi, R. P. (1978) 'Marketing as exchange: a theory of transactions in the marketplace', *American Behavioural Scientist* 21 (4): 535–56.

Baker, M. J. (1992) *Marketing Strategy and Management*, 2nd edn, Basingstoke: The Macmillan Press.

Bell, D. (1974) *The Coming of a Postindustrial Age: A Venture in Social Forecasting*, London: Penguin Books.

Blake, R. R. and Mouton, J. S. (1964) *The Managerial Grid: Key Orientations for Achieving Production Through People*, Houston, TX: Gulf Publishing Company.

Brews, P. J. (2000) 'The challenge of the Web-enabled business', *FT Mastering Management supplement*, 24 November.

Brown, A. (1995) *Organisational Culture*, London: Pitman Publishing.

Brown, R. (1993) *Market Focus: Achieving and Sustaining Marketing Effectiveness*, Butterworth-Heinemann.

Carman, J. M. (1980) 'Paradigms for marketing theory', in Sheth, J. (ed.), *Research in Marketing*, Vol. 3, Greenwich, CT: JAI Press.

Carroll, A. B. (1993) *Business and Society: Ethics and Stakeholder Management*, 2nd edn, Cincinnati, OH: South-Western Publishing Co.

Christopher, M. G., Payne, A. and Ballantyne, D. (1991) *Relationship Marketing: Bringing Quality, Customer Service and Marketing Together*, Oxford: Butterworth-Heinemann/CIM.

Day, G. S. and Wensley, R. (1983) 'Marketing theory with a strategic orientation', *Journal of Marketing* 47, autumn, pp. 79–89.

Deetz, S. A. (1992) *Democracy in an Age of Corporate Colonization: Developments in Communication and the Politics of Everyday Life*, Albany, NJ: State University of New York Press.

Deetz, S. A. (1995) *Transforming Communication, Transforming Business: Building Responsive and Responsible Workplaces*, Creskill, NJ: Hampton Press.

Dilenschneider, R. L. (1991) 'Marketing communications in the post-advertising era', *Public Relations Review* 17 (3): 227–36.

Drucker, P. F. (1977) *Management: Tasks, Responsibilities, Practices*, New York: Harper's College Press.

Drucker, P. F. (1980) *Managing in Turbulent Times*, New York: Harper & Row.

Drucker, P. F. (1986) *The Frontiers of Management: Where Tomorrow's Decisions Are Being Shaped Today*, London: Heinemann/Guild Publishing.

Ehling, W. P., White, J. and Grunig, J. E. (1992) 'Public relations and marketing practices', in Grunig, J. E. (ed.), *Excellence in Public Relations and Communication Management*, Hillsdale, NJ: Lawrence Erlbaum Associates.

Evans, M. J., Moutinho, L. and van Raaij, F. (1996) *Applied Consumer Behaviour*, Harlow: Addison-Wesley.

Fuller, D. A. (1999) *Sustainable Marketing: Managerial–Ecological Issues*, Thousand Oaks, CA: Sage Publications.

Fulop, L. and Linstead, S. (eds) (1999) *Management: A Critical Text*, London: Macmillan Business. (Treats management as relational – the management of relationships rather than of things.).

Gayeski, D. (1993) *Corporate Communications Management: The Renaissance Communicator in Information-Age Organizations*, Boston, MA: Focal Press.

Goyder, M. (1998) *Living Tomorrow's Company*, Aldershot: Gower Publishing.

Gummesson, E. (1991) 'Marketing–orientation revisited: the crucial role of part-time marketers', *European Journal of Marketing* 25 (2): 60–75.

Halal, W. E. (1996) *The New Management: Democracy and Enterprise Are Transforming Organizations*, San Francisco, CA: Berrett-Koehler.

Handy, C. (1995) 'Balancing corporate power: a new federalist paper', in Handy, C., *Beyond Certainty: The Changing Worlds of Organizations*, London: Hutchinson, pp. 33–56.

Hawken, P. (1993) *The Ecology of Commerce: A Declaration of Sustainability*, New York: HarperBusiness.

Heath, R. L. (1994) *Management of Corporate Communication: From Interpersonal Contacts to External Affairs*, Hillsdale, NJ: Lawrence Erlbaum Associates.

Hollensen, S. (2001) *Global Marketing: A Market-Responsive Approach*, 2nd edn, Harlow: Pearson Education.

Kitchen, P. J. and Wheeler, C. (1997) 'Developments in marketing communications: a global perspective', paper presented at the 2nd International Conference on Marketing and Corporate Communication, University of Strathclyde, April.

Kotler, P. (1999) *Kotler on Marketing*, New York: The Free Press.

Kreps, G. L. (1990) *Organizational Communication*, 2nd edn, New York: Longman.

Lang, T. and Hines, C. (1993) *The New Protectionism: Protecting the Future Against Free Trade*, London Earthscan.

Leenders, M. R. and Blenkhorn, D. L. (1988) *Reverse Marketing: The New Buyer–Supplier Relationship*, London: Collier-Macmillan.

Levitt, T. (1969) *The Marketing Mode: Pathways to Corporate Growth*, New York: McGraw-Hill.

Maddox, K. (1999) 'Special report: P&G Interactive Marketer of the Year', *Advertising Age*, May, at www.adage.com.

Mattelart, A. (1995) 'Unequal voices', *UNESCO Courier*, February, pp. 11–14.

McDonagh, P. (1997) 'The ecocentric challenge for marketing communications in contemporary society', paper presented at the 2nd International Conference on Marketing and Corporate Communication, University of Strathclyde, April.

Mesdag, M. van (1991) *Think Marketing: Strategies for Effective Management Action*, London: Mercury Business Books.

Moore, J. F. (1996) *The Death of Competition: Leadership and Strategy in the Age of Business Ecosystems*, New York: HarperBusiness.

Ottesen, O. (1995) 'Buyer initiative ignored, but imperative for marketing management: towards a new view of market communication', Working Paper No. 15, Dept. of Business Administration, Stavanger (University) College, Norway.

RSA (1995) *Tomorrow's Company: The Role of Business in a Changing World*, London: The Royal Society of the encouragement of Arts, Manufactures and Commerce.

Sheth, J. N., Mittal, B. and Newman, B. I. (1999) *Customer Behavior: Consumer Behavior and Beyond*, Fort Worth, TX: The Dryden Press.

Simmonds, K. (1982) *Marketing as Innovation*, Research in Marketing Series, London: London Business School, July.

Statt, D. A. (1997) *Understanding the Consumer: A Psychological Approach*, London: Macmillan Business.

Swayne, L. and Ginter, P. (1993) *Cases in Strategic Marketing*, 2nd edn, Englewood Cliffs, NJ: Prentice-Hall.

Varey, R. J. (1998) 'Locating marketing within the corporate communication managing system', *Journal of Marketing Communications* 4 (3): 177–90.

Bibliography

Aaker, D. A. (1995) *Building Strong Brands*, New York: The Free Press.

Achrol, R. S. (1997) 'Changes in the theory of interorganisational relations in marketing: toward a network paradigm', *Journal of the Academy of Marketing Science* 25(1): 56–71.

Ackoff, R. L. (1998) 'Transforming organizations into market economies', in Halal, pp. 41–56.

Advertising Age, www.adage.com

Advertising Association, www.adassoc.org.uk

Advertising Standards Authority, www.asa.org.uk

Airtours Holidays Ltd (2000) 'The happening', issue 14, July–August, pp. 10–11 (employee magazine).

Ajzen, I. (1988) *Attitudes, Personality, and Behavior*, Chicago, IL: Dorsey Press.

Alger, D. (1998) *Megamedia: How Giant Corporations Dominate Mass Media, Distort Competition, and Endanger Democracy*, Oxford: Rowman & Littlefield Publishers.

Allen, D. E. (1978) 'Anthropological insights into consumer behavior', *European Journal of Marketing* 3: 45–57.

Alvesson, M. and Willmott, H. (1993) *Making Sense of Management: A Critical Introduction*, London: Sage Publications.

Anderson, P. F. (1982) 'Marketing, strategic planning, and the theory of the firm', *Journal of Marketing* 46: 15–26.

Anon. (1991) 'Benetton ads: a risqué business', *The Times*, 25 March, p. 13.

Anon. (1992) 'Shrinkage of stores and customers in US causes Italy's Benetton to alter its tactics', *Wall Street Journal*, 24 June.

Argyris, C. (1990) *Overcoming Organisational Defences*, New York: Simon & Schuster.

Arndt, J. (1979) 'Toward a concept of domesticated markets', *Journal of Marketing* 43: 69–75.

Assael, H. (1995) *Consumer Behavior and Marketing Action*, 5th edn, Cincinnati, OH: South-Western College Publishing.

Association for the Advancement of Relationship Marketing www.aarm.org

Back, K. and Back, K. (1982) *Assertiveness at Work: A Practical Guide to Handling Awkward Situations*, London: McGraw-Hill.

Bagozzi, R. P. (1978) 'Marketing as exchange: a theory of transactions in the marketplace', *American Behavioural Scientist* 21(4): 535–56.

Baker, M. J. (1992) *Marketing Strategy and Management*, 2nd edn, Basingstoke: Macmillan.

Baker, W. E. (1990) 'Market networks and corporate behavior', *American Journal of Sociology* 96(3): 589–625.

Ballantyne, D. (1991) 'Internal marketing, collaboration and motivation in service quality management', Cranfield School of Management working paper no. SWP 23/91.

Ballantyne, D. (1999) 'Dialogue and knowledge generation: two sides of the same coin in relationship marketing', paper presented at the Second WWW Conference on Relationship Marketing, November. (See www.mcb.co.uk/services/conferen/nov99/rm/paper3html.)

Barabba, V. P. and Zaltman, G. (1991) *Hearing the Voice of the Market*, Cambridge, MA: Harvard Business School Press.

Barich, H. and Kotler, P. (1991) 'A framework for marketing management', Sloan Management Review 32 (2): 94–104.

Barnes, B. (1995) *The Elements of Social Theory*, London: University College London Press.

Bartlett, C. and Ghoshal, S. (1991) *Managing Across Borders: The Transnational Solution*, Cambridge, MA: Harvard Business School Press.

Bauman, Z. (1998) *Work, Consumerism, and the New Poor*, Buckingham: Open University Press.

Belasco, J. A. (1990) *Teaching the Elephant to Dance: Empowering Change in Your Organization*, London: Random Century Books.

Bell, D. (1974) *The Coming of a Postindustrial Age: A Venture in Social Forecasting*, London: Penguin Books.

Bell, D. (1979) *The Cultural Contradictions of Capitalism*, New York: Basic Books.

Bennett, R. (1993) *The Handbook of European Advertising*, London: Kogan Page.

Bennis, W. (1989) *On Becoming a Leader*, London: Century Business Books.

Berger, P. L. and Luckmann, T. (1966) *The Social Construction of Reality: A Treatise in the Sociology of Knowledge*, Garden City, NY: Doubleday.

Bernstein, D. (1984) *Company Image and Reality: a Critique of Corporate Communications*, London: Cassell.

Bezjian-Avery, A., Calder, B. and Iacobucci, D. (1998) 'New media: interactive advertising vs. traditional advertising', *Journal of Advertising Research*, July–August: 23–32.

Blake, R. R. and Mouton, J. S. (1964) *The Managerial Grid: Key Orientations for Achieving Production Through People*, Houston, TX: Gulf Publishing Company.

Blattberg, R. and Deighton, J. (1991) 'Interactive marketing: exploiting the age of addressability', *Sloan Management Review* 32(1): 5–14.

Blythe, J. (2000) *Marketing Communications*, London: FT Prentice-Hall.

Bonoma, T. (1989) 'Managing performance – what do you expect?', *Harvard Business Review* September–October: 44–7.

Booms, B. H. and Bitner, M. J. (1981) 'Marketing strategies and organization structures for service firms', in Donnelly, J. H. and George, W. R. (eds) *Marketing of Services*, Chicago: AMA, pp. 47–51.

Boorstin, D. J. (1961) *The Image: or What Happened to the American Dream*, Harmondsworth: Pelican Books.

Boorstin, D. J. (1976) 'The rhetoric of democracy', *Advertising Age* 47(16), April.

Bowen, D. E. and Schneider, B. (1985) 'Boundary-spanning-role employees and the service encounter: some guidelines for management and research', in Congram *et al.* (1987).

Bradley, F. (1995) *Marketing Management: Providing, Communicating, and Delivering Value*, London: Prentice-Hall.

Brenner, J. G. (1999) *The Chocolate Wars: Inside the Secret Worlds of Mars and Hershey*, London: HarperCollinsBusiness.

Brews, P. J. (2000) 'The challenge of the Web-enabled business', *FT Mastering Management supplement*, 24 November.

Brierley, S. (1996) 'Trade unions', *Marketing Week*, 1 November: 36–9.

Britt, S. H. (1966) *Consumer Behavior and the Behavioural Sciences: Theories and Applications*, New York: John Wiley & Sons.

Britt, S. H. (1978) *Psychological Principles of Marketing and Consumer Behaviour*, Lexington, MA: Lexington Books.

Bromley, D. B. (1993) *Reputation, Image, and Impression Management*, Chichester: John Wiley & Sons.

Brown, A. (1995) *Organisational Culture*, London: Pitman Publishing.

Brown, R. (1993) *Market Focus: Achieving and Sustaining Marketing Effectiveness*, Butterworth-Heinemann.

Brownlie, D., Saren, M., Wensley, R. and Whittington, R. (eds) (1993) *Rethinking Marketing: New Perspectives on the Discipline and Profession*, Warwick Business School.

Burke, K. (1950/1969) *A Rhetoric of Motives*, Berkeley, CA: University of California Press.

Buttle, F. A. (1995) 'Marketing communication theory: what do the texts teach our students?', *International Journal of Advertising* 14: 297–313.

Buzzell, R. D. and Quelch, J. A. (eds) (1988) *Multinational Marketing Management: Cases and Readings*, Reading, MA: Addison-Wesley.

Carey, J. W. (1975) 'A cultural approach to communication', *Communication* 2: 1–22.

Carlsson, I. and Ramphal, S. (eds) (1995) *Our Global Neighbourhood*, Oxford: Oxford Paperbacks.

Carlzon, J. (1987) *Moments of Truth: New Strategies for Today's Customer-Driven Economy*, New York: Ballinger Publishing Corp.

Carman, J. M. (1980) 'Paradigms for marketing theory', in Sheth, 1980.

Carroll, A. B. (1993) *Business and Society: Ethics and Stakeholder Management*, 2nd edn, Cincinnati, OH: South-Western Publishing Co.

Carter, S. (1999) *Renaissance Management: The Rebirth of Energy and Innovation in People and Organisations*, London: Kogan Page.

Choi, C. J. and Kim, J.-B. (1996) 'Reputation, learning and quality uncertainty', *Journal of Consumer Marketing* 13(5): 47–54.

Christopher, M. G., Payne, A. and Ballantyne, D. (1991) *Relationship Marketing: Bringing quality, customer service, and marketing together*, Oxford: Butterworth-Heinemann/CIM.

Clampitt, P. G. (1991) *Communicating for Managerial Effectiveness*, London: Sage Publications.

Clarke, P. (ed.) (1973) *New Models for Communication Research*, Newbury Park, CA: Sage Publications.

Clough, B. (1992) 'Media: the posters shock ... but we all buy the knitwear: Benetton's ads may have turned stomachs, but they stick in consumers' minds. Patricia Clough meets the man who makes them', *The Independent*, 16 December.

Compton F. (1987) 'Internal marketing of marketing', in Congram *et al.* (1987), pp. 17–20.

Congram, C. A., Czepiel, J. A. and Shanahan, J. B. (1987) 'Achieving internal integration in service organisations: five propositions', in Congram *et al.* (1987), pp. 5–6.

Congram, C. A., Czepiel, J. A. and Shanahan, J. (eds) (1987) *The Services Challenge: Integrating for Competitive Advantage*, Chicago, IL: American Marketing Association.

Cook, A. (1994) 'The end of the line?', *Marketing*, 24 February, pp. 22–23.

Cosentino, G. (1982) 'The Benetton case – the top of the iceberg', *Panorama*, 15 December.

Covey, S. R. (1989) *The Seven Habits of Highly Effective People: Restoring the Character Ethic*, New York: Simon & Schuster.

Cowlett, M. (1996) 'Make it big with a small packet', *Marketing*.

Crainer, S. (1995) *The Real Power of Brands: Making Brands Work for Competitive Advantage*, London: FT Pitman Publishing.

Croft, R. and Dean, D. (1998) 'Interactive or hyperactive: advertising on the Internet', work-in-progress paper, 3rd International Conference on Corporate and Marketing Communication, University of Strathclyde, May.

Crosier, K. and Abbott, J. (1998) 'Net benefits: sizing up a marketing communications vehicle for the twenty-first century', paper presented to the 3rd International Conference on Marketing and Corporate Communications, University of Strathclyde, May.

Cutlip, S. M., Center, A H. and Broom, G. M. (1994/1999) *Effective Public Relations*, 7th/8th edns, Englewood Cliffs, NJ: Prentice-Hall.

Davidson, M. (1992) *The Consumerist Manifesto: Advertising in Postmodern Times*, London: Routledge.

Davis, H. L. and Silk, A. J. (eds) (1978) *Behavioral and Management Science in Marketing*, New York: Wiley.

Day, G. S. (1992) 'Marketing's contribution to the strategic dialogue', *Journal of the Academy of Marketing Science* 20: 323–9.

Day, G. S. and Wensley, R. (1983) 'Marketing theory with a strategic orientation', *Journal of Marketing* 47, autumn, pp. 79–89.

de Botton, A. (2000) *The Consolations of Philosophy*, London: Hamish Hamilton.

de Chernatony, L. (1993) 'The seven building blocks of brands', *Management Today*, March, pp. 66–8.

de Chernatony, L. and McDonald, M. H. B. (1992) *Creating Powerful Brands: The Strategic Route to Success in Consumer, Industrial and Service Markets*, Oxford: Butterworth-Heinemann.

Deetz, S. A. (1992) *Democracy in an Age of Corporate Colonization: Developments in Communication and the Politics of Everyday Life*, Albany, NY: State University of New York Press.

Deetz, S. A. (1995) *Transforming Communication, Transforming Business: Building Responsive and Responsible Workplaces*, Creskill, NJ: Hampton Press.

DeFoore, B. and Renesch, J. (eds) (1995) *Rediscovering the Soul of the Business: A Renaissance of Values*, San Francisco, CA: Sterling & Stone.

DeLozier, M. W. (1976) *The Marketing Communications Process*, New York: McGraw-Hill.

DePree, M. (1989) *Leadership is an Art*, New York: Doubleday. (Documents the leadership and commitment necessary for responsive and responsible business.)

Dewis, A. (1992) 'Image is more than skin deep', *Management Consultancy*, November, pp. 74, 76.

Dibb, S., Simkin, L., Pride, W. M., and Ferrell, O. C. (1999) *Marketing: Concepts and Strategies*, 3rd edn, Boston, MA: Houghton Mifflin Company.

Dichter, E. (1960) *The Strategy of Desire*, London: TV Boardman.

Dichter, E. (1966) 'How word-of-mouth advertising works', *Harvard Business Review*, 44, November–December: 147–66.

Dilenschneider, R L. (1991) 'Marketing communications in the post-advertising era', *Public Relations Review* 17(3): 227–36.

Dittmar, H. (1992) *The Social Psychology of Material Possessions*, Hemel Hempstead: Harvester.

Doward, J. (2000) 'Hearts – or just eyeballs', *Observer*, 15 October, p. 6.

Dowling, G. R. (1994) *Corporate Reputations: Strategies for Developing the Corporate Brand*, London: Kogan Page.

Dowling, G. R. (1995) 'Corporate reputations – the company's super brand', *Journal of Brand Management* 2(5): 377–85.

Drucker, P. F. (1973) *Management: Tasks, Responsibilities, Practices*, London: Heinemann.

Drucker, P. F. (1977) *Management: Tasks, Responsibilities, Practices*, New York: Harper's College Press.

Drucker, P. F. (1980) *Managing in Turbulent Times*, New York: Harper & Row.

Drucker, P. F. (1986) *The Frontiers of Management: Where Tomorrow's Decisions Are Being Shaped Today*, London: Heinemann/Guild Publishing.

Duncan, T. and Moriarty, S. E. (1998) 'A communication-based marketing model for managing relationships', *Journal of Marketing* 62: 1–13.

Dwyer, F. R., Schurr, P. H. and Oh, S. (1987) 'Developing buyer–seller relationships', *Journal of Marketing* 51, April: 11–27.

Eadie, D. R. and Kitchen, P. J. (1999) 'Measuring the success rate: evaluating the marketing communications processes and marcomm programmes', in Kitchen, P. J. (ed.) *Marketing Communications: Principles and Practice*, London: International Thomson Business.

East, R. (1997) *Consumer Behaviour: Advances and Applications in Marketing*, London: Prentice-Hall.

Economist, The (1991) 'Britain's most admired companies: top marks', 26 January, pp. 66–7.

Edwards, G. (1997) 'A reputation to uphold', *Scottish Communications Review*, pp. 4–5.

Edwards, M. (2000) 'Stairway to heaven.com', *The Sunday Times Magazine*, April, p. 23.

Ehling, W. P., White, J. and Grunig, J. E. (1992) 'Public relations and marketing practices', in Grunig (ed.) (1992), pp. 357–93.

Ehrenberg, A. S. C. (1997) 'How do consumers come to buy a new brand?', *Admap*, March, pp. 20–24.

Ehrenberg, A., Barnard, N. R. and Scriven, J. A. (1997) 'Differentiation or salience', *Journal of Advertising Research* 37: 7–14.

Ehrenberg, A., Barnard, N. R., Scriven, J. A. , Kennedy, R. and Bloom, H. (1999) 'Brand advertising as publicity', research report 4, the Business School, South Bank University, London.

Emler, N. (1990) 'A social psychology of reputation', in Stroebe and Hewstone (1990).

Engel, J. F., Blackwell, R. D. and Miniard, P. W. (1993) *Consumer Behavior*, 7th (international) edn, Fort Worth, TX: The Dryden Press.

Engel, J. F., Blackwell, R. D. and Miniard, P. W. (1995) *Consumer Behavior*, 8th edn, Fort Worth, TX: The Dryden Press.

Engel, J. F., Warshaw, M. R., and Kinnear, T. C. (1994) *Promotional Strategy: Managing the Marketing Communication Process*, 8th edn, Burr Ridge, IL: Irwin.

Ess, C. and Sudweeks, F. (eds) (1998) *Proceedings of the Cultural Attitudes Towards Technology and Communication Conference*, London, August.

Evans, I. G. and Riyait, S. (1993) 'Is the message being received? Benetton analyzed', *International Journal of Advertising* 12(4): 291–301.

Evans, M. J., Moutinho, L. and van Raaij, F. (1996) *Applied Consumer Behaviour*, Harlow: Addison-Wesley.

Eysenck, M. W. and Keane, M. T. (2000) *Cognitive Psychology: A Student's Handbook*, 4th edn, Hove: Psychology Press.

Fabre, M. (1964) *A History of Communications*, London: Prentice-Hall.

Fang, I. (1997) *A History of Mass Communication: Six Information Revolutions*, Boston, MA: Focal Press.

Feare, T. (1999) 'Building a new kind of online business', *Modern Materials Handling*, August.

Fearnley, M. (1992) 'Companies fail to live up to their reputation', *Management Consultancy*, November, pp. 35–36.

Festinger, L. (1957) *A Theory of Cognitive Dissonance*, New York: Harper & Row.

Festinger, L. (1964) *Conflict, Decision and Dissonance*, Stanford, CA: Stanford University Press.

Fill, C. (1995) *Marketing Communications: Frameworks, Theories and Applications*, London: Prentice-Hall.

Fill, C. (1999) *Marketing Communications: Contexts, Contents, and Strategies*, 2nd edn, London: Prentice-Hall.

Fisk, G. (ed.) (1986) *Marketing Management Technology as a Social Process*, New York: Praeger.

Fiske, R. P., Brown, S. W. and Bitner, M. J. (1993) 'Tracking the evolution of the services marketing literature', *Journal of Retailing* 69(1): 61–103.

Fletcher, W. (1994) *How to Capture the Advertising High Ground*, London: Century Business Books, pp. 1–17.

Fombrun, C. (1996) *Reputation: Realizing Values from the Corporate Image*, Cambridge, MA: Harvard Business School Press.

Fombrun, C. and Shanley, M. (1990) 'What's in a name? Reputation building and corporate strategy', *Academy of Management Journal* 33(2): 233–58.

Fortune (1993, 1994) 'Corporate reputations', 8 February/7 February.

Foxall, G. R. (1992) 'The behavioral perspective model of purchase and consumption: from consumer theory to marketing practice', *Journal of the Academy of Marketing Science* 20 (2): 189–98.

Freeman, R. E. (1984) *Strategic Management: A Stakeholder Approach*, Boston, MA: Pitman Publishing.

Friedman, M. (1970) 'The social responsibility of business is to increase its profits', *New York Times Magazine*, 13 September.

Fromm, E. (1942) *The Sane Society*, New York: Rinehart & Co.

Fromm, E. (1966) *The Heart of Man*, London: Routledge & Kegan Paul.

Fromm, E. (1978) *To Have or to Be?*, London: Abacus Books.

Fuller, D. A. (1999) *Sustainable Marketing: Managerial-Ecological Issues*, Thousand Oaks, CA: Sage Publications.

Fulop, L. and Linstead, S. (eds) (1999) *Management: A Critical Text*, London: Macmillan Business. (Treats management as relational – the management of relationships rather than of things.)

Gable, W. (1998) 'Market-based management at Koch Industries', in Halal, 1998, pp. 69–78.

Gabriel, Y. and Lang, T. (1995) *The Unmanageable Consumer: Contemporary Consumption and its Fragmentation*, London: Sage Publications.

Galbraith, J. K. (1958) *The Affluent Society*, London: Hamish Hamilton.

Gardener, E. and Trevidi, M. (1998) 'A communications framework to evaluate sales promotion strategies', *Journal of Advertising Research* May–June: 67–71.

Gatarski, R. and Lundkvist, A. (1998) 'Interactive media face artificial consumers and marketing theory must re-think', *Journal of Marketing Communications* 4 (1): 45–59.

Gates, S. (1995) *The Changing Global Role of the Marketing Function*, Brussels: The Conference Board Europe.

Gavaghan, K. (1993) 'The power of knowledge', *Marketing Week*, 2 April, p. 31.

Gay, S. (1997) 'Affinity and beyond', *Marketing Week*, Promotions and Incentives supplement, 8 May, pp. v–vii.

Gayeski, D. (1993) *Corporate Communications Management: The Renaissance Communicator in Information-Age Organizations*, Boston, MA: Focal Press.

Ghoshal, S. and Bartlett, C. A. (1997) *Individualized Corporation: A Fundamentally New Approach to Management*, London: William Heinemann.

Gilligan, C. (1995) *Marketing Communications: Planning, Implementation and Control*, Oxford: Butterworth-Heinemann.

Gilmore, A. and Carson, D. (1995) 'Managing and marketing to internal customers', in Glynn, W. J. and Barnes, J. G. (eds) *Understanding Services Management*, Chichester: John Wiley & Sons, pp. 295–321.

Goffman, E. (1959) *The Presentation of Self in Everyday Life*, London: Penguin Books.

Goffman, E. (1969) *Where the Action Is*, London: Allen Lane.

Goleman, D. (1985) *Vital Lies, Simple Truths: The Psychology of Self-Deception*, London: Bloomsbury.

Goyder, M. (1998) *Living Tomorrow's Company*, Aldershot: Gower Publishing.

Grönroos, C. (1983) *Strategic Management and Marketing in the Service Sector*, Bromley: Chartwell-Bratt.

Grönroos, C. (1990) *Service Management and Marketing: Managing the Moments of Truth in Service Competition*, Lexington, MA: Lexington Books.

Grönroos, C. (2000) *Service Management and Marketing: A Customer Relationship Management Approach*, Chichester: John Wiley & Sons.

Gray, J. (1986) *Managing the Corporate Image*, New York: Quorum Books.

Grossberg, L., Wartella, E. and Whitney, D. C. (1998) *MediaMaking: Mass Media in a Popular Culture*, Thousand Oaks, CA: Sage Publications.

Grunig, J. E. (ed.) (1992) *Excellence in Public Relations and Communication Management*, Hillsdale, NJ: Lawrence Erlbaum Associates.

Grunig, J. E. (ed.) (1992) *Excellence in Public Relations and Communication Management*, Hillsdale, NJ: Lawrence Erlbaum Associates.

Grunig, J. E. and Hunt, T. (1984) *Managing Public Relations*, New York: Holt, Rinehart & Winston.

Guiltinan, J. P. and Paul, G. W. (1994) *Marketing Management: Strategies and Programs*, 5th (international) edn, New York: McGraw-Hill.

Gummesson, E. (1991) 'Marketing–orientation revisited: the crucial role of part-time marketers', *European Journal of Marketing* 25(2): 60–75.

Gummesson, E. (1993) 'Marketing according to textbooks: six objections', in Brownlie *et al.* (1993).

Gummesson, E. (1999) *Total Relationship Marketing: Rethinking Marketing Management – From 4Ps to 30Rs*, Oxford: Butterworth-Heinemann.

Habermas, J. (1984) *The Theory of Communicative Action: Volume 1, Reason and the Rationalization of Society*, Boston, MA: Beacon Press.

Halal, W. E. (1996) *The New Management: Democracy and Enterprise Are Transforming Organizations*, San Francisco, CA: Berrett-Koehler.

Halal, W. E. (ed.) (1998) *The Infinite Resource: Creating and Leading the Knowledge Enterprise*, San Francisco: Jossey-Bass.

Hall, E. T. (1961) *The Silent Language*, New York: Anchor Books.

Hall, E. T. and Whyte, W. F. (1960) 'Intercultural communication: a guide to men of action', *Human Organisation* 19(1).

Handy, C. (1995) 'Balancing corporate power: a new federalist paper', in Handy, 1995, pp. 33–56.

Handy, C. (1995) *Beyond Certainty: The Changing Worlds of Organisations*, London: Hutchinson.

Hardt, H. (1992) *Critical Communication Studies: Communication, History & Theory in America*, London: Routledge.

Hargie, O. and Tourish, D. (eds) (2000) *Handbook of Communication Audits for Organisations*, London: Routledge.

Harris, P. and McDonald, F. (eds) (1994) *European Business and Marketing: Strategic Issues*, London: Paul Chapman Publishing.

Harris, R. and Carman, J. M. (1983) 'Public regulation of marketing activity', *Journal of Macromarketing* 3(1).

Harris, T. L. (1991) 'Why your company needs marketing public relations', *Public Relations Journal* September: 26–27.

Hart, N. A. (1995) *Strategic Public Relations*, London: Macmillan Business Books.

Hawken, P. (1993) *The Ecology of Commerce: A Declaration of Sustainability*, New York: HarperBusiness.

Hayek, F. A. (1990) *The Fatal Conceit: The Errors of Socialism*, Chicago, IL: University of Chicago Press.

Haywood, R. (1994) *Managing Your Reputation: How to Plan and Run Communications Programmes that Win Friends and Build Success*, Maidenhead: McGraw-Hill.

Heath, R. L. (1994) *Management of Corporate Communication: From Interpersonal Contacts to External Affairs*, Hillsdale, NJ: Lawrence Erlbaum Associates.

Hefzallah, I. M. and Maloney, W. P. (1979) 'Are there only six kinds of TV commercials?', *Journal of Advertising Research* 19(4): 57–62.

Heider, F. (1958) *The Psychology of Interpersonal Relations*, New York: John Wiley & Sons.

Herbig, P. and Milewicz, J. (1996) 'To be or not to be ... credible that is: a model of reputation and credibility among competing firms', *Corporate Communications: An International Journal* 1(2): 19–29.

Heskett, J. L. (1987) 'Lessons in the service sector', *Harvard Business Review* 65: 118–26.

Heskett, J. L. and Signorelli, S. (1988) 'Case 1.3 – Benetton', in Buzzell and Quelch, 1988, pp. 47–76.

Heyman, R. (1994) *Why Didn't You Say That in the First Place?: How to Be Understood at Work*, San Francisco, CA: Jossey-Bass.

Hickman, C. R. and Silva, M. A. (1984) *Creating Excellence – Managing Corporate Culture, Strategy and Change in the New Age*, London: George Allen & Unwin.

Hoffman, D. L. and Novak, T. P. (1996) 'Marketing in hypermedia computer-mediated environments: conceptual foundations', *Journal of Marketing* 60(3): 50–68.

Hofstede, G. (1981) *Culture's Consequences: International Differences in Work Related Values*, London: Sage Publications.

Hofstede, G. (1991) *Cultures and Organizations: Software of the Mind. Intercultural Cooperation and Its Importance for Survival*, New York: McGraw-Hill.

Holbrook, M. B. and Hirschman, E. C. (1982) 'The experiential aspects of consumption: consumer fantasies, feelings, and fun', *Journal of Consumer Research*, September, pp. 132–40.

Holland, K. A. (1994) 'How to sell marketing to your company', *Marketing Intelligence & Planning* 12(11): 22–25.

Hollensen, S. (2001) *Global Marketing: A Market-Responsive Approach*, 2nd edn, Harlow: Pearson Education.

Homans, G. C. (1961) *Social Behaviour: Its Elementary Forms*, London: Routledge & Kegan Paul.

Hope, J. and Hope, T. (1997) *Competing in the Third Wave: The Ten Key Management Issues of the Information Age*, Cambridge, MA: Harvard Business School Press.

Howard, J. A. and Sheth, J. N. (1969) *The Theory of Buyer Behaviour*, New York: John Wiley & Sons.

Hughes, G. D. (1980) *Marketing Management: A Planning Approach*, Reading, MA: Addison-Wesley.

Jackson, T. (1997) *Inside INTEL: How Andy Grove Built the World's Most Successful Chip Company*, London: HarperCollins.

Jacobs, J. (1992) *Systems of Survival: A Dialogue on the Moral Foundations of Commerce and Politics*, London: Hodder & Stoughton.

Jefkins, F. and Yadin, D. (2000) *Advertising*, 4th edn, London: FT Prentice-Hall.

Jones, J. P. (1986) *What's in a Name?: Advertising and the Concept of Brands*, Lexington, MA: Lexington Books.

Jones, J. P. (1998) *How Advertising Works*, London: Sage Publications.

Jones, N. (1996) 'Talking pages', *Marketing Week*, 26 July, pp. 37–40.

Joyce, T. (1991) 'Models of the advertising process', *Marketing & Research Today*, November, pp. 205–12.

Kale, S. H. (1991) Culture-specific marketing communications: An analytic approach, *International Marketing Review* 8(2): 18–30.

Kashani, K. (2000) 'The essence of building an effective brand', *FT Mastering Management supplement*, 14 December.

Katz, E. and Lazarsfeld, P. (1955) *Personal Influence: The Part Played by People in the Flow of Mass Communications*, New York: The Free Press.

Kay, J. (1993) *Foundations of Corporate Success: How Business Strategies Add Value*, Oxford: Oxford University Press.

Kelley, W. T. (1968) *Marketing Intelligence: The Management of Marketing Information*, London: Staples Press.

Kellogg, R. T. (1995) *Cognitive Psychology*, London: Sage Publications.

Kelman, H. C. (1961) 'Processes of opinion change', *Public Opinion Quarterly* 25: 57–78.

Kent, K. (1996) 'Communication as a core management discipline: The relationship between new management trends and the need for new perspectives in education in both management and public relations', *Journal of Communication Management* 1(1): 29–36.

Kikoski, J. F. and Kikoski, C. K. (1996) *Reflexive Communication in the Culturally Diverse Workplace*, Westport, CN: Quorum Books.

King, S. (1984) *Developing New Brands*, London: J. Walter Thomson (advertising agency).

Kitchen, P. (1993) 'Marketing communications renaissance', *International Journal of Advertising*, 12: 367–86.

Kitchen, P. J. and Wheeler, C. (1997) 'Developments in marketing communications: a global perspective', paper presented at the Second International Conference on Marketing and Corporate Communication, University of Strathclyde, April.

Klapper, J. T. (1960) *The Effects of Mass Communication*, New York: The Free Press.

Kline, S. (1993) *Out of the Garden: Toys and Children's Culture in the Age of TV Advertising*, London: Verso, especially Chapters 1 and 2.

Kotler, P. (1982) *Marketing for Non-Profit Organizations*, 2nd edn, Englewood Cliffs, NJ: Prentice-Hall.

Kotler, P. (1986) 'Megamarketing', *Harvard Business Review* 64 (2): 117–24.

Kotler, P. (1991) *Marketing Management: Analysis, Planning, Implementation & Control*, 7th edn, London: Prentice-Hall.

Kotler, P. (1996) *Principles of Marketing*, 2nd European edn, London: Prentice-Hall, case study no. 19.

Kotler, P. (1999) *Kotler on Marketing*, New York: The Free Press.

Kotler, P. (2000) *Marketing Management: International Millenium Edition*, London: Prentice-Hall.

Kotler, P. and Andreasen, A. R. (1991) *Strategic Marketing for Non-profit Organisations*, Englewood Cliffs, NJ: Prentice-Hall.

Kreps, G. L. (1990) *Organizational Communication*, 2nd edn, New York: Longman.

Krugman, H. E. (1988) 'Point of view: Limits of attention to advertising', *Journal of Advertising Research* 38: 47–50.

Labich, K. (1983) 'Benetton takes on the world', *Fortune*, 13 June, p. 114.

Labovitz, G. and Rosansky, V. (1997) *The Power of Alignment: How Great Companies Stay Centered and Accomplish Extraordinary Things*, New York: John Wiley & Sons.

Lang, T. and Hines, C. (1993) *The New Protectionism: Protecting the Future Against Free Trade*, London Earthscan.

Langer, E. J. (1989) *Mindfulness: Choice and Control in Everyday Life*, HarperCollins.

Lannon, J. (1985) 'Advertising research: New ways of seeing', *Admap*, October: 520–27.

Lannon, J. (1992) 'Asking the right questions – what do people do with advertising?', *Admap*, March: 11–16.

Lannon, J. and Cooper, P. (1983) 'Humanistic advertising', *International Journal of Advertising* 2: 195–213.

Laskey, H. A., Day, E. and Crask, M. R. (1989) 'Typology of main message strategies for television commercials', *Journal of Advertising* 18(1): 36–41.

Lauzen, M. M. (1991) 'Imperialism and encroachment in public relations', *Public Relations Review* 17(3): 245–55.

Lavenka, N. M. (1991) 'Measurement of consumers' perceptions of product quality, brand name, and packaging: candy bar comparisons by magnitude estimation', *Marketing Research* 3(2): 38–46.

Leaver, R. (1995) 'The commonwealth organization: healing the world's ailing soul', in DeFoore and Renesch (1995), pp. 257–72.

Lee, H. and Varey, R. J. (1998) 'Analysing cultural impacts of computer-mediated communication in organisations', in Ess and Sudweeks (eds), 1998, pp. 259–64.

Leeds-Hurwitz, W. (ed.) (1995) *Social Approaches to Communication*, New York: Guilford Press.

Leenders, M. R. and Blenkhorn, D. L. (1988) *Reverse Marketing: The New Buyer–Supplier Relationship*, London: Collier-Macmillan.

Lefkwith, E. F. and Clark, T. (1988) 'In services, what's in a name?', *Harvard Business Review* September–October: 28–30.

Leiss, W., Kline, S. and Jhally, S. (1986) *Social Communication in Advertising: Persons, Products, and Images of Well-Being*, London: Methuen.

LETSLINK (1999) LETS Information Pack, available from LETSLINK UK, 2 Kent Street, Portsmouth PO1 3BS, England (see www.letslinkuk.demon.co.uk).

Levitt, T. (1962) *Innovation in Marketing*, London: McGraw-Hill.

Levitt, T. (1969) *The Marketing Mode: Pathways to Corporate Growth*, New York: McGraw-Hill.

Linton, I. and Morley, K. (1995) *Integrated Marketing Communications*, Oxford: Butterworth-Heinemann.

Lloyd, T. (1990) *The 'Nice' Company: Why 'Nice' Companies Make More Profits*, London: Bloomsbury Publishing.

Luck, D. J., Ferrell, O. C. and Lucas, G. S. (1989) *Marketing Strategy and Plans*, 3rd edn, London: Prentice-Hall.

MacNamee, B. and McDonnell, R. (1995) *The Marketing Casebook: Short Examples of Marketing Practice*, London: Routledge.

Maddox, K. (1999) 'Special report: P&G Interactive Marketer of the Year', *Advertising Age*, May, at www.adage.com

Maile, C. A. and Kizilbash, A. H. (1977) 'A marketing communications model', *Business Horizons*, November: 77–84.

Management Today (1994, 1995, 1996) Britain's Most Admired Companies.

Manasco, B. (2000) *Cutting Edge Companies Cultivate Learning Relationships: One-to-One Learning Strategies Enable Firms to Effectively Collaborate with Customers*, article in Knowledge Inc. newsletter @ www.webcom.com/quantera/One2One.html

Maney, K. (1995) *Megamedia Shakeout: The Inside Story of the Leaders and the Losers in the Exploding Communications Industry*, New York: John Wiley & Sons.

Mantovani, G. (1996) *New Communication Environments: From Everyday to Virtual*, London: Taylor & Francis.

March, J. G. and Simon, H. A. (1958) *Organisations*, John Wiley & Sons.

Marketing Business (1994) 'About face for corporate image', February, p. 5.

Mason, R. S. (1998) *The Economics of Conspicuous Consumption: Theory and Thought Since 1700*, Cheltenham: Edward Elgar Publishing.

Massie, R. K. (1969) *Nicholas and Alexandra*, London: World Books.

Mattelart, A. (1991) *Advertising International: The Privatisation of Public Space*, trans. M. Chanan, New York: Routledge.

Mattelart, A. (1995) 'Unequal voices', *UNESCO Courier* February: 11–14.

Mattelart, A. (1996) *The Invention of Communication*, trans. S. Emanuel, Minneapolis, MN: University of Minnesota Press.

Maynard, H. B. and Mehrtens, S. E. (1996) *The Fourth Wave: Business in the 21st Century*, San Francisco, CA: Berrett-Koehler.

McDonagh, P. (1997) 'The ecocentric challenge for marketing communications in contemporary society', paper presented to the Second International Conference on Marketing & Corporate Communication, University of Strathclyde, April.

McDonagh, P. (1998) 'Towards a theory of sustainable communication in risk society: relating issues of sustainability to marketing communications', *Journal of Marketing Management* 14: 591–622.

McDonald, M. H. B. (1992) *The Marketing Planner*, Oxford: Butterworth-Heinemann/CIM.

McEwen, W. J. and Leavitt, C. (1976) 'A way to describe TV commercials', *Journal of Advertising Research* 16(6): 35–39.

McGuire, W. J. (1978) 'An information processing model of advertising effectiveness', in Davis and Silk (eds), 1978.

McKenna, R. (1991) *Relationship Marketing: Own the Market Through Strategic Customer Relationships*, London: Century Business Books.

McLuhan, H. M. (1964) *Understanding Media: The Extensions of Man*, New York: Signet Books.

McLuhan, H. M. and Powers, B. (1989) *The Global Village: Transformations in World Life and Media in the Twenty-First Century*, Oxford: Oxford University Press.

McQuail, D. (1987) *Mass Communication Theory: An Introduction*, London: Sage Publications.

McQuail, D. (2000) *Mass Communication Theory*, 4th edn, London: Sage Publications.

Mercer, D. (1992) *Marketing*, Oxford: Blackwell Business Books.

Mesdag, M. van (1991) *Think Marketing: Strategies for Effective Management Action*, London: Mercury Business Books.

Miles, L. (1991) 'Mix and match', *Marketing Business* October: 32–4.

Mitchell, A. (1995) 'Evolution', *Marketing Business* November: 33.

Mitchell, A. (1995) 'The distribution revolution: Relationship building', *Marketing Business* March: 14–18.

Mitchell, A. (1996) 'Evolution', *Marketing Business* October: 38.

Mitchell, A. (1996) 'How will the loyalty card evolve now?', *Marketing Week*, 30 August: 20–21.

Mitchell, A. (1997) 'The future of marketing: putting customers first', *Marketing Business* April: 18–21.

Mohr, J. and Nevin, J. R. (1990) 'Communication strategies in marketing channels: a theoretical perspective', *Journal of Marketing* 54: 36–51.

Moore, J. F. (1996) *The Death of Competition: Leadership and Strategy in the Age of Business Ecosystems*, New York: HarperBusiness.

Moran, W. T. (1990) 'Brand presence and the perceptual frame', *Journal of Advertising Research* 30 (5), October–November.

Morgan, N. A. (1991) *Professional Services Marketing*, Oxford; Butterworth-Heinemann.

Moriarty, S. E. (1994) 'PR and IMC: the benefits of integration', *Public Relations Quarterly*, autumn, pp. 38–44.

Mulgan, G. (1997) *Connexity: How to Live in a Connected World*, London: Chatto & Windus.

Nelson, F. (1999) 'Littlewoods to kill off names in rebranding', *The Times*, 30 June, p. 34.

Nelson-Horchler, J. (1991) 'The magic of Herman Miller', *Industry Week*, 18 February: 11–17.

Newsom, D., Carrell, B. J. and Rossbach, A. (1997) 'Cultural conflicts and corporate responsibility in the international marketplace', *Journal of Communication Management* 1(4): 379–87.

Normann, R. and Ramirez, R. (1994) *Designing Interactive Strategy: From Value Chain to Value Constellation*, New York: John Wiley & Sons.

NorthWest Business Insider (1994, 1995, 1996) *The North West Top 250 Companies*, Manchester: Newsco Publications.

O'Keefe, B J. (1988) 'The logic of message design: individual differences in reasoning about communication', *Communication Monographs* 55: 80–103.

O'Shaughnessy, J. (1987) *Why People Buy*, Oxford: Oxford University Press.

O'Shaughnessy, J. (1988) *Competitive Marketing: A Strategic Approach*, London: Routledge.

O'Sullivan, T. (1993) 'School projects: could do better', *Marketing Week*, 3 December: 23–24.

Olson, J. (ed.) (1980) *Advances in Consumer Research*, Vol. 7, Ann Arbor, MI: The Association for Consumer Research.

Ortony, A. (ed.) (1993) *Metaphor and Thought*, 2nd edn, Cambridge, MA: MIT Press.

Ottesen, O. (1995) 'Buyer initiative ignored, but imperative for marketing management: Towards a new view of market communication', working paper no. 15, Dept. of Business Administration, Stavanger (University) College, Norway.

Page, C. and Kinsey, D. (1997) 'A co-orientational model for reputation management', Proceedings of the IABC Research Foundation Conference, Los Angeles.

Parkinson, C. N. and Rowe, N. (1977) *Communicate: Parkinson's Formula for Business Survival*, London: Pan Books/Prentice-Hall.

Paudler, S. (1997) *A Proposed Model Combining Communication Theory with an Integrated Marketing Approach*, unpublished MSc dissertation, The Management School, University of Salford.

Peattie, K. (1992) *Green Marketing*, London: Pitman/M&E Handbooks.

Peck, M. S. (1987) *The Different Drum: Community Making and Peace*, New York: Simon & Schuster.

Peppers, D. and Rogers, M. (1993) *The One-to-One Future: Building Business Relationships One Customer at a Time*, New York: Doubleday.

Peppers, D. and Rogers, M. (1997) *Enterprise One-to-One: Tools for Building Unbreakable Customer Relationships in the Interactive Age*, London: Piatkus Books.

Peppers and Rogers Group – Marketing 1to1 at www.1to1.com

Percy, L. and Woodside, A. (eds) (1983) *Advertising and Consumer Psychology*, Lexington, MA: Lexington Books.

Pettigrew, A. M. and Whipp, R. (1991) *Managing Change for Competitive Success*, Oxford: Blackwell Business Books.

Petty, R. E. and Cacioppo, J. T. (1983) 'Central and peripheral routes to persuasion: application to advertising', in Percy and Woodside (eds), 1983.

Plender, J. (1997) *A Stake in the Future: The Stakeholding Solution*, London: Nicholas Brealey.

Prus, R. (1989) *Making Sales and Pursuing Customers*, Newbury Park, CA: Sage Publications.

Purdom, N. (1996) 'Securing write of way from editors', *PR Week*, 3 May: 11–13.

Rackham, N. (1988) *SPIN Selling*, Maidenhead: McGraw-Hill.

Ransdell, E. (1998) 'Streamline delivers the goods', *Fast Company* 16: 154–56.

Ransmayr, C. (1991) *The Last World: With an Ovidian Repertory*, London: Paladin Books.

Ray, M. (1973) 'Marketing communication and the hierarchy of effects', in Clarke (ed.), 1973.

Ray, M. (1982) *Advertising and Communication Management*, Englewood Cliffs, NJ: Prentice-Hall.

Rayport, J. F. and Svikola, J. J. (1995) 'Managing in the marketspace', *Harvard Business Review* November–December: 141–50.

Reddy, M. J. (1993) 'The conduit metaphor: a case of frame conflict in our language about our language', in Ortony, A. (ed.) 1993, pp. 284–324.

Reid, L. and Rotfeld, H. (1976) 'Toward an associative model of advertising creativity', *Journal of Advertising* 5(4): 24–29.

Richardson, P. (2001) 'An investigation into integrated communications and its use in UK organisations', unpublished MPhil thesis, Corporate Communication Research Unit, School of Management, University of Salford.

Riel, C. M. B. van (1995) *Principles of Corporate Communication*, London: Prentice-Hall.

Ries, A. and Trout, J. (1985) *Positioning: The Battle for Your Mind*, New York: McGraw-Hill.

Ritson, M. (2000) 'Integration as the way ahead for marketing', *FT Mastering Management supplement*, 7 December.

Roberts, J. H. and Lattin, J. M. (1997) 'Consideration: review of research and prospects for future insights', *Journal of Marketing Research* 34: 406–10.

Robinson, K. (2000) 'Britain's best kept secrets', *The Independent on Sunday*, 18 June.

Rogers, E. M. (1983) *Diffusion of Innovations*, 3rd edn, New York: Diffusion of Innovations.

Rogers, E. M. (1986) *Communication Technology: The New Media in Society*, New York: The Free Press.

Rogers, E. M. and Kincaid, D. L. (1981) *Communication Networks: Towards a Paradigm for Research*, New York: The Free Press.

Rosenberg, M. J. (1960) *Attitude, Organisation and Change*, New Haven, CT: Yale University Press.

Rosengren, K. E. (1999) *Communication: An Introduction*, London: Sage Publications.

Rossiter, J. and Percy, L. (1997) *Advertising, Communications, and Promotion Management*, 2nd edn, New York: McGraw-Hill.

Rothenberg, R. (1998) 'The Net's precision accountability will kill not only traditional advertising, but its parasite, big media. Sniff', *Wired*, January, located at www.wired.com/wired/archive/6.01/rothenberg.html

RSA (1995) *Tomorrow's Company: The Role of Business in a Changing World*, London: Royal Society of the Encouragement of Arts, Manufactures and Commerce.

Russell, P. (1982) *The Awakening Earth: Our Next Evolutionary Leap*, London: Routledge & Kegan Paul.

Rust, R. T. and Oliver, R. W. (1994) 'The death of advertising', *Journal of Advertising* 23 (4): 71–7.

Saunders, J., Brown, M. and Laverick, S. (1992) 'Britain's most admired companies', Loughborough University Business School research series, paper no. 1992:26.

Schenk, C. and Holman, R. (1980) 'A sociological approach to brand choice: the concept of situational self-image', in Olson (ed.), 1980, pp. 610–15.

Schmidt, R., Vignali, C. and Davies, B. (1994) 'Case 1 – Benetton: Risk and Reward in Franchise Distribution', in Harris and McDonald (eds), 1994, pp. 90–97.

Schramm, W. A. (1948) *Mass Communications*, Urbana, IL: University of Illinois Press.

Schramm, W. A. (1971) 'The nature of communication between humans', in Schramm and Roberts (eds), 1971.

Schramm, W. A. and Roberts, D. F. (eds) (1971)*The Process and Effects of Mass Communication*, Urbana, IL: University of Illinois Press.

Schultz, D. E. and Schultz, H. F. (1998) 'Transitioning marketing communication into the twenty-first century', *Journal of Marketing Communications* 4: 9–26.

Schultz, D. E., Tannenbaum, S. I., and Lauterborn, R. F. (1993) *Integrated Marketing Communications: Putting It Together and Making It Work*, Lincolnwood, IL: NTC Business Books.

Schultz, D. E., Tannenbaum, S. I., and Lauterborn, R. F. (1995) *The Marketing Paradigm: Integrated Marketing Communications*, Lincolnwood, IL: NTC Business Books.

Sheth, J. N. (ed.) (1980) *Research in Marketing* 3, Greenwich, CT: JAI Press.

Sheth, J. N., Gardner, D. M. and Garrett, D. E. (1988) *Marketing Theory: Evolution and Evaluation*, London: John Wiley & Sons.

Sheth, J. N., Mittal, B. and Newman, B. I. (1999) *Customer Behavior: Consumer Behavior and Beyond*, Fort Worth, TX: The Dryden Press.

Shimp, T. A. (1976) 'Methods of commercial presentation employed by national television advertisers', *Journal of Advertising* 5(4): 30–36.

Shimp, T. A. (1997) *Advertising, Promotion and Supplemental Aspects of Integrated Marketing Communications*, 4th edn, London: The Dryden Press.

Signorelli, S. (1984) 'Benetton: case study 9-685-014', Boston, MA: Harvard Business School.

Simmonds, K. (1982) *Marketing as Innovation*, Research in Marketing Series, London: London Business School, July.

Simon, H. A. (1957) *Administrative Behaviour: A Study of Decision Making Process in Administrative Organisations*, New York: The Free Press.

Simon, L. J. (1971) *The Management of Advertising*, Englewood Cliffs, NJ: Prentice-Hall.

Singh, J. (1988) 'Consumer complaint intention and behaviour: definition and taxonomica issues', *Journal of Marketing* 52(1): 93–107.

Skerlos, K. and Blythe, J. (2000) 'Ignoring the audience', paper presented at the Fifth International Conference on Corporate and Marketing Communications, Erasmus University, Rotterdam, May.

Skinner, B. F. (1938) *The Behavior of Organisms*, New York: Appleton-Century-Crofts.

Smith, P. R. (1998) *Marketing Communications: An Integrated Approach*, London: Kogan Page.

Smith, P. R., Berry, C. and Pulford, A. (1997) *Strategic Marketing Communications: New Ways to Build and Integrate Communications*, London: Kogan Page.

Smythe, J., Dorward, C. and Reback, J. (1992) *Corporate Reputation: Managing the New Strategic Asset*, London: Century Business Books.

Snell, R. (1999) 'Managing ethically', in Fulop, L. and Linstead, S. (eds) *Management: A Critical Text*, London: Macmillan Business, pp. 335–63.

Sobol, M. G. , Farrelly, G. E. and Taper, J. S. (1992) *Shaping the Corporate Image: An Analytical Guide for Executive Decision Makers*, London: Quorum Books.

Statt, D. A. (1997) *Understanding the Consumer: A Psychological Approach*, London: Macmillan Business.

Streamline Inc. www.streamline.com

Stroebe, W. and Hewstone, M. (eds) (1990) *European Review of Social Psychology*, Vol. 1, Chichester: John Wiley & Sons.

Strong, E. K. (1925) *The Psychology of Selling and Advertising*, New York: McGraw-Hill.

Strong, S. (1997) 'The ENO soldiers on for art's sake', *PR Week*, 31 January.

Sutherland, M. (1993) *Advertising and the Mind of the Consumer*, St Leonards, NSW: Allen & Unwin.

Swayne, L. and Ginter, P. (1993) *Cases in Strategic Marketing*, 2nd edn, Englewood Cliffs, NJ: Prentice-Hall.

Tannen, D. (1999) *The Argument Culture: Changing the Way We Argue and Debate*, London: Virago.

Tannenbaum, R. and Schmidt, W. H. (1973) 'How to choose a leadership pattern', *Harvard Business Review* 51(3): 162–75.

Tapp, A. (2000) *Principles of Direct and Database Marketing*, 2nd edn, London: FT Prentice-Hall.

Taylor, F. W. (1929) *Scientific Management in American Industry*, New York: Harper & Brothers.

Thayer, L. (1968) *Communication and Communication Systems in Organization, Management, and Interpersonal Relations*, Homewood, IL: Richard D. Irwin.

Thayer, L. (1997) *Pieces: Toward a Revisioning of Communication/Life*, London: Ablex Publishing Corporation.

Tomlinson, A. (ed.) (1994) *Consumption, Identity, and Style: Marketing, Meanings, and the Packaging of Pleasure*, London: Routledge.

Toffler, M. (1970) *Future Shock*, London: Bodley Head.

Toor, M. (1993) 'Sony hits home with database', *Marketing*, 30 September.

Tynan, C. (1997) 'A review of the marriage analogy in relationship marketing', *Journal of Marketing Management* 13(7): 695–704.

Usunier, J.-C. (1993) *International Marketing: A Cultural Approach*, New York: Prentice-Hall.

van Raaij, F. (1998) 'Interactive communication: consumer power and initiative', *Journal of Marketing Communications* 4 (1): 1–8.

van Waterschoot, W. and Van den Bulte, C. (1992) 'The 4P classification of the marketing mix revisited', *Journal of Marketing* 56, October: 83–93.

Vandermerwe, S. and Rada, J. (1988) 'Servitization of business: adding value by adding services', *European Management Journal* 6(4): 314–24.

Varey, R. J. (1995) *Corporate Communication and Business Performance*, Cheltenham: Stanley Thornes.

Varey, R. J. (1996) A Broadened Conception of Internal Marketing, unpublished PhD thesis, Manchester School of Management.

Varey, R. J. (1996) 'Capitalist society, social character, and communication attitude', unpublished paper, Corporate Communication Research Unit, the Graduate School of Management, University of Salford.

Varey, R. J. (1996) 'Communicating to compete?: Report of the 1996 IABC Survey of Corporate Communications Practitioners', unpublished research report, Corporate Communication Research Unit, University of Salford.

Varey, R. J. (1997) 'Identification in a co-operative community: internal marketing to build corporate image and reputation', Stern School of Management Conference on Corporate Reputation, Image, and Competitiveness, New York University, January.

Varey, R. J. (1998) 'Locating marketing within the corporate communication managing system', *Journal of Marketing Communications* 4(3): 177–90.

Varey, R. J. (1999) 'Marketing, media, and McLuhan: rereading the prophet at century's end', *Journal of Marketing* 63(3): 148–53.

Varey, R. J. (2000) 'A contemporary communication theory for marketing communication', paper presented to the 29th European Marketing Academy Conference, Erasmus University, Rotterdam, The Netherlands, 23–26 May.

Varey, R. J. (2000) *Corporate Communication Management: A Relationship Perspective*, London: Routledge.

Varey, R. J. (2000) 'A critical review of conceptions of communication evident in contemporary business and management literature', *Journal of Communication Management* (4): 328–40.

Varey, R. J. (2000) 'The integrated total communication system: a response to Hartley and Picton's "mindscape of marketing communications"', paper presented at the Fifth International Conference on Corporate and Marketing Communications, Erasmus University, Rotterdam, The Netherlands, 22–23 May.

Varey, R. J. (forthcoming) *Relationship Marketing: Dialogue and Networks in the E-commerce Era*, Chichester: John Wiley & Sons.

Varey, R. J. and Lewis, B. R. (eds) (2000) *Internal Marketing: Directions for Management*, London: Routledge.

Varey, R. J. and Wood, G. (2001) 'Brand management in the ethical communication system: a reflection on ethical progress with respect to relaters to e-brands', paper submitted to the 14th Annual Congress of the European Business Ethics Network entitled Business Ethics in the Information and Communication Society, Valencia, 12–14 September 2001.

Veblen, T. ([1899] 1963) *The Theory of the Leisure Class*, New York: Allen & Unwin.

Vickers, G. (1984) *Human Systems Are Different*, London: Harper & Row.

Visser, M. (1991) *The Rituals of Dinner: The Origins, Evolution, Eccentricities, and Meaning of Table Manners*, London: Viking Books.

Watson, J. B. and Raynor, R. (1920) 'Conditioned emotional reactions', *Journal of Experimental Psychology* 3: 1–14.

Watts, A. (1972) *The Book: On the Taboo of Knowing Who You Are*, New York: Random House.

Weilbacher, W. M. (1993) *Brand Marketing*, Lincoln, IL: NTC Books.

Weiss, A. (1989) *Managing for Peak Performance: A Guide to the Power (and Pitfalls) of Personal Style*, New York: Ballinger Publishing Co.

Wells, H. G. (1951) *The Outline of History: Being a Plain History of Life and Mankind*, rev. edn, London: Cassell & Company.

Wells, W. D. and Prensky, D. (1996) *Consumer Behavior*, New York: John Wiley & Sons.

Wernerfelt, B. (1996) 'Efficient marketing communication: helping the customer learn', *Journal of Marketing Research* 33, May: 239–46.

White, J. (1991) *How to Understand and Manage Public Relations: A Jargon-Free Guide to Public Relations Management*, London: Business Books.

Wikström, S. and Normann, R. (eds) (1994) *Knowledge and Value: A New Perspective on Corporate Transformation*, London: Routledge.

Williams, K. C. (1981) *Behavioural Aspects of Marketing*, Oxford: William Heinemann.

Williams, R. (1980) 'Advertising: the magic system', in *Problems of Materialism and Culture*, London: New Left Books.

Williamson, D. A. (1996) 'New Web ad model taps flexible pricing system', *Advertising Age*, 27 May, p. 26.

Wilson, C. A. (ed.) (1994) *Luncheon, Nuncheon and Other Meals: Eating with the Victorians*, Stroud: Allan Sutton Publishing.

Wilson, R. M. S., Gilligan, C. T. and Pearson, D. J. (1992) *Strategic Marketing Management: Planning, Implementation and Control*, Oxford: Butterworth-Heinemann/CIM.

Windahl, S., Signitzer, B., and Olson, J. T. (1992) *Using Communication Theory: An Introduction to Planned Communication*, London: Sage Publications.

Wolmar, C. (1997) 'Can Branson get back on track?', *New Statesman*, 7 November, pp. 12–14.

www.3com.com/technology/tech_net/white_papers

www.allen.com

www.ama.org (American Marketing Association)

www.cim.co.uk (The Chartered Institute of Marketing)

www.ffly.com

www.mad.co.uk/mw/ or www.marketing-week.co.uk (Marketing Week)

www.marketing.haynet.com (Marketing)

www.searchenginewatch.com/ereport/00/07-yahoo.html

Yeshin, T. (1999) *Integrated Marketing Communications: The Holistic Approach*, Oxford: Butterworth-Heinemann.

Zaltman, G. (1965) *Marketing: Contributions from the Behavioral Sciences*, New York: Harcourt, Brace & World, Inc.

Zandpour, F. and Harich, K. (1996) 'Think and feel country clusters: a new approach to international advertising standaradization', *International Journal of Advertising* 15: 325–44.

Index